Social Theory and the Urban Question

Second Edition

by the same author
An Introduction to British Politics
(with John Dearlove)
Property, Paternalism and Power
(with Howard Newby, Colin
Bell and David Rose)
Urban Politics: A Sociological Interpretation

Social Theory and the Urban Question

Second Edition

Peter Saunders

Professor of Sociology and Urban Studies,
School of Cultural and Community Studies,
University of Sussex

LONDON AND NEW YORK

First published 1981 by Unwin Hyman Ltd
Second edition 1986
Second impression 1989

Reprinted 1993
by Routledge
11 New Fetter Lane, London EC4P 4EE

Transferred to Digital Printing 2003
Routledge is an imprint of the Taylor & Francis Group

Printed and bound in Great Britain by
Selwood Printing Ltd, West Sussex

British Library Cataloguing in Publication Data
Saunders, Peter *1950–*
Social theory and the urban question. –
2nd ed.
1. Sociology, Urban
I. Title
307.7′6 HT151

ISBN 0–415–09116–0

Contents

Introduction to the second edition 7

1 Social theory, capitalism and the urban question 13

Marx and Engels: the town, the country and the capitalist mode of production – Max Weber: the city and the growth of rationality – Émile Durkheim: the city, the division of labour and the moral basis of community

2 The urban as an ecological community 52

Community and society – Human ecology is dead . . . – . . . Long live human ecology!

3 The urban as a cultural form 84

The metropolis and mental life – Urbanism and ruralism as ways of life – 'Real but relatively unimportant'

4 The urban as a socio-spatial system 114

Spatial structure and social structure – Urban managers: independent, dependent or intervening variables? – Housing distribution and class struggle

5 The urban as ideology 152

Henri Lefebvre: the humanist critique of urbanism – Manuel Castells: science, ideology and the urban question – Epistemological imperialism and the new urban sociology

6 The urban as a spatial unit of collective consumption 183

The urban system and the capitalist mode of production – Urban politics and the crisis of collective consumption – Production, consumption and the city

7 A non-spatial urban sociology? 240

Beyond a sociology of the city – The spatial aspect of economic organization – The spatial aspect of social organization

8 From urban social theory to a sociology of consumption 289

The politics of socialized consumption – Consumption sector cleavages and social restratification – Privatized consumption, self-provisioning and the dual society

Appendix A note on the empirical testing of theories 352
Further reading 363
References 369
Index 385

Introduction to the second edition

As a final year undergraduate student back in 1970, I chose to follow an option in urban sociology. I had very little idea of what to expect, and the course proved to be very varied. One week we would be looking at voluntary organizations in West African towns; the next at the power structure of Atlanta, Georgia. Extended families in Bethnal Green jostled for our attention with taxi-dance hall customers in Al Capone's Chicago. Ancient cities, medieval cities and modern cities, cities in capitalist countries, cities in socialist countries and cities in Third World countries, all were included in our broad intellectual sweep. Urban sociology, it soon transpired, could be about anything and everything – if you could find it happening in cities, then you could find it discussed somewhere in the urban sociology literature.

One major problem with all this was that none of the authors we considered seemed to be very clear about what a city was. To be sure, cities are places where large numbers of people live and work, but even this rudimentary definition is problematic. In North America and Australia, settlements which in Britain might be referred to as small towns, suburbs or even villages rejoice in a formally-designated city status. Just how big does a settlement have to be before it becomes urban?

Reflection on this problem immediately leads us into another, for in western capitalist countries, the boundaries between city and countryside, urban and rural, are generally indistinct. It is not just that we live in an age of the metropolis where cities have effectively 'joined up' as they have sprawled across the spaces which once divided them. It is also that we live in an age where people commute from outlying areas to work in city centres, and where, irrespective of their location, they tend to go to the same sorts of schools, to buy the same sorts of goods, to receive the same sorts of television programmes, to vote for the same sorts of political parties, and to lead much the same sorts of lives. Most of what we find going on in cities can, in a society like Britain, be found going on outside them too, and this makes it virtually impossible to identify any specific aspect of social life which is distinctive to cities – still less to focus on the city as an explanatory variable in the sense of identifying some causal factor or mechanism which may be said to generate particular kinds of social arrangements.

In the years since I did that urban sociology option, the subject itself has changed enormously. The attempt to trace and explain contrasts between 'urban' and 'rural' ways of life has now been recognized as largely futile. Other attempts to identify social processes which are distinctive to the particular spatial form of cities have been explored, but in my view, these too have been unsuccessful. By the late 1970s, when the first edition of this book was written, urban sociology had reached a point where it no longer seemed either possible or worthwhile to seek to identify any particular social process in western capitalist industrial societies as a phenomenon of cities. 'Urbanism' was everywhere, with the result that a sociology of urbanism was about everything.

Given such a conclusion, one might have expected the subject to disappear for there seems little point in continuing to offer courses, pursue research or write books in a field of study which has no distinctive object of analysis. In fact, however, urban sociology, and urban studies generally, have continued to grow. Not only this, but the field has arguably become one of the most stimulating and vibrant areas of the social sciences in the contemporary period. The explanation for this apparent paradox is, in my view, that urban studies has, in its long search for specifically 'urban' social phenomena, stumbled upon a distinctive and crucial research agenda. This agenda has little, if anything, to do with cities, but it has a lot to do with pressing problems of contemporary social organization in society as a whole. Urban sociology, in short, has developed into a sociology of consumption.

The first edition of this book was written in 1979–80 and published in 1981. In the final chapter of that edition, I outlined the bare bones of what this sociology of consumption might consist of. This was, however, little more than a conceptual skeleton, a first attempt to chart the contours of a newly-emerging research paradigm. In the years since then, a lot of things have happened and a lot of things have changed, and it is these changes and developments which have prompted me to revise and update the book.

One major change, of course, is that the political and economic conditions in most western societies, and certainly in Britain, have altered dramatically since the late 1970s. The economic recession has deepened with the result that in Britain, the officially-recorded unemployment rate has trebled to record levels while traditional industries have collapsed. This has coincided with the election in 1979, and re-election in 1983, of a 'radical right' Conservative government which has sought to reorganize the whole basis of state provision for consumption by cutting welfare expenditure, privatizing services and pursuing a market ideology which is the very antithesis of the corporatism and neo-Keynesianism which had grown up during the preceding period. It has also coincided with a stark polarization of British society which is expressed in a number of forms – the division between north and south, between inner city and suburb, between black and white, between unemployed and employed – and which has undoubtedly contributed to the sense of anger and frustration which spilled into the streets in 1981, when riots flared in London, Liverpool and other large cities, and again in 1985.

when Handsworth in Birmingham and Tottenham in London were the scenes of widespread arson, looting, vandalism and violence.

These social changes inevitably mean that some of the concerns addressed in the first edition of this book (e.g. the focus on corporatism) have at the very least to be reconsidered, while other issues which were not discussed there (e.g. the privatization of consumption) must now be given more prominence. Inevitably, social research takes its cue from the problems and developments of the time, and this new edition provides the opportunity to trace out a new research agenda which is relevant to the changed conditions of the mid 1980s.

A second change which has occurred since the first edition of this book was published has taken place within urban studies itself. The dominance achieved just a few years ago by the structuralist Marxist paradigm has now been shattered, not least as a result of the publication by one of its leading figures, Manuel Castells, of a book which overturns most of the philosophical, theoretical and political arguments which he had himself done so much to develop during the 1970s. Taken together with the publication of other major works by writers such as David Harvey, Ray Pahl, Anthony Giddens and Doreen Massey, this has shifted the whole agenda of urban studies by introducing new substantive concerns and by opening up new theoretical and methodological perspectives. In retrospect, it is now clear that the first edition of this book appeared at a pivotal time in the development of urban social theory, for while the old paradigm was visibly crumbling, the new had yet to develop. In this second edition, I have therefore been able to move beyond mere critique of structuralist Marxism (which was effectively where the first edition ended) and to address the problems and potential of new and exciting directions of theoretical research.

As I have already suggested, the most significant of these 'new directions' has been the growth of work exploring sociological aspects of consumption. Work such as that by Dunleavy (on consumption sector cleavages) and Pahl (on domestic self-provisioning) has been enormously significant in helping to establish this new research agenda. In addition, I have myself been able to put some empirical and theoretical flesh on the conceptual bones presented in the first edition of this book, and the results are assembled in Chapter 8.

Taken as a whole, the book has been thoroughly and fundamentally revised. Chapters 7 and 8, together with the major part of Chapter 6, are completely new and bear little resemblance to the chapters they have replaced, but the first five chapters too have been amended to a greater or lesser extent, and the appendix has been extended.

Chapter 1 considers the way Weber, Durkheim and Marx and Engels came to address the urban question in their historical works and in their analyses of contemporary capitalism. This chapter also provides the opportunity to outline the essentials of their different methodological approaches to social explanation, for it is basically these methodologies which form the basis of the various theories and approaches discussed in later chapters. My revisions to this chapter mainly consist of an attempt to simplify the discussion of Marx's method, although I have also revised the section which deals with Weber's difficult but important essay on the city.

The next five chapters cover what I see as the four main attempts this century to identify a sociological process which is distinctive to cities in the modern period. Chapter 2 discusses the theories of human ecology from Robert Park through to Amos Hawley, and this remains virtually unchanged from the first edition. In Chapter 3, I consider the various cultural theories of urbanism, concentrating in particular on the work of Georg Simmel and Louis Wirth, although in this edition I have also tried to give more careful consideration in addition to the well-known but rarely-read work of Ferdinand Tönnies. This is followed in Chapter 4 by a discussion of the Weberian urban sociology of John Rex and Ray Pahl, and the text here includes a substantial revision of the treatment of urban managerialist and corporatist theories in the light of the changed circumstances in Britain since 1979.

Chapters 5 and 6 consider some of the Marxist analyses of urbanism which developed from the late 1960s onwards. Chapter 5 compares the very different approaches of Henri Lefebvre and Manuel Castells, and here I have introduced various amendments, both in the light of a growing secondary literature on Lefebvre's work, and of subsequent changes in Castells's position. The shift in Castells's approach in recent years has necessitated a major re-write of Chapter 6 which not only traces this development, but also attempts to come to some conclusions regarding the methodological and theoretical arguments generated by his work over the years.

Chapters 7 and 8 have been written anew. Following a summary of the argument which has developed through preceding chapters, Chapter 7 considers two bodies of literature which attempt to theorize the social significance of space in contemporary capitalist or industrial societies. The first, associated with the Marxist geography of writers such as Soja, Harvey and Massey, basically explores the importance of space as a factor which helps to structure the opportunities for future capital accumulation. The second, associated more with sociologists such as Urry and Giddens, seeks to establish the importance of space in constituting social relations in the sense of enabling or constraining the development of social processes. The chapter concludes that, while space is important as an inherent feature of all social relations, it cannot itself form an object of theoretical analysis.

This then clears the way for the discussion in the final chapter of how urban sociology, stripped of its traditional preoccupation with spatial units such as cities or regions, may be developed through a substantive focus on the question of consumption. Beginning with an analysis of the politics of state consumption provision, in which the so-called 'dual politics thesis' is outlined and defended against its critics, the chapter goes on to analyse the implications of the current transition from a 'socialized' to a 'privatized' mode of consumption, arguing that a major social cleavage is now opening up between a relatively secure majority of the population and an increasingly marginalized minority. The chapter ends by considering how this division may be overcome and how consumption provision could be reorganized so as to extend the degree of autonomy and control which ordinary people may be able to assert in key areas of their everyday lives.

There have been times as I have been revising this book for this new edition when I have thought that it might have been easier to have started again from scratch. There is, I think, an analogy here with the argument developed by David Harvey in his analysis of contemporary capitalism, for just as, according to Harvey, capitalist firms encounter a major problem in reconciling their new requirements with existing patterns of investment, so too I have constantly encountered the problem of how to organize and present new materials and new ideas while all the time being constrained by a form of analysis and a framework laid down some years ago. That I have ended up with a revised edition of an existing book, rather than with a totally new work, reflects two fundamental elements of continuity between this and the first edition.

The first element concerns the core theme which ripples through most of these chapters. I suggested in the first edition, and I repeat with even more conviction here, that urban sociology, through its distinctive substantive focus on questions of consumption, has an enormous and as yet largely unrealized potential. The main reason why this potential has not been realized lies in the lingering and obstructive concern with relating urban social theory to the analysis of cities and/or space. It was my argument in 1981 and (despite considerable criticism) it remains my argument today that the traditional attempt to define urban sociology, or urban studies generally, in spatial terms (e.g. as the study of cities, regions or social-spatial interrelations) is both futile and diversionary. Urban sociology, like any other branch of social science, will address the peculiarities of space, just as it does those of time, but this cannot and must not be taken as its specific focus. Conceived as a sociology of consumption, urban sociology goes to the heart of some of the most significant questions regarding social organization in a country like Britain in the present period; conceived as a sociology of space, however, it is largely tangental to them.

The second source of continuity between this edition and the first is that it is still intended that this should be both a work *of* theory and a text *on* theory. In the chapters that follow, I have attempted not only to contribute to current debates and thinking in urban studies, but also to reflect on the tradition of urban social theory from the nineteenth century through to the present. A 'textbook' does not, I believe, have to limit itself to a dry and dispassionate reporting of existing ideas, for inevitably, while trying to discuss all approaches sympathetically, one is drawn into a critical engagement with them in the course of outlining them. What follows, therefore, is simultaneously an outline of, and an intervention in, what I believe is a fascinating and potentially very significant theoretical research tradition.

In the first edition, I acknowledged the help and influence of a number of friends and colleagues who had contributed in one way or another to my work on the book, and I am pleased to repeat those acknowledgements – to Jenny Backwell, Colin Bell, Alan Cawson, John Lloyd, Ray Pahl and Andrew Sayer – in this new edition. In the intervening years, of course, I have accumulated further intellectual debts, not least to other colleagues at Sussex University where the Urban and Regional Studies group remains an enormously stimulating context in which to work, but also to all those in Britain, North America, Australia and New Zealand with whom I have had the opportunity to discuss and exchange ideas over this period.

It is also usual to acknowledge the patience and understanding of the typist who painstakingly prepared the manuscript. In the present case, this is not appropriate since I prepared the manuscript myself on a home computer (a further example, perhaps, of the move to self-provisioning and privatized consumption which I discuss in Chapter 8). I will, however, thank Claire and Michael for the forbearance they have shown in watching me monopolize the machine while they have been waiting to play 'Beach-head' and 'The Staff of Karnath'. The least I can do is to dedicate this new edition to them.

Brighton
September 1985

1 Social theory, capitalism and the urban question

Most areas of sociology today are characterized by a certain degree of theoretical and methodological pluralism, and urban sociology is no exception. Thus there are distinctive Marxist urban sociologies, Weberian urban sociologies and so on, each differing according to the questions they pose and the criteria of adequacy or validity they adopt. What seems to be peculiar to urban sociology, however, is that these various approaches have rarely paid much attention to what the so-called 'founding fathers' of the discipline actually wrote about the urban question. Contemporary Marxist urban theories, for example, make considerable references to Marx's discussions of the method of dialectical materialism, the theory of class struggle and the capitalist state and so on, but rarely pay much attention to his discussions of the town–country division or the role of the city in the development of capitalism. Similarly, Weberian urban sociology has tended simply to ignore Weber's essay on the city and to concentrate instead on his discussions of bureaucracy and social classes. Whereas other branches of the discipline have generally developed directly out of the substantive concerns of key nineteenth-and early twentieth-century European social theorists (for example, the debates within industrial sociology over alienation and anomy, the concern with the question of bureaucracy in organizational sociology, the discussions of the state and political power in political sociology, the recurrent concern with secularization in the sociology of religion and with ideology in the sociology of knowledge), urban sociology has continually underemphasized the work of these writers on the city, and has tended instead to take as its starting point the theory of human ecology developed at the University of Chicago in the years following the First World War.

The reason for this is not hard to find, for it is not that Marx, Weber, Durkheim and other significant social theorists had little to say about the city (far from it, for as Nisbet (1966)* has suggested, this was in some ways a key theme in the work of all these writers), but rather that

*Full references quoted in the text are contained in the References beginning on p. 369.

what they did say tends to suggest that a distinctive urban sociology cannot be developed in the context of advanced capitalist societies.

The central concern of all of these writers was with the social, economic and political implications of the development of capitalism in the West at the time when they were writing. The rapid growth of cities was among the most obvious and potentially disruptive of all social changes at that time. In England and Wales, for example, the 'urban population' (administratively defined) nearly trebled in the second half of the nineteenth century with the result that over 25 million people (77 per cent of the total population) lived in 'urban' areas at the turn of the century (see Hall *et al.* 1973, p. 61). This sheer increase in size was startling enough, but it also came to be associated in the minds of many politicians and commentators with the growth of 'urban' problems – the spread of slums and disease, the breakdown of law and order, the increase in infant mortality rates and a plethora of other phenomena – all of which attracted mounting comment and consternation on the part of the Victorian middle classes.

Of course, Marx, Weber and Durkheim were each fully aware of the scale and significance of these changes, yet it is clear from their work that none of them considered it useful or necessary to develop a specifically urban theory in order to explain them. In other words, all three seem to have shared the view that, in modern capitalist societies, the urban question must be subsumed under a broader analysis of factors operating in the society as a whole. While cities could provide a vivid illustration of fundamental processes such as the disintegration of moral cohesion (Durkheim), the growth of calculative rationality (Weber) or the destructive forces unleashed by the development of capitalist production (Marx), they could in no way explain them. For all three writers, what was required was not a theory of the city but a theory of the changing basis of social relations brought about through the development of capitalism, and it was to this latter task that they addressed themselves.

When they did discuss the city, they did so only in one of two ways. First, all three saw the city as an historically important object of analysis in the context of the transition from feudalism to capitalism in western Europe. In his essay on the city, for example, Weber showed how in the Middle Ages the towns played a highly significant role in breaking the political and economic relations of feudalism and establishing a new spirit of rationality which was later to prove crucial for the development of capitalist entrepreneurship and democratic rights of citizenship. Similarly, Durkheim showed how the medieval towns helped break the bonds of traditional morality and foster the growth of the division of labour in society, while Marx and Engels saw the division between town and country in the Middle Ages as the expression of the antithesis between the newly developing capitalist mode of production and the old feudal mode in this period. However, it is clear that all three writers agree that the city was significant only at a specific period in history, and that neither the ancient city nor the modern capitalist city can be analysed in these terms. The city in contemporary capitalism is no longer the basis for human association (Weber), the locus of the division of labour (Durkheim) or the expression of a specific mode of production (Marx), in which case it is neither fruitful nor appropriate to study it in its own right.

The second context in which the city appears in the work of these writers is as a secondary influence on the development of fundamental social processes generated within capitalist societies. The city, in other words, is analysed not as a cause, but as a significant condition, of certain developments. The clearest example here concerns the argument found in the work of Marx and Engels to the effect that, although the city does not itself create the modern proletariat, it is an important condition of the self-realization of the proletariat as a politically and economically organized class in opposition to the bourgeoisie. This is because the city concentrates the working class and renders more visible the stark and growing antithesis between it and capital. In rather different vein, Durkheim's concern with the effects of an advanced division of labour on the moral cohesion of modern societies similarly takes urbanization as an important precondition of the development of functional differentiation. In both cases, therefore, a developmental theory (the growth of class struggle, the growth of new forms of social solidarity) is made conditional upon the growth of towns.

We can now appreciate why urban sociology has tended to pay so little attention to what Marx, Weber and Durkheim had to say about the city, for it is apparent in their work that the city in contemporary capitalism does not itself constitute a theoretically significant area of study. It is hardly surprising, then, that subsequent attempts to establish an urban sociology have drawn upon other aspects of their work while generally bypassing their discussion of the urban question. We shall see in later chapters, for example, how Durkheim's work on the social effects of the division of labour came to be incorporated into ecological theories of city growth and differentiation in the 1920s, how Weber's writings on political domination and social stratification formed the basis for a conceptualization of the city as a system of resource allocation in the 1960s, and how in the 1970s Marx's analysis of social reproduction and class struggle was developed as the foundation for a new political economy of urbanism. The influence of these three writers over the development of urban sociology has been pervasive yet selective.

The aim of this chapter is to retrace the way in which Weber, Durkheim and Marx and Engels all came to the conclusion that the city in contemporary capitalism was not a theoretically specific object of analysis. The paths followed by their respective analyses are divergent, yet the end-point is the same. In other words, although these writers differed radically in their methods, their theories and their personal political commitments and persuasions, their application of their different perspectives and approaches nevertheless resulted in conclusions that are broadly compatible. In each case, therefore, we shall consider first the methodological principles that guided their work, and second the results of the application of these principles to an analysis of the urban question.

Marx and Engels: the town, the country and the capitalist mode of production

Marx's method of analysis has been debated long and hard by subsequent generations. It is clear that Marx himself believed that his was a 'scientific' method in the sense that it led to the discovery of the forces which shaped the development of the social world, just as, for example, Darwin's work had led to the discovery of the forces shaping the evolution of the natural world. The problem, however, is that Marx did not devote much of his writing explicitly to elaborating this method, and it has therefore been left to later philosophers and theorists to specify precisely how such scientific discoveries could be accomplished.

Although Marx himself never used the term, his approach has often been designated by the label 'dialectical materialism'. The phrase is useful as it points to the two basic principles upon which Marx's method of analysis was based.

The principle of the dialectic is essentially that any 'whole' is comprised of a unity of contradictory parts, such that it is impossible to understand any one aspect of reality without first relating it to its context. We cannot, for example, understand the plight of wage labour under capitalism without also understanding the process leading to the augmentation of the wealth and power of capital, for capital and wage labour are tied together in an inescapable yet inherently antagonistic relation of mutual interdependence. A method of analysis which is dialectical, therefore, is a method which holds that no single aspect of reality can be analysed independently of the totality of social relations and determinations of which it forms a necessary part. Put another way, any explanation of the part can only be accomplished through an analysis of the whole. As Swingewood suggests, 'The dialectical approach in Hegel and Marx is preeminently a method for analysing the interconnections of phenomena, of grasping facts not as isolated, rigid and external data but as part of an all-embracing process' (1975, p. 33).

It is this claim to be able to analyse the totality of things which has helped to make Marxism so attractive to so many contemporary social scientists. In contrast to so-called 'bourgeois' social science with its irksome and petty disciplinary boundaries, Marxism holds out the promise of an all-embracing explanation which can relate the processes studied by the political scientist to those analysed by the economist or the sociologist. Its first claim to superiority, therefore, lies in its purported ability to transcend the inevitably partial and stunted knowledge of the specialist disciplines by means of an analysis of the totality of social relations in which changes in one sphere of life are explained with reference to changes in another.

There is, moreover, a second claim advanced on behalf of a Marxist method, and this had to do with Marx's 'materialism'. The term 'materialism' in this context is generally used in contradistinction to 'idealism', and it basically refers to the principle that the material world exists prior to our conceptions or ideas about it. Marx recognizes that the prevailing ideas which we share about what the world is like and how it works must bear some relation to the actual reality, for it is inconceivable that generations of people should collectively delude themselves entirely about the nature of a reality which daily confronts them in various forms and manifestations. Nevertheless, Marx also argues that reality may rarely be directly reflected in consciousness. The way the world appears to us, in other words, may conceal or distort its essential character. Indeed, if this were not the case, there would be no need for science since all knowledge of reality would be immediately available to us through our everyday unmediated experience of living in the world. What science does, according to Marx, is to penetrate the forms of appearance in which reality cloaks itself in order to discover the essential causal relations which lie behind and give rise to such appearances. As Derek Sayer puts it, 'Unlike phenomenal forms, Marx holds, essential relations need not be transparent to direct experience. Phenomenal forms may be such as to mask or obscure the relations of which they are the forms of manifestation' (1979, p. 9).

We are now in a position to understand Marxism's claims relative to 'bourgeois' social science. First, a Marxist method will understand the total context of interrelations and mutual determinations which shape the social world, whereas bourgeois approaches will remain partial and thus fail to achieve any clear overall understanding of the causes of the changes they are studying. And second, a Marxist method will penetrate the phenomenal forms of appearance in which the world presents itself to our consciousness while bourgeois approaches will remain stuck at the level of these appearances and fail to analyse the underlying essential relations which generate them. It was precisely in these terms that Marx attacked the bourgeois economists of his day, for in his view, any theory which fails to relate the operation of the economy to processes taking place in society as a whole (e.g. as in economists' fascination with Robinson Crusoe models of economic life), and which adopts as its tools of analysis the categories of everyday experience (e.g. land, labour and capital as three 'factors of production' which exchange freely as equivalents) while failing to analyse the processes which underpin these experiences (i.e. the creation of value by labour and its expropriation by capitalists and landowners) will simply end up reproducing in more elaborate terminology the existing and muddy conceptions characteristic of any given period. Such theories, in other words, are no more than ideologies. It is the task of science to go beyond the world of common-sense experience: 'The forms of experience are reproduced directly and spontaneously, as current and usual modes of thought; the essential relation must first be discovered by science' (Marx 1976, p. 682).

All of this, of course, raises the obvious question of how Marx's method of dialectical materialism can analyse the totality and come to discover its essential features when all other methods are doomed to remain partial in their scope and superficial in their insight. How do we get from our existing knowledge, which is inevitably partial and superficial, to a scientific knowledge which claims to be holistic and essential? And (just as important), having made this transition from common sense to science, how are we to know that the totality is as the theory tells us, and that the essential determinations which it has discovered are actually present and operating, when all that we can ever 'see' are the 'parts' and the 'appearances'?

It is clear from Marx's own writings that he believed that scientific understanding derived both from theoretical critique and development of existing ideas and from empirical investigation of existing conditions. There is, in other words, a dialectical interplay between theory and observation, the development of generalizations and a concern with specifics, the elaboration of abstractions and the analysis of concrete cases. Seen in this way, Marx's science is a product both of his mulling over musty texts in the British Museum and of his observation of conditions in the European capitalist countries of his time. McBride summarizes this method as, 'A movement from broad generalizations to endless specifics to generalities qualified by facts' (1977, p. 56).

Now this is all very well, but it does not take us very far. The problem still remains: *how* is the scientific knowledge produced and *how* is it to be evaluated? If the scientific knowledge is a product first and foremost of Marx's theorizing, then why should we accept his ideas as in any way more insightful or valid than anyone else's? Are we to accept, for example, that Marx had some privileged insight into reality, an 'inside track' denied to other mortals who, in their reflections on the world, fail to get beyond partiality and phenomenal forms of appearance? If, on the other hand, the knowledge is primarily a function of observation and experience, then how was Marx able to construct valid and all-embracing generalizations out of his own selective and partial biographical experience? How, for example, could he derive his theoretical constructs and abstractions directly and necessarily from his observations when, as he himself argues, such observations necessarily obscure or even invert the essential reality which lies behind them?

Despite the manifold attempts over the last hundred years to demonstrate the epistemologically superior starting point of Marxist analysis, it is clear that any approach which attempts to analyse the whole when all that can be experienced are the parts, and which attempts to discover essential causes when all that can be experienced are phenomenal forms, can never be more than conjectural. What Marx offers, in other words, is not a special insight into the truth, but a distinctive approach based upon what Sayer has termed a 'method of retroduction'.

Sayer resolutely denies the claims which have often been advanced by Marxists that a Marxist method starts from theoretical abstraction.

As he points out, any mode of investigation that began with a battery of abstractions would have to be premised on the assumption of some prior magical or privileged insight into the essence of reality, yet it is precisely this essence which the method is supposed to discover. It follows, therefore, that the starting point for investigation must be empirical:

> Marx's historical categories ... are generated neither from 'simple abstractions' in general, nor from transhistorical categories in particular. They are emphatically *a posteriori* constructs, arrived at precisely by abstraction from the 'real and concrete'. Marx had no mysteriously privileged starting point (D. Sayer 1979, p. 102).

This then raises the question of how Marx derives his abstractions from observation of 'concrete' conditions. How does he penetrate the phenomenal forms of appearance to reveal the essential relations which lie behind them? Sayer's answer is that he only ever develops conjectural knowledge of the essential relations. In other words, the logic of Marx's approach is to suppose the existence of certain relations which, *if they did exist*, would account for the observed phenomenal forms. 'The "logic" of Marx's analytic', says Sayer, 'is essentially a logic of hypothesis formation, for what he basically does is to *posit* mechanisms and conditions which would, if they existed, respectively explain how and why the phenomena we observe come to assume the forms they do' (p. 114). This method is neither deductive (since there are no *a priori* covering laws or transhistorical generalizations from which essential relations can be deduced), nor inductive (since the discovery of regularities in the phenomena under investigation cannot itself imply the existence of certain essential causes). Rather, it is a 'retroductive' method.

The logic of retroductive explanation involves the attempt to explain observable phenomena by developing hypotheses about underlying causes. It cannot support *any* conjecture, since the hypothesized causes must be able to explain evidence at the level of appearances, but it is equally a weak form of inference since the hypotheses can never be directly tested. In other words, it is never possible finally to demonstrate that a posited 'law' of capitalist development is actually true since such a law refers to processes which, even if they do exist, remain hidden. Furthermore, it is never possible to demonstrate that the essential relations posited by the theory are the correct ones since there is always the possibility that other essences could be put forward which could explain phenomenal forms equally as well.

Marx's method, understood as a method of retroduction, thus carries no guarantees of truth and no privileged insight into the inner workings of society. There is no warrant in this method for dismissing alternative theories that can also explain phenomenal appearances, nor for claiming a monopoly over the 'correct' scientific mode of analysis. Equally, of course, it makes no sense to attack this method on the grounds that its results cannot be directly tested against experience, since its very purpose is to theorize processes that by definition cannot be amenable to direct observation. The results of the application of such a method must be evaluated on its own terms (for example, does the posited essence explain phenomenal forms? are the predictions – as opposed to the prophecies – that arise out of this method borne out historically? how well does the theory explain comparative variations between societies? and so on). As Sayer concludes,

> If we require all the propositions in a scientific explanation to be open to empirical refutation, we must conclude that Marx was no scientist. If, on the other hand, we demand merely that it must be possible to provide independent empirical evidence which bears on its truth or falsity, then we may reasonably regard *Capital* as a paradigm of scientific research (D. Sayer 1979, p. 141).

In short, Marx's method can be used fruitfully to generate theories that are plausible to a greater or lesser extent but can never finally be demonstrated, and it follows that there is no necessary and compelling reason to accept such theories other than one's own political values and purposes. Marxism, in other words, is as much a guide to political practice as a method of scientific analysis.

The distinction drawn in Marxist methodology between phenomenal appearances and the essential relations of which they are an expression is crucial to any understanding of how Marx and Engels themselves analysed the phenomenon of urbanism. Both writers argued that the division between town and country had characterized all human societies from antiquity to modern capitalism. Historically this separation was second only to the division between men and women as the cornerstone of social organization, and for Marx, it was thus a primordial expression of the social division of labour: 'The foundation of every division of labour which has attained a certain degree of development, and has been brought about by the exchange of commodities, is the separation of town from country. One might well say that the whole economic history of society is summed up in the movement of this antithesis' (1976, p. 472). Yet having said this, the essence of the relation between city and countryside was different in different periods of human history. The town–country antithesis is, in other words, a phenomenon which has to be analysed in the context of the underlying mode of production which sustains and is sustained through it in any given period of human history. The analysis of the city and its relation to the countryside is thus premised on the analysis of class relations inscribed within specific modes of production, for urbanism assumes a different significance in different social contexts.

According to Marx, the first real class society was that of the ancient city (notably Rome). Roman society was based on a slave mode of production in which the wealth of the ruling class was founded on agricultural land ownership. Ownership of the means of production became increasingly concentrated into great estates – the *latifundiae* – as a result of the progressive collapse of the independent peasantry, but although the great landowners lived in the city itself, the mode of production remained rural: 'Ancient classical history is the history of cities, but cities based on landownership and agriculture' (Marx 1964, p. 77).

In antiquity, therefore, the city never became the locus of a new mode of production. The relation of Rome to its provinces was entirely political; the city was nothing more than an administrative centre superimposed upon a slave–agriculture mode of production. It followed from this that internal struggles could destroy this political bond but that there was no basis in this society for the development of a qualitatively new mode of production out of the ruins of the old: 'Rome, indeed, never became more than a city; its connection with the provinces was almost exclusively political and could, therefore, easily be broken again by political events' (Marx and Engels 1970, p. 90). Rome collapsed, it was not transcended, and this is because the tension between town and country, centre and periphery, was never more than political. Ancient society disappeared 'without producing a different mode of production, a different society ... Why? Because the town in antiquity consisted of a closed system. Internal struggle could only harm it from the inside without being able to open up another practical reality' (Lefebvre 1972, p. 40). With the collapse of Rome, the break-up of the *latifundiae* and the fall of a slave mode of production, all that happened was a return to individual peasant agriculture.

The history of human societies up to the Middle Ages is therefore a history of the countryside. In the feudal or Germanic period, however, this begins to change: 'The middle ages (Germanic period) starts with the countryside as the locus of history, whose further development then proceeds through the opposition of town and country; modern history is the urbanization of the countryside, not, as among the ancients, the ruralization of the city' (Marx 1964, pp. 77–8). In other words, in the feudal era, for the first time, the division between town and country comes to express an *essential contradiction* which eventually brings about the transcendence of feudalism itself.

According to Marx, the growth of a merchant class in the established towns during the Middle Ages had the important effect of extending trading links between different areas, thereby facilitating a division of labour between different towns and stimulating the growth of new industries: 'The towns enter into relations with one another, new tools are brought from one town into the other, and the separation between production and commerce soon calls forth a new division of production between the industrial towns, each of which is soon exploiting a predominant branch of industry' (Marx and Engels 1970, p. 72). However, the development of industrial capital was hindered by the existing relations of production in the established towns, for the guild system both restricted entry into manufacture and regulated the movement of labour. Capitalist manufacture, based originally on weaving, was thus propelled out of the corporate towns and was at the same time attracted into the countryside where there was water power to drive the new machinery and labour power to work it:

> The money capital formed by means of usury and commerce was prevented from turning into industrial capital by the feudal organization of the countryside and the guild organization of the towns. These fetters vanished with the dissolution of the feudal band of retainers, and the expropriation and partial eviction of the rural population. The new manufacturers were established at sea-ports, or at points in the countryside which were beyond the control of the old municipalities and their guilds (Marx 1976, p. 915).

The new system of capitalist manufacture, facilitated by merchants' capital in the medieval towns, thus took root in the countryside, and the great cities of the Industrial Revolution grew up around it. Whereas the towns of antiquity had represented a closed system, these new industrial towns represented an opposition to the mode of production that had spawned them. The hierarchical obligations of feudalism and the corporate regulation of the medieval towns were here replaced by relations based entirely on the cash nexus. The new social relations of capitalism thus became established as the antithesis to the old social relations of feudalism, and the contradictions between them, expressed in the class antagonism between industrial bourgeoisie and feudal landowners, came to be represented directly and vividly in the conflict between town and country.

In the feudal period, therefore, the division between town and country not only reflected the growing division of labour between manufacture and agriculture, but was also the phenomenal expression of the antithesis between conflicting modes of production. Although the new industrial towns were not themselves the cause of the transcendence of feudalism, they were the form it took. In this sense, the town was at this time an historical subject:

> For Marx, the dissolution of the feudal mode of production and the transition to capitalism is attached to a *subject*, the town. The town breaks up the medieval system (feudalism) while transcending itself . . . the town is a 'subject' and a coherent force, a partial system which attacks the global system and which simultaneously shows the existence of this system and destroys it (Lefebvre 1972, p. 71).

The stark contrast between town and country is, of course, in no way overcome by the establishment of a capitalist mode of production. Indeed, Engels suggests that this contrast is 'brought to its extreme point by present-day capitalist society' (1969b, p. 333). However, the significance of this division changes with the development of capitalism, for the essential contradiction within the capitalist mode of production (that between capital and labour) no longer corresponds to the phenomenal forms of town and country in the way in which that between capital and feudal landownership once did. Once capitalism has become established, it permeates throughout social production, and (in time) agriculture becomes characterized by capitalist social relations just as manufacturing industry does. The town and the country are thus no longer the real subjects of analysis or of political struggle, for although the separation between them becomes ever more vivid, it does not itself set the parameters within which the struggle for socialism is to be waged. Put another way, the struggle between proletariat and bourgeoisie extends across urban–rural boundaries as workers in town and countryside are increasingly drawn into the capital relation.

Having said that, it is nevertheless the case that Marx and Engels look to the *urban* proletariat to lead the struggle for socialism. As Williams (1973) has pointed out, there is something of an ambivalence in their analysis of the role of the city in capitalist societies, for they argue on the one hand that the city expresses most vividly the evils of capitalism, and on the other that it is within the city that the progressive forces of socialism are most fully developed. What this indicates is not so much an 'emotional confusion' (as Williams 1973, p. 37, suggests) as a dual focus in their work on capitalist urbanization. In other words, Marx and Engels study the capitalist city in two ways: first as an illustration or a microcosm of processes occurring at a different rate throughout capitalist society, and second as an important condition of the development of certain specific processes within that society.

When they discuss the city as a microcosm, their concern is not with the city *per se* but with capitalist processes that are most clearly revealed in an urban context: 'From this perspective, seen in this light, the town provides the backcloth; on that backcloth lots of events and notable facts come to pass which analysis detaches from their relatively unimportant decor' (Lefebvre 1972, p. 106). It is, in other words, not the city that is held responsible for the poverty and squalor of the urban proletariat, but the capitalist mode of production. Engels makes this abundantly clear both in his early work on the condition of the English working class, where he argues that 'the great cities really only secure a more rapid and certain development for evils already existing in the germ' (1969a, p. 150), and in his later essay on the housing question. In both works the city is portrayed as the hothouse of capitalist contradictions, the exaggerated expression of essential tendencies within capitalism itself, and in both Engels leaves us in no doubt that urban poverty can be overcome only through a transformation of the society as a whole.

As his work developed, so his treatment of the urban question became every more firmly grounded in a critique of capitalism. In his essay on the housing question (written some thirty years after his discussion of the condition of the English working class), he states explicitly that 'The housing shortage from which the workers and part of the petty bourgeoisie suffer in our modern big cities is one of the innumerable *smaller* secondary evils which result from the present day capitalist mode of production' (Engels 1969b, p. 305). And whereas in his earlier work, written before he met Marx, he had been tempted to suggest that the 'Big Whigs' of Manchester were perhaps in part responsible for perpetuating the pattern of urban deprivation in that city (see Engels 1969a, pp. 80–1), he is clear in his later essay that it is the capitalist system itself, and not the conscious and deliberate actions of individual capitalists, that explains the deplorable conditions under which large sections of the proletariat are obliged to live. Indeed, he argues that the bourgeoisie has sometimes attempted (out of self-interest) to alleviate these conditions, but that such attempts necessarily fail as the logic of capitalism constantly reasserts itself:

> Capitalist rule cannot allow itself the pleasure of generating epidemic diseases among the working class with impunity. . . . Nevertheless the capitalist order of society reproduces again and again the evils to be remedied, and does so with such inevitable necessity that even in England the remedying of them has hardly advanced a single step (Engels 1969b, p. 324).

This notion of an 'inevitable necessity', an inexorable capitalist logic, recurs throughout this essay. There is, according to Engels, no possibility of resolving the housing question within capitalist society. Every attempt at what today would be termed 'urban renewal' results in the eradication of slums in one area and their simultaneous reappearance in another:

> The breeding places of disease, the infamous holes and cellars in which the capitalist mode of production confines our workers night after night, are not abolished; they are merely shifted elsewhere! The same economic necessity which produced them in the first place produces them in the next place also! As long as the capitalist mode of production continues to exist it is folly to hope for an isolated settlement of the housing question or of any other social question affecting the lot of the workers. The solution lies in the abolition of the capitalist mode of production (Engels 1969b, pp. 352–3).

The city is not, however, only a reflection of the logic of capitalism, for Marx and Engels also see in the development of urbanization the necessary condition for the transition to socialism. This is not because the city is the locus of a new mode of production, as was the case in the medieval period, but because it is in the city that the revolutionary class created by capitalism, the proletariat, achieves its 'fullest classic perfection' (Engels 1969a, p. 75). Precisely because the tendencies within capitalism are most fully developed in the great cities, it is there that the conditions for effective struggle against capital reach their maturity:

Since commerce and manufacture attain their most complete development in these great towns, their influence upon the proletariat is also most clearly observable here. Here the centralization of property has reached the highest point . . . there exist here only a rich and a poor class, for the lower middle class vanishes more completely with every passing day (Engels 1969a, p. 56).

The tendencies for capital to become concentrated and for the classes to polarize develop in the cities, and it is therefore in the cities that the concentration and common deprivation of the proletariat is most likely to result in the growth of class consciousness and revolutionary organization:

If the centralization of population stimulates and develops the property-holding class, it forces the development of the workers yet more rapidly. The workers begin to feel as a class, as a whole. . . . The great cities are the birthplaces of labour movements; in them the workers first began to reflect upon their own condition and to struggle against it; in them the opposition between proletariat and bourgeoisie first made itself manifest. . . . Without the great cities and their forcing influence upon the popular intelligence, the working class would be far less advanced than it is (Engels 1969a, p. 152).

Here, then, is the source of the ambivalence noted by Williams, for although the city represents a concentration of the evils of capitalism, it also constitutes the necessary conditions for the development of the workers' movement that will overthrow it. The conditions of life in the countryside cannot sustain a coherent class challenge to the bourgeoisie because 'the isolated dwellings, the stability of the surroundings and occupations, and consequently of the thoughts, are decidedly unfavourable to all development' (Engels 1969a, p. 291). This is why Marx and Engels develop the well-known argument in the *Communist Manifesto* to the effect that the bourgeoisie has rendered a service to the workers' movement by creating large cities which have 'rescued a considerable part of the population from the idiocy of rural life' (1969, p. 112).

It is important to recognize, however, that it is not urbanization itself that forges a revolutionary working class any more than it is urbanization that gives rise to poverty, squalor and disease. The development of potentially revolutionary conditions is a tendency inherent within the development of capitalism, and the growth of cities is a contingent condition influencing whether and how such conditions come to be acted upon by the working class. The city is only of secondary significance in Marx's analysis of capitalism and the transition to socialism.

What this means, of course, is that there is no basis in the work of Marx and Engels for the development of a specific theory of urbanism in capitalist societies. The city may illustrate the manifestations of essential tendencies within capitalism, and it may even influence the way in which these manifestations come to be articulated in political struggle, but it is not the essential cause of such developments, nor is it the phenomenal form of an underlying contradiction as was the case in feudal society. A Marxist analysis that seeks to go beyond the level of appearances and to posit the existence of essential relations will not take the city as an object of analysis, but will rather consider the phenomena that become manifest in cities in terms of the underlying relations and determinations of which they are but one manifestation.

From a Marxist perspective, then, there seems little basis for developing a theory of urbanism. Even Marx's analysis of the role of the cities in fostering a nascent capitalism during the medieval period has been challenged by writers such as Abrams (1978) and Holton (1984) who argue that the cities were generally part of the feudal system rather than antithetical to it, and that the transition to capitalism took place as much in the countryside (through the struggle between serfs and their lords) as in the towns (where the burghers often enjoyed the patronage of the feudal landed nobility). Whether or not the medieval city represents what Lefebvre calls an 'historical subject', however, it is clear from Marx's work that the capitalist city does not. For Marx and Engels, it is capitalism rather than urbanism which constitutes the essential object of analysis in the contemporary period. Any analysis which seeks to attribute causal powers to the city (e.g. through explanations couched in terms of 'urban problems' or 'urban processes') is thus little more than an ideology, for in the context of modern capitalism, the urban is a common-sense category with no scientific status.

Max Weber: the city and the growth of rationality

Weber's approach to sociological explanation represents almost a total reversal of Marx's method. While Marx emphasized totality, the need to relate everything to everything else, Weber argues that only partial and one-sided accounts are ever possible. Where Marx seeks to identify essential causes behind phenomena, Weber's concepts represent logical purifications of phenomenal forms. Marx's notion of praxis, the inherent fusion of scientific analysis and political struggle, is directly opposed to Weber's insistence on the separation of science and politics, facts and values. And while Marx is interested in individuals only in so far as they are personifications of objective relations, Weber sees individual actions and individual consciousness as the very base of sociological analysis.

The basic concept in Weber's sociology is that of the human subject endowed with free will who, in interaction with others, attempts to realize certain values or objectives. He recognizes that not all human actions are rational since individuals may be unaware of certain possibilities for realizing their aims, and their actions may in any case be contaminated by habit or emotion. Sociology in his view can therefore perform a technical service by clarifying what people want to achieve (e.g. by pointing to inconsistencies between different sets of values to which they are committed), and by indicating which strategies are most likely to result in the required effects.

At the heart of Weber's sociological enterprise, therefore, is the attempt to relate subjective motives to particular courses of action. It follows from this that the explanation of social action will be premised upon an understanding of the subjective meaning that that action has for the individual concerned. Hence Weber's well-known definition of sociology as 'A science concerning itself with the interpretative understanding of social action and thereby with a causal explanation of its course and consequences' (1968, p. 4). By social action, Weber means human action which is subjectively meaningful and which takes account of the actions of others.

Implied in this definition is a rejection of any attempt to explain social phenomena as the result of anything other than subjectively meaningful human actions:

> Action in this sense of subjectively understandable orientation of behaviour exists only as the behaviour of one or more *individual* human beings . . . collectivities must be treated as *solely* the resultants and modes of organization of the particular acts of individual persons, since these alone can be treated as agents in the course of subjectively understandable action (Weber 1968, p. 13).

Thus, when using collective concepts such as 'social class', or 'state', the sociologist should always remember that it is not a class or a state that acts, but rather the individuals who comprise it.

The explanation of social action involves two stages. First, the sociologist must attempt to provide a plausible account of the actors' motives. This is possible because certain types of subjective meanings are generally attached to certain types of actions in certain types of situations (e.g. chopping wood on a cold day may be indicative of a desire to light a fire). There is, of course, no guarantee that the posited motive is the actual motive (the more rational the action, the greater is the likelihood that we will understand it correctly), and having adduced a possible motive, the sociologist must then go on to show that this individual tends to act in similar ways in other similar situations. In other words, an adequate sociological explanation must attempt both to understand the meaning of a given action for those involved, and to demonstrate the probability of its occurrence in particular types of situations. As Weber puts it,

> If adequacy with respect to meaning is lacking, then no matter how high the degree of uniformity and how precisely its probability can be numerically determined, it is still an incomprehensible statistical probability, whether we deal with overt or subjective processes. On the other hand, even the most perfect adequacy on the level of meaning has causal significance from a sociological point of view only insofar as there is some kind of proof for the existence of a probability that action in fact normally takes the course which has been held to be meaningful (Weber 1968, p. 12).

Correlations and generalizations explain nothing if we fail to understand what lies behind them, just as understanding of subjective meanings is useless if we cannot predict typical patterns of action.

Two points in particular should be noted about this argument. The first is that Weber only ever talks of *adequate* explanations; even when the attribution of meaning is successfully combined with an analysis of probability, we can never be certain that the explanations we put forward are correct. Furthermore, the element of free will in social life means that there must always be an element of uncertainty in the explanation of social action, for if individual actions are not determined then the most that sociology can achieve is statements of probability regarding the likely occurrence of certain types of actions in certain types of situations. It follows from this that laws of social life (including Marxist laws) are impossible, since each action is a unique (though often predictable) event. The so-called 'laws' of the social sciences (for example, the law of supply and demand) are in fact statements of typical probability regarding the likelihood of certain types of action occurring in certain types of situations.

The second point is that, although all social events are historically unique, there is clearly a need for some means whereby social phenomena can be classified in general terms, for only in this way is it possible to understand typical motives and to recognize typical patterns of action. It is, in other words, necessary to generalize in order to explain unique events. In Weber's sociology, this function of generalization is fulfilled through the construction of *ideal types*. These are mental constructs which serve to specify the theoretically most significant aspects of different classes of social phenomena. They may be either 'individual' types (Calvinism, capitalism, bureaucracy, etc.) or generic types (such as the four different types of social action). As Burger has pointed out, individual types clearly refer to numerous empirical cases (for example, there are many different capitalist societies): 'This type of ideal type is not called "individual" because it refers to one individual phenomenon, but because the occurrence of the constellation of elements decribed in it characterizes, from the point of view adopted by the historian, a class of phenomena occurring in a distinct unique, i.e. individual, historical epoch' (1976, pp. 131–2). Generic types, on the other hand, are ahistorical and serve to specify the elements from which individual types are constructed. One of the defining features of Weber's ideal type of the spirit of capitalism, for example, is goal-oriented rational action (one of four generic types of social action). As Torrance suggests, 'On the whole, Weber's position appears to be that types are constructed out of general conceptual elements, but may be additionally defined by a specific historical reference to times, places or persons' (1974, p. 136).

Weber insists that ideal types are indispensable in sociological explanation and that we constantly construct and use them whether or not we realize it. Whenever we refer to 'capitalist societies', for example, we are employing an ideal type construct, for there are many variations between, say, France and the United States which we choose to ignore for the purposes of classification while emphasizing those aspects that they have in common and that appear most relevant for our theoretical purposes. Social reality is infinite, and we can never know all there is to know about a given phenomenon. When we come to study some aspect of social life, therefore, we are immediately confronted with a chaotic complexity of sense impressions, and the only way to impose order on this chaos in order to distinguish that which is relevant to our concerns from that which is not is through the application of conceptually pure types. Ideal types are the yardsticks by means of which empirical reality can be rendered accessible to analysis. In the absence of such constructs we would be left only with an infinite range of different unique cases, each with its own history and characteristics, and we would lack any criteria for determining which of these characteristics are significant for our theoretical purposes.

Although they are mental constructs, ideal types are not simply conjured up out of nothing in the mind of the researcher, but are developed on the basis of existing empirical knowledge of actual phenomena. They involve the logical extension of certain aspects of reality into a pure, artificial yet logically possible type against which existing phenomena can be measured and compared. While their basis lies in empirical reality, ideal types do not express that reality but rather exaggerate certain aspects of it while thinking away others. The only test of an ideal type consists in the assessment of its logical coherence. Since its purpose is to clarify reality in order to facilitate the development of hypotheses, it clearly makes no sense to criticize an ideal type on the grounds that it fails to reproduce the real world in all its bewildering complexity. Ideal types are not intended as descriptions. Indeed, it is quite possible to construct any number of different ideal types of the 'same' phenomenon according to which aspects of it are deemed most significant for any given purpose. While these different types may vary in their fruitfulness for research, they cannot be evaluated against each other in terms of their empirical validity since they will each involve extensions of different aspects of the phenomenon in question. Ideal types, in other words, are always partial: 'There is no absolutely "objective" scientific analysis of culture or . . . of "social phenomena" independent of special and "one-sided" viewpoints according to which – expressly or tacitly, consciously or unconsciously – they are selected, analysed and organized for expository purposes' (Weber 1949, p. 72).

Now it has often been suggested that this emphasis on the onesidedness of sociological constructs leads Weber into a hopeless relativism in which any one account is as good as any other. Hindess (1977), for example, finds in Weber's approach a 'systematic epistemological relativism' and concludes in relation to the ideal type method that 'There is no reason why the social scientist should not let his imagination run wild. He has nothing to lose but the chains of reason' (p. 38). Such arguments, however, ignore the fact that for Weber ideal types are simply the means of analysis, not its end product. It does not follow that a partial account cannot be objective, for although ideal types are subjective constructs and cannot be tested, the hypotheses developed on the basis of them can and must be: 'Essentially, all that Weber meant by objectivity was that, within the limits of the inescapably one-sided viewpoint, it is both possible and necessary to validate one's substantive propositions' (Dawe 1971, p. 50). All explanations are partial, but not all are valid (or to be more precise, adequate). Any sociological account must be demonstrated through historical and comparative evidence.

Where Weber does endorse relativism is not in the realm of facts but in the realm of values. Thus, although he argued that scientific explanations had to be evaluated in terms of their empirical adequacy, he denied that ethical judgements could ever be evaluated in the same way. For him, the moral realm necessarily consists of fundamental dilemmas which individuals must resolve for themselves. 'The ultimately possible attitudes toward life are irreconcilable, and hence their struggle can never be brought to a final conclusion' (Weber 1948a, p. 152). Science, therefore, can never legislate on moral questions, and the basic reason for this is that, as we have seen, science is itself partial in that the ideal types that it employs are constructed according to the relevance of particular aspects of reality for the scientist's own moral and practical concerns: 'The problems of the social sciences are selected by the value-relevance of the phenomena treated . . . cultural (i.e. evaluative) interests give purely empirical scientific work its direction' (Weber 1949, pp. 21–2). Sociology is therefore grounded in ethical concerns from the very outset: 'An attitude of moral indifference has no connection with scientific "objectivity" ' (1949, p. 60).

It follows from this, as Dawe suggests, that, 'Weber is arguing for the centrality of value to social science, not merely as a "principle of selection of subject matter", but as the *sine qua non of all meaningful knowledge of social reality*. Without the attribution of value, knowledge of social phenomena is inconceivable' (Dawe 1971, p. 42). This being the case, sociology clearly cannot be used to justify a particular value position, since, 'If sociology is shaped by value, it cannot become the justification for that value; the argument would be entirely circular' (pp. 55–6). Weber's concern is not to create a dry and morally indifferent social science, but rather to ensure that the inherently one-sided accounts of social science are not used to provide a spurious resolution to fundamental moral questions which individuals must confront for themselves: 'Weber is more concerned with defending the value sphere against the unfounded claims of science than with protecting the scientific process from valuational distortions' (Bruun 1972, p. 54).

Hindess suggests that Weber's method gives rise to 'plausible generalizations and plausible stories, nothing more' (1977, p. 48). This is true in the sense that, for Weber, there can be no final guarantee of truth (his criterion of science is one of adequacy, not truth), and there are many different sides to any one question. But as we saw in the previous section, Marx's logic of retroduction is similarly unable to offer guarantees of truth, and despite its emphasis on dialectical totality, it too may be seen as partial and one-sided (for example in the emphasis it places on economic factors). The significance of Weber's method is precisely that it recognizes the partiality of sociological explanations and thus takes account of the theoretical pluralism that has always characterized the social sciences. For Weber, no one approach ever enjoys a monopoly over 'correct' scientific knowledge of social reality. As we shall see in Chapter 5, attempts by Marxists to argue otherwise appear entirely unconvincing.

Weber's ideal type method is clearly evident in his study of the city; indeed, one commentator has suggested that this study contains 'the most fully worked out typology' in his economic sociology (see Freund 1968, p. 168). As we shall see later (p. 95), Weber begins by rejecting the idea found in Simmel and others that size constitutes an adequate basis for conceptualizing the city, and he goes on to suggest that questions of economic and political organization are much more significant. As regards the former, he suggests that cities are defined by the existence of an established market system: 'Economically defined, the city is a settlement the inhabitants of which live primarily off trade and commerce rather than agriculture . . . the city is a market place' (Weber 1958, pp. 66–7). He then distinguishes between consumer, producer and commercial cities on the basis of this economic criterion, adding that 'It hardly needs to be mentioned that actual cities nearly always represent mixed types' (p. 70) and that these are therefore ideal constructions that enable classification.

As regards the political dimension, he suggests that partial political autonomy is a key criterion: 'The city must . . . be considered to be a partially autonomous association, a "community" with special political and administrative arrangements' (p. 74). On this basis, he distinguishes the 'patrician city', run by an assembly of notables, and the 'plebeian city', run by an elected assembly of citizens. He further suggests that, in its pure form, political autonomy entails some independent basis of military power in the form of a fortress or garrison, although he recognizes at various points in the study that, in the Middle Ages, the political autonomy of the cities in northern Europe was achieved on the basis of economic rather than military power.

Taking these two dimensions together, Weber then constructs his ideal type city:

> To constitute a full urban community a settlement must display a relative predominance of trade-commercial relations with the settlement as a whole displaying the following features. 1. a fortification; 2. a market; 3. a court of its own and at least partially autonomous law; 4. a related form of association; and 5. at least partial autonomy and autocephaly, thus also an administration by authorities, in the election of whom the burghers participated (Weber 1958, pp. 80–1).

Clearly this is an ideal type which is useful only in the analysis of the city at particular historical periods. This reflects Weber's concerns in this study which are basically to trace the significance of the medieval European city in the development of western capitalism, and to show why cities in ancient times and those in other parts of the world in the Middle Ages failed to create these conditions. As Bendix (1966) recognizes, this study is therefore an essential complement to Weber's earlier work on the Protestant ethic, and it reflects the same historical interest in the question of the peculiar origins of western capitalism.

Essentially, Weber's essay sets out to show how the medieval cities in western Europe sustained a fundamental challenge to the feudal system which surrounded them, and thus paved the way for the subsequent development of a rational–legal, capitalistic social order. This challenge emanated partly from the erosion of traditional values and the development of new forms of individualism, and partly from the usurpation of traditional powerful landed interests and their replacement by new forms of domination on the part of wealthy merchants and the urban nobility (as in the 'patrician cities') or later (and especially in Italy), on the part of entrepreneurs and artisans organized through urban guilds (as in the 'plebeian cities'). As Elliott and McCrone suggest, the essay 'depicts the medieval cities as places of revolution, as centres in which legitimate forms of political authority were challenged and overthrown, as places where new classes and strata appeared and contrived first to usurp power and subsequently to establish some legitimation for their own system of rule. These struggles...represented the piecemeal efforts to transform the economic and political systems that we call feudalism' (1982, p. 37). It is this concern with the struggle for political hegemony and the break from traditional values and patterns of domination which explains Weber's emphasis in his ideal type on the military, economic, legal, social and political autonomy and distinctiveness of western medieval urbanism, and his dismissal as insignificant of factors such as demographic structure or physical layout, for his concern throughout is not to develop a theory of urbanism, but to generate an historical understanding of the roots of modern capitalism.

Having developed this ideal type, Weber notes that general approximations to it are found only in the Occident. Thus, although there are many similarities between East and West, both in antiquity and in the Middle Ages, it was only in the West in the medieval period that the city came to be the basis of human association. In other places and in previous times, urban residents formed associations on the basis of kinship and estate, but in the western city in the Middle Ages, they came together for the first time as *individuals*:

> Here, in new civic creations burghers joined the citizenry as single persons. The oath of citizenship was taken by the individual. Personal membership, not that of kin groups or tribe, in the local association of the city supplied the guarantee of the individual's personal legal position as a burgher (Weber 1958, p. 102).

This contrasts with both the ancient city, where 'the individual could be a citizen . . . but only as a member of his clan' (p. 101), and with the Oriental and Asiatic city, where 'when the urban community appears at all it is only in the form of a kin association which also extends beyond the city' (p. 104).

Weber argues that a major factor explaining this difference was Christianity, for it helped dissolve clan associations while other religions such as Islam reinforced clan and tribe structures: 'By its very nature the Christian community was a confessional association of believing individuals rather than a ritualistic association of clans' (p. 103). It was also significant that there was no centralized hierarchical bureaucracy in the West as there was, for example, in China, for this meant that there were no religious or political barriers to the development of the city as an association of individuals.

The main form of association that emerged in the western medieval cities was the guild (and, later, the corporation). As time went on, the guilds became less and less associated with particular crafts and businesses, and more and more associated with the *de facto* political control of the city. Citizenship rights became dependent upon guild membership, and non-urban, non-industrial classes such as the large nobles and bishops had therefore to join the guilds in order to achieve access to political power: 'The English guild often bestowed the civic rights. . . . Nearly everywhere the guild was actually, though not legally, the governing association of the city' (Weber 1958, p. 134). Like Marx, therefore, Weber sees the city in the Middle Ages as highly significant in the break with feudalism and the foundation of the conditions for the development of capitalism: 'Neither modern capitalism nor the modern state grew up on the basis of the ancient cities while medieval urban development, though not alone decisive, was carrier of both phenomena and an important factor in their origin' (p. 181).

This significance was both economic and political. Economically, the guilds laid the basis for the development of economic rationality: 'Under the domination of the guild the medieval city was pressed in the direction of industry on a rational economic model in a manner alien to the city of antiquity' (p. 223). This is not to suggest that capitalist industry developed within the guild system, for Weber agrees with Marx that 'the new capitalistic undertakings settled in new locations' (p. 189) away from the traditional forms of enterprise and the constricting organization of labour represented by the city guilds and corporations. The economic importance of the western medieval city was not, therefore, that it spawned capitalist industry, but that it created the ideological and institutional legacy that 'formed the urban population of medieval Europe into a "ready-made" audience for the doctrines of the great Reformers' (Bendix 1966, p. 79). In other words, the development of the spirit of capitalism from the sixteenth century onwards, which Weber traces to the influence of puritanism, can be seen as the germination of a seed sown some 400 years earlier in the medieval city.

Just as important as the development of a rational and individualistic ethos in economic affairs was the development of new legal and political forms. Weber shows, for example, how rational codes of law came to be drawn up and administered by a formally-disinterested class of specialist administrators whose job it was to arbitrate between feuding factions within the patrician ruling class. Not only did this enable disputes to be settled according to some set of 'objective' criteria, rather than by force of arms or personal decree from on high, but it also facilitated the spread of common legal institutions between different cities, thereby underpinning inter-urban trade and contacts.

Furthermore, as power shifted from the military might of the nobility to the economic power of the entrepreneurial class, so new forms of political representation developed, based on the guilds and later the corporations, in which a rudimentary form of democratic self-government came to be established: 'In the Middle Ages resident citizen entrepreneurs and small capitalistic craftsmen played the politically central role. Such strata had no significant role within the ancient citizenry' (p. 204). In this way, the medieval city in Europe was the place where the crucial political as well as economic break from feudalism was accomplished.

Weber is clear that the city became the basis of human association and the spearhead of social transformation only at a specific historical period. In antiquity the basis of association, even within the cities, was kinship; in the modern period it is the nation-state. As Elliott and McCrone suggest, Weber's concern is thus directed at a fleeting yet crucial period of urban autonomy sandwiched between the city's subordination to feudal lords prior to the thirteenth century and its subordination to the absolute monarchies of the newly-emerging nations from the sixteenth century. Like Marx, therefore, Weber shows no interest in analysing the city in modern capitalist societies, and there is no basis in his work for developing a theory of urbanism as such. Just as Marx denies the theoretical significance of contemporary urbanism on the grounds that the town–country division no longer expresses an underlying class contradiction, so Weber denies it on the grounds that the city is no longer a meaningful and autonomous unit of economic and political association. Both writers thus cast a long shadow of doubt over the possibility or fruitfulness of developing an urban theory in the context of modern capitalist societies.

Émile Durkheim: the city, the division of labour and the moral basis of community

Durkheim's method provides a direct contrast to the approaches of both Marx and Weber. Like Marx, he accepts that the essence of social reality may be hidden and distorted by everyday common-sense ideas about it, but unlike Marx he suggests that the appearance of phenomena can nevertheless be taken as the expression of their essence if such phenomenal appearances are directly observed without conceptual encumbrances. In other words, Durkheim rejects the Marxist method of theorizing essences, and argues instead that essences can be directly ascertained through pure observation of appearances. Like Weber, therefore, Durkheim assumes that reality is given in observation, but unlike Weber he denies the necessity for any conceptual abstraction of partial aspects of that reality and he asserts the ability of sociology to penetrate to the essence of social phenomena. Put simply, it is Durkheim's commitment to empiricism that most sharply separates his approach from that of the other two writers discussed in this chapter, for what is specific to his method is the assertion of observation as the basis of knowledge and the consequent denial of any *a priori* theorization or conceptualization as a condition of knowledge.

Durkheim's firm commitment to empiricism has often led commentators to suggest that his is a positivist sociology. To some extent this is correct, for his endorsement of a purely experiential basis for knowledge, his equation of the logic of explanation between the natural and social sciences and his rejection of actors' ideas about the world as an important aspect of sociological explanation are all commonly associated with sociological positivism (see Giddens 1974). Against this, however, Durkheim rejects the positivist prescription of value-freedom and ethical neutrality of science, arguing that if science cannot prescribe ends then it loses all point, and that valuations of good and bad can be derived from observation of normal and pathological forms of phenomena. He also rejects individualistic explanations in favour of those that seek the causes of phenomena in collective forces which are not themselves directly observable. As Keat and Urry argue, it is therefore too simple to summarize his method as positivist since 'there are in Durkheim elements of both positivist and realist conceptions of science' (1975, p. 81). As we shall see, it is precisely the strain between these two conceptions that results in the final internal incoherence of his approach.

Basic to Durkheim's method is his argument that reality cannot be known through ideas about it. Science must address itself to the facts themselves if it is to avoid the ideological contamination of commonsense ideas, and this entails the eradication of all preconceptions: 'We must, therefore, consider social phenomena in themselves as distinct from the consciously formed representations of them in the mind; we must study them objectively as external things' (Durkheim 1938, p. 28). Science thus begins with 'a complete freedom of mind' (1933, p. 36) in which the objectivity of social facts can impress itself upon the senses. Only then is it possible to develop definitions of social facts which can identify their essential and inherent qualities: 'In order to be objective, the definition must obviously deal with phenomena not as ideas but in terms of their inherent properties. It must characterize them by elements essential to their nature' (1938, p. 35).

Sociological definitions are thus built up inductively, for it is only by observing a range of cases that the common elements essential to them all can be ascertained. Theory, in other words, plays no part in the definition, identification and classification of phenomena, but rather is developed on the basis of prior empirical observation. The classic problem of induction, of course, is that we can never be sure that we have identified an element common to all cases since the next empirical observation may prove to be an exception. Durkheim, however, denies that this is a problem for his method, and argues explicitly that there is no need even to aim for completeness of observation:

> A satisfactory method must, above all, aim at facilitating scientific work by substituting a limited number of types for the indefinite multiplicity of individuals. . . . But for this purpose it must be made not from a complete inventory of all the individual characteristics but from a small number of them, carefully chosen (Durkheim 1938, p. 80).

The reason why exhaustiveness is not required (and, incidentally, why this method is far removed from the conceptual partiality of Weber's ideal types) is that, for Durkheim, observable cases provide the means for identifying the common essence that lies behind them. The inductive analysis of a small number of cases is therefore sufficient to establish the common essential element of which each case is an expression.

Durkheim is careful to argue that the initial definition of social facts does not itself penetrate to their essence. All that is possible at this first stage is the identification of the surface features of phenomena: 'Since the definition in question is placed at the beginnings of the science, it cannot possibly aim at a statement concerning the essence of quality; that must be attained subsequently. The sole function of the definition is to establish contact with things' (1938, p. 42). Social facts, in other words, leave visible traces which provide indications of their essence; different types of social solidarity, for example, give rise to and are therefore indicated by different types of law, so that it becomes possible to distinguish the moral basis of different societies by means of an initial definition of legal forms (see below, pp. 45–6). Sociology therefore relies on observable phenomena as indicators of the essence of social facts, just as, say, the physicist relies on observation of the movement of mercury in a thermometer to indicate temperature.

This argument, of course, assumes that there is a direct causal link between indicator and essence – that what we can observe is the direct expression of social facts that remain hidden. In order to establish such a link, Durkheim advances two principles of causality. The first is that social phenomena have social causes: 'The determining cause of a social fact should be sought among the social facts preceding it and not among the states of the individual consciousness' (1938, p. 110). The explanation of social facts cannot therefore be reduced to an analysis of individual actions any more than the explanation of biological facts can be found in the analysis of the chemical composition of living organisms. Social facts, the collective phenomena of social life, have an existence external to individuals, and individual actions are constrained by them in various ways (for instance by the moral authority of laws, by the determinacy of socialization, by the 'currents' generated in collective life, and so on). It follows that there exists a distinct social reality which sociology alone can study, and that the causes of social phenomena cannot be sought through psychology or any other science: 'Products of group life, it is the nature of the group which alone can explain them' (1933, p. 350).

The second principle of causality is that any social fact has only one social cause: 'A given effect can maintain this relationship with only one cause, for it can express only one single nature' (1938, p. 127). If there appear to be several causes, then this can only mean that there are, in fact, several different phenomena to be explained. For example, if, as Durkheim (1952) suggests, there are three principal causes of suicide, then there must be three types of suicide corresponding to them. The morphological classification of social facts can therefore be followed by analysis of the causes of each of the facts identified.

Taken together, the argument that social phenomena are *sui generis*, and that single facts have single causes, enables Durkheim to assert the inherent connection between visible indicators and the essences of which they are a function. To return to our previous example, if there are two types of law then there must be two distinct types of social phenomena that have given rise to them. The question then is how are these social causes to be discovered?

Durkheim's answer is that the discovery of causes proceeds through the method of 'concomitant variation': 'We have only one way to demonstrate that a given phenomenon is the cause of another, viz., to compare the cases in which they are simultaneously present or absent, to see if the variations they present in these different combinations of circumstances indicate that one depends on the other (1938, p. 125). If a consistent correlation is found in a number of different cases, then a real relationship is to be assumed between them: 'As soon as one has proved that, in a certain number of cases, two phenomena vary with one another, one is certain of being in the presence of a law' (p. 133). Observable correlations therefore point to the existence of an essential causal relation.

It is only at this point that theory plays a part in the analysis, for having demonstrated concomitant variation, the sociologist must attempt to explain it:

> When two phenomena vary directly with each other, this relationship must be accepted. . . . The results to which this method leads need, therefore, to be interpreted. . . . We shall first investigate, by the aid of deduction, how one of the two terms has produced the other; then we shall try to verify the result of this deduction with the aid of experiments, i.e., new comparisons. If the deduction is possible and if the verification succeeds, we can regard the proof as completed (Durkheim 1938, p. 132).

The example given by Durkheim concerns the statistical relationship between levels of education and suicide rates. Since education cannot itself explain an increase in the tendency to suicide, we must attempt to identify some common factor that can account for both. Such a factor is the break-down of traditional religion, which increases both the desire for knowledge and the tendency towards suicide, and the task is then to show that wherever such religions have been eroded, both education and suicide increase accordingly. If this is demonstrated, then a sociological proof has been established.

The major question that must be posed to Durkheim's method, however, is whether theory really is limited to the secondary role that he attributes to it, and thus whether he has in fact developed an objective empirical science freed from contaminating preconceptions. The first point to be noted is that the initial process of classification and identification of visible phenomena is itself dependent upon theoretically derived criteria. The identification of 'facts' is theoretically derived:

> 'Facts', supposedly, can be identified and classified on the basis of 'experience' and 'observation' alone, without prior theory or interpretation.

Classification is, however, a theory-dependent exercise. It requires observation and comparison, of course, but it also requires a knowledge of its field of operation, criteria of identity, difference and relevance for characteristics of the 'objects' classified (Benton 1977, p. 89).

Durkheim's phenomenalism thus reveals the classic weakness of positivist approaches which rest on the assumption of a purely experiential basis of knowledge.

There is, however, also a second problem which derives from his attempt to assert this postulate of phenomenalism while at the same time drawing the distinction between observable phenomena and their hidden essences. The point, quite simply, is that, far from discovering essences through the method of concomitant variation and theoretical deduction, Durkheim's method assumes their existence from the outset. The existence of essences, and their relation to observable phenomena, is therefore pre-established in the assumptions on which the method is premised. Thus Durkheim's starting point, that observable phenomena are significant as expressions and embodiments of an essential reality to which they are causally linked, depends upon a prior theory of essences and their relation to appearances which is, according to his own prescriptions for eradicating preconceptions, illegitimate. As Hirst shows, he can only assert the phenomenal as the basis of knowledge by positing an essence theoretically: 'Durkheim's sociology . . . is a theoretical mechanism for the reproduction of the "given". It is a device for "saving" the phenomena of immediate experience: at one and the same time it promotes these phenomena to primacy ("the given") and it installs an essence behind their groundless existence' (Hirst 1975, p. 103). The result of the application of such a method is, as Hirst suggests, self-confirming, since Durkheim's sociology begins by identifying 'social facts' on the basis of unacknowledged theoretical criteria, and then asserts the necessity of these facts by 'discovering' essential causes which are similarly the product of prior theoretical assumptions: 'The essence to which we refer tells us nothing but what we already know' (p. 101).

This problem of the prior role of theory in positing the existence of an underlying essence as the basis for phenomenal forms is, in fact, explicitly recognized by Durkheim in his study of suicide (1952). There he argues that the method of morphological classification cannot be followed since it is not possible to identify different types of suicide on the basis of the empirical study of individual cases (i.e. the official records do not distinguish different types of suicide). He therefore proposes to reverse the order of study and to proceed from a *theoretical* identification of the different causes of suicide (anomy, egoism and altruism) to an empirical classification of the different types (see pp. 145–7). In other words, he assumes that his theory, which argues for three causes of suicide, is correct in order to identify different types of cases on the basis of which the theory can be tested. While he apparently sees this problem as specific to this particular analysis (in that available data are inadequate for the purposes of classification), it is clear that his procedure in this study is in fact entailed in his very method, the difference being that the theory-dependency of classification and of the identification of the essential causes of phenomena is here made explicit.

To summarize, then, Durkheim's method is inherently contradictory. If he wishes to assert the theoretical neutrality of observation of social facts as the basis for subsequent sociological explanation, then there is no ground in his method for the identification of essences causally linked to such facts. If, on the other hand, he wishes to assert the existence of an essential social reality to account for phenomenal appearances, then there is no basis in his method for rejecting the role of theory in constituting knowledge. This dilemma between phenomenalism and realism is irresolvable within the terms of Durkheim's method, and as we shall see in Chapter 2, it is a dilemma that recurs in the work of the Chicago school of human ecology whose exponents, like Durkheim, attempted to hold to a positivist approach to the source of knowledge while at the same time explaining observed phenomena as the result of unobservable hidden forces in human society.

Durkheim's method was set out most explicitly in *The Rules of Sociological Method* (1938), but as Giddens notes, this work 'explicates the methodological suppositions already applied in *The Division of Labour*' (Giddens 1971, p. 82). This latter text, Durkheim's first major work, is the most significant of his writings as regards our present concern with the role of the city in Durkheim's sociology.

The theme of the book concerns the moral basis of social solidarity, that is the social origins and foundation of the social cohesion of collective life. In it, Durkheim is concerned to show that social solidarity may be a function of either homogeneity or heterogeneity, of similarly between the 'parts' comprising the social whole or of the complementary differences between them. The problem, however, is that the moral basis of social life is not itself directly observable. The resolution to this problem, in line with his methodological prescriptions, is to identify an observable indicator that reveals it:

> Social solidarity is a completely moral phenomenon which, taken by itself, does not lend itself to exact observation nor indeed to measurement. To proceed to this classification and this comparison, we must substitute for this internal fact which escapes us an external index which symbolizes it and study the former in the light of the latter. This visible symbol is law (Durkheim 1933, p. 64).

His argument, therefore, is that different types of law, which can (he suggests) be classified directly through observation, are the effects of different types of solidarity: 'Since law reproduces the principal forms of social solidarity, we have only to classify the different types of law to find therefrom the different types of social solidarity which correspond to it' (p. 68).

The two types of law he identifies are 'repressive' (the imposition of punishment through suffering or loss) and 'restitutive' (the restoration of normality to counterbalance an infraction). Both are social in origin but their forms are different (indicating that they arise from different social conditions).

Repressive law is indicative of the existence of strong, generalized collective sentiments in society – a strong 'collective conscience' – to which all normal members of the society subscribe. An offence against this collective morality is thus not merely an offence against an individual, but is a transgression of something that is felt to be sacred and above any individual. Repressive law is thus the means by which the collectivity avenges itself: 'Since these sentiments are collective it is not us they represent in us, but society. Thus, in avenging them, it is surely society and not ourselves that we avenge, and moreover, it is something superior to the individual' (p. 101). Clearly, such a law based on a generalized collective morality can derive only from a society based on 'essential social likenesses' (p. 105), for it is only in such a society that a high degree of moral conformity and collective sentiment can be sustained. Repressive law, in other words, is both a product of and indicative of what Durkheim terms social bonds of 'mechanical solidarity'. Such a society is maintained and perpetuated on the basis of the similarity between its members, and challenges to this solidarity meet with a strong collective response through the use of repressive sanctions.

Restitutive law, by contrast, does not reflect a strong collective conscience (although its origin remains social) in that an offence against such law does not provoke a generalized moral outrage but merely an attempt to rectify the wrong that has been done. The only collective sentiment expressed in restitutive law relates to the ethic of individualism: 'The only collective sentiments that have become more intense are those which have for their object, not social affairs, but the individual' (p. 167). This type of law, therefore, is indicative of a society that derives its solidarity from the complementary differences between individuals and in which mechanical bonds of similarity have been replaced by 'organic' relations of interdependence. In such a society, the force of collective sentiments has given way to a positive union of co-operation brought about by the social division of labour: 'It is the division of labour which, more and more, fills the role that was formerly filled by the common conscience. It is the principal bond of social aggregates of higher types' (p. 173). The bonds of interdependence forged by the growth of the division of labour are infinitely stronger than the mechanical bonds of similarity, and the development of advanced societies is the history of the transition from the latter to the former.

Having classified the two types of social solidarity, Durkheim then considers the causes of the growth of the division of labour which brings about the transition from one to the other. It is at this point that the analysis of the city becomes important.

His argument is that two factors give rise to an increased division of labour in society: 'material density' (by which he means density of population in a given area) and 'moral density' (which refers to the increased density of interaction and social relationships within a population). In *The Division of Labour* (1933) he argues that the two are in practice inseparable and that 'it is useless to try to find out which has determined the other' (p. 257), although he later revised this view, arguing that social concentration cannot simply be deduced from physical concentration (since this would be to admit to the origins of a social fact in a physical rather than a social cause), and that the key cause of the division of labour was therefore an increase in moral density (see 1938, p. 115).

The increase in moral density of a society is expressed through urbanization: 'Cities always result from the need of individuals to put themselves in very intimate contact with others. There are so many points where the social mass is contracted more strongly than elsewhere' (1933, p. 258). In simple segmental societies characterized by only the most rudimentary division of labour and by mechanical bonds of solidarity, cities do not exist. The history of the advanced societies, on the other hand, reveals a continuous expansion of urban life which. 'Far from constituting a sort of pathological phenomenon...comes from the very nature of higher social species' (p. 259). Urbanization, together with the associated development of new means of transportation and communication, is the cause of the division of labour. The reason is simple; a concentrated human population can survive only through differentiation of functions: 'In the same city, different occupations can co-exist without being obliged mutually to destroy one another, for they pursue different objects . . . all condensation of the social mass, especially if it is accompanied by an increase in population, necessarily determines advances in the division of labour' (pp. 267–8). As we shall see in the next chapter, this explicit application of Darwinian principles to the analysis of functional differentiation in human societies is one of the principal themes that later urban sociologists abstracted from Durkheim's work.

There is, however, no guarantee that an increase in moral density will result in increased division of labour, since it may simply lead to, say, the collapse of the society or to the elimination of weaker competitors within it. Moral density is, in other words, a necessary but not a sufficient condition. What is necessary in addition is that the moral weight of the collective conscience be weakened, since 'the progress of the division of labour will be as much more difficult and slow as the common conscience is vital and precise' (p. 284). Here too, however, the development of the city performs an important role. This is because cities grow principally through immigration rather than through natural increase and thus attract new residents from surrounding areas whose attachment to traditional beliefs and values is thereby weakened: 'Nowhere have the traditions less sway over minds. Indeed, great cities are the uncontested homes of progress . . . When society changes, it is generally after them and in imitation . . . no ground is more favourable to evolutions of all sorts. This is because the collective life cannot have continuity there' (p. 296).

Durkheim's characterization of the city as a force for change presents what has since become a very familiar analysis of the nature of urban life. His argument that the city undermines traditional controls, that the collectivity cannot possibly impose a single code of moral conduct over the diverse spheres of action in which the urbanite becomes involved, that the individual enjoys freedom as a result of the necessary anonymity of the city, that small moral communities may develop in different parts of the city but that their sphere of influence over the individual is circumscribed, that the city extends its influence over the surrounding countryside and thus 'urbanizes' the society as a whole – all of this is reflected in the work of the Chicago school of urban ecology (Chapter 2), in Wirth's essay on urbanism as a way of life (Chapter 3) and in countless community study monographs up to the present day. And what these subsequent developments have also taken over from Durkheim is the recognition that, while the city is undoubtedly a force for progress and individual freedom, it may also become associated in the most vivid way with the pathological aspects of modern society.

It is Durkheim's concern to show that, while the development of the division of labour contains within it the possibility for a new and stronger basis of social solidarity, it may nevertheless come to be expressed through 'abnormal' forms. In other words, the erosion of collective morality that it entails may, in certain circumstances, result not in a new organic solidarity of interdependence, but in a state of moral deregulation or anomy. Where this occurs (i.e. where the division of labour has not become sufficiently institutionalized as the moral basis of social life), the moral cohesion of society itself is threatened, and according to Durkheim this was the explanation of the malaise of the advanced societies at the time when he was writing. Given the role of the city as the primary force for change, it is naturally in the cities themselves that the anomic character of modern societies becomes most evident: 'The average number of suicides, of crimes of all sorts, can effectively serve to mark the intensity of immorality in a given society. . . . Far from serving moral progress, it is in the great industrial centres that crimes and suicides are most numerous' (pp. 50–1). This is why (as we noted at the start of this chapter) the cities tend to be associated with social 'problems', for they are the most developed expression of the pathology generated as a result of moral deregulation in the society as a whole.

Given his commitment to a science of ethics, Durkheim attempts in *The Division of Labour* to diagnose the causes of this social malaise and to prescribe a remedy. The latter he finds in the establishment of a modern form of occupational guild system, nationally organized. His argument here is particularly relevant to our present concern with the urban question, for he suggests that the medieval guilds and corporations were at that time the 'normal mould' for the organization of economic interests (p. 20) and that the town was thus the cornerstone of medieval society. However, as large-scale capitalist industry developed, so the urban corporation of merchants and traders became less and less suited to its organizational needs:

While, as originally, merchants and workers had only the inhabitants of the city or its immediate environs for customers, which means as long as the market was principally local, the bodies of trades, with their municipal organization, answered all needs. But it was no longer the same once great industry was born. As it had nothing especially urban about it, it could not adapt itself to a system which had not been made for it . . . An institution so entirely wrapped up in the commune as was the old corporation could not then be used to encompass and regulate a form of collective activity which was so completely foreign to the communal life (Durkheim 1933, p. 22).

The erosion of the corporation of the Middle Ages (which in France was finally completed in the Revolution of 1789) has, however, left a vacuum precisely at the time in history when economic life has become central to collective existence. This vacuum cannot be filled by the state, for it is too remote from individuals and is ill-equipped to regulate the complexity of modern economic relations. Nor can it be filled by a resurrection of the medieval guild system, since this is totally inappropriate to a society in which the advanced division of labour has become extended far beyond the locality:

There are not many organs which may be completely comprised within the limits of a determined district, no matter how far it extends. It almost always runs beyond them. . . . The manner of human grouping which results from the division of labour is thus very different from that which expresses the partition of the population in space. The occupational environment does not coincide with the territorial environment any more than it does with the familial environment (Durkheim 1933, pp. 189–90).

It can, therefore, be filled only by nationally organized occupational corporations which alone can regulate the moral basis of economic life and thereby overcome the anomic condition of modern industrial societies.

It is clear from this argument that, like Marx and Weber, Durkheim does not consider the modern city relevant to the key concerns of social theory in advanced capitalist societies. Like them, he argues that it is only in the Middle Ages that the city was significant in itself since it was only during that period that it provided the organizational expression for functional economic interests. Just as Marx and Weber see the city in antiquity as theoretically unimportant, so too does Durkheim, arguing that 'Rome was essentially an agricultural and military society' (p. 19), and that the basis of association was familial rather than urban. And just as Marx and Weber deny the theoretical significance of the modern city (since for Marx it no longer expresses essential class relations, and for Weber it is no longer the basis for human association), so too Durkheim argues that the distinction between the city and the society as a whole in the modern period is no longer meaningful, that the society itself can now be likened to one great city (p. 300), and that localism has been undermined by the extension of the occupational and social division of labour. As he puts it,

> As advances are made in history, the organization which has territorial groups as its base (village or city, district, province, etc.) steadily becomes effaced.... These geographic divisions are, for the most part, artificial and no longer awaken in us profound sentiments.... Our activity is extended quite beyond these groups which are too narrow for it, and, moreover, a good deal of what happens there leaves us indifferent (Durkheim 1933, pp. 27–8).

Like the other two theorists discussed in this chapter, Durkheim therefore addresses the urban question in two ways. First, he sees the city as an historically significant condition for the development of particular social forces (that is to say, it creates a social concentration which stimulates the division of labour, while at the same time it facilitates this development by breaking down the bonds of traditional morality); second, he sees in the modern city the expression of the current (abnormal) development of these forces (pathological disorganization reflecting the anomic state of modern society). What appears as the most striking (and, given the divergences in their methods, astonishing) feature of any comparative reading of the works of Marx, Weber and Durkheim in relation to the urban question is thus their unanimity in their approach to the city, for all three see the medieval city as historically significant while addressing the modern city simply as the most visible expression of developments in the society as a whole.

The lesson from these three writers should be clear. There may or may not be a case for treating the city as an object of analysis in historical context. Even here, it is apparent that caution is needed, for in most places and at most times, the city has not functioned autonomously of the society of which it forms a part. The image of medieval urban autonomy is one which has been disputed (e.g. by Abrams (1978) who recommends that urban sociologists and historians alike 'get rid of the concept of the town' from their disciplines – p.10), and to the extent that it is valid, it applies (as Weber recognized) only to certain western cities over just a few hundred years. As Sjoberg notes in his classic study of feudal urbanism, 'Such a generalization, except perhaps for a narrow time period and a restricted locale in western Europe, is untenable for feudal societies in general . . . the city, shaped as it is by the enfolding socio-cultural system, whether preindustrial or industrial, must be taken as a *dependent* rather than an independent variable' (1960, p. 15). But if caution is needed in the field of urban history, then the lesson from Marx, Weber and Durkheim is surely even stronger in the case of urban sociology, for there appears to be no coherent rationale for studying cities as such in the context of modern industrial societies where cities have seemingly lost all sociological significance. As we shall see in the following chapters, urban sociologists over most of this century have ignored this lesson in their attempts to conceptualize contemporary urbanism. The result has, in most cases, been conceptual confusion and a series of theoretical dead-ends.

2 The urban as an ecological community

In his review of various attempts by sociologists to develop a specifically urban theory, Leonard Reissman suggests that the ecological perspective advanced between the wars by Robert Park and his colleagues at the University of Chicago remains 'the closest we have come to a systematic theory of the city' (1964, p. 93). Certainly human ecology was the first comprehensive urban social theory, and in the United States it has some claim to have been the first comprehensive sociological theory, for it developed at a time when American sociology was gaining institutional recognition as a discipline but lacked an indigenous body of theory. As Hawley observes, 'The reformist phase of sociology was drawing to a close and the subject was gaining acceptance as a respected discipline in the curricula of American universities. . . . Ecology opportunely provided the necessary theory' (1968, p. 329).

From its very inception, therefore, human ecology exhibited a certain tension as regards the scope of its applicability. On the one hand, it was represented as a theory of the city and thus as an attempt to develop an explanation of patterns of city growth and urban culture. In this sense, human ecology could be seen as a sub-discipline within sociology with its own object of study; while some sociologists studied education and others studied the family, those interested in human ecology studied the city. On the other hand, however, it claimed to be a discipline in its own right with its own distinctive body of theory. Indeed, the human ecologists argued that the ecological perspective addressed a problem that could not be subsumed under any other discipline, including sociology. Human biology studied the individual organism, human psychology the individual psyche, human geography the organization of space, and the various social sciences the different aspects, economic, political or cultural, of social organization. In contrast with all of these, human ecology was concerned with the specific theoretical problem of how human populations adapted to their environment. As we shall see, it then followed from this formulation that human ecology was the basic social science that established the framework within which economic, political and moral phenomena could be investigated. As one of Park's students was later to suggest, 'Human ecology, as Park conceived it, was not a branch of sociology but rather a perspective, a method, and a body of knowledge essential for the scientific study of social life and hence, like social psychology, a general discipline basic to all the social sciences' (Wirth 1945, p. 484).

This tension between human ecology as an approach within urban sociology, and human ecology as a distinct and basic discipline within the social sciences, runs throughout the work of the Chicago school. It is basically a tension between defining the perspective in terms of a concrete, physical, visible object of study – the community – and defining it in terms of a theoretically specific problem – the adaptation of human populations to their environment. Whenever Park addressed himself to such methodological questions (which was not very often), he adopted, as Wirth suggests, the latter position, arguing that a science was defined by the theoretical problem it posed rather than the concrete object it studied. Yet throughout his writings, Park nevertheless emphasized the ecological concern with the community as a visible and real entity. This confusion, which lies at the heart of the problems associated with human ecology, is reflected in, and was exacerbated by, the ambiguity inherent in Park's concept of 'community', for this term is employed to refer both to the physical community and to the ecological process. In the former case it refers to an empirical object of analysis, in the latter to a theoretical one.

Community and society

Many different intellectual influences can be discerned through an examination of Park's writings, among them those of Simmel, Comte, Spencer and W. I. Thomas. However, it does appear that two writers were especially significant. At risk of some oversimplification, it may be suggested that it was from Émile Durkheim that Park derived his methodological framework, and from Charles Darwin that he derived his theory.

Durkheim's influence can be found first in Park's ontological assumptions regarding 'human nature' and the relationship between the individual and society. In his first important statement of the ecological perspective in 1916, for example, Park wrote, 'The fact seems to be that men are brought into the world with all the passions, instincts and appetites uncontrolled and undisciplined. Civilization, in the interests of the common welfare, demands the suppression sometimes, and the control always, of these wild, natural dispositions' (1952, p. 49). Just as Durkheim sought the conditions for social stability and cohesion in the subordination of the individual to the moral authority of society, so Park takes as his starting point the tension between individual freedom and social control. Like Durkheim, Park explains personal and social disorganization in terms of the erosion of moral constraints, for *Homo ecologicus* is an inherently egoistical and unsocial creature who needs to be kept in check by society for his or her own good and for the good of others.

Of course, Park recognized that the social control of human nature was not, and never could be, total. Indeed, in the same way that Durkheim noted that social disorganization (within limits) was the necessary price to be paid for human progress, and that too much moral constraint was as bad as too little since it resulted in individual fatalism and social stagnation, so Park found in the break-down of traditional moral controls a cause for both concern and celebration. On the one hand, he saw that the growth of the cities had undermined the social cohesion once maintained by the family, the church and the village, and he pointed to the threat of the mob 'swept by every new wind of doctrine, subject to constant alarms' (1952, p. 31). Yet on the other, he saw the potential for individual freedom and self-expression that the city represented, and he noted how disorganization could be seen as a prelude to reorganization at a new level of human organization involving new modes of social control.

Human nature and moral constraint thus constantly confronted each other, and it followed that any form of human organization was necessarily an expression of both. This was certainly true of the city, for despite the regular geometrical form of many American cities, which suggested artificial rather than natural causes, Park maintained that 'The structure of the city . . . has its basis in human nature, of which it is an expression', and that, because of this, 'There is a limit to the arbitrary modifications which it is possible to make (1) in its physical structure and (2) in its moral order' (1952, p. 16). In other words, the city is as much a manifestation of natural and invariant forces as it is of political and conscious choices, and it is no more possible to abolish the ghettos and the dens of iniquity than it is to programme people's passions or eliminate their instincts.

For Park, then, human society involves a double aspect. On the one hand, it is an expression of human nature, and this is revealed in the competition for survival in which relationships with others are entirely utilitarian (a view that Park finds in the work of Herbert Spencer). On the other, it is an expression of consensus and common purpose (a view that he traces to Comte). On one level individual freedom is supreme; on the other individual will is subordinated to the 'collective mind' of society as a superorganism (to what Durkheim termed the *conscience collective*). The first level Park terms 'community', and the second 'society'; 'The word community more accurately describes the social organism as Spencer conceived it. Comte's conception, on the other hand, comes nearer to describing what we ordinarily mean by society' (1952, p. 181).

As we shall see later, this distinction between community as the biotic level of social life and society as its cultural level proved highly problematic. In particular, Park's writings on the subject exhibit some inconsistency as regards the methodological status of the dichotomy, for on some occasions he refers to community and society as analytical categories, while on others he treats them as empirical realities. The distinction is, however, basic to his ecological approach, for it enables Park to identify the peculiar concerns of human ecology in relation to the other social science disciplines. 'Ecology', he writes, 'is concerned with communities rather than societies, though it is not easy to distinguish between them' (1952, p. 251). The ecological approach to social relations, therefore, was characterized by an emphasis on the biotic as opposed to the cultural aspect of human interaction, the Spencerian rather than the Comtean view of social relations. This did not mean that human ecology denied the relevance of consensus and culture in the study of social life; only that it concentrated on the unconscious and asocial aspects as its specific area of interest.

By thus delimiting the field of ecological inquiry, Park was able to draw upon the work of Darwin in order to show how the forces that shape plant and animal communities also play a significant role in the evolution of human communities. Central to Darwin's thesis was the notion of a 'web of life' through which all organisms were related to all others in ties of interdependence or 'symbiosis'. This balance of nature was a product of the tooth and claw struggle for survival which served to regulate the population size of different species and to distribute them among different habitats according to their relative suitability. Competition for the basic resources of life thus resulted in the adaptation of different species to each other and to their environment and hence to the evolution of a relatively balanced ecological system based upon competitive co-operation among differentiated and specialized organisms. Needless to say, this was an entirely natural and spontaneous process.

It was Park's contention that the same process operated in the human community: 'Competition operates in the human (as it does in the plant and animal) community to bring about and restore the communal equilibrium when, either by the advent of some intrusive factor from without or in the normal course of its life history, that equilibrium is disturbed' (1952, p. 150). Competition between individuals, he argued, gave rise to relations of competitive co-operation through differentiation of functions (division of labour) and the orderly spatial distribution of these functions to the areas for which they are best suited. His analysis, in other words, is both functional and spatial: 'The main point is that the community so conceived is at once a territorial and a functional unit' (1952, p. 241).

His discussion of the development of functional differentiation and interdependence in the human community draws heavily on Durkheim's analysis of the origins of the division of labour. Just as Durkheim argues that the transition from a relatively homogeneous to a relatively differentiated society is effected by an increase in material and moral density, so too Park suggests that an increase in population size within a given area, together with an extension of transport and communication networks, results in greater specialization of functions (and thus stronger ties of interdependence). Park then goes on to argue, however, that this functional differentiation is also expressed spatially, for competition not only stimulates a division of labour, but also distributes the different economic groups to different niches in the urban environment. The pattern of land use in the city therefore reveals the pattern of economic interdependence.

The ecological concept that explains the congruence between spatial and economic differentiation is that of dominance. Again with reference to Darwin, Park suggests that 'In every life community there is always one or more dominant species' (1952, p. 151). The beech tree, for example, has achieved dominance over its natural habitat in the sense that only those plants, such as bluebells, that flower at a time when the tree has no leaves can flourish under its branches. In the human community, analogously, industry and commerce are dominant, for they can outbid other competitors for strategic central locations in the city. The pressure for space at the centre therefore creates an area of high land values, and this determines the pattern of land values in every other area of the city, and thus the pattern of land use by different functional groups. As Park puts it, 'The struggle of industries and commercial institutions for a strategic location determines in the long run the main outlines of the urban community . . . the principle of dominance . . . tends to determine the general ecological pattern of the city and the functional relation of each of the different areas of the city to all others' (1952, pp. 151–2). Differences in land values are thus the mechanism by which different functional groups are distributed in space in an orderly, efficient yet unplanned manner.

It follows from all this that the natural state of the ecological community, be it human or otherwise, is one of equilibrium. Change, which may result either from internal expansion or from external disruption, is represented as basically a cyclical and evolutionary process involving, first, a destabilization of the existing equilibrium; second, a renewed outburst of competition; and, finally, the development of a new (and 'higher') stage of adaptation. Basic to this conception are two assumptions. The first is that, having reached a 'climax' stage (an optimal point at which population size and differentiation is most closely adapted to environmental conditions), a community will remain in a state of balance unless some new element emerges to disturb the *status quo*. The second is that the process of community change involves an evolution from the simple to the complex through the adaptive process of differentiation of functions. This theory of community change was most explicitly set out by one of Park's colleagues at the University of Chicago, Roderick McKenzie.

McKenzie (1967) argued that the size of any human community is limited by what it can produce and by the efficiency of its mode of distribution. Thus a primary service community (such as one based on agriculture) cannot grow beyond a population of around 5000, whereas an industrial town can grow to many times that size provided its industries are serviced by an efficient system of market distribution. It was McKenzie's contention that any particular type of community tended to increase in size until it reached its climax point at which the size of population was most perfectly adjusted to the capacity of the economic base to support it. The community would then remain in this state of equilibrium until some new element (e.g. a new mode of communication or a technological innovation) disturbed the balance, at which point a new cycle of biotic adjustment would begin involving movement of population, differentiation of functions, or both of these processes. Competition, in other words, would again sift and sort the population functionally and spatially until a new climax stage was reached.

Drawing again on Darwin's work, the human ecologists referred to this process of structural community change as succession – 'that orderly sequence of changes through which a biotic community passes in the course of its development from a primary and relatively unstable to a relatively permanent or climax stage' (Park 1952, p. 152). Just as in nature one species succeeds another as the dominant life form in a particular area, so too in the human community the pattern of land use changes as areas are invaded by new competitors which are better adapted to the changed environmental conditions than the existing users. Such a process of invasion and succession is reflected in the human community in changes in land values with the result that competition for desirable sites forces out the economically weaker existing users (e.g. residents) who make way for economically stronger competitors (e.g. business). Following a successful invasion, a new equilibrium is then established and the successional sequence comes to an end.

It is these related processes of competition, dominance, succession and invasion that provide the basis for the well-known model of community expansion proposed by Burgess (1967). He suggested that the city could be conceptualized ideally as consisting of five zones arranged in a pattern of concentric circles. The expansion of the city occurred as a result of the invasion by each zone of the next outer zone, so that the central business district tended to expand into the surrounding inner-city zone of transition, which in turn tended to expand into the zone of working-class housing around it, and so on. This physical process of succession therefore results in the segregation of different social groups in different parts of the city according to their suitability: 'In the expansion of the city, a process of distribution takes place which sifts and sorts and relocates individuals and groups by residence and occupation. . . . Segregation offers the group, and thereby the individuals who compose the group, a place and a role in the total organization of city life' (pp. 54 and 56).

This constant process of change and adjustment, invasion and succession, disorganization and reorganization, is especially marked in the inner-city zone of transition. The outward pressure of the central business district accelerates the deterioration of the area around it by increasing the value of surrounding land while threatening the existing housing stock, and existing inhabitants progressively move out while their place is taken by new migrants into the city who find their niche in the decaying properties. In time, these migrants themselves move out and are replaced by later arrivals, and so the process of physical expansion and social turnover goes on. Burgess recognizes that mobility is therefore most pronounced in the inner-city areas that are in an almost constant state of flux, and he sees this as the explanation for the social disorganization (crime, vice, poverty, etc.) that tends to characterize these area. Mobility, in other words, is a source of change and of personal and social disorganization, and where mobility is greatest, so too is the lack of social cohesion and the demoralization of the human spirit.

All of these processes that we have described so far involve the natural and spontaneous response of human populations to changes in the environment in which they live. However, we noted earlier that Park and his colleagues recognized that human populations had certain characteristics that were not shared by plant and animal communities. In particular, human beings enjoyed scope for mobility which plants did not possess, and they had a capacity for consciously changing their environment which had no parallel in the plant and animal worlds. As McKenzie observed, 'The human community differs from the plant community in the two dominant characteristics of mobility and purpose, that is, in the power to select a habitat and in the ability to control or modify the conditions of the habitat' (1967, pp. 64–5). Human beings, in other words, shared a culture.

According to the Chicago ecologists, the cultural aspect of human organization, which they associated with the concept of society as opposed to community, developed at the point where the biotic struggle for existence had established a natural equilibrium. Competition led naturally to one form of human organization by forcing increased functional and spatial differentiation and thereby creating utilitarian ties of mutual interdependence (symbiosis). Once distributed functionally and territorially, however, the members of a human population were then in a position to develop new and qualitatively different bonds of cohesion based not on the necessities of the division of labour but on common goals, sentiments and values. From its origins in unconscious competition, human organization thus developed a new basis in consensus and conscious co-operation, for while competition resulted in specialization and individuation, consensus involved communication and the subordination of the individual's primordial instincts to the collective consciousness. As Park writes,

> It is when, and to the extent that, competition declines that the kind of order which we call society may be said to exist. In short, society, from the ecological point of view, and in so far as it is a territorial unit, is just the area within which biotic competition has declined and the struggle for existence has assumed higher and more sublimated forms (Park 1952, pp. 150–1).

There are therefore two types of human association: the symbiotic, brought about by competition, and the social, brought about by consensus:

> The distinction is that in the community, as in the case of the plant and animal community, the nexus which unites individuals of which the community is composed is some kind of symbiosis or some form of division of labour. A society, on the other hand, is constituted by a more intimate form of association based on communication, consensus and custom (Park 1952, p. 259).

This does not mean, however, that at the level of society there is no competition or conflict, for although he never defines the term it is clear that for Park consensus refers to shared orientations rather than shared objectives, to a common frame of reference for action rather than universal agreement over what that action should be (see Weber 1968, appendix I, for a similar formulation of the concept). Thus Park suggests that, on the social level, competition takes the form of conflict (1952, p. 152), by which he means that competition becomes conscious and collectively organized (for example through political parties) and thereby patterned by cultural norms: 'In human as contrasted with animal societies, competition and the freedom of the individual is limited on every level above the biotic by custom and consensus' (1952, p. 156). Competition is therefore mediated by culture, but the cultural form does not fundamentally alter the underlying biotic process.

This distinction between the biotic and the cultural, community and society, is fundamental to the classical perspective of human ecology, for as we have seen it is on the basis of this dichotomy that Park identifies the specific area of concern that is peculiar to this approach. The methodological basis of this crucial distinction is, however, never clearly established.

On some occasions, Park refers to communities and societies as empirical categories and thus as real entities which can be distinguished (albeit with some difficulty) in empirical research. Following Durkheim, he designates communities and societies as 'things' which can be directly studied and which exist independently of our ideas and conceptualizations of them. Communities are in this sense identified as locally based functional systems which are irreducible to the elements (that is, to human individuals) from which they are composed. Communities are therefore visible objects which can be studied in their own right: 'The community is a visible object. One can point it out, define its territorial limits, and plot its constituent elements, its population and its institutions on maps' (1952, p. 182). Empirical research can therefore begin with the study of communities because community is the framework within which society develops, and because it is more immediately visible than society and thus more amenable to statistical analysis. From such a starting point, it should be possible to discover empirical regularities between different communities, and thereby inductively to develop plausible hypotheses and scientific generalizations.

Elsewhere, however, Park treats the community–society dichotomy as an analytical construct. This follows from his argument that a science is distinguished not by a specific object of study but by the theoretical problem it poses in relation to some aspect of that object: 'What things are for any special science or for common sense, for that matter, is determined largely by the point of view from which they are looked at' (1952, p. 179). This suggests that human ecology is defined, not by its empirical concern with communities, but by its mode of conceptualizing 'community'. In this sense, community refers to a specific aspect of human organization which is identified theoretically as the unorganized and unconscious process whereby human populations adjust to their environment through unrestricted competition. Community here is not a thing but a process, not a separate and visible area of human existence but a distinct perspective on human existence. Seen in this way, the concept of community is merely a shorthand term for the biotic forces operating in human society, in which case it is clearly not possible to distinguish it from society in any empirical research setting.

Of these two approaches, the latter appears to achieve more prominence in Park's writings. Like Durkheim, he is concerned to analyse the complexity of society by first tracing the simplest and most basic unit of human organization, and this he finds in the concept of community. Only through exhaustive analysis of the impact of biotic forces on human society is it possible to begin to identify the significance of cultural factors. As Wirth (1945) explained it, the basic physical and natural forces at work in human society establish the framework and the context within which people act, and human ecology is therefore basic and complementary to the analysis of social organization and social psychology: 'Human ecology is not a substitute for, but a supplement to, the other frames of reference and methods of social investigation' (p. 438).

Having first established the scope of the biotic in human affairs, Park then attempts to reconstruct the complexity of social reality by taking into account the additional significance of human technology and cultural values. While conceptually distinct, he therefore recognizes that the biotic and the cultural are empirically interrelated:

> Human ecology has, however, to reckon with the fact that in human society competition is limited by custom and culture. The cultural superstructure imposes itself as an instrument of direction and control upon the biotic substructure. Reduced to its elements the human community, so conceived, may be said to consist of a population and a culture, including in the term culture (1) a body of customs and beliefs and (2) a corresponding body of artifacts and technological devices. To these three elements or factors – (1) population, (2) artifact (technological culture), (3) custom and beliefs (non-material culture) – into which the social complex resolves itself, one should, perhaps, add a fourth, namely, the natural resources of the habitat. It is the interaction of these four factors that maintain at once the biotic balance and the social equilibrium when and where they exist (Park 1952, p. 158).

Having torn asunder the biotic and the cultural at the conceptual level, Park therefore reunites them at the level of empirical reality, for his four elements of the 'social complex' include ecological and cultural factors as inherently interrelated aspects.

Clearly, then, Park recognizes the mutual interdependence of the biotic and the cultural in the 'real' social world. Indeed, he takes the analysis further by suggesting that it is possible to conceptualize a hierarchy of constraints on the individual in terms of the operation of the ecological, economic, political and moral orders, such that the freedom of the individual is progressively restricted beyond the biotic level: 'The individual is more free upon the economic level than upon the political, more free on the political than the moral' (1952, p. 157). Such a formulation can be understood only analytically, and such an interpretation is reinforced in one of the last essays Park published where he developed a model of human society 'as a kind of cone or triangle, of which the basis is the ecological organization of human beings' (1952, p. 260). Furthermore, in this essay he added that on this basic ecological level 'the struggle for existence may go on, will go on, *unobserved* and relatively unrestricted' (p. 260; my emphasis), thereby demonstrating beyond doubt that the ecological community is not a thing but a theoretically defined aspect of social organization.

How, then, can a view of community as an empirical category – an observable and measurable object – be reconciled with the parallel view of community as an analytical construct? That both views are present in Park's writings cannot be doubted. That he never explicitly recognized their incompatibility is also apparent. His essays on human ecology span twenty-three years, yet in all that time he seemingly never felt obliged to address what appears as an obvious and fundamental confusion surrounding the dichotomy on which his entire approach was based.

The source of the confusion lies in the methodology that Park derived from Durkheim. As we saw in Chapter 1, this is basically an empiricist methodology, in that Durkheim (and Park) argues that knowledge is derived directly from the sense experiences and that phenomena must therefore be defined solely in terms of their external characteristics. It is for this reason that Park emphasizes community as an empirical and visible object. However, both Durkheim and Park are also committed to an holistic view of social collectivities in the sense that they wish to avoid reducing such collectivities to their individual components. Community (for Park) and society (for Durkheim) are therefore objects of study *sui generis*. There is an evident tension between these two postulates of phenomenalism and holism, for when we actually observe human communities and societies all we ever actually see are individuals. In other words, the very apprehension of a social collectivity as a thing is necessarily conceptual rather than phenomenal. The commitment to holism thus necessarily undermines the empiricist methodology by postulating a reality beyond direct experience. As Keat and Urry observe, 'When positivists seek to put into operation their methodology they often find themselves employing realist arguments or positing realist-type entities, albeit in an unsystematic and confused way' (1975, p. 82).

Such was the case with Durkheim in his study of the suicidogenic current which he saw as the underlying yet unobservable cause of the social suicide rate. Such is also the case with Park in his study of biotic forces as the underlying yet unobservable cause of functional and spatial organization. The way in which Durkheim side-stepped this problem was by reversing his own prescriptions as regards causal analysis. Because he was unable to observe the variations in the suicidogenic current, Durkheim inferred them from their supposed consequences in the suicide statistics (in other words, rather than tracing the effect of the current on the suicide rate,he deduced these effects from variations in the suicide rate, thereby developing an entirely tautological analysis). The way in which Park attempted to resolve what was essentially the same problem as regards the biotic forces behind human organization was by eliding an empirical category – community – which he argued could be observed, with an analytical one – the biotic level – which could not. In this way, he tried to fuse a phenomenal form with a realist concept. The way in which he did this was through the development of perhaps the most important concept of all in the ecological dictionary – that of 'natural area'.

We have seen that both Park and McKenzie argued that the biotic forces of competition always tend to produce a natural equilibrium at the point where the population is optimally adjusted to its environment. At this climax stage, the community is functionally and spatially differentiated such that different functional groups are located in different areas according to their relative suitability. As this unstable biotic equilibrium develops, so too do distinctive cultural forms corresponding to the different areas: 'The general effect of the continuous processes of invasions and accommodations is to give to the developed community well-defined areas, each having its own peculiar selective and cultural characteristics' (McKenzie 1967, p. 77). These different areas within the city, fashioned by competition and characterized by both functional and cultural differentiation, are termed 'natural areas'.

The significance of the concept of natural area for the Chicago school's human ecology is twofold. First, it overcomes the empirical problem associated with the biotic–cultural division by specifying an observable object – the ghetto, the red light district, the suburb or whatever – in which these two aspects of human organization have become fused. A natural area, that is, is also a cultural area. It is on the one hand an area characterized by division of labour and competitive co-operation, while on the other it is a moral area characterized by consensus and communication. It therefore represents an object, a 'thing', which can be studied both ecologically and sociologically, as a natural unit or as a social unit. Human ecology is therefore provided with an object of analysis in the sense that visible natural areas constitute a laboratory in which biotic processes of population change and adaptation can be studied.

The second point is related to this, for the natural area not only provides a concrete object of study, but also represents the conceptual framework within which such studies can be developed. Because natural areas are seen as the manifestations of natural forces operating in any and every human settlement, it follows that the different regions of one city should be directly comparable with those of another. Categories such as the ghetto or the suburb are treated generically, so that, for example, the cultural form of one ghetto should be similar to that of all others. Park writes,

> The natural areas of the city . . . serve an important methodological function. They constitute, taken together, what Hobson has described as 'a frame of reference', a conceptual order within which statistical facts gain a new and more general significance. They not only tell us what the facts are in regard to conditions in any given region, but in so far as they characterize an area that is natural and typical, they establish a working hypothesis in regard to other areas of the same kind. . . . Most facts that can be stated statistically, once they have been plotted in this conceptual scheme – this ecological frame of reference – can be made the basis of general statements which may be eventually reduced to abstract formulae and scientific generalizations (Park 1952, p. 198).

Empirical research is thus situated within a framework that enables the development of inductive generalizations (i.e. what Park sees as the transition from concrete fact to conceptual knowledge). Because biotic forces are assumed to be at work, the hidden causes of visible phenomena in natural areas, it is possible to develop scientific knowledge about them by studying their effects in different comparable locations: 'The result of every new specific enquiry should reaffirm or redefine, qualify or extend, the hypotheses upon which the original enquiry was based. The results should not merely increase our fund of information, but enable us to reduce our observations to general formulae and quantitative statements true for all cases of the same kind' (1952, p. 198).

Faced with the same methodological problems as Durkheim (how to develop knowledge of an underlying force in human society when the only valid knowledge is that grounded in experience of 'concrete facts'), Park therefore resorts to much the same solution (assume the existence of the force and search empirically for phenomena that are deemed to be manifestations of that force). Implicitly, however, Park seems to recognize that such an approach is hardly consistent with his positivist methodology, and it is for this reason that he also suggests that the natural area is itself an object of study in which the biotic as well as the cultural may be directly analysed.

This, then, is the source of the confusion referred to earlier between community as an empirical category and as an analytical construct. For Park it has to be both a thing that can be observed directly, and a force in human organization which can be theorized on the basis of such observation. The natural area concept is pressed into service to perform this dual function as both an observable object and a manifestation of an unobservable force. Once we recognize this uneasy tension in Park's methodology between positivism and realism, the analysis of communities and the theorization of the biotic forces that are at work within them, we can understand how it is that human ecology itself exhibits a dual identity, as on the one hand a sociological method for studying the city, and on the other a distinct discipline within the human sciences. Park's human ecology was from the very beginning set upon two stools. It was only a matter of time before the critics kicked them apart.

Human ecology is dead . . .

'By 1950, the ecological approach as developed by Park, his colleagues and students at the University of Chicago was virtually dead' (Berry and Kasarda 1977, p. 3). The demise was gradual and cumulative, brought about by a combination of essentially misguided criticisms (which nevertheless served to call the approach into question) and fundamental critiques.

What I term the 'misguided criticisms' fell into three categories. The first, stated most forcibly by Davie (1937), accepted the basic assumptions of human ecology – that city growth was the product of 'automatic forces' involving competition and selection – but took issue with Burgess's application of these ideas through the hypothesis of a concentric zone pattern. In a study of New Haven, Davie showed that patterns of residential location were largely a function of patterns of industrial location, and that industry located near lines of communication which exhibited no uniform pattern. Recognizing that Burgess's model was conceived as an ideal type, Davie nevertheless concluded that 'There is no universal pattern, not even of an "ideal type" ' (p. 161). His study then stimulated a series of other projects on other cities in which various authors engaged in increasingly elaborate mapping exercises, but this whole line of research and criticism inevitably led up a cul-de-sac since it was addressed only to the descriptive question of urban form. The theoretical problems of the ecological analysis of such forms remained unexamined. In retrospect it does seem that Burgess's famous paper has received disproportionate attention over the years, and this has resulted in widespread concern with the question of spatial distribution to the neglect of the more basic question of functional differentiation (a tendency which, as we shall see, was later 'corrected' by Hawley).

The second misconceived (yet in a different context very significant) criticism concerned the mode of statistical analysis in ecological research. Robinson (1950) drew a distinction between ecological correlations (correlations between aggregate phenomena such as that between the proportion of blacks in a population and the rate of illiteracy) and individual correlations (correlations between indivisible units). He then pointed to the fallacy of using an ecological correlation as evidence for an individual one, for the fact that there may be a strong correlation between the illiteracy rate and the proportion of blacks in a given population does not necessarily justify the deduction that it is the blacks who are illiterate. Indeed, Robinson showed that ecological correlations invariably overemphasized (and occasionally even reversed) individual ones.

Robinson's paper represents an important criticism of research which does aim to deduce individual statistical relationships from correlations based on aggregate data (one famous example being Durkheim's *Suicide*). This was not, however, the intention of the Chicago ecologists, for as Menzel (1950) pointed out, ecological correlations in their research were used to demonstrate 'a common underlying cause inherent not in the individuals as such but in inter-individual differences and relationships – properties of areas as such' (p. 674). Indeed, we saw in the previous section that Park was concerned to emphasize the irreducibility of the ecological community to its individual components. Thus a correlation between, say, divorce rates and crime rates would not be used to imply that divorcees are criminals, but as evidence of how the characteristics of a particular area (and in particular a high level of mobility) generate high levels of social disorganization which are reflected in the divorce rate, the crime rate and so on. Ecological correlation thus performed the same function as Durkheim's concomitant variation (which was discussed above, pp. 41–2).

The third criticism that is basically misguided is one developed by Alihan (1938), among others, to the effect that there is a disjuncture between the theoretical and the empirical products of the Chicago school. Reviewing the research monographs of those like Anderson (on the hobo) and Zorbaugh (on the slum), Alihan suggests that they invariably fail to distinguish biotic and cultural forces, and that they are no more than sociological studies in which territorial distribution is taken into account on a descriptive level: 'If we take a territorially demarcated unit as a basis of study, we do not discriminate between certain activities carried on within the area as those of "society" and others which are those of "community" (p. 82). Alihan's argument here is true but irrelevant, for while it certainly is the case that the various Chicago monographs do not draw this distinction, it is equally the case that it was never intended that they should. As we saw in the last section, such studies were premised on the assumption that the areas under investigation had been created by biotic forces, and their objective was to study the cultural forms that had developed as a result with a view to developing theoretical generalizations. The biotic–cultural division, in other words, provided the initial framework for such studies rather than their object of analysis. Thus Alihan's comment that Park and his colleagues 'waver between the complete scission of the two concepts on the one hand, and their fusion on the other' (pp. 69–70) cannot in itself be deemed a criticism, since it was precisely Park's intention to separate the two analytically and to fuse them empirically.

This line of attack was, nevertheless, pursued with much enthusiasm by critics of the Chicago school, and most notably by Firey (1945). He suggested that human ecology explained locational activity purely in terms of economic maximization, and argued against this that space may have a symbolic as well as economic value, and that locational activity may therefore reflect sentiment as much as economic rationality. Reporting his study of land use in Boston, he then showed how upper-class residents had remained in Beacon Hill for 150 years because of their sentimental attachment to the area and despite the economic advantages of selling up and moving out; how 'sacred sites' such as the common and civil war burial grounds had been preserved from development even though they occupied the most valuable ground in the city and caused economically wasteful traffic congestion; and how, even in an Italian slum, the first generation immigrants were loath to leave the area owing to their commitment to the values of family and *paesani* which were upheld in the slum but were threatened outside it. It followed from all this that cultural values and intersubjective meanings were clearly crucial variables in the explanation of patterns of land use, and that the ecological concern with biotic forces had therefore to be modified.

Park, however, never denied the empirical significance of cultural factors. Indeed, as we have seen, he included both technology and 'non-material' cultural factors as two of the four elements of the 'social complex'. In terms of empirical research, he and his colleagues never intended that community could be analysed separately from society (as Alihan's critique suggested), nor that distributional patterns should be explained solely in terms of ecological forces (as Firey claims). The most that can be said about the difference between Park and Firey is that they are primarily interested in different questions: for Firey, the interesting question is why and how Beacon Hill has resisted invasion from business uses for a century and a half; for Park, it would be why and how Beacon Hill came to be associated with the upper class in the first place.

Where the work of writers such as Alihan and Firey *does* pose an important challenge to human ecology is not in their atacks on the biotic–cultural dichotomy, but in the implications that their arguments have for the fundamental methodological division (which underpins this dichotomy) between the community as a visible object and the community as an analytical construct. These implications are in fact brought out by Alihan, who suggests in relation to the Chicago ecologists that

> One of their main difficulties lies in the confusion between abstraction and reality. Some of this confusion might have been avoided if the school had been familiar with the 'ideal type' method of investigation. The concept 'community' is approached in a way that denies its social attributes. In its very definition it is an abstraction of the asocial aspect of human behaviour. Yet the ecologists find themselves compelled in many ways to take account of the social factors which in reality are intrinsically related to and bound up with the asocial community. Had ecologists persisted in dealing with the concept of the 'natural order' as an abstraction, or as an 'ideal type', for the purposes of study these social factors could be treated apart from 'community', as conditioning, concomitant and intrusive phenomena of the 'natural order'. We would then have only the problem of the validity and scientific utility of a particular classification and of the particularistic philosophical ideology underlying the delimitation of the category 'community'. But ecologists do not pursue this course consistently; what is to them an abstraction at one time becomes a reality at another (Alihan 1938, pp. 48–9).

Alihan here summarizes the main point at issue. If Park had consistently approached the concept of 'community' solely as an abstraction, an heuristic device for analysis, then his approach would have been methodologically (though not necessarily theoretically) valid. We may still have wished to argue that it was not useful to approach human society from such a naturalistic perspective, and that to do so was to resort to unwarranted biological determinism (see Gettys 1940), but there would be no methodological grounds for disputing the biotic–cultural distinction. The fact that Park did not, and could not, limit the concept in this way was due to his commitment to the positivist postulate of phenomenalism. In other words, for him any abstraction had to have a direct empirical reference. He could no more accept the idealism implicit in Alihan's reference to ideal types than he could the realism inherent in the alternative view of abstractions as referring to a level of reality beyond the senses. Following Durkheim, the ecologists were concerned above all with things: 'Their universe of discourse became limited to externalities and the interpretation of social life hinged upon its most concrete aspects. Reducing social behaviour to a common denominator of the tangible and the measurable ... human ecologists became the expounders of the socially "given" ' (Alihan 1938, p. 6).

In the light of this critique, human ecology was confronted with two options. Either it could retain its foundation in a positivist methodology while rejecting attempts to theorize the underlying forces determining the mode of human organization, or it could attempt to develop and justify the concept of the ecological community as an abstraction while rejecting the search for an observable and physical reference point. Human ecology could no longer have its cake and eat it, and the two questions of spatial form and functional process, which Park had attempted to unite, had at last to be severed.

Different analysts, faced with this dilemma, chose different options. Those who chose the first continued to undertake research on the observable and external characteristics of human communities, but this was now divorced from any rigorous theoretical framework, and what Mills (1959) refers to as 'abstracted empiricism' was too often the result. Basically these studies fell into two categories: those concerned with statistical analyses of urban populations (tracing patterns of migration, mapping social phenomena, etc.) and those concerned with descriptive accounts of cultural forms (for example the tradition of community studies). Neither of these categories has provided coherent and cumulative data, for while the former merely amasses figures and trends, the latter provides a long series of non-comparable case studies on individual localities. Neither, in fact, can any longer be termed 'ecological', for while the first has disintegrated into the most descriptive demography, the second appears little different from cultural anthropology (see Hannerz 1980, ch. 2). In both, the theoretical specificity of the urban has disappeared.

Those analysts who chose the second option have fared somewhat better. This approach was first spelt out by Hawley (1944), who asserted (against the contemporary line of argument at that time) that human ecology was a viable theoretical perspective, but that it had been distorted by the Chicago school's emphasis on spatial distributions of social phenomena. Hawley sought to relocate human ecology in the mainstream of ecological thought, and in doing so he argued that space, far from being central, was incidental to the ecological problem. The traditional concern of the Chicago ecologists with the physical distribution of social phenomena (which, as we have seen, was the product of their commitment to the principle of phenomenalism) was, for Hawley, indicative not of a genuinely ecological framework but of a geographical one. Space, he suggested, was merely a factor that had to be taken into account by human ecology, just as it had to be taken into account by any other science. What was specific to human ecology was not, therefore, its concern with the physical human community, but rather its interest in a particular process; that of the adaptation of human populations by means of functional differentiation.

Six years after this article appeared, Hawley published a book which set out an ecological framework that has guided research in human ecology ever since. In the words of Berry and Kasarda, 'Hawley reformulated the ecological approach and initiated its present revival within the field of sociology' (1977, p. 3). So it was that human ecology re-emerged during the 1950s as a more modest, but methodologically more secure, approach than that first outlined by Park thirty-four years before.

. . . Long live human ecology!

Like Park, Hawley began from the position that a science should be distinguished according to its perspective rather than its object of study: 'A science is delimited by what it does rather than by any *a priori* definition of its field . . . it must bring into focus a set of problems not included within the scope of other disciplines to which scientific techniques can be, and are in fact being, applied' (1950, p. 10). The perspective that was specific to ecology was that which sought to explain how populations adapted collectively and unconsciously to their environment. This struggle to adapt was seen as a central problem for all species, including human beings, for although human beings had developed cultural artefacts which enabled them to adapt more efficiently and effectively than other species, the difference between them was quantitative rather than qualitative: 'The difference between men and other organisms in adaptive capacity, though great, seems to be a matter of degree rather than kind' (1950, p. 32). There was therefore no reason why the principles of ecological theory as a whole should not be applied to the analysis of adaptation by human communities in particular, and this is what Hawley set out to do.

It is important to recognize that Hawley does not suggest that an ecological approach to the human community is in any way exhaustive, for he argues that such communities are comprised of psychological and moral as well as functional relations, and that human ecology is concerned only with the latter. Nor does he suggest that these different aspects of social relationships can be empirically distinguished, for 'Sustenance activities and relationships are inextricably interwoven with sentiments, value systems and other ideational constructs' (1950, p. 73). Hawley never seeks to deny that values and individual motivations may play an important part in the development of human communities, but rather seeks to assert that this is irrelevant to the ecological problem. The theoretical objective of human ecology, he states, 'is to develop a description of the morphology or form of collective life under varying external conditions. With its problem stated in that manner, the irrelevance of the psychological properties of individuals is self-evident' (1950, p. 179). It is because human ecology is concerned with how human populations adapt collectively to their environment that questions of individual values and motivations have no place within it.

Hawley's analysis of adaptation is developed around the four ecological principles of interdependence, key function, differentiation and dominance. These principles are themselves derived and justified from certain 'cardinal assumptions' concerning the invariant conditions in which human populations are situated (see Hawley 1968). For example, every human population must afford some means whereby its members can achieve access to the environment in order to live; every human population develops some form of interdependence between its members; and so on. From such simple and seemingly non-contentious assertions, Hawley develops a complex and highly contentious theory. (It is worth noting here that Hawley's 'cardinal assumptions' are not dissimilar from those identified by Marx, for both writers emphasize the primacy of material production in society, and both stress the necessity for a system of social relations through which this can be accomplished. What is interesting about this is that, while both writers start from similar *a priori* assumptions regarding the conditions for social existence, they go on to develop very different theories, and this would tend to suggest that neither ecological nor Marxist theory can be justified simply in terms of logical deduction from general principles. As we saw in the discussion of Marx's methodology in Chapter 1, such abstract transhistorical generalizations are in fact very limited, and it follows from this that Hawley's claim to have 'deduced' the principles of ecological organization from such generalizations should be approached with some caution.)

The first of Hawley's ecological principles is interdependence, and he suggests that a major difference between his approach and that of earlier human ecologists concerns the relative emphasis on interdependence as opposed to competition. In any human population, the process of adaptation to the environment involves the development of interdependence among its members. This may take the form either of symbiotic relations (i.e. complementary relations between functionally dissimilar groups) or commensalistic relations (i.e. aggregation of functionally similar groups). In both cases, the combination of individual units increases their collective capacity for action beyond what would have been possible had they remained isolated. Thus a symbiotic union enhances the creative powers of human groups (for it enables specialization), while a commensalistic union enhances their defensive powers (for it increases numerical strength). Symbiotic unions are therefore productive while commensalistic unions are protective. Hawley terms the former 'corporate groups' and the latter 'categoric groups'. The main corporate groups in modern society are familial, associational and territorial, while the main categoric groups are those based on common occupation (for instance the trade unions).

The pattern of ecological organization of a given population within a given territory is therefore determined by the two axes of symbiosis and commensalism. The pattern will be far from simple, however, for Hawley recognizes that corporate groups (based on symbiotic interdependence) may sometimes function as categoric units (for example when responding to some external threat), while categoric groups (based on commensalistic aggregation) may sometimes develop corporate characteristics (for example by developing a specialized leadership stratum). Furthermore, the relations between various units may take either a symbiotic or commensalistic form, so that, for example, corporate units may establish categoric combinations while categoric units may develop symbiotic ties between them as a result of differentiation between their functions. Any human population therefore exhibits a complex pattern of interdependence between different units, but this complexity can nevertheless be analysed by means of the simple formal dichotomy between symbiosis and commensalism. For Hawley, in other words, the ecological community, which constitutes the object of analysis for human ecology, is the system of symbiotic and commensalistic relationships which enables a human population to carry on its daily life. As a system of interdependent relations, the ecological community is therefore irreducible to the units that comprise it: 'It is, in fact, the least reducible universe within which ecological phenomena may be adequately observed. . . . The community, then, is the basic unit of ecological investigation' (1950, p. 180).

Having thus identified the ecological community in terms of a system of functional and interdependent relationships, Hawley is then in a position to develop three further ecological principles. The first of these is the principle of the 'key function', by which he means that certain units within the system will tend to perform a more significant function in adapting the population to its environment than others: 'In every system of relationships among diverse functions, the connection of the system to its environment is mediated primarily by one or a relatively small number of functions' (1968, p. 332). Because the fundamental problem faced by human populations is that of adapting to the external environment, it follows that those units most centrally involved in this process must be the key functional units in the system. Although Hawley does not spell out the implications of this argument, it is clear from his work that the key function is therefore performed in a capitalist society by private enterprise firms which mediate both between the population and its natural environment (through material production) and between the population and its surrounding social environment (through trade).

The performance of the key function is crucial to the two remaining ecological principles identified by Hawley. The first of these is functional differentiation, the extent of which depends upon the productivity of the key function. Thus, while the low productivity of hunting and gathering societies inhibits the development of functional differentiation and specialization, the high productivity of societies organized around the key function of industry means that there is in principle no upper limit on the extent to which differentiation may proceed. This is significant because differentiation, involving an increasingly complex mode of social organization, is the principal way in which human populations adapt to their environment. In other words, given adequate productivity of the key function, differentiation restores the balance between population and environment where this is disturbed by competition (in the way Park suggested) or by improvements in transport and communications (in the way Durkheim suggested in his discussion of moral density).

The final ecological principle – that of dominance – is similarly dependent upon the key function, for the dominant positions within the ecological system are assumed by those units that contribute most to the key function: 'Dominance attaches to the unit that controls the conditions necessary to the functioning of other units. Ordinarily that means controlling the flow of sustenance into the community' (1950, p. 221). Interestingly, Hawley recognizes that one implication of this view is that the dominant units in a human population are likely to be economic rather than political:

> It is commonly assumed that government assumes the dominant position.... Yet its dominance is not without qualification ... government, especially in the United States, plays a passive part in the sustenance flow to the community. In effect, government shares and is in competition for the dominant position with associational units whose functions enable them to exert a decisive influence on the community's sustenance supply (Hawley 1950, p. 229).

The functional dominance of business within the ecological system is therefore expressed politically through business influence over community decision-making; a conclusion that Hawley later re-affirmed (1963) in a study of concentrated business power in relation to urban renewal programmes.

The functional dominance of business is expressed not only politically, but also spatially and temporally. It is expressed spatially through centrality, for the centre of human settlements is the point at which functional interdependence is integrated and administered. Dominant units performing the key function therefore occupy central sites, while other units performing lesser functions are distributed according to their relative contributions: 'In general, units performing key functions have the highest priority of claim on location. Other units tend to distribute themselves about the key function units, their distances away corresponding to the number of degrees of removal separating their functions from direct relation with the key function'

(Hawley 1968, p. 333). The functional hierarchy is thus expressed in the form of a spatial gradient, and although Hawley notes that the spatial distribution of different functional units may be affected by factors such as topography and transport routes, his analysis nevertheless results in a very familiar conclusion: 'A noticeable tendency appears for each class of land use to become segregated in a zone situated at an appropriate distance from the centre. The resulting series of more or less symmetrical concentric zones represents in general outline a universal community pattern' (1950, p. 264). Burgess's famous description of the pattern of land use is therefore reaffirmed by Hawley, but his analysis is not, for Hawley explains this pattern as the result of *functional* dominance rather than central dominance *per se*. Where business performs the key function in the system, it will be found at the centre of human settlements, but where other units (e.g. household units in pre-industrial societies) perform the key function, they will occupy the central locations. Thus, while evidence relating to the spatial pattern of pre-industrial cities appears to refute Burgess's model, it is entirely consistent with Hawley's.

The temporal dimension of dominance is revealed in the way in which the rhythm of the principal sustenance unit in the community becomes imposed upon other activities. Just as business dominance is expressed spatially in the pattern of land use, so it is expressed temporally in the rhythm of community activities, the most obvious example of this being the rush-hour.

The significance of these four principles of interdependence, key function, differentiation and dominance is that together they explain how it is that human populations exhibit a constant tendency towards functional equilibrium in their relationship with their environment. Thus Hawley suggests that these four factors tend to bring about a situation where 'development has terminated in a more or less complete system that is capable of sustaining a given relationship to environment indefinitely' (1968, p. 334). In such a closed system, differentiation of functions has been maximized (relative to the productivity of the key function) and organized in terms of corporate and categoric units; the performance of the key function itself has been concentrated in just one unit (or a categoric grouping of units) in order to maximize efficient control of other units of the system; all functions are mutually complementary and are organized at maximum efficiency so that the number of individuals involved in performing each function is just enough to maintain it adequately; and the different functional units have been arranged in space and time so that accessibility is directly proportional to the frequency of exchanges between them.

The tendency towards such an optimally adjusted and maximally efficient system is, however, only a tendency. The fact that such systems are never actually realized is due first to 'immanent change' (that is, change in the environment, such as a decline in non-replaceable natural resources, which necessitates constant readjustment of the ecological system), and second to 'cumulative change' (expansion of the system itself consequent upon the growing productivity of the key function). Because the ecological system is never static it never attains a state of closure, but the underlying tendency within the ecological community is nevertheless always towards the re-establishment of equilibrium. System change is thus fundamentally an evolutionary process involving expansion and readjustment of the ecological system.

This emphasis on evolutionary change lies at the heart of contemporary ecological theory. It is found, for example, in the work of Otis Dudley Duncan, one of the leading exponents of Hawley's approach to human ecology, who writes, 'The most fundamental postulates of human ecology still are best elucidated in an evolutionary framework' (1964, p. 45). Like Hawley, Duncan conceptualizes the ecological community as 'equilibrium-seeking' (Duncan 1959). He suggests that the ecological system may be understood as a functionally interdependent 'ecological complex' consisting of population, environment, human technology and human organization. All four of these variables interact upon each other, although in general population and organization tend to be dependent while environment and technology are independent. In other words, just as Hawley traces the source of system change to external environmental conditions or to internal expansion of productivity, so too Duncan emphasizes the significance of environmental and technological changes in the evolution of the ecological complex as a whole. Changes in these two factors, together with associated changes in population size and organizational capacity, bring about the expansion of the system as a whole: 'Ecological expansion . . . may be characterized by a formula, the four terms in which have been called the "ecological complex": technological accumulation at an accelerated rate; intensified exploitation of environment; demographic transition (now popularly known as "population explosion"); and organizational revolution' (Duncan 1964, p. 75).

Contemporary human ecology is thus characterized above all by its emphasis on the tendency to equilibrium (homeostasis) and the evolutionary nature of system change. In both respects, it has come very close to the functionalist paradigm in sociology. Indeed, there are other parallels between ecological and functionalist perspectives, for not only do they both address themselves to the same problems of the maintenance of equilibrium and the evolutionary development of social systems, but both are oriented towards the analysis of system features rather than individual values and motivations (see Beshers 1962, ch. 2), and both attach considerable significance to patterns of functional interdependence between different units in social systems and to the process of cybernetic feedback within systems (for example through the mutual interaction of the four elements in Duncan's ecological complex). Duncan himself has recognized this close affinity between the two approaches, and has even argued that the ecological perspective may help to clarify some of the areas of confusion within functionalist sociology as a whole (see Duncan and Schnore 1959).

Given this affinity between ecological and functionalist approaches, it is not surprising that many of the familiar criticisms made against functionalist theory have also been made against post-war human ecology. Two in particular deserve mention. The first concerns the problem of teleology and tends to involve the argument that analysis of social systems cannot be accomplished without reference to the subjectively meaningful purposive actions of individual members. The second concerns the question of ideology and tends to involve the assertion that theories that are addressed to the problem of system maintenance are grounded in inherently conservative postulates.

The problem of teleology is that collectivities do not act purposefully, which renders problematic any explanation of a given phenomenon couched in terms of the social purpose, or function, it serves. According to Hawley, however, human ecology does not encounter the problem of teleology found in structural functionalism because it theorizes the control and regulation mechanism within ecological systems: 'As an organization attains completeness it acquires the capacity for controlling change and for retaining its form through time (1968, p. 331). In other words, as the ecological community develops towards a closed system, so there evolves a centralized and concentrated key function which effectively controls the development of other units within the system.

What remains unclear in this analysis, however, is how this control and integration on the part of the key functional unit is achieved. Thus according to Robson (1969), any such analysis of the functional role of institutions must implicitly resort to an analysis of the purposive actions of the individuals within them: 'A viewpoint which emphasizes the functional role of social institutions, as does Hawley's, makes assumptions as to motivations, attitudes, sentiments and values which must at least be recognized and considered' (p. 23). Hawley, however, seeks to develop a theoretical perspective which can put to one side questions of individual motives and values, yet according to Robson he conspicuously fails to demarcate the line between the cultural aspects which he does not wish to study and the ecological aspects which he does. Robson's argument is precisely that this line cannot be drawn and that any ecological analysis must take account of the subjective values and purposes of individual actors.

This sort of criticism is at one and the same time both profound and irrelevant. It is profound because it points to a basic problem in urban sociology in particular (see Chapter 4 on urban managerialism and Chapter 6 on the state and the urban system) and in sociology in general; namely, the division between the 'two sociologies' of system and action discussed by Dawe (1970).

Yet it is also irrelevant for the same reason, for it fails to articulate theoretically with the ecological perspective. As Castells (1977a, ch. 8) has suggested, criticisms of the ecological perspective that are grounded in a commitment to an action frame of reference represent less of a critique and more of an inversion. Human ecology is criticized not for what it is, but for what it is not. The debate between voluntaristic action theorists and deterministic systems theorists is as old as sociology itself, and it does not therefore appear particularly useful to criticize human ecology on these grounds.

The argument that human ecology is ideological is one that has more often been made in relation to the pre-war than the post-war literature. Alihan (1938), for example, suggested that the Chicago school's emphasis on competition as 'the process basic to all other processes' (p. 91) was little more than an ideological judgement reflecting the core competitive ethic of American capitalism at the time when Park and his colleagues were writing. Similarly Gettys (1940) pointed to the biologistic and naturalistic claims of the Chicago school as fundamentally misrepresenting and mystifying what were essentially social processes – a criticism that has subsequently been developed more fully by Castells (1977a), who has suggested that the apparently 'natural' forces identified by Park must rather be explained as forces specific to the capitalist mode of production (see Chapter 5).

With the work of Hawley and Duncan, however, the emphasis on competition as a basic process in human organization has been replaced by an emphasis on interdependence, while assertions about the natural basis of ecological processes have become blurred as a result of the attempt to dispense with the biotic–cultural dichotomy. Nevertheless, post-war human ecology is still open to the charge of ideology for much the same reason as the work of the Chicaco school was, for fundamental to the claims of contemporary ecological theory is the view that certain processes are constant and invariant. Human ecology, in other words, is still concerned to identify transhistorical generalities – forces and processes that invariably operate in all human societies.

We noted earlier that the range of transhistorical generalizations that can safely be made concerning necessary features of all societies appears very limited, and that Hawley's set of cardinal assumptions (that individuals must have access to the environment; that this access must involve some degree of interdependence; that individuals are time-bound; and so on) do not take us very far. The problem is that Hawley believes that other principles can logically be deduced from these initial assumptions (for example principles of dominance and the key function) and that these principles are also invariant. It is in this respect that his work can be attacked as ideological, for there appear no necessary logical grounds for arguing that, for example, certain groups must exercise a dominant function and must therefore attain political, spatial and temporal dominance in society, or that dominant groups must always occupy central locations from which they can control the whole system. Although Hawley avoids discussion of natural biotic forces, the whole thrust of his analysis is nevertheless towards the conclusion that centralized power and extreme division of labour are natural and necessary. Indeed, his conceptualization of the closed ecological system, towards which all systems are said to exhibit a constant tendency, appears as much a political as a theoretical 'ideal', and it is one that, with its implications of extensive corporate power and all-embracing political control, many people are concerned to work and fight against.

Like structural functionalism, therefore, human ecology has tended to develop theoretical explanations (and hence, implicitly, justifications) for a particular mode of political and economic organization. It is a theory of the *status quo* that supports arrangements by explaining them as the outcome of invariant principles. Its concerns are the concerns of the dominant groups in society – it talks of maximizing efficiency but has nothing to say about increasing accountability, it talks of maintaining equilibrium through gradual change and readjustment and rules out even the possibility of fundamental restructuring. In one sense, the ecological perspective can be enlightening in that it points to the processes that need to be addressed by those seeking social change. But in another sense it is totally restricting and inhibiting in that it denies the possibility of acting on these processes. At best it is mildly reformist; at worst it is fatalistic in its conservatism.

Whether all this is sufficient to dismiss human ecology as ideological depends on how ideology is conceptualized, and this in turn depends on whether it is possible to distinguish science and ideology. This is a question that is taken up in Chapter 5. For the moment, the least that can be said is that this body of theory presents a picture of the social world that is likely to prove particularly unattractive to those who are committed to working for change.

As regards its contribution to the development of a specifically 'urban' social theory, however, we are in a position to draw more definite conclusions regarding the claims and achievements of human ecology. It is clear from Duncan's work that the application of the ecological perspective to the urban question is now problematic. For a start, Duncan (1959) argues convincingly against Hawley's claim that the community represents a microcosm which can be studied in its own right as the smallest indivisible ecological unit, for he points out that the scope of the interdependency between the four elements of the ecological complex now extends far beyond the community to the 'supra-local'. Indeed, it may be suggested that, given the interdependency of localities, regions and states in the world today, the only viable ecological unit is the world system! Clearly urban sociology loses its specificity entirely when the theoretical processes in which it is interested, and the objects of study that it is concerned to analyse, can only be represented quite literally as the world and its entire contents.

Second, it is also clear from Duncan's work that ecology has become a theoretical perspective which has no necessary connection with urban analysis. In a defence of the ecological perspective, for example, Duncan and Schnore (1959) suggest that it can fruitfully be applied to the study of any aggregate phenomenon, and they cite as examples the analysis of bureaucracy and stratification as well as urbanization. The distinctiveness of the ecological approach, in other words, lies solely in its emphasis on the problem of how human aggregates adapt to changing conditions, and there is nothing specifically 'urban' about that.

Appreciation of this point enables us to situate human ecology more precisely in terms of its relationship to structural functionalism, for it is apparent that ecology has become merely one specialized area of study *within* the functionalist paradigm. The problem that it poses is one of the four key functional problems identified by Parsons in his famous 'AGIL' scheme, the other three being goal definition (which on a societal level refers to the political system), integration (which refers to institutions performing social control functions) and latency or pattern maintenance (which refers to the process of socialization) (see Parsons, Bales and Shils 1953). For Parsons, adaptation, the fourth cell in the typology, is achieved by the economic system, for this mediates between the social system as a whole and its external non-social environment.

It is interesting in the light of this to note that, in his attempt to distinguish the theoretical concerns of human ecology from those of other social science disciplines, Hawley (1950, ch. 4) encounters the greatest difficulty in distinguishing it from economics, and he resolves his problem only by claiming that ecology is broader than economics in that it focuses on interdependencies beyond those grounded in mere exchange values. It may be, therefore, that the ecological system should replace the economic system in Parson's AGIL typology, for what is clear is that Parsons's theoretical identification of the problem of adaptation coincides exactly with the theoretical concerns of the postwar human ecology.

Once human ecology is located as a sub-discipline within structural–functionalism, its significance for urban analysis can more readily be evaluated. We have seen in this chapter that, as originally developed by the Chicago school, human ecology represented an attempt to generate both a distinct theoretical approach to human society and a specific theory of the city, and that the irreconcilable tension between these two resulted eventually in its collapse. Hawley was able to resurrect human ecology only by jettisoning its specific relevance to the city, and his development of the ecological approach as a sociological perspective rather than as an urban theory was then taken further by Duncan with the result that the relation between ecological theory and urban theory became purely contingent. Now that ecology has found its niche within the functionalist paradigm, we may debate its validity and its usefulness in that context, but irrespective of the conclusions we draw from such a debate, it is clear that human ecology is no longer essentially an urban theory and that it cannot provide a conceptual framework within which a specifically urban social theory can be developed.

3 The urban as a cultural form

There is in Anglo-Saxon culture a deep and enduring tension between the image of the town and that of the countryside. The imagery is that of opposites, for the virtues of rural life – family, traditional morality, community – are mirrored in the vices of the city – egoism, materialism, anonymity – while the advantages of urban living are similarly reflected in the disadvantages of rural existence. As Raymond Williams observes,

> On the country has gathered the idea of a natural way of life: of peace, innocence and simple virtue. On the city has gathered the idea of an achieved centre: of learning, communication, light. Powerful hostile associations have also developed: on the city as a place of noise, worldliness and ambition; on the country as a place of backwardness, ignorance, limitation. A contrast between country and city, as fundamental ways of life, reaches back into classical times (Williams 1973, p. 1).

While the prevailing image of the city, which can be traced in literature and, more recently, in film, includes both positive and negative aspects – progress as well as pollution, liberty as well as loneliness – it does appear that evaluation is more often hostile than favourable: 'Life in the countryside is viewed as one of harmony and virtue. The town is disorganized; the countryside is settled. The town is bad; the countryside is good' (Newby 1977, p. 12). In part this may be the legacy of the fear of the town by the dominant classes in the nineteenth century, for as Glass (1968) has argued, the expanding Victorian cities represented a concentration of the industrial proletariat which the guardians of the *status quo* viewed with some apprehension. Then as now, industrialists, philanthropists and visionary planners sought to re-establish the moral bonds of the small community by developing company towns and new model communities which would reintegrate the individual into society and demobilize the mob (see Dennis 1968, Heraud 1975). Yet this is far from a complete explanation for the durability and pervasiveness of anti-urban sentiment in western cultures, for as Williams demonstrates, the tendency to compare the urban present with an idyllic version of a rural past has been in evidence for centuries. We shall consider Williams's own explanation for this later in this chapter.

Not surprisingly, the tension between the urban and the rural and between the values that each represents has found expression not only in cultural forms, but also in social theory and philosophy, where it is revealed most clearly in the concept of community. Nisbet (1966) has suggested that community constitutes 'the most fundamental and far-reaching of sociology's unit-ideas' (p. 47), and this is the case because it is indicative of what appear to be some of the most basic dilemmas in social relationships. If, as Nisbet suggests, community encompasses relationships of personal intimacy, depth, commitment and continuity, then, either implicitly or explicitly, it represents a vivid contrast with other types of relationships which are characterized by indifference, superficiality, segmentalism and brevity. It is the contrast between emotion and intellect, altruism and egoism, affection and instrumentalism, and so on.

Such contrasts are basic to sociological analysis for they help to define the range of types of action in which people may engage in different situations. When we come to study the social relationships involved in families, street gangs, factories, churches or state bureaucracies, we inevitably make use of such ideal type conceptual contrasts in order to describe and analyse the patterns of social interaction which we find there. Herein lies the usefulness of such well-known conceptual schema as Parsons's 'pattern variables'. Parsons (1951) identifies a series of dilemmas which confront actors when they enter a given situation. Should they, for example, display emotion towards others or should they maintain emotional indifference? Should they accept a wide range of obligations towards others or should their concern be more specific? Should they apply universal criteria when evaluating other people's actions or are the particular qualities of others more relevant in determining how to behave towards them? And should they relate to others in terms of what they do or in terms of who they are?

According to Parsons, such dilemmas are usually resolved for us as a result of our socialization – we 'know' in most situations what the appropriate role behaviour should be. Indeed, these dilemmas tend to cluster into typical patterns – within the family, for example, we will normally be expected to act emotionally, to accept a wide range of obligations, to be concerned with the particular qualities of other family members and to relate to each other in terms of ascribed rather than achieved characteristics, whereas such a pattern of action would normally be entirely inappropriate within, say, a formal bureaucratic organization.

Parson's pattern variables represent an elaboration and refinement of a fundamental dualism which runs through much social theory over the last hundred years or more. We see it, for example, in Durkheim's contrast between mechanical and organic solidarity, or in Weber's distinction between traditional and rational action. Such contrasts have often been used in one or both of two ways: either as a basis for developing a theory of social change in which human societies are said to 'evolve' from one typical pattern to the other over time, or as a basis for developing a theory of social geography in which different types of human settlements are distinguished according to their conformity to one or other typical pattern. In the first case, the contrasts are ranged at either end of a time continuum – societies are said to change (or often 'develop') from traditionalistic, affectual, homogenous and undifferentiated structures at one time to modern, rational, heterogenous and highly differentiated structures at another. In the second, the contrasts are ranged at either end of a space continuum in which human settlements are said to vary between generally small-scale units where interaction takes place at a face-to-face level and is governed by strong bonds of communality and tradition, and much larger human aggregates where intimacy has been replaced by formal role requirements and personal modes of social regulation and obligation have given way to impersonal systems of social control and to communities of limited liability in which egoism and self-interest come to the fore.

Often, the time and space continua have been combined into a single theory. Such is the case, for example, in Tönnies's classic study of *gemeinschaft* and *gesellschaft*, originally published in 1890 and republished with a new introduction in 1931.

Tönnies described it as his purpose 'to study the sentiments and motives which draw people to each other, keep them together, and induce them to joint action' (1955, p. 3). To this end, he drew a basic distinction between what he termed 'natural will' (the sensations, feelings and instincts which derive from physiological and psychological processes and which he believed to be 'inborn and inherited' – p. 121) and 'rational will' (the deliberate, goal-oriented and calculative product of the use of intellect). In common parlance, the distinction is that between the heart and the head. While recognizing that the two types can never be totally disentangled in empirical situations, Tönnies argued that it was possible to distinguish predominant tendencies in human affairs towards one or the other. To the extent that social relationships were governed mainly by natural will, he spoke of '*gemeinschaft*'; to the extent that they were governed by rational will, he designated them as '*gesellschaft*'.

It was Tönnies's fundamental thesis that human societies had changed over time from forms of association based on *gemeinschaft* to those based on *gesellschaft*, and that the factor which had more than any other produced this shift had been the extension of trade and the development of capitalism. Indeed, at one point he characterizes *gesellschaft* as 'bourgeois society' (p. 87). The unity of sentiment which characterizes *gemeinschaft* and which flows from the 'natural' bonds of blood, neighbourhood and religious belief is disrupted by the growth of industrial capitalism which puts in its place a precarious unity based on monetary calculation and the resolute pursuit of self-interest: 'The possibility of a relation in the Gesellschaft assumes no more than a multitude of mere persons who are capable of delivering something and consequently of promising something . . . In Gesellschaft every person strives for that which is to his own advantage and affirms the actions of others only insofar as and as long as they can further his interest' (p. 88). In such a context, the only source of unity is the state, but the modern state lacks the natural authority which characterizes the paternalistic rule of fathers, village elders or clerics in the *gemeinschaft*. Instead, it serves the interests of the propertied class by exercising a formal, legalistic authority which comes to be experienced by ordinary people as alien.

What Tönnies is outlining in his book is a rudimentary evolutionary theory of social change. Indeed, like Marx, he tries to extrapolate his theory of change into the future, for while he recognizes that a return to *gemeinschaft* is impossible, he nevertheless suggests that the association of *gesellschaft* which characterizes modern day capitalism may be developed into a more cohesive and less alienative union of *gesellschaft* through the emergence of worker co-operatives and similar structures which may transcend the individualistic era of competitive capitalism.

There is, however, in this work also a rudimentary theory of social geography (what Bell and Newby, 1976, rightly see as his most mischievous legacy). Thus, not only do *gemeinschaft* and *gesellschaft* appear at opposite ends of a time continuum, but they also appear by the end of the book at opposite ends of a space continuum. *Gemeinschaft*, we are told, is physically located in the house, the village and the town, and it is 'almost entirely lost' with the development of the city (which is 'typical of Gesellschaft in general') and the metropolis (the 'highest form' of *gesellschaft*). As the urban centres grow, so the *gemeinschaft* of the rural hinterland is eclipsed and undermined. Family life and village communalism are replaced by urban individualism and state power which itself carries the seeds of a future development of socialist union.

By the end of the book, it is impossible to disentangle the effects of capitalism from those of urbanism. Change over time has become inextricably interwoven with change over space, for the *gemeinschaft/gesellschaft* dualism is applied equally to both. The significance of Tönnies's work as regards the later development of urban sociology is that it blended and confused these two dimensions and thereby opened up the possibility of developing theories of urbanism around the classic polarities of nineteenth-century evolutionary social thought. Concepts which had previously been applied to the analysis of different types of societies at different points in time could hereon equally be applied to different types of settlement within the same society at different points in space. The potential for confusion was, needless to say, considerable, and the confusion began shortly after the publication of Tönnies's book when the German sociologist, Georg Simmel, published an essay on metropolitan life which, for all its undoubted insights, hopelessly muddled up the analysis of the effects of modern capitalism with that of the effects of urban concentration. It was to take urban sociology some sixty years to sort out the difference.

The metropolis and mental life

It has often been suggested that Simmel's sociology is highly personal, wilfully eclectic and internally incoherent. However, the wide diversity of his writings does reveal a certain methodological unity and a degree of substantive continuity. The methodological unity is a function of his commitment to formalistic analysis and to the principle of the dialectic (the unity of opposites), while the substantive continuity is revealed in his recurring concern with the questions of individuality and freedom, modernity and the division of labour, and intellectual rationality and the money economy. All of these concerns are expressed in his essay on the metropolis and mental life.

Simmel's methodology was fundamentally neo-Kantian. Like Weber, he believed that knowledge of the world could be achieved only through the active mediation of a knowing subject – that is, through a prior mental process of selection of relevant aspects of concrete reality and of classification of these aspects through analytical constructs. The sociologist, in other words, imposed a conceptual order upon the world in order to understand it.

For Simmel, this order was achieved through the analytical separation of form and content. While the content of specific human actions could be explained only psychologically (the question of why certain individuals choose to embark upon certain courses of action was for Simmel a psychological question), the social form through which they were expressed was a sociological phenomenon. For example, in his analysis of the triad (the forms taken by three-person interaction), he identified three different forms that interaction between the parties could take. One party could adopt the role of referee or mediator between the other two, or could attempt to profit from the conflict between the other two while remaining non-aligned, or could adopt a strategy of divide and rule. These formal possibilities are inscribed in the properties of triadic interaction and may appear in a wide variety of contexts (e.g. interaction within families, within legislatures, between nations, and so on). While sociologists cannot explain why one party chooses to adopt one strategy rather than another (for the mainsprings of action lie in the spontaneity of individual personality), they can analyse the forms which action may take – forms which both facilitate and constrain action and which in a sense take on a life of their own. In this way, it becomes possible to generalize about cultural forms divorced from their specific historical contexts.

Sociology, therefore, is the science of the forms of human association as abstracted from real-world interaction. Just as grammar studies the forms of language rather than what is actually said, and epistemology studies the forms of knowledge rather than what is actually theorized, so sociology studies the forms of interaction rather than what is actually done (see Levine 1971, introduction). Sociology is the geometry of social forms, for its relationship to the content of social action is 'like that of geometry with regard to physico-chemical sciences of matter: it considers form, thanks to which matter generally takes an empirical shape – consequently a form that exists in itself only as an abstraction' (Simmel, quoted in Freund 1978, p. 160).

Simmel's commitment to dialectical analysis emerges out of his methodological formalism, for he suggests that social forms are at one and the same time the means whereby individual actions come to be expressed and the source of constraint upon them. Not only is the individual in society, but society is in the individual. Society (in the sense of the forms of human association) is both the source and the negation of individuality:

> Social man is not partially social and partially individual; rather his existence is shaped by a fundamental unity which cannot be accounted for in any other way than through the synthesis or coincidence of two logically contradictory determinations: man is both social link and being for himself, both product of society and life from an autonomous centre (Simmel; quoted in Coser 1965, p. 11).

Social life is thus founded in an irresolvable paradox, for the expansion of society is both the condition of and the challenge to the growth of individuality.

This analysis becomes clearer in Simmel's discussion of the sociological significance of number. As we have seen, the difference between a group of two and a group of three is, according to Simmel, qualitative as well as quantitative. In the dyad, each partner can rely on only one other, and this results in intense commitment to the relationship and to the knowledge that no superpersonal level of constraint is operating. In the triad, however, it becomes possible for the first time for the group to prevail over the individual, for the individual can be outnumbered. 'Simmel put his finger on a fundamental sociological phenomenon: series really begin only with the number three' (Freund 1978, p. 163); for the transition from two to three is qualitative, whereas transitions thereafter are quantitative.

There is, however, another qualitative shift at the indeterminate point at which a small group becomes a large group. In the large aggregate, new phenomena are needed that are not necessary in smaller groupings:

> It will immediately be conceded on the basis of everyday experiences that a group upon realising a certain size must develop forms and organs which serve its maintenance and promotion but which a small group does not need. On the other hand, it will also be admitted that smaller groups have qualities, including types of interaction among their members, which inevitably disappear when the groups grow larger (Simmel; in Wolff 1950, p. 87).

The unity of the group is no longer preserved by direct interaction among its members, and the personal and emotional commitments of members of small groups are replaced by formal means of control such as agencies of the law. If custom is characteristic of small groups, law is characteristic of large ones. In the large group, therefore, the individual is more restricted by the operation of superpersonal agencies that confront him and are seemingly beyond his control. However, the individual's commitment to the large group is correspondingly less, for as groups expand, so different social circles begin to intersect and the individuals spread their commitments across each. The result is that the increasing constraint within large groups is offset by the growing area of individual freedom across them: 'The increased restriction is more bearable for the individual because, outside of it, he has a sphere of freedom which is all the greater' (in Wolff 1950, p. 102).

An increase in the size of a social group has implications not only for the scope of individual freedom, however, but also for the degree of individual distinctiveness. As a group expands, so it threatens to immerse the individual within the mass: 'It pulls the individual down to a level with all and sundry' (in Wolff 1950, p. 31). The intellect of the individual is eroded by the emotion of the masses, and social interaction is debased as social life becomes grounded in the lowest common denominator. The larger the group, the more impersonal group interaction becomes, and the less concerned members become with the unique personal qualities of others. Faced with this assault on their individuality, people in the metropolis come to emphasize their own subjectivity, both to others (e.g. by distancing themselves from the crowd by exaggerating their particular attributes or displays) and to themselves (e.g. by adopting a blasé attitude of indifference or antipathy towards others which highlights the distinctiveness of self). In the large group, the individual stands alone – isolated yet rejoicing in the privacy which the metropolis affords. 'When the individual's relations begin to exceed a certain extensiveness, he becomes all the more thrown back upon himself' (in Levine 1971, p. 290). In the large group, the individual increasingly stands alone.

Simmel's work on the social effects of size thus leads to the conclusion that, in a large group (such as the modern city), custom is replaced by formal social control mechanisms, the individual's commitments become extended across a number of different social circles, the scope of individual freedom is increased, the character of social relations is highly impersonal, and the individual's consciousness of self is heightened. Exploration of the significance of number for social life is, however, only one theme in Simmel's sociology, and it is complemented by a second major concern which relates to the analysis of the social effects of modernity. Of particular significance here is the development of an advanced division of labour in society, together with the establishment of a money economy.

The growth of the division of labour in modern societies has three main effects for the forms of human association. First, it fragments and segmentalizes social life. In small-scale relatively homogeneous societies, the individual's group memberships form a concentric pattern; the individual belong to a guild, which belongs to a confederation, etc. Individuals are therefore vertically integrated into their society, and the pattern of association becomes total, enveloping all aspects of their lives. With an advanced division of labour, however, the social circles in which individuals move become tangential to each other, and their involvement in any one of them is partial and specific. As Simmel puts it, 'The point at which the individual momentarily touches the totality or the structure of the whole no longer pulls parts of his personality into the relationship that do not belong there' (in Levine 1971, p. 293).

Second, the division of labour reinforces the self-consciousness engendered by an increase in size. This is because, in a highly differentiated society, the individual is constantly exposed to an infinite variety of changing situations and sensations in which his or her own unique personality is the only constant factor:

> The more uniformly and unwaveringly life progresses, and the less the extremes of sensate experience depart from an average level, the less strongly does the sensation of personality arise; but the farther apart they stretch, and the more energetically they erupt, the more intensely does a human being sense himself as a personality (in Levine 1971, p. 291).

The division of labour therefore encourages egoism and individualism.

Third, the development of the division of labour in society fosters an alienation of individuals from the cultural world which they have created. For Simmel, such alienation is unavoidable in modern life (see Mellor 1977, p. 185), for it is the division of labour (and not simply capitalism) which leads to the reification of all humanly-created cultural products.

The world of things that individuals have created thus confronts them as an objective spirit, while the essential creativity of individuals is increasingly impoverished. Increasingly, the objective spirit comes to dominate the subjective spirit: 'The price of the objective perfection of the world will be the atrophy of the human soul' (Coser 1965, p. 23).

These characteristics of modernity are expressed in, and reinforced by, the development of a money economy. Money is totally depersonalized, for its exchange leaves no trace of the personality of its previous owner. It is a leveller, for it reduces all qualitative values to a common quantitative base. It is a source of individual freedom and independence, for the development of a cash economy enables social expansion upon a world level on the one hand, yet individual freedom of choice on the other. It confronts the individual as an objective power. It is, in short, the finest expression of the rationality of the modern world.

We find in Simmel's work, therefore, a recurrent concern with three core themes: size, division of labour and money/rationality. At the risk of some oversimplification, it may be suggested that these three constitute the 'independent variables' of his analysis of the forms of human association in the modern world. It is for this reason that the metropolis assumes a central significance for Simmel, for it is here that the effects of size, differentiation and the money economy on social relationships are most immediately visible and most intensely felt. As Nisbet observes, 'The direction of history is toward metropolis, which for Simmel is the structure of modernism, performing for his thought the role that democracy does for Tocqueville, capitalism for Marx, and bureaucracy for Weber' (1966, p. 308). The metropolis is the crystallization of the objective spirit.

These three variables are prominent in his essay on the metropolis and mental life. According to Simmel, the sheer *size* of the metropolis is significant because it gives rise to 'one of the few tendencies for which an approximately universal formula can be discovered' (in Wolff 1950, p. 416). As we have seen this formula is that larger social circles increase the scope of individual freedom while reducing the quality of relationships with others:

> The reciprocal reserve and indifference and the intellectual life conditions of large circles are never felt more strongly by the individual in their impact upon his independence than in the thickest crowd of the big city. This is because the bodily proximity and narrowness of space makes the mental distance only the more visible. It is obviously only the obverse of this freedom if, under certain circumstances, one nowhere feels as lonely and lost as in the metropolitan crowd. For here as elsewhere it is by no means necessary that the freedom of man be reflected in his emotional life as comfort (Wolff 1950, p. 418).

Similarly, the effects of *differentiation* are most pronounced in the metropolis, for 'cities are, first of all, seats of the highest economic division of labour' (Wolff 1950, p. 420). This extreme differentiation is itself a function of size, for Simmel argues (consistently with Spencer and Durkheim) that only large human aggregates give rise to and can support a wide variation of services. Because of this close association between the city and the economic division of labour, the effects of division of labour in terms of individuality and alienation are most clearly revealed there. Individuals are driven constantly to exaggerate their own uniqueness and to 'adopt the most tendentious peculiarities, that is, the specifically metropolitan extravagances of mannerism, caprice and preciousness' (p. 421) in order to gain attention and assert their personality. The change and flux that characterize city life intensify nervous stimulation and lead to greater consciousness of self: 'The city sets up a deep contrast with small town and rural life with reference to the sensory foundations of psychic life. The metropolis extracts from man as a discriminating creature a different amount of consciousness than does rural life' (p. 410). Yet precisely because new sensations become the norm in the metropolis, the individual develops a blasé attitude towards them. As nerves are blunted by continual stimulation, we become incapable of reacting to new sensations with the appropriate enthusiasm and energy. We become 'sophisticated' as a defence against the assault on our senses: 'The finite psyche becomes overloaded with mental images' (Smith 1980, p. 108).

This devaluation of the world 'in the end drags one's own personality down into a feeling of the same worthlessness' (p. 415). Art, technology, science and other aspects of human culture all become devalued and grow increasingly distant from the individual whose creation they are: 'The individual has become a mere cog in an enormous organization of things and powers which tear from his hands all progress, spirituality and value in order to transform them from their subjective form into the form of a purely objective life' (p. 422). Other individuals, too, are devalued and urbanites develop an aversion and antipathy towards others as a shield against others' indifference towards them. Metropolitan life thus becomes impersonal and calculative, and again Simmel points to the contrast with small-town life.

This impersonality is reinforced by the third defining feature of the metropolis, the *money economy*. 'The metropolis', argues Simmel, 'has always been the seat of the money economy' (in Wolff 1950, p. 411). Money is both the source and the expression of metropolitan rationality and intellectualism, for both money and intellect share a matter-of-fact attitude towards people and things and are indifferent to genuine individuality. Metropolities are guided by their heads rather than their hearts, by calculation and intellect, not affection and emotion. 'Throughout the whole course of English history, London has never acted as England's heart, but often as England's intellect and always as her moneybag!' (p. 412). Money also contributes to urbanites' devaluation of the things and people around them, for it is the 'most frightful leveller' in its capacity to express all variations in terms of a single measure of equivalence: 'Money expresses all qualitative differences of things in terms of "how much?" Money, with all its colourlessness and indifference, becomes the common denominator of all values' (p. 414).

In the metropolis, therefore, are found the basic dilemmas of social life. It is here that the struggle is waged by the individual 'to preserve the autonomy and individuality of his existence in the face of overwhelming social forces (p. 409). It is here that the tension is most clearly revealed between the eighteenth-century ideal of the freedom of the individual from traditional bonds, and the nineteenth-century ideal of individuality in the face of the mass. The metropolis is for Simmel the crucible of modern life.

Many aspects of Simmel's work have attracted considerable criticism over the years. He has been attacked for his formalism, for his exclusive concern with the minutiae of social life, for his empiricism and for his assumption of the inevitability of the patterns of social relationships that he identifies (see, for example, Mellor 1977, ch. 5). His claims regarding the invariant relation between size and the quality of social relationships (his so-called 'universal formula') have been challenged, not least by Weber, who argued in the opening paragraph of his essay on the city that 'various cultural factors determine the size at which "impersonality" tends to appear' (1958, p. 65). From our present perspective, however, the basic question to which we must address ourselves is how far Simmel's work constitutes a specific theory of the city as opposed to a theory of social relations in modern industrial capitalist societies. Leaving aside questions of its empirical validity, its theoretical consistency and its methodological adequacy, therefore, we need to consider the extent to which Simmel's approach to the analysis of the metropolis provides the framework for a distinctive urban sociological theory.

Clearly it is a different approach from that adopted by Weber, Durkheim or even Tönnies, for the contrasts drawn by these theorists relate mainly to changes in patterns of social relations over time following on the growth of rationality, the expansion of the division of labour, or whatever in society as a whole. This is not the case with Simmel, for although the distinction between cause and effect is far from clear in his analyses, it does seem that he sees in the metropolis itself the source of at least some of the features of modern life. He does not refer to the city merely as an illustration of the rationality, impersonality and the like that characterize social relationships in the modern era, but rather sees it as a causal factor in its own right in the explanation of such social forms. What is crucial here, and what separates Simmel from the other writers discussed, is his unique emphasis on the sociology of number. The metropolis is above all a large human agglomeration, and according to Simmel's writings on the sociological significance of size, this fact alone should be expected to create different patterns of human association from those found in small settlements such as rural villages. With regard to his emphasis on size, therefore, Simmel's essay does represent an attempt to theorize the city *per se*.

Equally clearly, however, Simmel draws on other factors apart from size (namely, the division of labour and the money economy) to explain the depersonalized and utilitarian character of social relationships in the city, and although these additional factors are, according to his argument, historically associated with the metropolis, they are not peculiar to it or explained by it. They are, in other words, features of the mode of organization of society as a whole. It is because his theory of metropolis includes factors that are 'social' rather than specifically 'metropolitan' that Simmel is obliged to define the city in other than merely geographical or numerical terms: 'A city consists of its total effects which extend beyond its immediate confines' (in Wolff 1950, p. 419). But applying this definition, we soon end up with an equation between the concepts of metropolis and society, in which case the arguments about the effect of size become irrelevant (since society includes both small and large settlements) and the use of the term 'metropolis' becomes redundant. With regard to his emphasis on the effects of division of labour and the money economy, therefore, Simmel's essay cannot be represented as a specifically urban theory.

This latter interpretation of Simmel's essay lies behind Becker's assertion that

> Simmel never thought of urbanization as an explanatory formula. . . . On the contrary, the cities that he had in view were exclusively of the kind

manifesting an elaborate division of labour, a money economy, a wage system, marked industrialization and other characteristics peculiar to the western world from the fifteenth century until very recent times (Becker 1959, p. 230-1).

But Becker's argument that Simmel was 'really' writing about a particular type of society rather than a particular type of settlement pattern ignores the central significance accorded to the fact of size in his work. When we consider Simmel's essay on the metropolis, therefore, we are confronted with a classic (though unintended) Simmelian dualism, for it is on the one hand an analysis of the city, and on the other an analysis of modern western society.

These two dimensions must be treated separately, yet in Simmel's work they are inextricably confused. As it stands, Simmel's essay on the metropolis appears highly plausible as a description, yet hopelessly muddled as an analysis. Any attempt to develop a theory of the city must be able to include the common essential features of all cities, irrespective of the mode of production in which they are located. As Louis Wirth observed, 'It is particularly important to call attention to the danger of confusing urbanism with industrialism and modern capitalism' (1938, p. 7). It was precisely such a confusion that characterized Simmel's approach, and it was just this confusion that Wirth, thirty-five years later, set out to correct.

Urbanism and ruralism as ways of life

Wirth's paper, 'Urbanism as a way of life' (1938) is arguably the most famous article ever to have been published in a sociology journal. Its intellectual pedigree is explicit, for it reflects on the one hand the influence of Simmel and on the other that of Park. Having said that, it should be noted that it is therefore the product of rather intense inbreeding, for Park was himself a student of Simmel's at Berlin, and his sociology was strongly (though by no means entirely) influenced by Simmel's work (see the introduction to Levine 1971 for a discussion of the connections and disjunctions between Park and Simmel). As is often the case with the products of inbreeding, the essay reflects the weaknesses of its parentage.

In many ways, Wirth's essay can be seen as an extension, modification and development of Simmel's paper on the metropolis (a paper that Wirth described as 'the most important single article on the city from the sociological standpoint' – 1967, p. 219). From

Simmel he derives a concern with the forms of human association in the city, with the dualism between town and country, and with the subjective experience of urban life. Like Simmel, he identifies size as a key explanatory variable, although Simmel's analysis of the division of labour is replaced in Wirth's paper by an analysis of heterogeneity, while the effects of a money economy are dropped from the analysis altogether.

As a student of Park's, on the other hand, Wirth also drew upon some of the insights developed by the Chicago human ecologists as regards the effects of density on human organization and the dominance achieved by the city over its hinterland. He saw human ecology as one of three significant perspectives on the city (the other two being organizational and socio–psychological, concerned respectively with forms of social relationships and personality characteristics), and argued that all three should complement each other: 'Human ecology is not a substitute for, but a supplement to, the other frames of reference and methods of social investigation' (Wirth 1945, p. 488). It was his intention, therefore, to develop a theory of the city that could account for the ecological, organizational and social–psychological characteristics of urbanism. Put another way, he set out to synthesize Park's human ecology and Simmel's analyses of the forms of association and the development of urban personality.

Wirth believed that such a systematic theory of the city was possible but had yet to be achieved (Weber and Park had, in his view, come closest to fulfilling this objective, but neither of their essays on the city provided an ordered or coherent framework for analysis). He was highly critical of contemporary work, which proceeded on the basis of arbitrary classifications of urban settlements – usually that employed by the American census, which defined an urban area as one of a certain population size – for he argued that such classifications were mechanical and unsophisticated and in no way correspond with actual entities. 'What we look forward to', he wrote in a paper shortly before he died, 'is not the piling up of a vast body of reliable, continuous information if this labour is to be largely wasted on a basic system of classification such as we have used up to now. The factor-by-factor analysis of any problem in terms of which rural and urban settlements have shown significant differences . . . leads to sterile results' (Wirth 1964, p. 224). The size of settlement was not in itself of any sociological interest unless it could be shown to affect forms of association: 'As long as we identify urbanism with the physical entity of the city, viewing it merely as rigidly delimited in space, and proceed as if urban attitudes abruptly ceased to be manifested beyond an arbitrary boundary line, we are not likely to arrive at any adequate conception of urbanism as a mode of life' (1938, p. 4).

For Wirth, therefore, the urban–rural dichotomy referred to two ideal types of human community, two basic patterns of human association that characterized the modern age. Different types of settlements were thus more or less urban or more or less rural: 'We should not expect to find abrupt and discontinuous variation between urban and rural types of personality. The city and the country may be regarded as two poles in reference to one or the other of which all human settlements tend to arrange themselves' (1938, p. 3). There is, in other words, a continuum between the urban and the rural, and the differences between any two existing settlements are differences in degree along this continuum (Wirth 1964, p. 224). The important point to note about this is that differences between different settlements have therefore to be determined empirically. The role of Wirth's ideal types is to provide a framework for such analysis which (unlike government census classifications) is relevant to sociological concerns and which can provide the basis for hypothesis formation: 'To set up ideal-typical polar concepts such as I have done, and many others before me have done, does not prove that city and country are fundamentally and necessarily different. . . . Rather it suggests certain hypotheses to be tested' (1964, p. 223).

The hypothesis that Wirth advances is that variations in patterns of human association may be explained as the effects of three factors – size, density and heterogeneity. These three constitute the parameters of his conceptualization of the urban: 'For sociological purposes a city may be defined as a relatively large, dense and permanent settlement of socially heterogeneous individuals' (1938, p. 8). The task for urban sociology is then to analyse the extent to which each of these three variables gives rise to definite forms of social relationships: 'We may expect the outstanding features of the urban social scene to vary in accordance with size, density and differences in the functional type of cities' (p. 7).

It is important to recognize, however, that Wirth emphasizes that 'folk' ways of life may still be found in cities, for previously dominant patterns of human association are not completely obliterated by urban growth, and also to recognize that 'urban' ways of life are likely to spread beyond the boundaries of the city, given the ecological dominance of the city over its hinterland. Furthermore, he notes that technological developments in transport and communications have led to the spillover of the city into the countryside and to a new accessibility of the city to rural dwellers, and that the pace of such changes has 'made such notions as we have about rural and urban likenesses and differences obsolete' (1964, p. 221). All this merely reinforces his argument that the designation of different localities as more urban or more rural is a conceptual exercise, and that while we should expect larger, denser and more heterogeneous settlements to exhibit more urban characteristics than smaller, more scattered and more homogeneous ones, this remains an empirical question which should not be 'resolved' by the *a priori* identification of urbanism with particular physical locations.

Wirth's analysis of the social effects of *size* closely reflects that of Simmel. Thus he develops the familiar argument that larger size means greater variation, and then draws upon the ecological tradition to suggest that this in turn will be reflected in the spatial segregation of different groups according to ethnicity, race, status, occupation and so on. He also suggests, *pace* Simmel, that an increase in size reduces the chances of any two individuals knowing each other personally, and that this leads to segmentalism in social relationships, an emphasis on secondary rather than primary contacts, and a corresponding indifference towards others:

> The contacts of the city may indeed be face to face, but they are nevertheless impersonal, superficial, transitory and segmental. The reserve, the indifference and the blasé outlook which urbanites manifest in their relationships may thus be regarded as devices for immunising themselves against the personal claims and expectations of others (Wirth 1938, p. 12).

It is important to note that Wirth does not claim that primary relationships disappear in the city; in his earlier study of a Jewish ghetto in Chicago, for example, he concluded that it formed a 'cultural community' with a communal way of life (1927, p. 71). Nor does he suggest that the urbanite knows fewer people than the country dweller; the reverse may well be the case. All that he is arguing here, therefore, is that in a large settlement, the individual will be personally acquainted with a smaller proportion of those with whom he or she interacts, and that this fact alone explains the development of the social distance that characterizes urban life.

Like Simmel, Wirth recognizes that size engenders a tension between individuality and individual freedom, for a large human group undermines the former while encouraging the latter: 'Whereas the individual gains, on the one hand, a certain degree of emancipation or freedom from the personal and emotional controls of intimate groups, he loses, on the other hand, the spontaneous self-expression, the morale and the sense of participation that comes with living in an integrated society' (1938, pp. 12–13). Life in large groups thus tends to become anomic, and moral deregulation is countered by the development of more formal agencies of control and participation such as the mass media.

The effects of *density* on social relationships are a function of the growth of differentiation. Wirth follows Durkheim and the Chicago ecologists in arguing that differentiation is the way in which any population responds to an increase in numbers in a given area. The effects of an increase in density are therefore clearly related to those of size, and Wirth notes that 'Density thus reinforces the effect of numbers in diversifying men and their activities and in increasing the complexity of the social structure' (1938, p. 14).

Complex differentiation of functions within a human aggregate creates forms of interaction in which people relate to each other on the basis of their specific roles rather than their personal qualities: 'We see the uniform which denotes the role of functionaries, and are oblivious to the personal eccentricities hidden behind the uniform' (p. 14). It therefore fosters an instrumental attitude towards others who are treated merely in terms of the role they perform, and the resulting spirit of mutual exploitation has therefore to be regulated by law and other mechanisms of formal control. However, Wirth also notes that homogeneous sub-groups created in the process of differentiation tend to congregate together in different parts of the city, forming what Park and his colleagues termed 'natural areas'. Predatory relationships within the city as a whole may therefore come to be mediated within different parts of the city by the development of more personal and emotional ties: 'Persons of homogeneous status and needs unwittingly drift into, consciously select,or are forced by circumstances into the same area. The different parts of the city acquire specialized functions and the city consequently comes to resemble a mosaic of social worlds in which the transition from one to the other is abrupt' (p. 15).

If Wirth's discussion of density relies heavily on Park, his analysis of the effects of *heterogeneity* leads him to return once again to Simmel. The analysis of social heterogeneity is couched largely in terms of Simmel's geometry of social circles. Individuals participate in many different circles, none of which can command their undivided allegiance. These circles are tangential and intersecting (in contrast to the concentric totality of the rural community), and individuals enjoy a different status, and perhaps even a different identity, in each of them with the result that instability and personal insecurity becomes a norm. The urban personality easily becomes disorganized, and rates of mental illness, suicide and so on increase accordingly.

Heterogeneity also leads to a process of social levelling in which the individual is subordinated to the mass: 'If the individual would participate at all in the social, political and economic life of the city, he must subordinate some of his individuality to the demands of the larger community and in that measure immerse himself in mass movements' (p. 18). Action, to be effective, has to be collective, and political participation is achieved through representation. The individual is 'reduced to a state of virtual impotence' (p. 22), and official agencies assume responsibility for a wide range of provisions and services on which the urbanite increasingly depends.

Wirth's description of urbanism as a way of life, and in particular his diagnosis of the urban personality, is overwhelmingly bleak, yet neither he nor Simmel could be described as rural romantics. Wirth was as aware of the positive aspects of city life as he was of the negative aspects of the countryside. Nevertheless, his work did serve to bring social theory closer to the rural nostalgia and virulent anti-urbanism that has been so characteristic of western culture, for his description of urban life as anonymous, impersonal, superficial, instrumental and so on was entirely consistent with the imagery portrayed in English novels and poetry for generations. The difference, of course, is that Wirth deduced these characteristics from an analysis of the sociological significance of three variables, and thereby established the traditional imagery of the city in the form of a hypothesis: 'The deductive inferences sound plausible, principally because they point to the characteristics that have for so long been accepted as typically urban' (Reissman 1964, p. 143). As with Simmel's work. Wirth's essay appears intuitively plausible as a description of city life, but the question, as we shall see, is whether his simple explanation in terms of the necessary effects of size, density and heterogeneity does in fact account for the phenomena he describes.

Support for Wirth's thesis came just three years after the publication of his essay from another of Park's students, Robert Redfield. Redfield (1941) studied four communities in the Yucatan peninsula of Mexico, ranging from the small, homogeneous and very isolated settlement at Tusik to the largest town in the region, Merida.

On the basis of this study, he argued that the less isolated and more heterogeneous the settlement, the more it became characterized by cultural disorganization, secularization and the growth of individualism. On the basis of this and other studies, Redfield (1947) then proceeded to develop an ideal type of the 'folk society' which complemented Wirth's analysis by identifying the cultural characteristics of communities at the other end of the rural–urban continuum.

According to Redfield, 'Folk societies have certain features in common which enable us to think of them as a type – a type which contrasts with the society of the modern city' (1947, p. 293). He saw the city as a 'vast complicated and rapidly changing world' (p. 306), and contrasted this with the folk society as 'small, isolated, non-literate and homogeneous with a strong sense of group solidarity' (p. 297). The ideal type folk society was small, isolated, intimate, immobile, pre-literate, homogeneous and cohesive. It had only a rudimentary division of labour based mainly on a rigid differentiation of sex roles; the means of production were shared; and economic activity was contained within the community. The culture of the folk society was strongly traditional and uncritical. It was grounded in social bonds based upon kinship and religion, and its internal coherence derived from custom rather than formal law. Patterns of interaction were based on ascribed status, and social relationships were personal and diffuse. In such relationships, added Redfield somewhat wistfully, 'There is no place for the motive of commercial gain' (p. 305).

Taken together, the work of Wirth and Redfield exhibits two main themes. The first is that patterns of human relationships can be conceptualized in terms of a pair of logically opposite ideal types (the contents of which are open to discussion) such that any empirical case can be located at some point between them and compared with other cases against some purely conceived yardstick of urbanism or ruralism. It should be noted that the characterization of the ideal types themselves is variable, for some researchers may choose to emphasize one aspect while others may select other aspects. It is not a valid criticism of Wirth's approach to suggest that cities exhibit certain features that are different from those he identified in his paper, for Wirth's characterization of urbanism is a logical construct, not an empirical description. It is a construct designed to facilitate empirical research on actual cities by providing a conceptual criterion of urbanism, and like all ideal types, it may therefore be evaluated in terms of its usefulness but not its empirical validity.

Wirth's paper, of course, attempts to go beyond a simple exercise in conceptualization and to develop an explanation of empirical variations in ways of life between different settlements. This provides the second theme to emerge out of his and Redfield's work: namely that variations in patterns of human relationships between different communities are to be explained in terms of differences in their size and density, their degree of internal homogeneity, and the extent of their isolation from other centres of population.

The first of these themes is therefore a concern with conceptualization, while the second is an attempt at explanation. It follows that this line of work has to be evaluated on two levels, for the exercise in conceptualization may be assessed only in terms of its logical consistency and its fruitfulness for empirical research, while the attempt at explanation has to be examined in terms of its theoretical adequacy. Unfortunately, as we shall now see, much of the subsequent work that has claimed to refute Wirth has failed to recognize this distinction.

'Real but relatively unimportant'

Just as the critics of the Chicago school in the 1930s were led up an empiricist blind alley by attempting to refute Burgess's concentric zone model of urban growth while ignoring the theoretical adequacy of the ecological postulates that lay behind it, so too much of the debate over Wirth's thesis since the war has been theoretically sterile. There is now, as Pahl points out, 'an almost overwhelming body of evidence that the central areas of cities differ from what Wirth and many others have suggested' (Pahl 1968, p. 267). Yet such evidence is of only marginal relevance to an evaluation of Wirth's theory, for it has generally been cited as part of an ultimately misguided and futile attempt to refute an ideal type with empirical data.

Such evidence falls mainly into two categories. The first concerns those studies (e.g. Young and Willmott 1957, Gans 1962, Abu-Lughod 1961) that have documented the existence of 'rural' ways of life (such as close kinship links or personal friendships among neighbours) in the centre of large cities (in the case of these writers, London, Boston and Cairo respectively). There is now a lot of evidence from a lot of different cities which indicates that what Gans terms 'urban villages' are fairly common, and that Wirth's description of urban ways of life in terms of anonymity, impersonality and so on is not applicable to them.

The second category of evidence concerns studies that have documented 'urban' ways of life in the countryside. Mann (1965, p. 106) provides one such example when he suggests that the residents of the small Sussex village of Forest Row exhibit more 'urban' characteristics in terms of sophistication and a blasé attitude than do the inhabitants of a northern town such as Huddersfield. More pertinently, Lewis (1951) studied the same Mexican village of Tepoztlan that Redfield had studied twenty years earlier (and from which he had derived many of his original conceptions regarding folk society) and found not 'rural' harmony, tranquility and consensus, but rather a 'pervading quality of fear, envy and distrust in inter-personal relations' (p. 429).

Two points need to be made about these and other similar studies. The first is that, despite the claims often made for them, they are not necessarily inconsistent with Wirth's characterization of urban and rural types. Evidence on the existence of urban villages and what Abu-Lughod terms the 'ruralization of the city' is encompassed by Wirth's argument that one effect of increased density is precisely the creation of a 'mosaic of social worlds' in which groups of similar race, class, status, etc., congregate. Similarly, studies of rural areas that find elements of urban culture can readily be explained in Wirth's approach as the result of the dominance achieved by the city over its hinterland. It is a source of some surprise, therefore, that evidence like this has so often been used in an attempt to counter the description of city life that Wirth provides.

The second point is that, even if such data were not consistent with the image of urban life that Wirth presents, they would not constitute a refutation of his theory, but only a criticism of the usefulness of his concepts. As Sjoberg has recognized, 'We must not confuse an analytical distinction with empirical reality' (1964, p. 131). To repeat once again, Wirth did not argue that ways of life in cities were necessarily anonymous, superficial, transitory and segmental; only that it was in terms of such characteristics that he wished to conceptualize the notion of urbanism. If Bethnal Green is not like that then, from this perspective, Bethnal Green is not highly urban (though from another perspective, such as one that conceptualized urbanism in terms of atmospheric pollution or mileage of made-up roads, it clearly would be).

This, however, does raise the first significant question-mark against Wirth's approach, in that we may validly ask how useful or fruitful such a conceptualization of the urban really is. We cannot disprove an ideal type, but if we doubt its relevance to empirical research we are most certainly justified in ignoring it.

One problem with his conceptualization of the urban, and with the very notion of a continuum between two ideal types of urban and rural, is that it is indiscriminate. This has been recognized both by those who defend an approach based on rural–urban distinctions (e.g. Miner 1952, Jones 1973) and by those, such as Lewis, who attack it. The problem is that many different variables are clustered together at each pole of the continuum, but it cannot be assumed that they are all interdependent and that they will all vary consistently with each other. Lewis, for example, suggests that it is logically and empirically possible for a society to exist with both a high degree of homogeneity and of individualism, and he concludes that 'The concept "urban" is too much of a catchall to be useful for cultural analysis' (1951, p. 434). This argument was subsequently reinforced by Duncan (1957), who showed not only that 'urban' and 'rural' characteristics did not always vary consistently with each other, but also that they did not even exhibit a continuous gradation.

A second problem with this mode of conceptualization, also noted by Lewis, is that it appears too narrow to be useful. Thus Lewis accounted for much of the difference between his and Redfield's descriptions of Tepoztlan in terms of the limitations imposed upon the scope of Redfield's observation by his commitment to the organizing principle of the folk–urban continuum. According to him, the process of change in Mexican society is far too complex to be reduced to a single principle: 'There is no single formula which will explain the whole range of phenomena' (Lewis 1951, p. 445). Of course, Weber argued when he developed the ideal type as the distinctive method of sociological analysis that an all-embracing view of the social world was impossible, and that it was precisely the function of an ideal type to identify and isolate those aspects of reality that the researcher found most relevant to his or her concerns. Lewis's argument is that the use of urban and folk types fails to identify the most significant aspects for study.

A third criticism concerns not so much the usefulness of the concepts of urban and rural as their evaluative character. To quote Lewis's critique of Redfield once again, 'Again and again in Redfield's writings there emerges the value judgement that folk societies are good and urban societies bad. It is assumed that all folk societies are integrated while urban societies are the great disorganizing force' (1951, p. 435). This is a common criticism made against those who employ rural–urban contrasts, although it appears less applicable in the case of Wirth (who was careful to point to the positive aspects of urbanism, especially the growth of individual freedom, as well as its negative side) than it does to Redfield. Without wishing to enter the long debate over value-freedom in the social sciences (which I have discussed briefly in Saunders 1979, pp. 338–46), it should nevertheless be noted that the ideal type method is inherently evaluative (see Chapter 1). The decision to emphasize certain aspects of 'urbanism' and to ignore others is a decision that is necessarily grounded in value, and while we may wish to take issue with the values that guide and interpret work such as that by Redfield or Wirth, it is hardly a valid criticism to attack them for an evaluative bias *per se*.

Despite these various criticisms, therefore, it may be suggested that the main problems with Wirth's approach concern not his mode of conceptualization but the adequacy of his theoretical explanation. The problem here is that Wirth fails to demonstrate that size, density and heterogeneity are the key determinants of the ways of life he describes; both Morris (1968) and Reissman (1964) argue that the same characteristics could be deduced from many other variables that are similarly commonly associated with cities (for example technology, economic rationality and so on). This line of criticism has been developed most fully by Gans and Pahl.

Gans levels three fundamental criticisms against Wirth's analysis:

> First, the conclusions derived from a study of the inner city cannot be generalised to the entire urban area. Second, there is as yet not enough evidence to prove – nor, admittedly, to deny – that number, density and heterogeneity result in the social consequences which Wirth proposed. Finally, even if the causal relationship could be verified, it can be shown that a significant proportion of the city's inhabitants were, and are, isolated from these consequences by social structures and cultural patterns which they either brought to the city, or developed by living in it (Gans 1968, pp. 98–9).

Of these three points, the third is ultimately most significant.

Gans illustrates his first point, concerning Wirth's spurious generalization from statements about the inner city to a theory of the city as a whole, by citing evidence on social relationships in outer city and suburban areas which shows that ways of life in these areas, though not entirely intimate, are nevertheless not entirely anonymous and impersonal either. Gans then coins the term 'quasi-primary' to describe these relationships in which 'interaction is more intimate than a secondary contact, but more guarded than a primary one' (1968, p. 104).

His second point, which relates to the dubious adequacy of size, density and heterogeneity as explanatory variables in those cases where ways of life do approximate Wirth's ideal type of urbanism, is developed by arguing that the key characteristic of parts of the inner city is their residential instability, and that this factor (which itself gives rise to heterogeneity) constitutes a more adequate explanation than Wirth's three variables:

> Under conditions of transience and heterogeneity, people interact only in terms of the segmental roles necessary for obtaining local services. Their social relationships thus display anonymity, impersonality and superficiality. The social features of Wirth's concept of urbanism seem therefore to be a result of residential instability, rather than of number, density or heterogeneity (Gans 1968, p. 103).

The important implication of this argument is that 'urban' ways of life may be expected to develop wherever there is residential instability, irrespective of whether it occurs in the city or in the countryside. Gans's second point therefore throws into doubt the validity of any attempt to develop a theory of the city in order to account for ways of life found within it, and it is this theme that is developed more fully by his third point.

His third argument is that, even if Wirth's three variables could be shown to affect the quality of social relationships, this can be the case only where certain social and cultural factors obtain. To illustrate this point, he distinguishes between five types of inner city residents, all of whom live in densely populated and socially heterogeneous surroundings. The cosmopolites, such as students, intellectuals and professionals, choose to live in the inner city because of its proximity to the cultural centre. Young unmarrieds and childless couples, on the other hand, tend to live there until they start a family, at which point they remove to the suburbs. Both of these first two groups therefore reside in the inner city by choice but are largely detached from it, either because their interests lie outside their immediate environment, or because they are located there only temporarily. The third group is the urban villagers, who are in, but not of, the city, and who form a relatively self-contained and homogeneous enclave within which ways of life continue relatively unaffected by the surrounding urban environment. Like the first two groups, therefore, they too remain virtually immune from the effects Wirth described. Only the last two groups – the deprived (who are forced by their material circumstances to live in inner-city slum areas) and the trapped (usually elderly people who remain behind in deteriorating inner neighbourhoods) – are susceptible to the sorts of factors Wirth analysed, for they are not detached from their surrounding environment.

What emerges from this argument is that, even in the inner city, many residents enjoy a choice as regards their physical location and the way of life they adopt, and that, the greater the choice available, the less significant do Wirth's three variables become. Gans therefore shifts analysis of social relationships in the city from identification of the determinants of ways of life to the study of choice as a way of life. In this way, he suggests that the most significant factors explaining variations in social relationships are the sociological variables of class and life-cycle: 'If people have an opportunity to choose, these two characteristics will go far in explaining the kinds of housing and neighbourhoods they will occupy and the ways of life they will try to establish within them' (p. 111).

For Gans, then, where people do not enjoy choice their ways of life will reflect the degree of residential instability of their neighbourhoods, and where they do social patterns will be a function of factors such as class and life-cycle. In neither case will size, density and heterogeneity appear as particularly significant explanatory variables. It follows from this that the explanation of social and cultural forms in the city cannot be accomplished through an analysis of inherent characteristics of the city: 'If ways of life do not coincide with settlement types, and if these ways are functions of class and life-cycle stage rather than of the ecological attributes of the settlement, a sociological definition of the city cannot be formulated. . . . The sociologist cannot, therefore, speak of an urban or suburban way of life' (pp. 114–15).

This conclusion is reasserted by Pahl, who argues that the explanation of social patterns in any given locality can be achieved only through analysis of social structure. Concepts of urban and rural thus appear of little value as analytical frameworks, and are positively misleading when used as explanatory variables: 'It is clear it is not so much communities that are acted upon as groups and individuals at particular places in the social structure. Any attempt to tie particular patterns of social relationships to specific geographical milieux is a singularly fruitless exercise' (Pahl 1968, p. 293).

Pahl therefore agrees with Gans that social relationships have to be explained with reference to sociological factors, and that geographical and environmental theories are essentially misconceived. However, he also takes Gans's argument several stages further, first by pointing to factors other than class and life-cycle which must be taken into account in any analysis (e.g. divisions between traditional residents and newcomers and the different patterns of social networks between locals and cosmopolitans), and second by indicating the direction in which urban sociology should develop. For Pahl, local social processes are important in affecting people's lives, and what Stacey (1969) later termed 'local social systems' are therefore an important area of study. But both Pahl and Stacey emphasize that the analysis of localities must take into account the relationship that exists between them and the wider society, for 'in any locality study some of the social processes we shall want to consider will take us outside the locality' (Stacey 1969, p. 145). It follows from this that the important distinction around which research should be oriented concerns not whether a particular locality is 'urban' or 'rural', but rather the relationship between the local and the national: 'I can find little universal evidence of a rural–urban continuum, which even as a classificatory device seems to be of little value. Of much greater importance is the notion of a fundamental distinction between the local and the national' (Pahl 1968, p. 285). As we shall see in Chapter 4, this distinction lies at the heart of Pahl's subsequent attempt to specify a distinctive area of interest for urban sociology, for he argues that 'Since people will always have their lives shaped by a combination of national and local influences and processes, a sub-discipline will continue – and this implies a convergence between rural and urban sociology – under whatever name' (p. 287). It is Pahl's view, in other words, that while an urban sociology cannot be founded upon the notion of a distinctive urban culture, there is nevertheless a conceptual space for a sub-discipline which focuses upon the combination of local and national processes and their effects on individuals' life chances.

Before we proceed to consider this claim in the next chapter, we should however pause to consider two final questions regarding the arguments discussed in this. The first is why, if the rural–urban distinction is essentially spurious, it nevertheless occupies such a central place in western culture? Ideas like this cannot achieve dominance in people's conceptions of their world unless they are in some way related to aspects of their everyday experience of that world. So we must ask to what, if anything, does the urban–rural dichotomy refer? Second, and in part related to this, we should also consider whether physical factors such as the size of human settlements are really totally irrelevant to an understanding of different patterns of social relationships, for there is a danger in following the critiques offered by writers such as Gans and Pahl that we throw the (albeit small) baby out with the bathwater.

On the question of why rural–urban imagery remains so pervasive in western culture, we can do no better than refer to Williams's argument in the final chapter of *The Country and the City* (1973). Williams suggests that the resilience of this imagery points to a real division in our experience and to a fundamental need which that division creates: 'Clearly the contrast of country and city is one of the major forms in which we become conscious of a central part of our experience and of the crises of our society . . . the persistence indicates some permanent or effectively permanent need, to which the changing interpretations speak' (1973, p. 289). It is through reference to the physical forms of the country and the city that 'experience finds material which gives body to the thoughts' (p. 291).

According to Williams, the experience from which this imagery derives and to which it relates is that of social relationships in a capitalist society. Capitalism divorces a necessary materialism from a necessary humanity, and this division is expressed, not only in the dichotomy of work and leisure, week and weekend, society and individual, but also in that between town and country:

> The pull of the idea of the country is towards old ways, human ways, natural ways. The pull of the idea of the city is towards progress, modernisation, development. In what is then a tension, a present experienced as tension, we use the contrast of country and city to ratify an unresolved division and conflict of impulses, which it might be better to face on its own terms (Williams 1973, p. 297).

Leading our everyday lives in the context of a capitalist mode of production, we come to accept as normal the 'modes of detached, separated, external perception and action: modes of using and consuming rather than accepting and enjoying people and things' (p. 298). Alienation is the accepted condition. Yet elements of the suppressed humanity remain – in childhood memories, in occasional communality when collectively we are threatened, and so on. It is this recurring sense that 'one is not necessarily a stranger and an agent, but can be a member, a discoverer, in a shared source of life' (p. 298) which becomes displaced into the representation of the country and the subsequent antithesis between it and the town: 'Unalienated experience is the rural past and realistic experience is the urban future' (p. 298). The rural–urban contrast is therefore the ideology through which we live and interpret our alienated existence under capitalism. It follows from this, of course, that those sociological theories that are premised upon this contrast are themselves in their function 'ideological' (see Chapter 5).

This need not imply, however, that these theories have no basis in reality. It is one thing to argue that differences in the size and density of human settlements cannot provide an adequate explanation for variations in ways of life, but quite another to conclude from that that they are therefore irrelevant. Simmel's analysis of the changes wrought by an increase in the size of any human aggregate undoubtedly has some validity, and Gans appears to recognize this when he notes that social differences between residents cannot entirely account for variations in social patterns which 'must therefore be attributed to features of the settlement' (Gans 1968, p. 112). Similarly Pahl (1968, p. 273) notes that status group interaction will tend to be more marked in a small settlement, while elsewhere (1975, p. 91) he lists some of the significant differences in life chances (e.g. in terms of availability of local services, the range of occupational choice and so on) between urban and rural areas which follow directly from the differences between them in terms of population density. While we are surely right to reject the division between rural and urban cultures as the basis for an urban social theory, it does nevertheless appear that there are certain differences between them that can be explained in terms of factors such as size and density.

What is basically at fault with the theories of Simmel, Wirth, Redfield and other similar writers is not that they chose to focus their attention on, say, the question of how size affects the pattern of social relationships, but that they failed to recognize the very limited scope of such an approach and in consequence attempted to explain a wide range of culturally variable phenomena through an illegitimate physical reduction. As Dewey recognized some years ago, 'The inclusion of both population and cultural bases in the term "urbanism" renders it useless except for labelling time-bound phenomena' (1960, p. 64).

Dewey argues that, other things being equal, variations in the size of human settlements do tend to be reflected in the degree of anonymity, differentiation, heterogeneity, impersonality and universalism of social relationships within them, but that the sorts of cultural factors that have been identified by various writers as 'urban' or 'rural' have nothing to do with size:

> There is no such thing as urban culture or rural culture, but only various culture contents somewhere on the rural–urban continuum. The movement of zoot suits, jass and antibiotics from city to country is no more a spread of urbanism than is the transfer or diffusion of blue jeans, square dancing and tomatoes to the cities a movement of ruralism to urban centres (Dewey 1960, p. 65).

If Dewey's argument is accepted, then it does seem that we should draw back a little from Pahl's somewhat sweeping assertion that the analysis of social relationships in terms of physical location is a singularly fruitless exercise. The size and density of settlement does have some effect on patterns of social relationships and, indeed, on the distribution of life chances. However, it also follows from Dewey's analysis that the scope of these effects is limited, for it does not take us very far to suggest that anonymity is more characteristic of life in cities than of life in small rural settlements, or that social differentiation tends to be more marked in large towns than in small villages. As Dewey observes, 'No evidence suggests that these concepts can acquire more than incidental importance in the understanding of the complexities of human relations in cities or hamlets' (1960, p. 66). Furthermore, 'It may occur to one that, if this be all that there is to the rural–urban continuum, it is of minor importance for sociology. He would be quite correct' (p. 66).

The most judicious conclusion, then, would appear to be that, while there is no distinctively urban culture and thus no basis in the work of Simmel or Wirth for development of a specifically urban social theory, it is nevertheless possible to identify a small range of questions in which the issue of population size and density remains pertinent. It is, however, doubtful whether such questions can constitute the basis for a specific theory or sub-discipline, for not only are the social implications of size very limited, but it may also be suggested that any attempt to analyse them will involve not an urban theory but a social–psychological theory in which spatial factors are taken into account as one among several variables. In other words, the size of human settlements is just one factor among many which may have some effect on the pattern of social relationships, and there appears little justification for isolating it as the object of intensive and specialized study. It is for this reason that we may endorse Dewey's argument that the effects identified by cultural theories of urban–rural differences are 'real but relatively unimportant'.

4 The urban as a socio-spatial system

For many years following the Second World War, urban sociology was unmistakably in decline as it became increasingly isolated from developments within the discipline as a whole. Following the demise of Chicago ecology and the lingering but finally inevitable collapse of the rural–urban continuum, urban sociology staggered on as an institutionally recognized sub-discipline within sociology departments, yet its evident lack of a theoretically specific area of study resulted in a diverse and broad sweep across a range of concerns that shared nothing in common save that they could all be studied in cities. Urban sociology became the study of everything that happened in 'urban' areas – changing patterns of kinship, political controversies over land use, educational deprivation among the working class, social isolation in council tower blocks – and it therefore became indistinct from the sociological analysis of advanced, industrial capitalist societies. The 'urban' was everwhere and nowhere, and the sociology of the urban thus studied everything and nothing. As Pahl observed, 'It is as if sociologists cannot define urban without a rural contrast: when they lose the peasant they lose the city too' (1975, p. 199).

Given this context, it is not surprising that urban sociologists (in Britain at least) reacted with considerable enthusiasm and not a little gratitude to the publication in 1967 of a book that aimed partly to contribute to the sociology of race relations, but which also set out to develop a new sociological approach to the analysis of the city. *Race, Community and Conflict*, written by John Rex and Robert Moore, reported a study of housing and race relations in an inner-city area of Birmingham called Sparkbrook. In it they developed a theoretical framework which represented a fusion between Burgess's work in Chicago on the zone of transition and Weber's sociological emphasis on the meaningful actions of individuals, and in this way they laid the foundations for an urban sociology which could retain its distinctive concern with the spatial dimension to social relationships while at the same time drawing upon a body of theory located within mainstream sociology in order to analyse such relationships.

Spatial structure and social structure

For Rex and Moore, the significance of the Chicago school in general, and of the work of Burgess in particular, lies in their recognition that, in the course of its historical development, the city becomes differentiated into distinct sub-communities which are spatially segregated into various zones or sectors, and which are associated with particular types of residents who collectively exhibit particular kinds of culture. Rex and Moore take this insight as the starting point for their theory of the city, and they suggest that 'In the initial settlement of the city, three different groups, differentially placed with regard to the possession of property, become segregated from one another and work out their own community style of life' (1967, p. 8). These three groups are, first, the upper middle-class, who own relatively large houses located near the cultural and business centre but away from the factories and other negative urban amenities; second, the working class, who rent small terraced cottages and whose common experience of economic adversity generates a strong sense of collective identity and mutual support; and, third, the lower middle class, who rent their houses but who aspire to the way of life of the bourgeois home-owners.

Like Park and Burgess, Rex and Moore suggest that the process of city growth involves the migration of population from central to outlying areas. In part this is due to the expansion of the central business district, but it is also due to the widespread pursuit of a middle-class way of life which becomes associated with the newly developing suburbs. Thus, while the professionals and the 'captains of industry' move out to detached houses in the inner suburbs, the lower middle class (who can gain access to credit for house purchase) move further out to semi-detached suburbia, and the working class (whose growing political muscle comes to be reflected in the provision of state housing) similarly relocate to a 'new public suburbia' (p. 9). As a result of this 'great urban game of leapfrog' (Rex 1968, p. 213), the various types of nineteenth-century housing around the city centre are abandoned to new users. The imposing homes of the bourgeoisie become swallowed up by the encroaching central business district, while the houses once occupied by the lower middle class are bought up and sublet as lodging houses accommodating new migrants into the city. In this way, inner-city zones like Sparkbrook are gradually transformed into 'twilight areas', characterized by physical decay of short-life properties and by growing concentrations of immigrant populations.

Central to Rex and Moore's theory is their assertion that 'the city does to some extent share a unitary status-value system' (1967, p. 9) in the sense that the move to the suburbs is an aspiration that is general among all groups of residents: 'The persistent outward movement which takes place justifies us in saying and positing as central to our model that suburban housing is a scarce and desired resource' (Rex 1968, p. 214). If suburban housing is widely desired, however, it is clear that it is not widely available. It is a scarce resource, and access to it is unequally distributed among the population. Two key points follow directly from this. First, if desirable housing is in short supply, then the means whereby it is allocated to different sections of the population become crucial to an understanding of the distribution of life chances in the city. Second, it is clear that the pattern of housing distribution constitutes the basis for at least potential conflict between different groups demanding access to the same resource. It was by pointing to the significance of these two questions of access and conflict that Rex and Moore provided urban sociology with a new orientation to the analysis of urban processes; an orientation that was inherently political in the fundamental concerns it raised.

Their analysis of the question of access to scarce and desirable housing indicated the importance of two principal criteria. The first was size and security of income, for it was largely on this basis that those institutions (e.g. the building societies) that controlled the allocation of credit for house purchase determined whether or not individuals could achieve access to the private owner-occupied housing sector. In general, the income criterion could be expected to operate in favour of middle class and relatively well paid skilled manual workers. The second criterion related to 'housing need' and length of residence, for need and residence qualifications were laid down by local authorities as conditions of access to good standard public housing. Thus, in Birmingham at the time of the research, the housing department operated a five-year residence rule which effectively rendered recent immigrants from the West Indies and the Indian sub-continent ineligible for council housing. Furthermore, even those immigrants who could satisfy the local authority's criteria then had to negotiate a further hurdle represented by the housing visitor whose job it was to grade applicants according to their suitability for different qualities of council accommodation, and this often resulted in black families being offered sub-standard short-life housing in inner-city clearance areas. The only other means of access to council housing was by being rehoused as part of a local authority slum clearance programme, and even this channel was often closed off to immigrants as a result of the council's apparent policy of clearing predominantly white areas while leaving areas of black concentration to continue deteriorating.

Rex and Moore's analysis of access to desirable housing thus suggested that, while the white middle class could generally gain entry to the owner-occupied sector in the suburban areas through the market mode of allocation, and while the white working class could usually secure access to council housing on suburban estates via the bureaucratic mode of allocation, there was nevertheless a residual group in the population (in which immigrants were heavily over-represented) that was effectively deprived entry to either of these desirable housing tenures. This third category could not therefore fulfil the general aspiration for suburban life, and was instead obliged to seek accommodation in the inner-city zone of transition.

According to Rex and Moore, the first cohort of immigrants to arrive in the city, faced with their effective exclusion from both the owner-occupied and local authority sectors, were forced either to seek private rented accommodation or to purchase the large deteriorating houses in areas like Sparkbrook which had been vacated owing to the middle-class flight to the suburbs. Because such purchases could not be arranged through building societies, however, they had therefore to turn to alternative sources of finance which entailed their accepting short-term loans at high rates of interest. The high repayments on such loans in turn necessitated sub-division and multi-occupation of the houses: 'Buying a house of this kind was possible only if the owner proceeded to let rooms. Once he did this he found himself meeting a huge demand from other immigrants' (1967, p. 30). Certain areas thus soon became characterized by multi-occupation, and the housing stock began to deteriorate even more quickly. Furthermore, as more immigrants moved into an area, so more indigenous families moved out. In Birmingham, as elsewhere, particular inner-city areas thus swiftly became associated with large concentrations of minority groups living in poor quality lodging houses.

In contrast to suburban owner-occupation, which is legitimated by the core values of a 'property-owning democracy', and purpose-built council housing, which is legitimated by values of welfare statism, such lodging house areas are, according to Rex and Moore, deemed to be illegitimate forms of tenure by radicals and conservatives alike:

'Both unite . . . in condemning the "bad landlords" who operate the system, and also the tenants for their failure to obtain better housing' (p. 40). The response of the local authority is therefore to insulate such areas in an attempt to stop them spreading into surrounding neighbourhoods, and thus to consolidate the formation of ghettos. The local authority therefore acts against the very group – the lodging house landlords – who provide housing for those (like themselves) who fall between the two stools of market and bureaucratic allocation: 'The city, having failed to deal with its own housing problem, turns on those upon whom it relies to make alternative provision, and punishes them for its own failure' (p. 41). Immigrant landlords, who were forced into landlordism because of the lack of alternative strategies for achieving accommodation, thus become convenient scapegoats for the inadequacies of the housing system.

It follows from Rex and Moore's analysis that the twilight zones of the city come to be populated by four distinct housing groups: tenants of nineteenth-century working-class housing, inhabitants of short-life slum property (often owned by the local authority) awaiting demolition, lodging-house landlords, and lodging-house tenants. While there are obvious sources of conflict between these groups (for instance between tenants and landlords over rents, repairs, etc.), all four appear disadvantaged as compared with suburban owner-occupiers and council tenants on purpose-built estates. All four are frustrated in their general desire for suburban living. The effect of local authority planning and public health policies, which are designed to restrict the growth of the twilight areas, and of its housing policies, which function to prevent certain groups from gaining access to more desirable forms of housing, is to exacerbate this comparative disadvantage and to foster the conditions for more intense conflict over the housing issue: 'Any attempt to segregate the inhabitants of this area permanently is bound to involve conflict. The long term destiny of a city which frustrates the desire to improve their status by segregationist policies is some sort of urban riot' (Rex and Moore 1967, p. 9).

The basic social processes within the city therefore relate to the allocation of scarce and desirable housing, both through the market and by bureaucratic means, and to the resulting struggle over housing by different groups located at different points in the housing hierarchy. As we shall see later, Rex and Moore suggested that this struggle over housing could be analysed as a class struggle over the distribution of life chances in the city. In other words, just as class struggles occurred in the world of work with respect to the distribution of life chances, so too they occurred in the realm of consumption of housing.

The significance of Rex and Moore's study is twofold. First, by emphasizing housing as an important, and analytically distinct, area in which individuals' life chances were determined, they located the theoretical concerns of urban sociology firmly within the traditional concerns of mainstream sociology with the sources of inequality and class conflict (see Harloe 1975, p. 2). Second, they showed how the spatial structure of the city articulated with its social organization through the system of housing allocation: 'The housing market represents, analytically, a point at which the social organisation and the spatial structure of the city intersect' (Haddon 1970, p. 118). In this way they laid the foundations for a new approach to urban sociology, although it was left to Pahl to draw out a conceptualization of the urban system which remained largely implicit in their study.

Like Rex and Moore, Pahl argues that the city is a source of new inequalities over and above those generated in the world of work, although like them he also recognizes that wage inequalities are an important factor determining urban inequalities. His argument is that individuals' life chances are affected by their relative access to sources of indirect, as well as direct, income; those who have to travel long distances to work (such as central city service workers who cannot afford to live in central areas) are therefore worse off than those who can choose to live near their employment, just as those who live near to positive public resources such as shops, parks and so on are better off than those who live near to negative ones such as gasworks or motorways. While high wages enable people to buy privileged access to positive urban resources, it is also the case that, in a country like Britain, allocation of public resources by the state is also important in distributing life chances. The task of urban sociology, therefore, is to study the distributional patterns of urban inequalities as these are affected by both market and bureaucratic processes: 'Urban sociologists are concerned with the basic constraints which affect people's life chances in urban areas, in so far as these fall into a pattern' (Pahl 1970, p. 53).

For Pahl, as for Rex and Moore, the city can be conceptualized as a relatively discrete local social system (see Elliott and McCrone 1975, p. 32). This does not imply that the city can be studied independently of the wider society of which it forms a part (the fact that Pahl recognizes that people's position in the occupational structure strongly influences their position in the urban system indicates his awareness of the need to understand the relationship between city and society). Indeed, Pahl has criticized traditional urban sociology for making precisely this assumption: 'Paradoxically, the fundamental error of urban sociology was to look to the city for an understanding of the city. Rather, the city should be seen as an arena, an understanding of which helps in the understanding of the overall society which creates it' (1975, pp. 234-5). Like Stacey (discussed above, page 110), therefore, Pahl's position is that, while the urban system cannot be divorced from the wider society, there are nevertheless important processes within it which can be identified and analysed in their own right.

The most fundamental of these processes concerns the distribution of scarce urban resources. Thus Pahl defines the city as 'A given context or configuration of reward-distributing systems which have space as a significant component' (1975, p. 10). There are three main implications of this approach.

First, space remains an important factor in Pahl's analysis. It has consistently been a basic feature of his approach that space is inherently unequal since no two people can occupy the same location in relation to the provision of any facility. This is why, according to his definition, an urban resource must have a spatial component. Urban sociology does not, therefore, study all allocative or distributive systems: 'Housing and transportation are elements in my view of the city; family allowances and pension schemes are not' (p. 10). The specificity of urban sociology lies in its concern with the patterns of distribution of those resources that are inherently unequal owing to their necessary location in a spatial context.

Given that inequalities in the distribution of urban resources are inevitable, it follows that spatial constraints on life chances will always operate to some extent independently of the mode of economic and political organization in society: 'It is central to my argument that these spatial constraints on the distribution of resources operate to a greater or lesser degree independently of the economic and political order. . . . These constraints can be ameliorated by political intervention but such intervention cannot totally negate their effects' (Pahl 1975, p. 249). Both capitalist and socialist societies are confronted with the operation of this spatial logic, and both may therefore encounter similar problems with regard to the distribution of urban facilities: 'The process of resource allocation has certain common elements no matter what the scale of organization or the specific mode of production with which we are concerned' (Pahl 1979, p. 34). It is for this reason that the results of state intervention in the urban system may be similar in very different types of society, and that the actual effects of policies may fall far short of the original intentions behind them' (see Pahl 1977a, p. 154).

Pahl does not, however, argue for a spatial or ecological determinism, for the second implication of this approach is that, although urban resources will always be unequally distributed, the question of *how* they are distributed is largely a function of the actions of those individuals who occupy strategic allocative locations in the social system. A pattern of social distribution is thus superimposed upon an underlying spatial logic. In the urban system, there are various 'gatekeepers' whose decisions determine degrees of access of different sections of the population to different types of crucial urban resources, and the task of urban sociology is therefore to study their goals and values in order to explain resulting patterns of distribution: 'We agree that certain urban resources will always be scarce and that social and spatial constraints will mutually reinforce one another whatever the distribution of power in society may be, However, given that certain managers are in a position to determine goals, what are these goals and on what values are they based? (Pahl, p. 208).

The third implication of Pahl's approach is that conflict over the distribution of urban resources is inevitable in any society. This is because such resources are crucial in the determination of individuals' life chances, yet are inevitably scarce and unequally distributed: 'Fundamental life chances are affected by the type and nature of access to facilities and resources and this situation is likely to create conflict in a variety of forms and contexts' (Pahl 1975, p. 204). Whether or not this conflict becomes manifest through conscious and politically organized struggles is for Pahl an open question, for distinct patterns of urban inequalities are not always immediately visible, and different groups may appear to be relatively more privileged in respect of the allocation of one type of resource and less privileged in relation to another. However, Pahl does suggest that, in future years, consciousness of common urban deprivations may develop, in which case conflicts between the managers and the managed in the urban system will increase: 'I am not certain whether a distinctive class struggle over the means of access to scarce urban resources and facilities could emerge . . . but increasingly political pressure may be less to reduce inequalities at the work place than to reduce inequalities at the place of residence' (1975, p. 257).

These three elements – spatial constraints on, social allocation of, and conflict over, the distribution of life chances in the urban system – together constitute Pahl's framework for urban sociological analysis. For Pahl, the urban is to be conceptualized as a socio-spatial system which generates patterns of inequality in the distribution of life chances over and above the inequalities generated in the sphere of production. He summarizes his perspective in the following terms:

> (a) There are fundamental *spatial* constraints on access to scarce urban resources and facilities. Such constraints are generally expressed in time/cost distance. (b) There are fundamental *social* constraints on access to scarce urban facilities. These reflect the distribution of power in society and are illustrated by: bureaucratic rules and procedures [and] social gatekeepers who help to distribute and control urban resources. (c) . . . The situation which is structured out of (a) and (b) may be called a socio-spatial or socio-ecological system. Populations limited in this access to scarce urban resources and facilities are the *dependent* variable; those controlling access, the *managers* of the system, would be the independent variable. (d) Conflict in the urban system is inevitable (Pahl 1975, p. 201).

Taken together, the work of Rex and Moore and Pahl provides a distinctive focus for urban sociology which combines an emphasis on the sociological significance of spatial distribution of population and resources with the familiar Weberian concerns with the goals and values of individual actors and the distribution of life chances in society. In particular, this body of work has served to focus attention within urban sociology on two questions: first, the significance of urban managers as allocators of life chances, and, second, the significance of patterns of urban resource distribution for the development of new forms of class struggle. It is to an examination of these two themes that the remainder of this chapter is devoted.

Urban managers: independent, dependent or intervening variables?

We have seen that, in his original conception, Pahl saw urban managers as the independent variables of analysis. In other words, the explanation of any given pattern of resource distribution could be achieved through analysis of the goals and values of strategically placed allocators and controllers of the stock of scarce and desired urban facilities. Thus: 'A truly *urban* sociology should be concerned with the social and spatial constraints on access to scarce urban resources and facilities as dependent variables and the managers or controllers of the urban system, which I take as the independent variable' (Pahl 1975, p. 210). This position was, of course, entirely consistent with that of Rex and Moore, who identified the actions of housing managers, housing visitors, planners, building society managers and so on as the source of the inequalities of opportunity in Birmingham's housing system.

As regards the identification of crucial urban managers, Pahl's original work suggested that a wide range of individuals, working in both the private and the public sectors, controlled access to key urban resources such as housing, and that the task for research was to discover the extent to which these different gatekeepers shared common ideologies and therefore acted consistently with each other in generating and perpetuating definite patterns of bias and disadvantage in respect to different sections of the population:

> The crucial urban types are those who control or manipulate scarce resources and facilities such as housing managers, estate agents, local government officers, property developers, representatives of building societies and insurance companies, youth employment officers, social workers, magistrates, councillors and so on. These occupations and professions should be studied comparatively to discover how far their ideologies are consistent, how far they conflict with each other and how far they help to confirm a stratification order in urban situations (Pahl 1975, p. 206).

This perspective stimulated and encompassed much fruitful research (see Williams 1978 for a brief summary). Some studies focused on gatekeepers in the private sector; Ford (1975), for example, showed how building society managers were socialized into a value system that defined certain types of applicants for mortgages as bad risks; Elliott and McCrone (1975) analysed the motives and values of private landlords in Edinburgh; and so on. Other research concentrated on the actions of political leaders and state employees in local government; Davies (1972), for example, showed how planners in the Rye Hill area of Newcastle imposed their values in the name of the client population; Young and Kramer (1978) showed how the ideologies of suburban political elites in London led them to frustrate attempts by the Greater London Council to decentralize council housing; and so on. Some research (notably that by Harloe, Issacharoff and Minns 1974) took up Pahl's call for comparative research and engaged in analysis of both private and public sector gatekeepers in order to discover how far a comprehensive housing policy was possible.

Increasingly, however, such research encountered two problems on which Pahl's urban managerialism thesis provided little effective guidance. The first concerned the identification of urban managers. Should research address itself to the values and goals of those in the top positions in bureaucratic hierarchies who were formally responsible for deciding policies, or should it focus instead on lower-level employees who actually worked at the interface with the client population? Furthermore, should studies of urban managerialism consider the actions of public sector gatekeepers as more significant than those of individuals in private sector agencies or vice versa? What such problems pointed to was the fact that, although he had urged sociologists to consider the actions of crucial urban managers, Pahl had failed to provide any theoretically rigorous criteria by means of which the relative significance of different types of managers could be assessed. As Norman (1975) pointed out, his identification of urban managers was achieved descriptively rather than analytically. Research grounded in this perspective could thus easily degenerate into mindless empiricism, studying one set of empirically determined urban managers after another with no coherent theoretical rationale other than some vague recognition that they all appeared to enjoy some degree of control over allocation of some resource.

The second problem concerned the autonomy of those managers who were selected for study. Pahl did, of course, recognize that, although they could be treated as independent variables in analysis, urban managers were nevertheless constrained to some degree by the operation of a spatial logic which contained its own inherent inequalities. Later research, however, indicated that the context of constraint was much broader than this. Harloe *et al.* (1974), for example, found that, while the ideologies of those involved in the supply of housing were important in determining their actions, so too were the organizational constraints upon them, in terms both of the availability of resources such as land and finance, and of the limitations imposed on their choice of action by other organizations with which they interacted. What this and other studies tended to suggest, therefore, was that urban managers in the public sector at least were restricted in their actions by the operation of market processes in the private sector (for example, land for public housing had to be purchased at current market prices, finance for such schemes had to be raised from the private capital market at current rates of interest, and so on), and by the organizational structure in which they were located (for example, many areas of policy were strictly regulated by higher-level governmental agencies). Given such constraints, the designation of urban managers as independent variables began to look somewhat dubious.

These two problems of identification and autonomy led Pahl to introduce two important refinements in his later work on urban managerialism. First, he distinguishes between managers in the private sector and those in the local state sector and restricts his definition of urban managers to those in the latter category. Second, he recognizes that local state bureaucrats have to operate under the constraints imposed by their relations with the private sector and central government. In this way, he moves from an analysis of urban managers as independent variables to one that conceptualizes them as intervening variables mediating between, on the one hand, the contradictory pressures of private sector profitability and social needs, and on the other the demands of central government and the local population:

> It seems to me that one set of urban managers and technical experts must play crucial *mediating roles* both between the state and the private sector and between central state authority and the local population. Another set of private managers control access to capital and other resources. . . . The attempt to focus on the relationship between market distributive systems and 'rational' distributive systems, seeing the urban managers as the essential mediators between and manipulators of the two systems, is extremely interesting (Pahl 1977c, p. 55).

This shift in Pahl's approach is a significant one, for while he continues to see the analysis of the goals, values and actions of local state employees as a valid and useful area of research, he does so only in so far as such an analysis is situated in a broader theoretical framework in which the key variables are the state and the capitalist economy. Thus he criticizes his own earlier formulation for its focus on the 'middle dogs' to the exclusion of the 'top dogs', and for its neglect of the constraints imposed upon public policy by the operation of national and international capitalism. At best, he suggests, local authority officers 'only have slight, negative influence over the deployment of private capital, and their powers of bargaining with central government for more resources from public funds are limited' (Pahl 1975, p. 269). To locate responsibility for urban inequalities and the urban crisis in the actions of local state employees is, he argues, 'rather like the workers stoning the house of the chief personnel manager when their industry faces widespread redundancies through the collapse of world markets' (1975, p. 284). Clearly we have moved a long way from an analysis of urban managers as the independent variables of the subject.

In this revised formulation, therefore, urban managers are significant as allocators of resources, but it is recognized that the initial availability of such resources depends upon decisions made by central government and by those who control investment in the private sector. It follows from this that an adequate explanation of the distribution of life chances in the urban system can be achieved only by combining an analysis of the process of allocation at the local level with an analysis of the production of resources in society as a whole. Put another way, if urban managers are no longer the independent variables, then it is necessary to identify those individuals or groups that are. For Pahl, this entails analysis of the changing role of the state in an advanced capitalist society like Britain.

Pahl's argument is that, in Britain at least (for he denies the possibility of developing a single theory of *the* capitalist state given the wide variations between different capitalist societies), lack of investment in the private sector, coupled with the growing intensity of international competition, has increasingly resulted in a qualitative change in the relation between the state and private capital. Britain, he suggests, is developing into a corporatist society:

> In general it could certainly be argued until fairly recently that the state was subordinating its intervention to the interests of private capital. However, there comes a point when the continuing and expanding role of the state reaches a level where its power to control investment, knowledge and the allocation of services and facilities gives it an autonomy which enables it to pass beyond its previous subservient and facilitative role. The state manages everyday life less for the support of private capital and more for the independent purposes of the state. . . . Basically the argument is that Britain can best be understood as a corporatist society (Pahl 1977a, p. 161).

His discussion of the role of the state in the new corporatist society is located firmly within the Weberian tradition of political sociology. In particular it reflects three basic themes in Weber's writings: namely, a conceptualization of the state as an apparatus controlled by individuals with definite aims and motivations; a view of the state's mode of operation in which officials and technical experts are deemed to prevail against elected political leaders; and a commitment to a theory of politics as a realm autonomous of economic class relations.

We saw in Chapter 1 that Weber's approach to sociological explanation rests on the analysis of the goals and values that guide individuals' actions in relation to others. We also noted his ontological commitment to a view of the social world as a moral realm in which individual actors are constantly confronted with choices between irreconcilable values (Weber's 'warring gods'). From these two basic orientations, it is clear that the question of power was central to Weber's entire sociology, for as soon as individuals attempt to achieve transcendent goals (that is, to impose their objectives against those of others), conflict becomes inevitable and power becomes crucial. Thus in Weber's view, power involves the ability of any one actor within a social relationship to realize his or her will, if necessary against the opposition of others. It is, in other words, a function of the relationship between individuals. When the power of one actor in relation to others becomes sufficiently well established that there is a recurring probability that his or her commands will be obeyed by them as a matter of course, Weber identifies a relationship based on domination.

Domination over others may be achieved on the basis of economic power (through control of goods and services in demand by others) or of political power. Weber insisted that these two spheres of domination in society were analytically distinct. He denied the Marxist claim that there was a necessary correspondence between them, for although he recognized that historically those who controlled economic resources often also controlled the instruments of state power, he argued that this did not reveal any historical necessity. While economic power is achieved through control of commodity or labour markets, political power is achieved through control of the state and therefore refers to 'the leadership, or the influencing of the leadership, of a political association, hence today of a state' (Weber 1948b, p. 77). Political power, in other words, entails the pursuit of given goals or values by those individuals who are in a position to control or influence state policies. Thus we arrive at the first of Weber's key principles that is carried over into Pahl's analysis: political domination is autonomous of economic class domination.

The second principle develops directly out of this, for it is apparent that, for Weber, the state is a 'thing' to be controlled by individuals. More accurately, it is a particular type of political association which is characterized by a legally sanctioned monopoly over the use of physical coercion:

> Ultimately one can define the modern state sociologically only in terms of the specific means peculiar to it, as to every political association, namely the use of physical force. . . . Of course, force is certainly not the normal or the only means of the state – nobody says that – but force is a means specific to the state . . . a state is a human community that (successfully) claims the monopoly of the legitimate use of physical force within a given territory (1948b, pp. 77–8).

Political domination is therefore achieved by individuals through privileged access to the instruments of state power. In order to understand state policies, therefore, it is necessary to understand the goals and values of certain key individuals. This is reflected in Pahl's argument that the state today manages society according to its own independent purposes. It is also, of course, the logic behind his search for crucial urban managers.

The third aspect of Weber's work that recurs in Pahl's analysis concerns the role of state officials. We saw earlier that, in his reformulation of the concept of urban managers, Pahl came to focus exclusively on the actions of bureaucrats and technical experts who are in the employment of the state. Similarly in his discussion of corporatism, it is clear that Pahl traces the 'independent purposes' of the state to the objectives set by the state bureaucracy through the establishment of various agencies of social and economic planning. This emphasis on the role of the bureaucracy reflects Weber's argument that the growing rationalization and complexity of modern capitalist (or socialist) societies must increasingly be reflected in the rationalization of the state's administration of these societies: 'The question is always who controls the existing bureaucratic machinery. And such control is possible only in a very limited degree to persons who are not technical specialists' (Weber 1968, p. 224).

Weber is resolutely sceptical as regards the claims made on behalf of modern representative democracy, for he argues that direct democratic control over a large and complex state is impossible. Representative assemblies perform just two functions: they are the means for mobilizing the consent of the masses to their own subordination, and they provide the means whereby new political leaders can emerge. Weber therefore rejects the notion of parliaments representing the 'will of the people', and argues instead that the masses vote for leaders rather than policies, and out of emotion rather than calculation. The most successful political leaders are those who have mastered the art of demagogy: 'Democratisation and demagogy belong together' (1968, p. 1450). Elected on the basis of plebiscitary democracy, it is then the task of strong political leaders to attempt to counter the deadening hand of bureaucracy by introducing a spark of creativity into the political process. Political administration in modern society thus exhibits a recurring tension between the official and the charismatic leader, the ethic of responsibility and the ethic of conviction, bureaucracy and democracy, rational administration and value-commitments, in which the power of expertise generally prevails over the power of ideals.

The picture that emerges from Weber's political writings is that of a centralized state imposing goals of efficiency in its administration of ever-widening areas of social and economic life. It is precisely this picture that is developed in Pahl's work on the development of a corporatist society in Britain and which underpins his more recent discussions of the role of urban managers.

Pahl's work on corporatism is contained mainly in two articles (Pahl 1977a and b), although it resonates through much of his writing in the late 1970s (e.g. 1977c, 1979) and should be read in conjunction with papers by Winkler (1976, 1977) who was originally responsible for developing the key elements of the theory to which Pahl refers. Taking all this work together, we may discuss the corporatism thesis in terms of the three questions of the causes, functions and mode of operation of the new corporatist state.

There are basically four factors that explain the increased role of the state in managing the British economy. The first is the growing concentration of capital into a small number of large oligopolies such that the fate of the economy as a whole is now bound up with the fate of a handful of companies. The state must therefore act to ensure that these companies continue to generate an adequate rate of return on investment, but in underwriting their profits it must also ensure that it does not create a 'licence to plunder'. Profits, in other words, must be both guaranteed and regulated. Second, the falling rate of profit in the economy as a whole (which the theory does not itself explain) has resulted in private companies seeking state financial aid as alternative sources of investment dry up. In providing capital (for example through the National Enterprise Board), the state has therefore been able to exert its influence over patterns of investment in the private sector. Third, new technological developments, which have themselves spurred on the process of industrial concentration, have generated new problems which have necessitated further state regulation of, and participation in, the private sector. Research and development costs, for example, have escalated to a point where even the largest companies require state aid, while the social implications of new technology in terms of pollution, public safety, levels of employment and so on have necessarily led to increased state involvement. Finally, as we have already seen, the growing intensity of international competition has led private sector firms to seek the support and protection of the state in their search for new markets and their need to consolidate existing ones.

These four factors have not only resulted in a quantitative increase in state economic activity, but have provoked a qualitative shift in its role in relation to the private sector: 'Stripped to its essentials, corporatism is principally defined by one particularly important qualitative change, the shift from a supportive to a directive role for the state in the economy' (Winkler 1976, p. 103). It is fundamental to Pahl's and Winkler's position that the developing corporatist society represents a mode of political and economic organization that is different from that of both capitalism and socialism: while capitalism entails the private control of private property, and socialism entails state control of collective property, corporatism 'is an economic system of private ownership and state control' (ibid., p. 109).

The change in the state's role from the support to the direction of the private sector thus involves a new set of state functions which to some extent challenge some of the basic principles of capitalism. Corporatism replaces the 'anarchy' of the free market with the order of the rational plan; it substitutes predictability for profit maximization; and it undermines traditional elements of capitalist property rights by dictating uses (such as investment) and restricting benefits. In place of the principles of free enterprise and competition, the corporatist state imposes four principles of its own: unity (collaboration and co-operation between the functional interests of capital and labour), order (stability and discipline in, for example, industrial relations), nationalism (defence of the national interest both domestically, against sectional interests, and internationally, against foreign competitors) and success (the dominance of the principle of means by the pragmatism of ends – notably in ensuring efficiency). Not only, therefore, does the state extend its sphere of economic influence and control, but it increasingly directs the economy according to its own non-capitalist criteria.

The mode of corporatist control is hierarchical but essentially non-bureaucratic in the sense that a premium is placed upon flexibility of administration. The state dictates policy but attempts to find others to carry it out, preferably on a 'voluntary' basis. Thus, for example, agreements are reached with the trade union leadership over wages policy, and it is then left to the union bureaucracies to impose or sell the policy to the rank-and-file. Similarly, planning agreements are secured with the largest companies as the means of controlling the economy as a whole. As Winkler puts it,

> What appears to be happening is a formalisation of interest group politics; an institutionalisation of pluralism. And, indeed, within co-optive institutions, the state will have to bargain and make compromises. But the ultimate purpose of such institutions is to give the state some measure of control over what were previously autonomous private organisations (Winkler 1977, p. 54).

The corporatist state is therefore centralized, hierarchical and co-optive.

It is in this context that the role of urban managers – local state officials – has to be analysed. On the one hand, they are agents of a centralized corporatist state, and this leads Pahl to reject the view that they are responsible for the policies that they carry out: 'The previous work on local decision-makers "running" a town overtly or covertly seems curiously inadequate and dated' (Pahl 1979, p. 42). On the other hand, however, it is in his view inevitable that the peripheral agents of a centralized state must enjoy a certain degree of discretion in determining how policies are to be carried out: 'Those who administer these systems of allocation we may term the managers, and generally they have considerable discretion either in determining the rules or in administering the rules determined elsewhere' (1979, p. 39). It follows from this that, while they are certainly not the independent variables in any analysis of the pattern of urban resource distribution, they must be taken into account as significant intervening variables: 'The urban managers remain the allocators of this surplus; they must remain, therefore, as central to the urban problematic' (1975, p. 285).

The argument that Pahl continually emphasizes is that the state, both at national and local levels, cannot be studied merely in terms of the 'needs' of capital. In other words, state policies do not always or necessarily reflect the interests of capital but are rather the outcome of 'managerial bargaining' between agents representing different types of organizations. Like Weber, therefore, he is concerned to stress, first, that political power is not simply a reflection or derivation of economic power but can be and is used to direct, control and influence key economic interests, and, second, that such power has ultimately to be analysed as a function of relationships between individuals:

'Specific *agents* ultimately control and allocate resources' (1979, p. 43). Analysis of political outcomes must therefore begin with the goals, values and practical purposes of those individuals who control access to key resources, and then must attempt to identify the constraints that limit the potential scope of their actions.

In the case of urban managers, this necessitates carrying the analysis beyond and outside the urban system: 'It is no longer possible to consider "urban" problems and "urban" studies separately from the political economy of the society as a whole' (Pahl 1975, p. 6). Thus, by arguing that urban managers perform a dual mediating role between the private sector and the welfare sector on the one hand, and between the central state and the local population on the other (see page 125), Pahl identifies the context of political and economic constraints within which the allocators of resources within the urban system must operate. In other words, not only are their actions limited by the operation of an inequitable spatial logic within the urban system (for throughout his work Pahl has consistently reiterated his argument that territorial inequalities are inevitable in any society), but they are also constrained by the power of a centralized interventionist state and by decisions taken by private sector firms outside it. None of these three factors – ecological, governmental and economic processes – can be said to *determine* the pattern of urban resource distribution (theories that deny the relevance of urban managers are therefore every bit as inadequate as those that assert their autonomy), but all three together constitute the system of constraints within which the actions of urban managers must be studied and understood.

Williams has pointed out that 'Urban managerialism is not a theory, nor even an agreed perspective. It is instead a framework for study' (1978, p. 236). The question, therefore, is how useful this framework appears for empirical study.

The first point to make is that Pahl's whole approach was very much a product of its time. The concern with urban managers was a clear reflection of the context of the 1960s and early 1970s – a period of enormous expansion in state spending on consumption provisions such as housing, health and education, and a time when public sector bureaucracies were growing and professional autonomy and power was expanding. These were the years of massive urban renewal projects when millions of people saw their homes designated as 'slums' and were forcibly removed to system-built high-rise flats by zealous 'evangelistic bureaucrats'; when public services in Britain were fundamentally restructured and 'modernized' through managerial upheavals affecting local government, personal social services, health and the schools and higher education; and when the rediscovery of poverty and the growing fear of racial disturbances led to a variety of interventionist programmes designed to break the so-called 'cycle of deprivation' in the inner-city areas. Against such a context, a focus on urban managers – on the people who seemingly had it in their power to allocate millions of pounds of public money and to determine policy priorities and outputs – appeared not only plausible but crucial if the pattern of urban inequalities of life chances was to be analysed.

Similarly, Pahl's interest in corporatist state theories in the later 1970s also reflected important economic and political developments in British society at that time. Under the 1974–9 Labour government, for example, attempts were made to draw big capital and organized labour into regular negotiation and consultation with government, and the Industry Acts of 1972 and 1975, taken together with the so-called 'Social Contract' governing wages, investment and public spending, seemed to many to herald the consolidation of an irreversible shift towards public sector regulation of private sector economic activity.

Much of this context against which the managerialist and corporatist theses were developed has subsequently changed. The onset of a sustained recession from the mid 1970s, coupled with the election in 1979, and re-election in 1983, of a radical-right Conservative government, led in a few short years to dramatic reductions in certain areas of welfare spending (notably housing), a resurgence of economic liberalism coupled with an outright attack on state planning agencies, and an unprecedented erosion of local state autonomy from the centre. In the light of such changed conditions, we may indeed ask how useful Pahl's framework has been for empirical analysis.

It has immediately to be said that the strong corporatist thesis developed by Pahl and Winkler has been disproved in so far as any social science theory can be disproved. Winkler's brave but, in retrospect, foolhardy prediction in 1977 that 'Corporatist institutions should be reasonably well established in Britain by around the end of the 1980s' (p. 57) now seems faintly ludicrous, but even back in the 1970s, there was probably little evidence to sustain such confident futurology. As various critics pointed out at the time, the planning agreements system introduced in the 1975 Industry Act was effectively toothless from the start, price controls were mainly cosmetic and incomes policies soon foundered on the inability of the union leaderships to police their own rank-and-file. As Westergaard (1977), Hill (1977) and others pointed out, the supposedly new 'corporatist' society did not look very different from the old 'capitalist' one it was said to be replacing. 'Why', asked Hill rhetorically, 'call Britain corporatist rather than state capitalist?' (p. 42).

While rejecting the claim that Britain is developing into a corporatist society, however, it is important to recognize that a somewhat weaker version of corporatist theory may still be extremely useful in contemporary political analysis. In this version (e.g. Cawson 1982, Jessop 1982) corporatism is understood, not as a type of society or even type of state system, but rather as one among several modes through which particular functional interests may achieve privileged access to state power and themselves take on specific responsibilities for administering policies agreed with government. Corporatism as a distinct mode of interest representation and mediation has, it seems, survived the ravages of recession and the anti-planning ideology of successive governments, and flourishes in particular areas of the state system including land use planning (Flynn 1981, Simmie 1981, Reade 1984). The growth of non-elected urban service agencies such as the water authorities, the health authorities and the urban development corporations in Britain from the 1970s onwards has also facilitated the emergence of exclusive corporatist forms. In London's derelict docklands, for example, local residents and trade union groups were kept at arms length by the Development Corporation set up by the government to redevelop and 'revitalize' the area, while various business and professional interests seem to have been closely involved in formulating and executing the redevelopment strategy (see Duncan and Goodwin 1985). Similarly, the non-elected regional water authorities, which took over responsibility for water services from local councils in 1974, have developed clear corporatist strategies in their relations with key users such as farmers, industrialists and developers while participation on the part of domestic and other consumers (e.g. amenity groups) has been little more than token and ritualistic (see Saunders 1985a).

Evidence like this suggests that a modified concept of corporatism may still have a place in the lexicon of urban studies. However, it is clearly important not to over-extend the concept, for not all urban services are managed and provided in this way. In the British health authorities, for example, there is little evidence of corporatist forms, the prevailing pattern here being that of managerial and professional domination within a strongly centralized system in which central government controls the purse strings. And in other areas of urban policy, especially those under the control of elected local authorities, it is still possible for, say, residents, tenants, trade unions or other voluntary citizens' groups to achieve some input and influence. Furthermore, services characterized by one form of control and mediation at one point in time may shift to another pattern at another time, just as the pattern found in one country may vary from that found in another. The point is, then, that corporatism, managerialism and pluralism represent three possible systems for determining urban policy outputs, and we should be wary of any general theory which claims that any one of these is general or universal across all services at all times in all places (I return to this issue in Chapter 8).

Where does all this leave Pahl's urban managerialism thesis? The importance of the thesis in my view lies in its recognition that the state, whether at central or local level, now plays a crucial role in a country like Britain in shaping or influencing people's life chances. Precisely because we are so familiar with its presence in so many aspects of our everyday lives, it is easy to forget just how pervasive the state has become. One-third of British households live in accommodation rented from the state; nineteen out of every twenty children in Britain are educated (compulsorily) in state schools; the vast majority of people rely on the state health service when they fall ill; millions rely on the state-run bus and train services to get them to work, to the shops or wherever; and everyone relies on the state to provide roads and other aspects of physical infrastructure such as water, sewerage, gas and electricity, and so on. In addition, some 7 million people rely on the state for their employment (in local government, the public services, the nationalized industries, etc.) while millions more rely on it for cash benefits such as housing allowances, family allowances, pensions, unemployment benefits, supplementary benefits and the rest. It is the essential strength of an urban managerialist perspective that it asks who, if anyone, controls this vast resource system, how they seek to direct it, and to whose benefit?

Now it is clear that Pahl's initial answer to such questions – namely that the managers of the services represent the 'independent variables' – is crude and naïve. However, his later formulation, in which local state bureaucrats and professionals are seen as playing a crucial mediating role at the intersection of strong cross-cutting pressures – those between the central authority and the local population, and between the private sector and the welfare system – seems altogether more fruitful in that it avoids what Pahl himself came to term the 'managerial heresy' (1975, p. 7). It is no longer true, for example, that 'The managerialist approach, in concentrating on studying the allocation and distribution of "scarce resources", fails to ask why resources are in scarce supply' (Gray 1976, p. 81), for the actions of urban managers are now to be seen in the wider context of relations between government and the private sector. Similarly, the argument developed by Lambert and his colleagues (1978) to the effect that the importance of urban managers lies not in the content of their policies but in the style with which they administer them is not entirely inconsistent with Pahl's later formulation in which managers are seen as juggling the pressures and expectations imposed from above against the demands and aspirations coming up from below.

Yet having said all this, there remains a fundamental problem with this whole approach, and that concerns the limits to managerial autonomy and discretion. Pahl's claim that the allocation of 'urban' resources can do much to ameliorate or exacerbate existing inequalities arising out of the operation of the labour market represents a seemingly 'obvious' yet nevertheless crucial insight. Sociology has long been preoccupied with the significance of occupational class and labour market situation in shaping people's lives, yet the majority of people in a country like Britain do not engage in waged work (e.g. school students, the retired, 'housewives', the unemployed, the sick and so on), and of those that do, many are still in receipt of significant state support in cash or in kind. Clearly, then, the use of state power and the allocation of state resources is likely to be as, if not more, significant in determining patterns of inequality and life chances as the operation of market power in the formal economic system. Furthermore, Pahl's additional claim that the 'logic' dictating the way this state power is used may be different from that underpinning the operation of the economic system is also crucial and incontrovertible. As Weber recognized, economic or market power and political or state power are analytically distinct bases of domination in the modern world, and although each may influence and set limits upon the other, it is surely fascile to assume that we can simply read off from one the logic which dictates the other. While one is necessarily subject to the operation of what Marxists term 'the law of value' (simply, nothing can or will be produced in the long run which does not generate a normal rate of profit), the other is to some extent subject to political will and human volition (simply, governments may and frequently do commit themselves to providing certain things irrespective rather than because of cost or profitability calculations). In so far as the urban managerialist perspective serves to direct our attention to these often neglected principles, it represents an enormously significant corrective to those approaches which all too often forget that the system of power and domination analysed by Marx over a hundred years ago has been dramatically modified by an unprecedented extension of state power into every nook and cranny of people's lives.

The problem, however, remains that this approach gives no indication of where the power of state managers to shape resource distribution ends and the logic of the capitalist market system takes over. For all its faults, the original managerial thesis was at least clear in the assertions which it was making. But once Pahl recognized (mainly under pressure from Marxist critics) that managers were constrained by the political–economic system in which they were obliged to function, the thesis effectively lost its analytical cutting edge. As Pickvance suggests:

> Pahl's starting point was a strong statement that urban managers could be seen as independent variables. . . . But in response to Marxist critics he abandoned this claim and introduced two typologies. The outcome of urban management could now be to narrow, reflect or widen income inequalities . . . and resource allocation might be carried out by urban managers, central government, capitalists or some combination. . . . Whereas there was an underlying logic to the initial claim, viz. that it was the professional ideologies of urban managers that led them to reduce income inequalities, this coherence disappears as soon as the typologies are introduced since they cater for every eventuality (1984, p. 43).

Putting the same point another way, the more realistic the thesis became, the less it explained. Thus it is undoubtedly true that the state at both national and local level is hedged in by constraints, many of which derive from the operation of a capitalist logic in the markets for land, finance, labour and so on, just as it is also true (as we have seen) that state managers may play important roles in allocating some resources while being virtually insignificant in allocating others. But having recognized all this, we end up with an extremely weak form of theory in which virtually everything is found to be contingent. That managers may enjoy *some* autonomy from the dictates of central government and the constraints imposed by the need to safeguard capital accumulation may be taken as axiomatic: the problem then still remains to theorize how far and in which situations this autonomy may be exercised.

This Pahl fails to do. To the extent that he offers an answer to the problem, it is that it is an empirical question to be resolved by empirical research. This, however, is inadequate, for it is a recipe for extremely dubious inductive generalization, the conclusion to which is likely to be no more than the observation that things are different in different places at different times. If we start out on an empirical investigation merely on the assumption that managers are constrained to some extent, then not only will we lack any criteria for determining where to begin looking for the origins of any given policy, but we shall also lack the theoretical means for explaining variations between the different cases we observe. Indeed, Pahl's revised urban managerialism thesis will simply open up without resolving the familiar problem of the receding locus of power: the actions of urban managers can only be understood in the context of national state policy; national state policy can only be understood in the context of the operation of a complex mixed economy; the operation of the economy can only be understood in the context of the world economic system. In this way, the researcher who starts out by trying to explain, say, housing inequalities in Birmingham swiftly ends up by trying to analyse the determination of Middle Eastern oil prices or the impact of American budgetary strategies on the international terms of trade.

The point of this example is not to deny that such 'wider' factors are important – of course they are – but to show how, in an attempt to meet the criticisms made against his original formulation, Pahl's later revisions effectively undermined the distinctiveness of his focus on the urban system as a resource and power system. It was therefore no accident that, having shifted his position on urban managers, he soon ended up studying, not the urban system, but the national political economy. His work on corporatism, in which he attempted (wrongly as it turned out) to analyse what he saw as a fusion of private ownership and state control in the national economy, was the inevitable end-point of what began, much less ambitiously, as a concern with the actions of local authority housing managers, social workers and other strategically-placed professionals and bureaucrats at the local level.

In this transition, any notion of the 'urban' as a distinct object of analysis was irretrievably lost. The simple yet compelling idea which stimulated Pahl's initial approach – that inequalities generated in the operation of the capitalist economy could be modified in crucial ways through processes operative in the urban system – was inexorably eclipsed as he fatally pursued the logic of his own thinking into the intellectual minefield of political economy. In this way, his work met the same fate as that of Park and McKenzie, Simmel and Wirth, before him, as the initial focus on the city crumbled into an indistinct and inevitably confused concern to understand the wider social processes which enveloped it.

The concern with urban management was, of course, just one aspect of the reformulation of the urban question which developed out of Rex and Moore's work in the 1960s. The other, complementary, aspect concerned the new and distinct patterns of social and political cleavages which were seen to arise around the process of urban resource allocation – cleavages which Rex and Moore themselves sought to analyse through their concept of a 'housing class' struggle. If the focus on urban managers eventually collapsed, it is now necessary to trace what happened to this second and related concern with the distinctively urban bases of class formation.

Housing distribution and class struggle

We saw in the first section of this chapter that the fundamental argument developed by Rex and Moore in their attempt to reformulate a sociology of the city was that the distribution of scarce and desired housing resources created new patterns of inequality of life chances that were analytically separate from those arising out of the occupational system. Drawing on Weber's analysis of class and class conflict, they then suggested that, just as struggles over access to wages could be seen in terms of class struggle, so too could competition over access to housing. The central principle of their urban sociology, therefore, was that

> There is a class struggle over the use of houses and that this class struggle is the central process of the city as a social unit. In saying this we follow Max Weber who saw that class struggle was apt to emerge wherever people in a market situation enjoyed differential access to property, and that such class struggles might therefore arise not merely around the use of the means of industrial production, but around the control of domestic property. . . . There will therefore be as many potential housing classes in the city as there are kinds of access to the use of housing (Rex and Moore 1967, pp. 273–4).

For Weber, the concept of class, like any other collective concept in sociology, can be understood only as referring to an aggregate of individual subjects. Class is a sociological construct which is imposed upon reality in order to clarify analysis – in reality there are only individuals, not classes, who act – although Weber did recognize that class may, in certain situations, become a meaningful concept for groups of individuals who may therefore come to designate themselves as a class and act accordingly. For Weber, therefore, it is fallacious to argue that classes exist and that 'the individual may be in error concerning his interests but that the "class" is "infallible" about its interests' (1968, p. 930), and this is the first of two crucial differences between his and Marxist approaches. Marx's distinction between a class in and for itself is alien to Weber's sociology; for Weber, class is ultimately only an idea, whether it be an idea used in sociological analysis or one to which groups of individuals orient their actions.

The second major difference between Weber's and Marx's analysis is that for Weber, the concept of class may usefully be applied to the analysis of any situation in which groups of individuals share roughly common life chances as a result of their economic power in labour or property markets. The relationship between employer and employee was therefore only one among several different class situations in which individuals may find themselves, and Weber drew a basic distinction between commercial classes, which referred to groups of individuals who typically shared common life chances as a result of their possession or non-possession of marketable skills, and property classes, which could be identified among groups whose life chances were a function of the ownership or non-ownership of resources that could be used to generate income. Unlike Marx, who analysed classes in terms of the relationship between those who owned and controlled the means of production in society and those who did not, Weber therefore located class analysis in the sphere of distribution rather than production relations, in the market rather than in the mode of production.

In arguing that competition over housing could be conceptualized in terms of a class struggle, Rex and Moore thus drew upon Weber's distinction between commercial and property classes by suggesting that, while power in the labour market was clearly an important factor in determining an individual's power in the housing market (including the mode of bureaucratic allocation), the distribution of housing nevertheless created a situation in which an individual could occupy one class situation in respect of the power to command a wage and another in respect of the power to command access to a desirable house. The formation of commercial classes in the world of work would not therefore necessarily be reflected in the formation of property classes in the city, in which case the task for urban sociology was, first to analyse the distribution of life chances consequent upon the differential power of different groups in the housing system and, second, to study the extent to which these groups come to recognize their common market situation and to mobilize politically in order to defend or improve it.

There was, however, a problem with this approach which was apparent from the outset and which derived directly from Rex and Moore's commitment to Weber's view of classes as distributionally defined aggregates of individuals. This concerned the identification of the main types of access to housing, and thus of the major housing class categories. It is an inescapable implication of Weber's formulation that, if classes are to be defined in terms of common degrees of market power among different individuals, then the number of potential classes that may be identified is almost infinite since no two individuals will ever share an exactly identical market situation. As Weber recognized, 'A uniform class situation prevails only when completely unskilled and propertyless persons are dependent on irregular employment' (1968, p. 302). The problem is thus to construct ideal types of different class situations which are mutually exclusive and relatively unambiguous. This was what Weber attempted to achieve with his concept of 'social class' which referred to a cluster of different market situations between which individuals could move relatively easily. As Giddens (1971) shows, he was then able to develop a model of the class system in which three main social classes were identified, consisting of an upper class with privileged access to property and skills, a lower class with little or no property and skills, and a middle class, comprising those with property but few skills and those with marketable skills but little property. Quite apart from the question of the usefulness of such a formal taxonomy in empirical research where the allocation of different individuals to different class categories is likely to remain a hazardous and somewhat arbitrary process, this mode of conceptualizing the class structure also left unexamined the problem of how the three social classes related to one another. Weber's work on class is descriptive rather than analytical, static rather than dynamic, positional rather than relational.

The same problems recur in the work of Rex and Moore (1967). For a start, it is never clear how the different housing classes are to be identified. At the beginning of *Race, Community and Conflict*, they suggest that the system of housing allocation gives rise to five housing classes: owner-occupiers, council house tenants, tenants of private landlords, owners of lodging houses and lodging house tenants (p. 36). By the end of the book (p. 274), however, they have added a sixth, namely those buying a house on mortgage, and have subdivided the 'class' of council tenants into those in long-life accommodation and those in slum stock. This subdivision was then subsequently represented as a distinct class division (Rex 1968, p. 215), bringing the total number of housing classes to seven, and in a still later study, Rex elaborated on this schema to identify four more classes or sub-classes, thereby bringing the grand total to eleven (Rex and Tomlinson 1979, p. 132). Yet there is no reason why taxonomic innovation should end there; for Moore (1977, p. 106) has suggested that two more classes could have been analysed in the Sparkbrook study, Rex (1977, p. 21) has argued that any group (such as one-parent families) that is discriminated against in housing may constitute a housing class, and Pahl (1975, pp. 242–3) has pointed out that the framework fails to take account of large landowners or of local authorities (who are, after all, more significant providers of housing than lodging house owners), both of which could, given the logic of Rex and Moore's approach, be included. There are, it seems, dozens of potential housing classes.

Part of the problem here derives not so much from the inherent pluralism of any Weberian class analysis as from a confusion, noted by Haddon (1970), between the conceptualization of housing classes and their empirical identification. While Rex and Moore's conceptual model stresses inequalities in *access* to scarce housing resources, their various taxonomies all refer to differences in current housing tenure: 'They equate this typology of housing with "housing classes" assuming that, analytically at least, people who are *at the present moment* in the same type of housing accommodation constitute a housing class' (Haddon 1970, p. 128).

In one sense, this criticism does not appear particularly cogent, for although there undoubtedly are some people who continue to live in relatively undesirable housing despite their ability to gain access to a more favoured type (for example the inner-city intellectuals and urban villagers identified by Gans – see page 108), these would appear to be in a small minority, in which case current housing situation may be taken as a reasonable indicator of potential power in the system of housing allocation. This, in fact, is how Rex and

Tomlinson counter Haddon's criticism: 'This seems on reflection to be an unreasonable criticism since the type of housing occupied is a very good indicator of the strength of its occupants in the housing market' (1979, pp. 20–1). Yet in another sense the criticism is highly pertinent, and Rex and Tomlinson's response to it misses the significant point. This is that the theoretical emphasis on inequalities of access to housing should lead in empirical research not to concern with housing groups as the units of analysis, but rather to a concern with different types of social groups. When Rex, for example, argues that fatherless families may constitute a housing class, he is clearly resorting to a very different mode of conceptualization from that employed when he identifies, say, council tenants in slum property as a housing class; single-parent families may be found in owner-occupied housing, on council estates, in rented rooms in the inner city and so on, and they cannot therefore be equated with a particular type of housing in the way in which council tenants obviously can be. Rex and Moore's application of the housing class concept is therefore confused. Indeed, it may be argued that their theoretical concern lies not with *housing* classes, but with different groupings within *social* classes (for instance, blacks, women, one-parent families, etc.) who, because of their peculiar *status* characteristics, experience greater difficulty in achieving access to certain types of housing than do other people who are in a similar market position with regard to the distribution of other types of resources in society. This is a crucial point, for it suggests that analysis of differential access to housing does not involve a sociology of the city at all, but rather entails analysis of the sources of inequality in society as a whole, in which case the distinctiveness of urban sociology disappears. This is the point to which we shall return at the end of this chapter.

A second problem with Rex and Moore's analysis concerns their assumption of a unitary value system in the city in which owner-occupation is valued above renting, council tenancies are valued above private tenancies, and suburban locations are valued above inner-city locations. This assumption was, it will be recalled, central to their theory of the city, since it was the foundation of their argument that the basic urban process was one of conflict between different classes desiring the same type of housing.

Subsequent research has, however, called this assumption into question. Davies and Taylor (1970), for example, report that in Newcastle ownership of lodging houses is positively desired by many Asians as a means of upward social mobility through property ownership. Indeed, no less than 75 per cent of the Asian population who owned the property in the Rye Hill area were landlords, and most of these were absentee landlords (indicating that, far from being pushed into lodging house ownership through lack of alternatives, many recent immigrants were opting for it as a means of capital accumulation). Furthermore, Davies (1972) went on to show that rented accommodation was generally despised by Asians to the extent that none of those interviewed had made any attempt to gain access to council housing and many had resisted attempts by the local authority to move them from inner-city clearance areas into council accommodation. He suggested that renting was rejected as a vulnerable form of tenure and that property ownership was embraced because of the security and opportunities for capital gains that it offered. He also claimed that few immigrants experienced unusual difficulties in gaining access to funds for house purchase: 'I have no evidence at all that the question of colour intruded into the economics of house buying in such a way as to *force* the immigrant into unwanted and oppressive methods of finance' (p. 32).

Further evidence against Rex and Moore's assumption is provided in a study of housing in the city of Bath by Couper and Brindley (1975). They show that one-third of all applicants for council housing in Bath would prefer a central to a suburban location, that one-quarter of all tenants in the city were in privately rented accommodation and would not apply for a council tenancy under any circumstances, and, perhaps most surprisingly of all, that 'There appear to be many people, not necessarily on low incomes, who prefer renting to owning' (p. 567) – indeed, one-half of all tenants in unfurnished accommodation said that they preferred to rent rather than to buy.

Such evidence appears very damaging to Rex and Moore's thesis, although, as Couper and Brindley themselves recognize, there is a methodological problem in such research in that the preferences that people articulate may reflect their (scaled-down) realistic aspirations as much as their ideal choices. Rex (1971), for example, criticizes the Davies and Taylor findings by suggesting that immigrant landlords may claim to have chosen this form of tenure even though they were in fact forced into it, although in the same article he concedes that 'multiple value systems do exist' (p. 297). He then argues, somewhat obscurely, that there may be a dominant value system among the competing value systems in the city, but this does little to rescue the original analysis since it appears that it is precisely those groups living in the supposedly 'undesirable' housing who do not subscribe to the dominant value system on which Rex and Moore founded their hierarchy of desirable housing types. Indeed, in his later research in the Handsworth area of Birmingham, he and Tomlinson have recognized that the desire to move to the suburbs is not prevalent among blacks living in the inner city, and they argue (rather lamely) that this 'does not alter the fact of the existence of housing classes (at least in themselves) since access is in effect denied to those who do wish to move' (Rex and Tomlinson 1979, p. 132). The point is however that, while this may not invalidate an ideal type model of housing classes, it does remove the very factor – competition over scarce resources desired by virtually all city dwellers – that made this model useful in urban research. By conceding that many of those in apparently disadvantaged housing conditions do not aspire to suburban living, Rex has therefore removed the grounds for arguing that the housing classes he identifies are in conflict with one another. As with Weber's ideal types of social classes, we are therefore left with a static positional description rather than a dynamic relational analysis.

In their Handsworth study, Rex and Tomlinson effectively attempted to rectify this by shifting the emphasis of their analysis of distribution of life chances in the city from an exclusive focus on access to housing to one that encompasses education and employment as well as housing opportunities. Their argument is that blacks in areas like Handsworth constitute a distinct 'underclass' in British society owing to the systematic inequalities they experience in competition with whites for jobs and for educational success, and that it is this broad area of disadvantage rather than discrimination in housing *per se* that creates the conditions for conflict. The significance of discriminatory housing policies is that they have created black concentrations in particular inner-city areas which enable the development of political organization separate from the white labour movement. In other words, the process of segregation in housing has produced the conditions – neighbourhood-based ethnic and kin ties – by means of which blacks can mobilize as an 'underclass-for-itself':

> Just as exploitation in industry gave rise to the trade union movement and more widely to the Labour movement amongst native British workers, so the fact of discrimination in housing has given rise to partially segregated areas, and to locally-based and relatively effective communal and ethnic organisations which are useful as a means of protecting the rights of minority groups. (Rex and Tomlinson 1979, p. 157).

In this later study, therefore, Rex and Tomlinson argue that situations of common housing deprivation are the means rather than the cause of conflict, and they document the growth in militancy of the West Indian organizations that are based in neighbourhoods like Handsworth. However, although this argument provides a convincing explanation of the sources of conflict, it does so largely at the expense of the housing class concept, for when Rex and Tomlinson discuss housing class mobilization, they are in fact referring to the mobilization of a black underclass on the basis of neighbourhood organization. Indeed, their emphasis on the common situation of disadvantage experienced by blacks in Handsworth in the job market and the educational system leads Rex and Tomlinson to deny the significance of tenure divisions among them, yet such divisions were the very basis of Rex's original housing-class concept. Thus they write: 'Private property owners and renters on the one hand, and immigrant council tenants on the other, have tended to be much the same sort of individual and, to all intents and purposes, we found very little differences in the observed attributes of those housed in the public and private sectors' (p. 144). The key factor, then, is not housing but race, and the focus of concern turns out not to be urban inequality but racial inequality. Once again, therefore, we find that the housing class concept does not constitute the basis for urban analysis but rather points to the need to understand sources of inequality in the society as a whole.

The third major criticism that can be levelled against Rex and Moore's discussion of housing classes is that it rests on a misinterpretation of Weberian class analysis. As we have seen, Weber applied the concept of class to the analysis of groups of individuals who share roughly common life chances as a result of their power in labour or commodity markets (that is, as a result of their ability to realize income from the sale of their skills or their property). He then distinguished between classes and status groups, defining the latter in terms of the distribution of social honour or prestige in society as reflected in different styles of life, and he argued that, while social honour (like political power) was often empirically closely related to patterns of economic inequality, it was nevertheless analytically separated and 'need not necessarily be linked with a class situation' (Weber 1968, p. 932). It followed from this that groups of individuals may come to act either as classes or as status groups, and that collective action on the basis of shared status characteristics could cross-cut class divisions.

Weber summarized the distinction between classes and status groups as basically that between the situation of individuals with respect to the distribution of life chances through the market, and their situation with respect to the distribution of life-styles through the process of consumption of goods and services. Seen in this way, it is clear that the groups that Rex and Moore identify as 'housing classes' are not classes at all but housing status groups. Different types of housing tenure are simply different modes of consumption of housing which may be differently evaluated according to the life-styles associated with them. The class situation of the council tenant with respect to the ability to realize returns in the housing market is the same as that of the private tenant, for both are, in Weber's terms, 'negatively-privileged' in the sense that neither owns property that can be used to generate income. The difference between them is a difference in their style of life – in other words, a status difference – rather than a difference in their market power. As Haddon puts it, 'Use of housing is an index of achieved life chances, not primarily a cause' (1970, p. 132).

This does not mean that a Weberian analysis of housing classes is not possible – Weber himself sees the ownership of domestic buildings as one type of property that may differentiate the market situation of various property classes (1968, p. 928) – but it does mean that Rex and Moore's emphasis on forms of tenure has to be replaced by an analysis grounded in the question of ownership and non-ownership of those types of housing that, potentially at least, may generate economic returns. This is the logic behind Pahl's reconceptualization of housing classes in which he distinguishes between large property owners (public or private), smaller landlords, owners of capital sufficient to buy their own houses, and those who lack property and are obliged to rent (Pahl 1975, p. 245). Similarly, I suggested in earlier works (1978 and 1979 ch. 2) that the application of a Weberian framework could lead to the identification of three housing classes according to whether people used housing as capital (e.g. landlords), as a pure means of consumption (e.g. tenants), or as both (e.g. in the case of owner-occupiers who may achieve considerable capital gains from ownership at the same time as they enjoy the use value of the house).

A major problem with all such formulations, however, is that they fail to explain the relationship between the 'housing class system' and the overall class structure. How, for example, does the class situation of a working-class owner-occupier differ from that of a comparable working-class council tenant? Furthermore, it is by no means clear why the exclusive focus should be on housing, for if it is the case that people's life chances are influenced by differential access to resources such as education, health care, personal transport and so on as well as to housing, then it would seem more fruitful to develop a mode of analysis which takes all such relations into account. As we shall see in Chapter 6, this is precisely what has happened with the development by Dunleavy (1979) and others of the concept of 'consumption sectors' – a concept which identifies a major cleavage in the modern period between those who are able to provide for their basic consumption needs through the market (e.g. by buying their house, running their own car, purchasing pre-school education for their children, paying into private pension schemes or whatever) and those who remain reliant on state provision. Seen in this way, the crucial basis of urban alignment is not housing tenure as such, but is the division between those with private property rights in key commodities or services (including housing) and those without.

Rex, however, remains resolutely sceptical about any attempt to reformulate the housing class concept around the question of property ownership, for, as we have seen, in his work with Tomlinson he argues both that owner-occupation among immigrants in the inner city may be no less a disadvantaged form of tenure than renting, and that the original conception of housing classes, suitably expanded to encompass groups such as homeless families and tenants of housing associations, remains a useful framework for analysis.

Such an assertion, however, simply ignores Haddon's argument that the housing class concept derives from a misreading of Weber and that the various groups that Rex identifies are in fact differentiated by status rather than by class situation. Rex has never answered this most fundamental criticism, yet it is crucial since it leads to the conclusion that housing struggles between different tenure groups can be understood only as status group conflicts, which may cross-cut and obscure more basic economic class divisions. It is but a short step from here to much of the contemporary Marxist literature on housing, which argues that divisions grounded in different forms of housing consumption are important only at the level of ideology in that the working class is fragmented by different types of provision, none of which alters the basic underlying class division between wage labour and capital. This sort of analysis (see Saunders 1979, ch. 2 for a resumé) totally ignores or devalues the significance of, for example, the capital gains which may accrue to owner-occupying households or the differential power and control experienced by those who buy commodities like housing as compared with those who rent from a public or private landlord. As we shall see in Chapter 8, such divisions arising out of patterns of consumption of crucial goods and services cannot simply be dismissed as 'superficial' or 'irrelevant', for their significance in influencing the quality of people's lives and the way they view their world can be enormous. There is a lot more of sociological significance in the spread of mass home ownership than simply the 'ideological partitioning' of the working class, but Rex's failure to reconceptualize the problem of housing cleavages around the issue of property ownership as opposed to tenure effectively closes off this avenue of analysis. Rex's Marxist critics are surely right when they dismiss tenure divisions as an important factor in reshaping the class system, but what both they and he apparently fail to consider is the deeper significance of the division between private and state provisioning.

The inescapable conclusion that suggests itself as a result of our discussion of the three major problems with Rex and Moore's work on housing classes is that the attempt to found a sociology of the city on this concept has now collapsed. Rex virtually admits as much in his book with Tomlinson, when he suggests that 'It was never claimed that the housing classes which seemed more relevant to explaining ethnic political conflict in Sparkbrook in the mid-1960s could be taken as a kind of inductive generalization covering all cases at all times' (Rex and Tomlinson 1979, p. 128). In other words, he now suggests that housing class is not a generic concept, yet this is clearly a retreat from his earlier position, in which he suggested that 'The *basic process* underlying urban social interaction is competition for scarce and desired types of housing', and that 'What is *common to all urban situations* is that housing, and especially certain kinds of desirable housing, is a scarce resource', for which different groups are in competition (Rex 1968, pp 214 and 216; emphases added). In his work with Moore (1967) Rex clearly saw the concept of housing classes as the basis for a new approach to the sociology of the city; in his work twelve years later with Tomlinson (1979) he equally clearly did not.

We have seen that there are three main reasons why a specifically urban sociology cannot be based upon the concept of housing class. First, the focus on access to housing means that housing classes cannot be equated with housing tenure groups and that analysis must focus not on a theory of the city but on a theory of social stratification which explains why different groups enjoy different degrees of access to the housing system. Second, the work by Rex and Tomlinson (1979) clearly demonstrates that the lack of a common value system with respect to desirable types of housing undermines an analysis of housing class conflict unless the application of the concept is restricted to particular groups (i.e. the black 'underclass') whose situation in other areas of life (namely the occupational and educational systems) creates the potential for conflict. In other words, the analysis of housing class struggles becomes merely a part of a sociological theory of race relations rather than the basis for a distinctive urban sociology. Third, the fact that, even from a Weberian perspective, the housing classes that Rex and Moore identify are not classes but status groups indicates that the analysis of housing divisions can be accomplished only through the attempt to theorize the significance of patterns of consumption for class relations, in which case what is needed is not a theory of the city but a sociological analysis of consumption as it affects class relations. In all three cases, therefore, we see that what appears to be the concern of urban sociology with housing class conflict is in fact the concern of a sociology of stratification, and that urban research premised upon this concept collapses into an analysis of questions of class structure, the relation between ethnicity and class, and the problem of consumption divisions and ideology.

Taking together the related concepts of housing class and urban managerialism, we can only endorse the conclusion reached by Lambert *et al.* (1978) in their study of housing allocation in Birmingham that we should 'reject the former notion and substantially redefine the latter' (p. 171). As they stand, neither concept provides a satisfactory foundation for a specifically urban sociology. A focus on urban managerialism soon leads beyond the city and into the complexities of national and international economic and political systems, while a focus on housing classes equally soon collapses into a more general concern with the system of social stratification in society as a whole in which the relation between social classes and consumption sectoral divisions appears central. But having said this, it obviously remains the case that the general themes addressed by writers such as Rex and Pahl through the 1960s and 1970s are of major significance for sociology. Unlike the legacy of the human ecologists and the cultural urbanists, that of Weberian urban sociology does contain within it the seeds of a coherent and important theoretical programme. At the heart of such a programme is the focus on the question of consumption in the context of contemporary capitalist societies where the state has come to play a central role in shaping people's lives. As we shall see, this concern with consumption became the focus for an important development in Marxist urban theory through the 1970s – a development which was to prove crucial in redefining urban sociology's object of analysis.

5 The urban as ideology

Since the late 1960s, there has been a tendency for western Marxist theory to broaden its traditional horizons in order to take account of various radical movements that have developed outside the process of production and which cannot simply be analysed in terms of the wage labour–capital relation. The growth of the feminist movement, for example, has spawned a considerable literature on the role of women and the family in capitalist societies and on the relationship between the women's movement and the labour movement. Similarly, the rise of black movements in the West and in the Third World and (to a lesser extent) the explosion of student radicalism in the 1960s both helped to undermine narrow conceptions of Marxist theory and political practice which sought to reduce all political struggles to that between bourgeoisie and proletariat.

It is in this context that Marxist theory has rediscovered the problem of the city, a problem that has been posed by the development of radical movements in the cities addressed to issues such as the decline of urban public services, environmental desecration and so on. The argument of Marx and Engels (discussed in Chapter 1) to the effect that the capitalist city is not in itself theoretically significant has therefore been reconsidered in recent years.

This reconsideration has involved two steps. The first is the critique of existing urban theories (such as human ecology) and urban practice (for instance, planning) as 'ideological'. The term 'ideology' has, however, meant different things for different writers, and this reflects two distinct (though related) meanings of the concept in Marx's work. Thus some writers have emphasized the notion of ideology as a means of legitimating class domination, and in this they have taken their cue from arguments such as that advanced in the *Communist Manifesto* that 'The ruling ideas of each age have ever been the ideas of its ruling class' (Marx and Engels 1969, p. 125). Current conceptions of urbanism and current explanations of urban problems are then termed ideological on the grounds that they reflect and are subordinated to the class interests of the bourgeoisie. Other writers, however, have seen this as too limited a conception of ideology and have attempted to develop a conception (also found in Marx) that contrasts 'theoretical ideologies' with 'scientific practice'. In other words, current theories are criticized on the grounds that they fail to break with the ideological appearances of material reality and thus reproduce ideological modes of thought in an elaborated theoretical form which is justified by a spurious claim to scientific status.

Having established the critique of existing conceptions of urbanism as ideological, the second step is to develop a theory that is not subordinate to dominant class interests or does not simply formalize existing ideological representations. Again, however, there are intense disagreements between different writers, and these tend to reflect a major division between humanist and determinist interpretations of Marxism. Thus, while one approach addresses the urban question in terms of the limitations and potential of 'urban society' for human liberation and individual self-realization, another is openly contemptuous of socialist humanism and rejects notions of the individual human subject as metaphysical. While the first conception sees the 'urban crisis' as central to advanced capitalism, the second sees it as secondary to the basic class struggle in industry. And while the former focuses on the question of the production of space (that is, on the way in which capitalist organization becomes extended and imprinted upon all aspects of everyday life), and hence on the need to develop new forms of struggle against capitalist domination of space, the latter sees the urban question as significant only in so far as urban crisis enables an extension of the traditional struggle against capitalist domination of industrial production.

It should be noted that these disagreements are not merely academic but reflect very different views regarding Marxist political strategy. As we shall see, the humanist approach seeks fundamentally to reorientate the workers' movement towards what it sees as the central question of the quality of everyday life, while the determinist approach seeks rather to encompass urban struggles within the existing workers' movement. The theoretical gulf between these two approaches cannot therefore be fully understood except in the context of recent debates within the European (and notably the French) communist parties regarding socialist strategy in the conditions of advanced capitalism. It is, in other words, no accident that the literature that we shall be discussing in this and the following chapter is almost entirely French and Italian in origin, for it is precisely in these countries that the question of communist strategy has been posed in its most practical terms since 1968.

In this chapter we focus on the way in which two Marxist theorists – Henri Lefebvre and Manuel Castells – sought to refashion the field of urban studies through the critique of existing approaches to and conceptions of 'the urban'. Although Castells has subsequently rejected much of his earlier work, his writings during this period were enormously influential in laying the basis for what became known as 'the new urban sociology', and it is difficult to over-estimate the significance of his legacy for the later development of the field.

Henri Lefebvre: the humanist critique of urbanism

Lefebvre's work on urbanism is not widely known in the English-speaking world. In part this appears to be due to the relative inaccessibility of his relevant work, for little of it exists in English translation. It is also due in part to the fact that Castells's text, *The Urban Question*, has been widely read and discussed, and this includes a heavily critical chapter on Lefebvre's theories. In other words, not only have the terms of academic Marxist debate (in Britain at least) been set largely by reference to Castells's framework, but also there has been little stimulus to examine Lefebvre's ideas since these were apparently demolished and transcended by Castells's work. In recent years, Lefebvre has begun to receive more attention through the work of Marxist urban geographers such as Harvey and Soja (discussed in Chapter 7), but his impact on urban sociology remains somewhat peripheral. This is probably due to its highly speculative, self-consciously 'utopian' character. Lefebvre's writings appear lively but also (sometimes at least) lacking in academic rigour. In places he clearly contradicts himself; the development of his argument often seems more arbitrary than logical; and the sense of spontaneity that pervades his writing stands in stark contrast to the painstaking formalism of a text such as *The Urban Question*. It is perhaps this difference in style (which itself clearly reflects a difference in their approaches to Marxism) that more than any other factor explains the differential response in Britain to Lefebvre and Castells, for the British intellectual tradition within and outside Marxism is one that has bred an extreme suspicion of academic speculation and spontaneity.

Lefebvre's critique of existing urban theories is premised on the argument that any theoretical system that guides human actions in such a way that they serve to maintain the existing system of social relations may be termed ideological: 'Any representation is ideological if it contributes either immediately or "mediately" to the reproduction of the relations of production. Ideology is therefore inseparable from practice' (1976, p. 29). He cites as an example the traditional ideology in capitalist societies that the system reproduces itself naturally, without the purposive interventions of human agents, for this not only serves to legitimate the system (what is natural is acceptable), but also denies the possibility of radical interventions to change it (what is natural is inevitable). Already, therefore, we see here the basis of Lefebvre's rejection of deterministic Marxist as well as of 'bourgeois' theories, for both have the practical effect of stunting the development of revolutionary action (that is to say, a deterministic Marxism that denies the effectivity of conscious human subjects denies also the potential for radical action and thus performs the same function as 'bourgeois' theories in undermining the practical struggle against capitalist domination).

Ideologies, therefore, are general social theories that have the practical effect of maintaining the dominance of particular class interests: 'It is the role of ideologies to secure the assent of the oppressed and exploited' (1968a, p. 76). This is achieved by masking the true interests of the dominated classes and thus curtailing their political struggle against the source of their domination. Marxism is not therefore ideological in this sense since it enables and facilitates such struggles; in other words, it is revolutionary in its practical effects: 'It discloses – not by some power of "pure" thought but by deeds (the revolutionary praxis) – the conditions under which ideologies and works of man generally . . . are produced, run their course and pass away' (1968a, p. 86).

In arguing that Marxism is not an ideology, Lefebvre does not seek to imply that it is therefore a science with a privileged insight into 'truth' and 'reality'. Far from it; for all theory, he suggests, is a mixture of truth and error, and there is no sharp distinction between science and ideology, truth and falsity. His discussion of ideology is not premised on the science/ideology distinction but on the distinction between those theories that have revolutionary practical effects and those that secure political consensus and containment. Lefebvre's views are echoed by Harvey, who criticizes 'the rather trivial view that there is one version of some problem that is scientific and a variety of versions which are purely ideological', and who asserts on the contrary that 'The principles of scientific method (whatever they may be) are normative and not factual statements. The principles cannot therefore be justified and validated by appeal to science's own methods . . . the use of a particular scientific method is of necessity founded in ideology' (Harvey 1974, p. 214). This reveals a crucial distinction between Lefebvre's view of Marxism and that of Castells, since for Lefebvre Marxism is not a science but a political theory of socialist practice. This is a view that the argument developed in the final section of this chapter will strongly endorse.

Given this view of Marxist theory, it follows that the development of radical ideas is crucial, not because ideas can wish away the material reality of capitalism, but because practical activity by individuals is guided and informed by the ideas that they have of that reality. This leads Lefebvre to designate himself as a 'utopian' on the grounds that 'Today more than ever there are no ideas without a utopia. Otherwise a person is content to state what he sees before his eyes' (1977, p. 349). Lefebvre's project, therefore, is to develop a set of ideas about urbanism that can stimulate radical action against what he sees as a new and all-embracing mode of capitalist domination of everyday life.

It is in this context that he develops his critique of urban planning and of the theory that underpins it. This is a theory that represents space as a purely scientific object and gives rise to a planning 'science' that claims to be as precise and objective as mathematics. It is a technocratic theory, in that spatial forms are taken as given and planning is conceived as a technical intervention which can bring about particular effects on the basis of a scientific understanding of a purely spatial logic. Urban theory and planning practice are thus premised on a denial of the inherent political character of space – politics are conceived as an irrational element that intrudes upon the spatial system from outside it rather than as an essential element in the constitution and perpetuation of spatial forms. This theory is thus ideological, for it sustains the *status quo* by depoliticizing the question of space and its use, and as an ideology it permeates throughout the society with the effect that political struggles over the use of urban space are defused:

> Urbanism, almost as a system, is now fashionable. Urban questions and reflections emanate from technical circles, from specialists and intellectuals who think of themselves as *avant garde*. They pass to the public sphere via newspaper articles and writings with various aims and objectives. Simultaneously, urbanism becomes ideology and praxis. Yet questions concerning the city and urban reality are not yet well understood or

recognized, they have not yet assumed a *political* importance in the same way as they exist in *thoughts* (in ideology) or in *practice* (Lefebvre 1968b, p. 9).

The task for a critical theory is to explode this urban ideology by showing how spatial forms and organization are the product of a specific mode of production – capitalism – and how they contribute to the reproduction of the relations of domination on which that mode of production depends:

> Space is political. Space is not a scientific object removed from ideology or politics; it has always been political and strategic. . . . Space, which seems homogeneous, which seems to be completely objective in its pure form such as we ascertain it, is a social product. The production of space can be likened to the production of any particular type of merchandise (Lefebvre 1977, p. 341).

It is precisely because space is a product of capitalism, and that it is therefore infused with the logic of capitalism (production for profit and exploitation of labour), that the urban ideology of space as a pure and non-political object is so crucial.

What is required, according to Lefebvre, is not therefore a science of space *per se*, but rather a theory of how space is produced in capitalist societies and of the contradictions that this process of production generates: 'We are not speaking of a science of space, but of a knowledge (a theory) of the production of space' (1976, p. 18). Such a theory will involve not a logical and physical theory of structures and systems, but rather a dialectical theory of contradictory processes which provide the basis for political struggle over the urban question. The basic contradiction in the production of space is that between the necessity for capital to exploit it for profit and the social requirements of those who consume it; in other words, the contradiction between profit and need, exchange value and use value. The political expression of this contradiction is found in the constant political struggle between individualistic and collectivistic strategies. It is this contradiction and this struggle that lies at the heart of Lefebvre's concern with the urban question.

Lefebvre argues that the contradiction identified by Marx between the forces and relations of capitalist production has been overcome in the advanced capitalist societies by spatial expansion. The development of capitalism, in other words, has not encountered its limits because capital has transformed space itself into a commodity: 'We now come to a basic and essential idea: capitalism is maintained by the conquest and integration of space. Space has long since ceased to be a passive geographical milieu or an empty geometrical one. It has become instrumental' (1970, p. 262). From a system where commodities are produced in a spatial setting capitalism has evolved into a system where space itself is produced as a scarce and alienable resource. Space, that is, is created as an homogeneous and quantifiable commodity:

Space, e.g. volume, is treated in such a way as to render it homogeneous, its parts comparable, therefore exchangeable. . . . The subordination of space to money and capital implies a quantification which extends from the monetary evaluation to the commercialization of each plot of the entire space. . . . Space now becomes one of the new 'scarcities', together with its resources, water, air and even light (Lefebvre 1970, pp. 261–2).

In this new era of capitalism, manufacturing industry is replaced by the construction and leisure industries as the pivotal points of the capitalist system of production:

Capitalism has not just integrated existing space, it has extended into completely new sectors. Leisure is becoming an industry of prime importance. We have conquered for leisure the sea, mountains and even deserts. The leisure industry and the construction industry have combined to extend the towns and urbanization along coastlines and in mountain regions . . . this industry extends over all space not already occupied by agriculture and the traditional production industries (Lefebvre 1970, p. 265).

In this way, the capitalist production of space has become integral both in generating surplus value (for these industries employ an immense and low-paid labour force and are characterized by a low organic composition of capital) and in realizing profits (since the commodification of space has created vast new markets). It is this gradual transition from an industrial to an urban base of modern capitalist production that Lefebvre refers to as 'the urban revolution', and he likens it to the earlier industrial revolution in which the main basis of production shifted from agriculture to manufacturing.

It is apparent from Lefebvre's concept of an urban revolution that he does not intend to equate the concept of the urban with the physical object of the city. It is precisely his argument that the urban revolution creates an urban society, in which case the physical separation of city and countryside becomes of less and less significance. Rather, the urban for Lefebvre consists of three related concepts, namely space, everyday life and reproduction of capitalist social relations. The urban, that is, is the global spatial context through which the relations of production are reproduced in people's everyday experience. Capitalist social relations are reproduced through the everyday use of space because space has itself been captured by capital and subordinated to its logic:

> The reproduction of the relations of production cannot be localized in the enterprise. . . . Reproduction (of the relations of production, not just the means of production) is located not simply in society as a whole but in space as a whole. Space, occupied by neo-capitalism, sectioned, reduced to homogeneity yet fragmented, becomes the seat of power (Lefebvre 1976, p. 83).

Because space bears the imprint of capitalism, it imposes the form of capitalist relations (individualism, commodification, etc.) on the whole of everyday life. The architecture of our cities symbolizes capitalist relations ('The Phallic unites with the political: verticality symbolizes power' (1976, p. 88)), our leisure space reflects capitalist relations (since it commercializes our non-work lives in line with our working lives), the dispersal of our homes in far-flung suburbs is a product of capitalist relations (central areas are taken over by commercial functions while residential use of space is relegated to the periphery), and so on. The organization of space – the essential similarity of different places, the fragmentation of life (e.g. work and home) between different places, and the hierarchy of control between dominant and subordinate places – thus carries within it the inner logic of capitalist hegemony. Capitalist social relations are reproduced in everyday life through this spatial patterning.

Lefebvre's analysis is by no means inherently pessimistic, however, for he argues that the urban revolution that overcomes one set of problems for capital gives rise to another. This is because the colonization of space by capital can proceed only by fragmenting and decentralizing the population: 'The centre attracts those elements which constitute it (commodities, capital, information, etc.) but which soon saturate it. It excludes those elements which it dominates (the "governed", "subjects" and "objects") but which threaten it' (1976, p. 18). This creates a political problem in so far as the city has traditionally been the cultural centre of the society – the principal source and location of the reproduction of social relations. If the city is fragmented and dispersed leaving only the economic and political offices of administration at the centre, then, while political power becomes centralized, cultural hegemony will necessarily become weakened:

> The spread of urban tissue is accompanied by the fragmentation of the town. And it is this that gives rise to one of the deepest contradictions of space. For the town not only represents a colossal accumulation of wealth, it is also the centre of birth and learning, the point of reproduction of all social relations. But it also becomes the place where these relations are threatened. . . . Should it be sacrificed, letting the urban tissue proliferate in disorder and chaos but thereby strengthening the decision-making centres? It is an unsettling contradiction for the reproduction of social relations (Lefebvre 1976, p. 28).

The effect of the progressive extension of the capitalist production of space is therefore to concentrate the decision-making centre while creating dependent colonies on the periphery: 'Around the centres there are nothing but subjugated, exploited and dependent spaces: neo-colonial spaces' (1976, p. 85). In France, for example, Paris presides over a system of internal colonialization in which the disparities between the underdeveloped regions of Brittany and the south and the over-urbanized metropolitan centre become ever more stark (see 1970, p. 258). Thus, while capitalism is consolidated through the exploitation of space, this very process engenders at the same time a contradiction which threatens to undermine capitalist domination: 'If space as a whole has become the place where reproduction of the relations of production is located, it has also become the terrain for a vast confrontation' (1976, p. 85). The political power of the centre is strengthened as key decision-making functions become concentrated there, yet at the same time the cohesion of the society is weakened as everyday life becomes dispersed to the periphery: 'Power suffers, as in Shakespearian tragedy: the more it consolidates, the more afraid it is. It occupies space, but space trembles beneath it' (1976, p. 86). The result, potentially at least, is a crisis of the reproduction of capitalist social relations.

This is a crisis that the bourgeoisie attempts to regulate and mediate by means of its control of the decision-making centres, and notably the state. Yet it is ultimately an irresolvable crisis, since the more capitalism becomes extended in space, the more it undermines the reproduction of the social relations on which its continuation depends. Lefebvre neatly summarizes the paradox by distinguishing between the extension of capitalist organization and the fragmentation of the organization of capitalism that results from it. The capacity of the productive forces to produce space on a large scale, and thus to extend capitalist organization into every corner of life, increasingly confronts the need to reproduce the relations of production, and thus to maintain the organization of capitalism. The hegemony of the bourgeoisie is threatened by the growing fragmentation of space and of everyday life, and the increasing power of the centre is challenged by the reaction of the periphery. It is in this way that Lefebvre explains the trend towards regional devolution in the advanced capitalist countries, for such a strategy involves the attempt by the ruling class 'to offload some of their responsibilities on to local and regional organisms while preserving the mechanisms of power intact' (1976, p. 87).

This basic contradiction in the new urban society is not only revealed in political struggles between centre and periphery, however, but is also expressed in a broadening concern with the quality of life. The traditional assumption that the development of the productive forces of capitalism would automatically involve an improvement in the qualitative conditions of everyday life has been undermined:

> This is what is new . . . that economic growth and social development can no longer be confused, as they have been before, by thinking that growth would bring development, that the quantitative would sooner or later bring the qualitative. . . . The ideology of growth has been mortally wounded. The vast ideological construct crumbles slowly but surely. Why? Because of the urban malaise, of the destruction of nature and its resources, because of blockages of all kinds which paralyze social development while enabling economic growth (Lefebvre 1970, p. 260).

The penetration of everyday life by capitalist organization has therefore revealed more clearly than before the contradiction between private profit and social need, between capitalist domination and social life. It is for this reason that Lefebvre sees the urban crisis as the central and fundamental crisis of advanced capitalism, for the struggle over the use of space and the control of everyday life goes to the heart of the conflict between the requirements of capital and social need.

The practical political implications of Lefebvre's analysis are clear; the workers' movement must organize in order to harness the productive forces to social needs, and this will involve a strategy that links the periphery (meaning not only the regions, but also 'urban peripheries' such as black city ghettos and migrant worker shanty towns, and international peripheries in the Third World) to the labour movement and organizes both production and everyday life in terms of self-management. However, he recognizes that the existing strategies of the French Communist Party represent the very antithesis of such a programme. This is because, first, the party is still waging the industrial battle in the urban era; that is, it interprets all political struggles in terms of a basic economic orientation to questions of the workplace, and thus fails to address the fundamental issue of advanced capitalism concerning the control of space and everyday life. The result is that it lacks a strategy for confronting the bourgeoisie over the most crucial question of advanced capitalism, and it approaches urban struggles armed with only the most 'infantile' concepts which seek to reduce such struggles to the traditional and superseded categories of the Marxist analysis of a century ago.

The second source of divergence between Lefebvre's position and that of orthodox Marxism is that he totally rejects the Leninist view of the role of the party and criticizes the Communists for their inherent conservatism in seeking merely to 'take over the baton' from the bourgeoisie. Against their orientation towards an appropriation of the power centres of the existing society, Lefebvre asserts the need for self-management which necessarily entails the abolition of central domination altogether. As Castells (1977a, p. 89) suggests, Lefebvre's position thus appears not only humanist but anarchist.

For Lefebvre, then, the critical struggle in the urban phase of capitalist development is the struggle to free everyday life from capitalist organization and to bring about the management of space by and for the masses. This is what he means by the title of one of his books, *The Right to the Town* (1968b), for the concentration of the power of capital in the centres and the consequent expulsion of the people to the periphery most vividly symbolizes the subordination of need to profit in the contemporary period. The potential offered by urban society for human liberation is immense, but this potential can be realized only through the struggle against the capitalist domination of space, and hence by transcending the technocratic ideology of space of the bourgeoisie and the narrow economistic ideology of the existing Marxist parties.

Manuel Castells: science, ideology and the urban question

Like Lefebvre, Castells has developed a critique of existing theories of urbanism as ideological. Unlike Lefebvre, however, he does not rest this argument on the identification of the functions of such theories in sustaining capitalist class relations, but rather explains this functional aspect of 'theoretical ideologies' as itself due to the failure of existing theories to transcend the ideological relations through which individuals live their relation to the real world. In other words, existing theories (and Castells includes Lefebvre's work in this category) are ideological in that they merely elaborate rather than break with the ideological forms of capitalist society, and therefore fail to establish the basis for a scientific analysis of the reality of that society. As Walther suggests, 'For Castells, the fact that urban sociology and its dispersed fields had bowed to social demand is not sufficient grounds to refute it as ideology. His critique of ideology in urban sociology delves to a more subtle level; it is essentially an *epistemological critique*' (1982, p. 16). Castells's critique of existing theories as ideological is thus premised on the argument that there is a scientific mode of analysis by means of which it is possible to identify ideological discourses.

It should be noted at the outset that, in the course of the development of his work, Castells had cause to amend his initial epistemological position quite considerably. In this section, however, we shall be concerned principally with his earlier work, since it is here that he develops his critique of urban sociology as ideological. The subsequent revisions to his epistemology were developed as a result of his attempt to apply his approach in empirical research, and this experience appears to have led him to reconsider his earlier conceptions of science and its relation to ideology. As we shall see, this reconceptualization has the effect of undermining any attempt at maintaining such a distinction and thus throws into question his earlier critique of alternative theories, although Castells himself has never explicitly re-examined his initial attack on these alternative theories in the light of his changed epistemological stance. The original critique of urban social theories was grounded in a relatively uncritical application of the Marxist philosophy of Louis Althusser to the urban question. Of particular significance was Althusser's argument that science develops out of an 'epistemological break' with existing ideological discourses – in other words that science involves a theoretical transformation of ideological concepts into scientific ones – for it was this that led Castells to engage in a critique of existing theories as the first step in developing a framework through which the 'real' question to which such theories were oriented could be identified and explored. As Althusser put it, 'The theoretical practice of a science is always completely distinct from the ideological theoretical practice of its prehistory: this distinction takes the form of a "qualitative" theoretical and historical discontinuity which I shall follow Bachelard in calling an "epistemological break"' (1969, pp. 167–8).

According to Althusser, the procedure whereby scientific practice comes to transcend prescientific ideological theories is implicit in Marx's own work, but is only ever made explicit in the 1857 Introduction in the *Grundrisse*. His argument is that Marx succeeded in breaking with ideology and founding a science of social formations when he developed his method of dialectical materialism, but that he never actually came to write the theory of this method. This is the task that Althusser takes upon himself and which he designates the Theory of Theoretical Practice.

The argument, which is derived mainly from a reading of the 1857 Introduction, begins by suggesting that the production of theory takes the same form as material production in society – that it involves the 'transformation of a determinate given raw material into a determinate product, a transformation effected by a determinate human labour, using determinate means (of production)' (Althusser 1969, p. 166). What this means is that scientific practice begins with certain raw materials of thought which it sets out to transform. These raw materials are existing general concepts, which may themselves be ideological or the products of earlier scientific practice. Althusser therefore endorses Marx's argument in the *Grundrisse* that science begins with abstractions, not with concrete reality itself: 'A science never works on an existence whose essence is pure immediacy and singularity ("sensations' or "individuals"). It always works on something "general" . . . a science always works on existing concepts. . . . It does not "work" on a purely objective "given", that of pure and absolute "facts"' (1969, pp. 183–4). Althusser's argument here reflects his resolute rejection of empiricist philosophy, for in his view, knowledge can never be derived directly from experience. It therefore follows that science starts out, not from observation, but from existing conceptual generalities (which he calls 'Generalities I').

These general concepts are transformed through the application of theoretical means of production (Generality II). Just as production in society involves the application of certain tools to certain raw materials, so too theoretical production involves the application of theoretical tools to prescientific concepts. This does not mean that theorists simply apply their own subjective ideas in order to produce scientific knowledge, for the theorist is seen by Althusser as the agent by means of which theoretical 'tools' come to be applied to a problem, just as the worker is the agent through which machines come to be applied in the production of commodities. Althusser is as opposed to idealism (the view that knowledge is a product of the individual human consciousness) as he is to empiricism (the view that knowledge is a reflection of concrete reality on to consciousness). Science involves neither the direct analysis of a given reality, nor the imposition of subjective constructs on to reality: 'The act of abstraction whereby the pure essence is extracted from concrete individuals is an ideological myth' (Althusser 1969, p. 191).

What this means, of course, is that the product of scientific practice (Generality III, knowledge) is the result of a theoretical transformation of existing concepts rather than of any direct articulation with the reality it claims to explain. For Althusser, it seems, there are two 'realities'; the reality that exists outside of thought, and remains unaffected by theoretical practice, and the reality that exists as a product of theoretical practice. There are, he says, 'two different concretes: the concrete-in-thought which is a knowledge, and the concrete-reality which is its object. The process which produces the concrete-knowledge takes place wholly in the theoretical practice' (1969, p. 186).

At this point, the obvious question concerns the relationship, if any, between the concrete reality and the concrete in thought. Althusser, however, rejects the premise on which such a question is based since the question makes sense only if we hold to an epistemology that distinguishes a knowing subject from the object of knowledge. His epistemology rejects this dualism since it rejects the notion of the knowing subject; as we have seen, the theorist is merely an agent of the theoretical transformation that takes place in scientific practice. This practice is itself *real* in that it involves a real transformation of ideology into knowledge:

> The critique which, in the last instance, counterposes the abstraction it attributes to theory and to science and the concrete it regards as the real itself, remains an ideological critique since it denies the reality of scientific practice, the validity of its abstractions and ultimately the reality of that theoretical 'concrete' which is a knowledge (Althusser 1969, p. 187).

In other words, Althusser defines scientific knowledge as the product of theoretical practice since it cannot be the product of pure experience, and further suggests that to deny the validity of such knowledge is to deny the validity of science itself and thus to collapse into ideology. As we shall see later, however, this all too neat solution to the problem still begs the question as to why dialectical materialism should provide the only correct guide to scientific practice – that is, why we should accept Althusser's epistemological legislation of scientific investigation in the first place.

It will be clear from this short exposition that, when Althusser turns to consider the question of ideology, his epistemology obliges him to reject the traditional argument that ideology involves the distortion of reality through ideas, since to argue thus would be to accept that knowledge is the product of the consciousness of human subjects (idealism), or to accept that reality is reflected in some way in our ideas about it (empiricism). Ideology is no more capable of distorting concrete reality than science is of representing it. Ideology, therefore, is not an ideal representation of reality, but is rather the way in which individuals relate to reality in their everyday lives: 'It is not their real conditions of existence, their real world, that "men represent to themselves" in ideology, but above all it is their relation to those conditions of existence which is represented to them there' (Althusser 1971, p. 154). Because the real relations in which individuals enter cannot themselves be directly known, individuals relate to their world by means of an imaginary relation. Thus, just as the product of scientific practice (the 'concrete-in-thought') is distinct from the concrete-reality, so too is the product of ideological practice (the 'imaginary lived relation').

One implication of this argument is that, although particular ideologies may change through history, ideology in general remains ever-present. Even in a communist society ideology would remain essential as the means whereby individuals lived their everyday lives, since reality itself will never become apparent. Ideology, therefore, is an inherent feature of social organization: in Althusser's terms, it is one 'instance' of the social totality (the concept of the social totality is considered in Chapter 6). It is also important to emphasize that, like science, ideology is a practice since it refers not to ideas about reality but to the very way in which we live that reality. Put another way, ideology is not ideal but material: 'Men "live" their ideologies as the Cartesian "saw" or did not see – if he was not looking at it – the moon two hundred paces away: not at all as a form of consciousness, but as an object of their "world" – as their "world" itself' (Althusser 1969, p. 233).

The most significant function of ideology, and one that serves to illustrate Althusser's argument, concerns what he terms the 'interpellation" of concrete individuals as subjects. By this he means simply that it is through our imaginary lived relation to the real world that we come to recognize ourselves and others as acting human subjects. In everyday life we act towards others, and others act towards us, as if we were subjects; that is, it is through ideological practices that we become constituted as subjects. The notion of the human subject, generating his/her own ideas from his/her own unique consciousness and imposing these ideas on the external world, is therefore a product of ideological practice in that subjects are constituted only through such practice: 'All ideology has the function (which defines it) of "constituting" concrete individuals as subjects. ... Like all obviousnesses ... the obviousness that you and I are subjects – and that that does not cause any problems – is an ideological effect, the elementary ideological effect' (Althusser 1971, pp. 160–1).

If the very notion of human subjectivity (with its related notions of human consciousness, human essence and so on) is a product of ideological practice, of our *imaginary* lived relation to the world, then it follows, of course, that scientific practice must involve a break with the category of the subject if it is to produce a knowledge that transcends ideology. For as long as theory retains the ideological concept of the human subject, it will remain incapable of developing a scientific knowledge of real, as opposed to 'imaginary', relations. Put somewhat crudely, such a theory will fail to see the wood (the totality of objective social relations) for the trees ('human subjects' constituted by such relations). Such a theory will be 'closed' in the sense that it will fail to open up the question of how the imaginary relation is itself constituted and is therefore destined merely to reproduce ideology in elaborated form. It is only when science breaks with ideology and becomes autonomous from it that it becomes possible to recognize ideology for what it is:

> Those who are in ideology believe themselves by definition outside ideology: one of the effects of ideology is the practical denegation of the ideological character of ideology by ideology: ideology never says, 'I am ideological'. It is necessary to be outside ideology, i.e. in scientific knowledge, to be able to say: I am in ideology (a quite exceptional case) or (the general case): I was in ideology (Althusser 1971, pp. 163–4).

It is now possible to understand the Althusserian critique of humanism as ideology, for it is not that humanist theories (those which set human subjects at the centre of the theoretical stage and endow them with consciousness and effectivity) are in some way false, but rather that they take categories constituted through ideological practice as the basic and unquestioned categories of analysis and thus preclude the possibility of explaining them: 'When I say that the concept of humanism is an ideological concept (not a scientific one), I mean that while it really does designate a set of existing relations, unlike a scientific concept it does not provide us with a means of knowing them' (Althusser 1969, p. 223). It is precisely this argument that Castells employs against Lefebvre.

Castells sets out to demolish Lefebvre's utopian concept of an urban society which he sees as in some ways a left version of Wirth's culturalist conception of urbanism (in that both see the city as structuring social relations rather than the reverse (Lebas 1980)). The demolition is effected, however, through an epistemological rather than theoretical critique, for Castells argues that Lefebvre's whole analysis stands or falls on the validity of his humanistic assumptions. Lefebvre's analysis, he suggests,

> indicates that space, like the whole of society, is the ever-original work of that freedom of creation that is the attribute of Man, and the spontaneous expression of his desire. It is only by accepting this absolute of Lefebvrian humanism (a matter of philosophy or religion) that the analysis might be pursued in this direction: it would always be dependent on its metaphysical foundation (Castells 1977a, p. 92).

Lefebvre's analysis is therefore little more than a theoretical ideology, since it is grounded in ideological (or 'metaphysical') categories which it simply elaborates. The consequence of this is that it prevents any breakthrough to science through its failure to recognize the determinate conditions of social life. Despite its radical flavour, therefore, it effectively hinders rather than aids scientific critique: 'This new urban ideology may thus serve noble causes . . . while masking fundamental phenomena that theoretical practice still finds difficult to grasp' (Castells 1977a, p. 94).

Castells develops much the same argument against other, less radical, urban theories which similarly seek to explain urban processes in terms of the actions of individual subjects. The (mainly American) community power literature, which is concerned to trace which individuals or groups at the local level enjoy the greatest power to determine policies, is one obvious example, since for Castells power cannot be conceptualized in terms of individual attributes or individual relationships (see Chapter 6). Another equally obvious example concerns the urban managerialist literature discussed in Chapter 4:

This perspective which, by virtue of the ease with which it responds to the concrete problems that face the 'decision-makers', is assuming increasing importance . . . rests entirely on an ideological base, for it is based on a metaphysical postulate, without which it becomes purely empirical description. This postulate is that 'ultimately one must place the accent on the freedom of man who remains, whatever his situation, an autonomous agent capable of negotiating his cooperation' (Castells 1977a, p. 250).

As we saw in Chapter 4, the basic problem encountered but not resolved in the urban managerialism approach concerns the need to theorize the limits on the autonomy of significant actors. Castells's analysis suggests that this problem must necessarily remain unresolved for as long as theory begins with the (ideological) category of individual subjects rather than with the question of the social totality that constitutes them as subjects: 'It is by situating the elements of social structure in a prior theoretical context that one will succeed in making significant the practices concretely observed and then, and only then, can one rediscover this supposed "autonomy" of the "actors"' (p. 251). For as long as analysis retains the actor as its focus of concern, it is doomed merely to reproduce but never to explain the imaginary relation of individuals to the real world:

The analysis that sets out from the concrete actors and their strategies necessarily ends up in an impasse: if these actors are simply empirical objects, the analysis becomes a mere description of particular situations; if they are first realities, therefore essences, the analysis is dependent on a metaphysics of freedom (Castells 1977a, p. 251).

For Castells, as for Althusser, the notion of the human subject consciously constituting his or her world must therefore be abandoned to the realm of prescience. He states his position most clearly in one of his earlier essays where he writes,

To identify the production of forms with their origin in action presupposes acceptance of the notion of actor-subjects, constructing their history in terms of their own values and aims. . . . This requires that one take as a starting point actors and combinations of actors, and thus that one accept the existence of primary essences, not deduced from social structures. . . . The theoretical issue is this: historical actors founding society through their action, or support-agents expressing particular combinations of the social structure through their practice. We will take for granted that the first approach belongs to the philosophy of history, and that only the second is capable of founding a science of society (Castells 1976b, pp. 77–8).

The practices of individuals thus can be explained only through a scientific theory of structure.

This emphasis on a theory of structure and of its elements explains the ironic feature of Castells's critique of urban sociology; namely that he is most implacably opposed to the most radical theories (for example those of Lefebvre and the elite theorists of community power) while finding much that is commendable in the most conservative theory (namely human ecology) and its later derivatives (mainly Wirth's theory of urbanism). As regards the ecological approach he writes, 'The attempt to explain territorial collectivities by the notion of an ecological system constitutes the most serious attempt to give urban sociology a specific theoretical field in conjunction with the functionalist approach' (1976b, p. 71); and he later extended the compliment to Wirth's work, which he sees as 'the most serious theoretical attempt ever made within sociology to establish a theoretical object (and consequently a domain of research) specific to urban sociology' (1977a, p. 77). The significance of Park and Wirth is that they not only avoided explanations couched in terms of human subjects (neither Park's biotic forces nor Wirth's size, density and heterogeneity made reference to the purposive actions of individuals in bringing about certain effects), but they also attempted to explain urban reality by developing a theory of determinate processes. In other words, their theoretical practice sought to identify a theoretically specific problem (what Castells terms a 'theoretical object') as the precondition for developing a scientific explanation of a concrete reality (the 'real object'). For them, as for Castells, the city or space cannot be known and explained directly but must be analysed in terms of a theoretically produced object. Park's theoretical object was integration (that is, the urban system was theorized in terms of the biotic forces operating to bring about social and system integration), while Wirth's was a specific cultural content (the urban was theorized in terms of the causal effect of demographic factors in bringing about anonymity, superficiality, etc.).

The problem with both of these theories, however, was that their theoretical objects, while valid in themselves, could not provide the basis for a distinctively urban theory that could be applied to the empirical study of the city. The problem of integration, for example, necessarily involved analysis of factors that bore no necessary relationship to urbanism: 'As soon as the urban context is broken down even into such crude categories as social class, age or "interests", processes which seemed to be peculiar to particular urban areas turn out to be determined by other factors' (1976a, p. 40). This resulted in the tension diagnosed in Chapter 2 between human ecology as a theory of the city and human ecology as a theory of adaptation, for there was no reason why the theoretical object of biotic processes of integration and adaptation should be confined to analysis of the city. Similarly, Wirth's problem of urban culture turned out on closer inspection to be a theory of the cultural forms of capitalism, for not only did research demonstrate that the cultures of pre-industrial and non-capitalist cities differ from that identified by Wirth, but the sorry history of the rural–urban continuum demonstrated that the factors that he took as adequate for explaining cultural differences between town and country in capitalist societies were in fact inadequate.

Neither of these theories therefore succeeded in producing a theoretical object by means of which the real object (urbanism, space) could be analysed. Rather, by equating a concept of urbanism with what was in fact a theorization of capitalism, they succeeded only in representing capitalist processes (competition, individualism, etc.) as inherent to the nature of cities: 'An urban sociology founded on urbanism is an ideology of modernity ethnocentrically identified with the crystallization of the social forms of liberal capitalism' (1976b, p. 70). In this way, these theories served an ideological function by providing a naturalistic explanation for people's everyday experiences: 'Such a "theory" is extremely useful to ruling political elites inasmuch as it conceptualizes social organization as depending less on social data, in particular class relations, than on natural, spatial, technical and biological data' (1977b, p. 62).

By this stage of his argument, Castells has effectively demolished the whole of urban sociology as ideological. The problem with previous work is twofold. First, theories such as those developed in the urban managerialist literature or that advanced by Lefebvre are grounded in the ideological category of the human subject and are therefore incapable of sustaining a scientific analysis (since such an analysis must be derived from a theory of the system and of its interrelated elements). Second, theories such as human ecology that avoid such categories have failed to develop a means of relating their real object of study (urbanism) to their overall theories of adaptation, and have therefore resulted in ideological effects (since they equate the effects of overall social processes within capitalism with the specific effects of urban processes). What is required, therefore, is a radical reformulation which can identify what is to be studied (the real object) and can provide a theoretical framework by means of which this real object can be studied in the context of its relationship to the system as a whole (a theoretical object).

As the first step towards such a reformulation, Castells suggests that, among the plurality of real objects which urban sociology has studied in the past, it is possible to identify two that, when taken together, constitute a legitimate focus for scientific concern. The first of these is space: 'The sociological analysis of space appears to us to be a quite legitimate field of study. However, it is not a theoretical object but a real object, since space is a material element and not a conceptual unit' (1976b, p. 70). Concern with space is, of course, the common feature of all previous approaches, but none of them has succeeded in demonstrating the coincidence of spatial units with social units. Thus spatial units do not coincide with distinctive cultural units (Wirth), with distinctive political units (Pahl), and so on, and this is why previous approaches have collapsed into a non-specific concern with culture in general, politics in general or whatever. It is therefore a precondition for any scientific reformulation of the 'urban question' that we establish the coincidence of a real spatial unit with a real social unit: 'What we would like to examine . . . is under what conditions a sociology could be defined as urban from the point of view of its scientific object. In our opinion this possibility exists when there is a coincidence between a spatial unit and a social unit' (1976a, p. 57).

The only candidate among the various social phenomena that have been studied by urban sociologists which can fulfil this requirement is what Castells terms 'collective consumption' units. As we shall see in the next chapter, his definition of collective consumption is by no means clear, and it undergoes various metamorphoses as his work develops, but in the early essays this term refers simply to 'consumption processes whose organization and management cannot be other than collective given the nature and size of the problems' (1976b, p. 75). The examples provided by Castells include housing, social facilities and leisure provisions. The basic assertion in his reformulation of the urban question is that, unlike units of production, which are organized on a regional (or even national or international) scale, units of consumption are socially organized and provided within the context of a spatially bounded system. The coincidence between a spatial unit and a social unit which has so often eluded urban sociology is therefore identified as that between spatial organization and the organization of collective consumption facilities. This is a relationship that has often been implicit in urban analysis but has never been made explicit as the definition of the urban real object: 'Urban sociology has in fact tended to tackle two types of problem: (1) relationships to space and (2) what may be termed the process of collective consumption. . . . Thus, as well as ideological themes and highly diverse real objects, the urban sociology tradition includes a sociology of space and a sociology of collective consumption' (1976b, pp. 74–5).

Having identified the real object as a (spatial) unit of collective consumption, Castells has prepared the ground for the rise of a new theoretical Phoenix with a secure scientific foundation from the ashes of the old urban sociology. It only remains for him to apply his ready-constituted theory of the total social system (a theory that he finds in Althusserian Marxism) in order to identify the theoretical element in that system to which collective consumption corresponds. As we shall see in Chapter 6, this is a relatively simple process since the theory breaks down the social totality into three analytical levels (the economic, the political and the ideological), and further breaks down the economic level into its constitutive elements of production, consumption and exchange. Each of these elements is defined through its functions within the system as a whole such that production entails the application of human labour to the material environment in order to create commodities; exchange involves the circulation of these commodities and thus (in capitalism) the realization of exchange value; and consumption involves the final utilization of these commodities by individuals as their means of life and sustenance. It is through the process of consumption, in other words, that individuals reproduce their labour-power (for example by consuming food, housing, recreation, education and so on) which then re-enters the system as a resource to be used in the process of producing new commodities. Consumption is therefore defined within this theoretical system in terms of its function in reproducing labour-power, and in this way its relation to the other elements (production, exchange) and levels (political and ideological) of the total system is established.

Castells, therefore, is now in possession of both a real object (the concrete reality of spatial units of collective consumption) and a theoretical object (the process of consumption as a functional element within the total social system involving the reproduction of the most fundamental resource in that system – labour-power). He is then in a position to analyse the real object by analysing the role of the theoretical object to which it corresponds within the total theoretical system. But before we consider the analysis that he offers, it is necessary to examine critically his claim that this new approach to the urban question is set upon a secure scientific basis which distinguishes it from the ideological character of all previous theories.

Epistemological imperialism and the new urban sociology

In choosing to attack existing approaches on epistemological grounds, by asserting their 'ideological' character in contrast to his own 'scientific' method, Castells clearly engaged in a very dangerous game, for it was then possible for others to criticize his perspective on exactly the same basis! As Lebas notes in a trend report on the new urban sociology, 'Contemporary discussion is truffled with allegations of bourgeois empiricism, ideal type classifications, not to mention rampant positivism, and such criticisms are more often directed at studies which claim to be Marxist in flavour if not in intent' (1982, p. 34). The problem with epistemological critique is that it encourages dismissal of people's work, not through addressing their arguments, but through the application of prior and inevitably arbitrary yardsticks of 'acceptable' scientific procedure. Castells was particularly vulnerable in this respect given that, first, his application of Althusser's epistemology was always somewhat inconsistent, second, the Althusserian distinction which he employed between 'science' and 'ideology' was ultimately unjustifiable, and, third, his work in any case developed in such a way as to undermine his initial epistemological principles. The remainder of this chapter will elaborate these three points.

The inconsistency in Castells's early work concerns his discussion of the real and the theoretical object. The latter appears relatively unproblematic within the context of the Althusserian schema, for it evidently refers to Althusser's notion of the 'concrete-in-thought' or scientific knowledge (which does not imply some 'final' state of knowledge or some absolute truth, but rather means that it is the foundation for the further development of scientific, as opposed to ideological, discourse). But what of the 'real object'? There appear to be two possibilities.

The first is that Castells intends this term to refer to what Althusser calls the 'concrete reality'. In this sense, spatial units of collective consumption exist in the real world but can never be directly known, either through experience or through ideal abstractions. But if this is what Castells means by a real object, then it would appear illogical to suggest, as he does on several occasions, that a science may be said to exist if it possesses *either* a real *or* a theoretical object: 'A scientific discipline is built either by a certain conceptual cutting up of reality, i.e. through the definition of a *scientific object*, or by a specific field of observation, i.e. through the choice of a *real object*' (Castells 1977b, pp. 61–2). Yet it is precisely Althusser's argument that the concrete reality can never itself be known, and Castells echoes this view when he warns that 'There is no such thing as a direct relationship between researcher and real object. All thought is more or less consciously shaped by a pre-existing theoretico-ideological field' (1976b, p. 83). The necessary consequence of this argument is that a science cannot be constituted through its possession of a real object, a 'specific field of observation', but rather constitutes itself through its theoretical practice. If we assume that Castells is following Althusser in his early work, then we must assume that the real object does not refer to the concrete reality, since for Althusser a science cannot be defined in terms of its empirical concern with some aspect of reality. Thus it will be recalled that he argues explicitly that 'The act of abstraction whereby the pure essence is extracted from concrete individuals is an ideological myth' (Althusser 1969, p. 191).

The second possibility is that Castells intends the real object to refer to the ideological raw materials of thought (Generalities I) which scientific practice transforms into theoretical knowledge. In this sense, the real object is not the concrete reality itself but the existing representations of the imaginary relation to the concrete. This is the interpretation of Castells offered by Pickvance when he suggests that 'The real object refers to some aspect of reality, ready-wrapped in preconceptions which are usually "ideological", while the science seeks knowledge in the form of a theoretical object' (Pickvance 1976a, p. 4). But if this is indeed what Castells means by the term, then it follows that spatial units of collective consumption are merely existing categories through which urban sociologists have conceptualized the real world, and that science will involve the transformation of these categories and hence their supersession. Clearly this is not what Castells intends, for he claims to have identified both a theoretical and a real object for his new scientific approach. His aim is not to transcend the real object but to study it. Collective consumption is not a prescientific category in his analysis but a constitutive category of his analysis.

We are forced to the conclusion that Castells's notion of the real object has no reference in Althusser's philosophy of scientific practice. Indeed, despite his protestations to the contrary, it is apparent that the whole thrust of Castells's critique of human ecology and of his subsequent reformulation of the field is premised upon an epistemology that Althusser himself rejects. Put simply, when Castells criticizes human ecology for failing to develop a theory specific to an urban real object, he has to assume that such a real object exists and can be known outside of theory, for how else can the lack of correspondence between the theory and the object be established? Similarly, when he sets out to identify a new real object (the coincidence of units of collective consumption with spatial units), he has first to assume that this can be identified unproblematically through observation before he can go on to show how it can be studied by means of his theoretical object. In short, both the critique and the reformulation are based on the argument that there must be a *correspondence* between some aspect of reality termed 'urban' and the theory that relates to it. Castells, in other words, has effectively re-introduced the knowing subject/object of knowledge dichotomy which Althusser sought to reject. By defining his science in terms of the relation between theory and reality, a theoretical object and a real object, he has fallen into what Althusser sees as the ideological trap of empiricism–humanism and has thereby re-opened the question of how a correspondence can be demonstrated between them. As we shall see in Chapter 6, Castells can therefore be criticized on precisely the same grounds as he criticized others; namely that his conceptualization of the urban does not 'fit' the reality observed. Thus Harloe has rightly noted the 'remarkable similarity between Castells's actual approach, as opposed to his intentions, and that of the bourgeois theorists he has criticized', for he ends up by imposing his theoretical categories on to reality in an attempt to relate the reality of the city to his pre-existing conceptual system (see Harloe 1979, p. 128).

As I shall suggest later (p. 223) Castells's approach actually owed more to Weber's method of ideal type construction than it did to Althusser's theoretical practice, for what it entailed was basically a one-sided conceptualization of one aspect of reality (the process of collective consumption) as the relevant object of study. That this procedure was wrapped up in Althusserian clothing perhaps reflects the fact that there is no warrant in Weber's sociology for drawing the distinction which Castells sought to employ between scientific and ideological modes of discourse. This is why Castells resorts to the formal structure of Althusserian scientific practice in his critique of urban sociology, even though his own method has little relation to this practice. Thus he begins with a critique of current conceptions of urbanism (the 'ideological' raw materials of thought); he then applies the theoretical tools of Marxist analysis to these conceptions (the theory of structure); and he ends up by producing a new scientific knowledge of the urban question (in terms of the function of collective consumption in reproducing labour-power). The move from Generalities I to Generalities III is reproduced in formal terms in his work, for it is only by means of this schema that he can claim to have developed a scientific knowledge that transcends ideological conceptions through an epistemological break with them.

There is, however, an irony in this attempt to hang on to the appearance of an Althusserian method, for even if Castells's approach had been consistent with that of Althusser, we should still have to reject the claim that it can distinguish between scientific and ideological theories. The reason for this, quite simply, is that no epistemology can legislate on the question of correct scientific method *per se*. The role of epistemology (as Castells was later to recognize in his article written jointly with Ipola) is to aid the clarification and subsequent resolution of problems confronted *within* particular discourses, not to referee what are basically irresolvable disputes over method *between* different discourses. It can, for example, point to obstacles of empiricism that may arise within approaches that seek to reject empiricism, but it cannot lay down with any final authority that empiricism is itself an 'incorrect' or 'invalid' approach to scientific knowledge (still less that it is inherently ideological).

My argument here closely reflects that developed in the work of Paul Hirst (1979). He has provided a detailed critique of Althusser's theory of ideology (including its later revisions) in the course of which he emphatically restates the critique of epistemological imperialism which he first developed in his work with Hindess. Basically, his argument is that no epistemology can establish a general principle, to be applied to all discourses, regarding the relation between theory and reality. This is because the relationship of any discourse to reality is defined within the discourse itself: 'Outside of epistemology what it is discourses and practices construct and refer to has no necessary common attributes; equally these constructions and referents are unintelligible except in and as discourse ... we deny any non-discursive level of "experience" or "consciousness"' (p. 20). It follows that epistemological principles that lay down the means of developing scientific knowledge cannot exist outside the theories that adopt and apply them, in which case Althusser's epistemology is applicable only within Althusser's theory (or, to put the same point in a different way, it has no general applicability and is not therefore an epistemology, in the sense of a general theory of the production of knowledge, at all).

If we abandon epistemology, then it follows that criteria of valid knowledge are always internal to theoretical systems:

> We would argue that discourses and practices *do* employ the criteria of appropriateness or adequacy (not of epistemological validity) but these are specific to the objectives of definite bodies of discourse and practice. None will pass muster as a general criterion of validity, but there is no knowledge process in general and, therefore, no necessity for such a criterion (Hirst 1979, p. 21).

This argument does not represent a collapse into relativism, both because relativism itself is only a problem within debates over general epistemological principles, and because different discourses may share common criteria of adequacy (in other words, criteria may be dependent upon, but not exclusively determined by, specific theories – see Andrew Sayer (1979, p. 9)).

The effect of this argument is to undermine any claim to epistemological privilege on the part of Marxist theories, and thus to demolish the division between science and ideology that such theories assert: 'Marxism is not a "science" (equally it is not a "non-science", science-ideology is an epistemological distinction), it has no privileged knowledge' (Hirst 1979, p. 6). This conclusion, of course, relates back to the discussion of Marx's method in Chapter 1, for there we noted that Marx has no privileged starting-point for analysing reality and that his method consists in hypothesizing certain relations as a means of providing a plausible explanation for the phenomena he identified in the real world. This is a perfectly acceptable method on its own terms, but it contains no means for asserting itself as the general and only scientific method for analysing social reality, nor does it establish any general criteria of scientificity against which other approaches may cavalierly be dismissed as ideological.

Even if Castells had remained faithful to the Althusserian position, therefore, there would be no warrant in his work for his epistemological distinction between scientific and ideological theories of the urban question. Yet, as we have already noted, in his later work he came to reject certain crucial elements of that position and thereby himself to undermine his original critique.

Of considerable significance here was a joint article originally published in 1972 and translated into English four years later. In this paper, Castells sought to retain Althusser's critique of humanism and subjectivism and his concept of the epistemological break while rejecting any general theory of science and ideology: 'We do refuse the abstract general thesis of an absolute and universal opposition between science and ideology and the consequences such a distinction entails' (Castells and Ipola 1976, p. 117). The authors went on to suggest that epistemology is limited in the scope of its intervention in scientific practice to clearing obstacles that are themselves epistemological; that is, it cannot determine the principles of scientific practice themselves but is rather an aid to clear analysis: 'A materialist epistemological intervention cannot be reduced to the application of pre-established rules according to a theoretical system: its relevance must be assessed after its effects and not after its ability to conform to any "principle" whatsoever' (p. 139). It followed from this that, rather than looking to epistemology to determine criteria of scientific truth, Marxism should develop its theories through concrete political struggles as the means of elaborating and realizing them.

The Castells and Ipola paper appears somewhat ambivalent towards Althusser's position (it is by no means clear, for example, how the epistemological break can be retained without a general theory of science and ideology), but Castells's drift away from Althusser became more marked in later work. The experience of applying the method in empirical research in the Dunkerque region was undoubtedly a chastening one, for in their theoretical and methodological introduction to this study he and Godard recognize the dangers of applying a preconstituted theoretical system to particular concrete cases: 'To fix a certain mode of theoretical analysis and to hold on to its internal logic and to the validity of the social laws already established by the general theoretical framework from which this mode of analysis derives is a considerable risk, or if you like, a gamble on its applicability' (Castells and Godard 1974, p. 14). Such a method would result simply in an unfounded attempt to reduce the complexity of the observed reality to the pre-existing system of concepts, and the authors reject such a sterile approach in favour of one that attempts to establish a correspondence between theory and reality:

> We have not 'operationalized' each concept as an indicator, following a one-to-one correspondence which would be perfectly illusory in the analysis of dynamic social processes, but we have traced the correspondence between a 'theoretical chain', through their logical articulation, such that the totality of facts becomes illuminated and interpreted in a coherent and theoretically significant way (Castells and Godard 1974, pp. 15–16).

Empirical research, in other words, is guided by and interpreted through theory, but theory is in turn itself developed and amended in the course of such research.

One year later, in his Afterword to *The Urban Question* (1977a), Castells underlined the significance of this break with Althusser's theoretical practice by explicitly rejecting the argument that knowledge involves a movement from the abstract to the concrete and arguing instead that the development of theory must be grounded in analysis of concrete cases from the very outset:

> What is involved is the very style of the theoretical work, the epistemological approach in question. One must choose between, on the one hand, the idea of a 'Great Theory' (even a Marxist one) which one then verifies empirically, and, on the other hand, the proposition of a theoretical work that produces concepts and their historical relations within a process of discovery of the laws of society given in their specific modes of existence. It is not only a question of 'carrying out empirical research'. It is a question rather of the fact that '*theory*' *is not produced outside a process of concrete knowledge* (Castells 1977a, p. 438; emphasis added).

This rethinking of his own method then led him to criticize his own theoretical work in this book as formalistic. He had, he reflected, simply 'coded' empirical reality by fitting aspects of the world into ready-made conceptual boxes, and this coding exercise had taken the place of any concrete analysis. As he explained in a later essay, 'The theoretical coding has been too rapid, too formal, the reality analysed was more complex than the models used' (Castells 1978, p. 12).

By 1983, when Castells published his major study of urban social movements, *The City and the Grassroots*, the shift away from his Althusserian origins had been completed. In the introduction to the book, he made plain his distrust of 'former experiences involving the useless construction of abstract grand theories' and he asserted his commitment to grounding 'theory-building on reliable research' in order to 'rectify the excesses of theoretical formalism that have flawed . . .our earlier work' (1983a, p. xvii). In contrast with the method and style of *The Urban Question*, this book sets up various tentative hypotheses which are to be evaluated, refined and developed through the comparative empirical study of urban movements across several different countries. In place of the painstaking discussions of epistemology, the book includes over fifty pages of methodological appendices setting out interview schedules, data sources and statistical profiles in order to show how 'All the facts had to be empirically established', and how 'All the relationships between these facts had to be empirically verified' (p. 341). And in place of the confident faith in the epistemological superiority of Marxist claims to knowledge, Castells launches a bitter assault on the Marxist tradition in urban research culminating in an attack on the 'Shameful pattern of constructing theories according to the party line' (p. 297).

Another notable feature of this dramatic change in Castells's whole approach is his endorsement of the role of human agency and subjectivity as central to social analysis and explanation. A major theme of the book lies in the exploration of how cities are created and transformed in response to the pursuit by people of their various values and objectives, and Castells even goes so far as to conceptualize the city in terms of the meanings which come to be assigned to it at different periods in history by different groups engaged in a struggle with one another. In this way, urban form is explained as the symbolic expression of social meanings imposed by various groups through struggle, while urban change is seen in terms of a successful redefinition of the meaning of the city consequent upon such struggles. In terms highly reminiscent of Lefebvre, Castells argues that:

> Spatial forms, at least on our planet, will be produced by human action, as are all other objects, and will express and perform the interests of the dominant class according to a given mode of production and to a specific mode of development. They will express and implement the power relationships of the state in a historically defined society. They will be realized and shaped by

gender domination and by state-enforced family life. At the same time, spatial forms will also be marked by resistance from exploited classes, oppressed subjects and abused women (1983a, pp. 311–12).

Not surprisingly, perhaps, Lefebvre himself, dismissed in *The Urban Question* as a 'millenarist utopian', is now reinstated as 'a great Marxist philosopher' (p. 15).

All of this raises an obvious question. If there are, after all, no epistemologically-privileged starting points, and if empirical research is an essential component of the development of scientific knowledge, and if grand *a priori* theories are to be dismissed as 'useless' or even 'shameful' while approaches grounded in the subjectivity of human actors are defended, then where does all this leave the original attack on urban social theories as 'ideological'? Castells has never really returned to this issue in the light of his later work (although some indication of his thoughts on this can be found in his 1985 paper), but it seems obvious enough that the logic of his argument has to be that such an epistemological mode of critique can no longer be sustained. Thus, while theories may be termed 'ideological' in the sense that they appear to reflect particular views of the world associated with particular kinds of interests, they cannot be dismissed scientifically through appeal to such criteria. Human ecology, for example, may be seen as 'ideological' in the sense that its concerns with competition and integration reflect the values and goals inscribed in American society at the time when the theory was developed, but even if such a label is applied, this tells us nothing of the theory's validity. Theories which appear to serve the interests of dominant groups may have some validity, just as those born of a sympathy with the oppressed may turn out to be worthless. As Giddens (1979, ch. 5) suggests, ideology is thus a matter of political theory, not epistemology.

Castells himself seems to recognize this when he argues that theories and perspectives can be justified in social science 'only by the fecundity of the research results acquired as a result of these new bases' (1977a, p. 450). The acid test of any urban theory, in other words, is its 'explicative capacity' (p. 454). It is to the question of this explicative capacity of recent Marxist analyses of the urban question that we now turn.

6 The urban as a spatial unit of collective consumption

Althusser's influence on Castells's reformulation of urban sociology was both epistemological and theoretical. We saw in the preceding chapter that the epistemological inheritance that provided the basis for Castells's critique of previous theories must be rejected on the grounds that no epistemology can be self-evident and self-justifying. We also saw that Castells himself was in any case never fully committed to this epistemology and that, as his work developed, so the separation between his and Althusser's method became increasingly explicit. The consequence of this is that the philosophical foundation of his work is now far from clear (for example, the notion of establishing a correspondence between 'chains of observation' and 'chains of theory' begs many familiar questions), and that his early critique of urban sociology as ideological has been undermined.

The rejection of Althusserian epistemology, however, does not in itself entail a rejection of the theoretical framework that Castells derived from Althusser and from other theorists (notably Nicos Poulantzas) influenced by his writings. This follows from the argument developed in the last chapter that theories must be evaluated on their own terms and cannot be upheld or rejected by reference to some set of external and eternal epistemological principles. Thus, while the critique of Althusser's attempt to legislate science and ideology necessarily leads us to reject the basis on which Castells attacked previous theories, it leaves open the question of the theoretical fruitfulness of Castells's own approach to the urban question.

Just as in the last chapter we saw how Castells moved away from his initial (half-hearted) endorsement of Althusser's method, so too we shall see in this chapter that his work has involved a progressive shift away from an initial commitment to Althusser's theoretical framework. In particular, we shall see how (in common with many other Marxist theorists) he has come to reject the uncompromising structural determinacy which characterized Althusser's position, and how he has attempted to take account of the various social interests and identities other than class which enter into social relations in the contemporary period. Central to this discussion will be the continuing focus in Castells's work on problems of consumption – a focus which has proved contentious yet which arguably provides the basis for a coherent urban sociology.

The urban system and the capitalist mode of production

Althusser's single most important contribution to the development of Marxist theory is arguably his critique of traditional interpretations of Marx's dialectic. Basically he suggests that the orthodox view that Marx 'inverted' Hegel's dialectic, thereby substituting a materialist theory of social development for an idealist one, is a gross oversimplification and misunderstanding of Marx's approach. Such a simple inversion would have led Marx to develop a theory of historical change based entirely on the development of the economic forces and relations of production and on the contradiction between them, just as Hegel's dialectic resulted in a theory based entirely on the development of a universal idea or spirit embodied in the state. Such an economistic theory does not, according to Althusser, bear any approximation to the theory of historical materialism that Marx did actually produce (although many later Marxist theorists have themselves interpreted Marx in such a way).

According to Althusser, Marx argued that the economic contradiction between the forces and relations of production (which in capitalism takes the form of the contradiction between capital and wage labour) was a necessary but not sufficient condition for historical transformations from one mode of production to another. What was necessary in addition was the development of other, secondary contradictions within the 'superstructure' of political and ideological relations, contradictions that could then act back upon the basic contradiction. In other words, although political and ideological relations derived out of the mode of economic organization, they developed to some extent independently of economic relations and generated their own effects within the system as a whole. The development of the economic contradiction thus takes place within the context of a unified system of contradictions and cannot be isolated from this system as a single motive force in history, for its development and effectivity is contingent upon the autonomous and uneven development of secondary contradictions elsewhere in the system (and, indeed, on the international context within which the system as a whole is situated). In Althusser's terminology, the basic economic contradiction is 'overdetermined' by contradictions developing at other points or 'instances' of the system, and the transformation from one mode of production to another is dependent upon the development of a 'ruptural fusion' of these different contradictions at a particular point in time ('historical conjucture'). It is in this way that Althusser explains the revolution in Russia in 1917, although it should be noted in passing that such a theory will always be *a posteriori* since, as Walton and Gamble (1972, p. 133) point out, it lacks any criteria by means of which we can identify a ruptural fusion of contradictions before a revolution takes place.

Althusser's theoretical framework constitutes a rejection of traditional Marxist concepts of an economic base determining a political and ideological superstructure. In its place he conceptualizes a complex system of three levels – the economic, political and ideological – in which contradictions develop both within and between each level. The system as a whole represents a specific mode of production in its pure form (that is, existing societies or 'social formations' always involve elements of different pure modes of production with the result that further contradictions develop between as well as within the different modes). Within any given mode of production, one of the three levels will perform the dominant role (for example, in a feudal mode of production the dominant level is the ideological, since religion performs the crucial function in maintaining the unity of the whole; in competitive capitalism the dominant level is the economic, because of the self-perpetuating character of commodity production; in ancient societies such as Rome the dominant level was the political, for the state was the crucial factor in maintaining the unity of the system as a whole). The system as a whole is thus termed by Althusser a 'structure in dominance' since it is a system that achieves its (contradictory) unity by means of a dominant level: 'The unity discussed by Marxism is the unity of the complexity itself . . . the complex whole has the unity of a structure articulated in dominance' (1969, p. 202).

The question of which of the three levels is to perform the dominant function in any particular mode of production is determined by the nature of the economic relations pertaining in that mode (feudal economic relations, for example, necessitated a dominant role for religion in maintaining the unity of the system; capitalist economic relations necessitate a dominant role for the economy itself; and so on). In other words, although the economic is not always dominant, it is always determinate in the sense that it determines the nature of the relations between the three levels and hence which is to perform the dominant role. This is what Althusser means by economic determinancy 'in the last instance'.

It is important to recognize that this ambiguous term should be understood analytically rather than temporally. Thus, when Althusser writes that 'From the first moment to the last, the lonely hour of the "last instance" never comes' (1969, p. 113), he does not mean (as interpreters have suggested) that economic determinancy never actually asserts itself, but rather that, while the economic *always* determines which level is to be dominant, it *never* determines how this level (or the other levels) is to develop. In other words, within a structure of dominance, the different levels develop in different ways and at different rates, and in the process they each affect the development of the others. Each level, that is, is *relatively autonomous* of each other level (only relatively so, since each level is necessarily affected by the specific effects of each other level; they exist only within a unified system, in which case total autonomy clearly becomes impossible). As we shall see later, this concept of relative autonomy has become crucial for Castells's application of the Althusserian system in his own theory.

Both in his early essays and in *The Urban Question*, Castells makes clear his theoretical debt to Althusser (e.g. Castells 1976c, pp. 149–50; 1977a, p. 125), and the development of his theory is premised upon a prior acceptance of Althusser's theory of the structure in dominance. Castells's starting point is therefore given in a theory of which the key elements are (a) the distinction between mode of production and social formation; (b) a concept of mode of production as constituted by three relatively autonomous levels; (c) a recognition of the dominance of one level, this being determined 'in the last instance' by the economic; and (d) an explanation of system change in terms of the identification of structural contradictions which are expressed in and through class practices. Taking this theory of structure as given, Castells then confronts the question of how the urban system relates to this structure.

He begins by arguing that the urban system is not something separate from the total system but is one aspect of it. It is, in other words, the specific expression of that system within a spatial unit of collective consumption: 'We shall use the term spatial structure (or "urban system" to conform to tradition) to describe the particular way in which the basic elements of the social structure are spatially articulated' (1976b, p. 78). The way in which the different levels of the total system articulate with one another must therefore correspond to their articulation in the urban system, and any change in the total system must be reflected in a similar change within the urban system: 'The urban system is not external to the social structure; it specifies that social structure, it forms part of it' (1977a, p. 263).

The first step in Castells's analysis therefore involves the application of the theory of the total system to the urban system. The urban system is thus to be constituted by three levels – the economic, the political and the ideological. The political level corresponds to urban administration (local government and other locally based agencies of the state) which performs the dominant function within the urban system of regulating the relations between the different levels in order to maintain the cohesion of the system. The ideological level corresponds to the 'urban symbolic' (the meanings emitted by socially produced spatial forms). Finally, the economic level is broken down into its three elements of production, consumption and exchange, each of which corresponds to different elements in the urban system (such as factories and offices, housing and recreation facilities, and means of transportation respectively).

The urban system thus contains all the levels and elements of the social system of which it forms a part, and these levels and elements are all structured in the same way as in the wider system. However, as we saw in Chapter 5, Castells argues that this system within a system is a theoretically significant object of study; it is not merely a microcosm of the total system but performs a specific function in relation to that system. As he puts it, 'It is necessary to refer back to the overall social structure (as a concept) to be able to define the urban system and give it a historical content' (1976b, p. 79). The way in which he identifies the theoretically important specific function that the urban system performs within the total social structure is by a process of elimination.

The urban system cannot be specified as a cultural unit (that is, with reference to the ideological level of the social structure), for as Castells's critique of Wirth demonstrated, there is no urban culture as such. Nor can it be specified as a political unit, for although (as we saw in Chapter 1) the medieval city was indeed a unit of political organization, the capitalist city cannot be so defined since political boundaries appear somewhat arbitrary and do not correspond to the contours of social units. It follows that its specific function within the total system must be economic.

As we have seen, the economic level consists of two main elements, production and consumption, which are mediated by a third, exchange. Castells argues that the urban system cannot refer to the production element since capitalist production is organized on a regional scale (for example, different stages in the production process may be located at different centres, factories in one town are administered from offices in another, and so on). It follows from this that it cannot be a specific system of exchange either. The function of the urban system must therefore lie in the process of consumption. Consumption, of course, performs a number of functions within the total capitalist system. It is, for example, the necessary end point of commodity production: 'Without production, no consumption; but also, without consumption, no production; since production would then be purposeless' (Marx 1973, p. 91). However, the principal function of consumption is that it is the means whereby the human labour-power expended in the production of commodities comes to be replaced. In other words, it is only by consuming socially necessary use values (housing, food, leisure facilities, etc.) that the work-force is able to reproduce its capacity for labour which it sells afresh each day.

The specific function of the urban system thus lies in the reproduction of labour-power. This is performed on a daily basis (through the reproduction of the labour-power of existing workers) and on a generational basis (through the production of new generations of workers to replace the existing one), and it entails both simple reproduction (recreation of expended labour-power) and extended reproduction (development of new capacities of labour-power). The means whereby such reproduction is realized are the means of consumption – housing and hospitals, social services and schools, leisure facilities and cultural amenities, and so on. Unlike the means of production, these means of consumption are specific to urban spatial units: '"The urban" seems to me to connote directly the processes relating to labour-power other than in its direct application to the production process. . . . The urban units thus seem to be to the process of reproduction what the companies are to the production process' (Castells 1977a, pp. 236–7).

Castells's justification for identifying the consumption process through which labour-power is reproduced as 'urban' is twofold. First, he suggests (somewhat tentatively) that the growing concentration of capital in advanced capitalist societies is paralleled by a growing concentration of the labour force, with the result that the processes of everyday life through which labour-power is reproduced (eating, sleeping, playing, etc.) are spatially delimited. Second, he argues that such spatial units of everyday life are increasingly structured by the requirements for the reproduction of labour-power within the capitalist system as a whole. For reasons that we shall consider in the next section, the provision of necessary means of consumption within advanced capitalist societies is a contradictory process, and the state has increasingly intervened and then taken responsibility for such provision upon itself. The result is that the means of consumption have not only become concentrated within specific spatial units, but have also become more and more collectivized, and it is this growing significance of the collective provision of the means of consumption that enables Castells to equate the urban system with the process of consumption since it gives rise to increased concentration and centralization:

> The organization of a process will be all the more concentrated and centralized, and therefore structuring, as the degree of objective socialization of the process is advanced, as the concentration of the means of consumption and their interdependence is greater, as the administrative unity of the process is more developed. It is at the level of collective consumption that these features are most obvious (Castells 1977a, p. 445).

Castells's argument may therefore be summarized as follows. (a) The urban system is an expression of the total system of which it forms a part, and it therefore consists of the same levels and elements, interrelated in the same way, as in the total system. (b) It nevertheless performs a significant and specific function within the total system, namely the reproduction of labour-power through the process of consumption. (c) The reproduction of labour-power within the social system as a whole is increasingly achieved within specific spatial units. (d) This is because the process of consumption is becoming concentrated as the population itself becomes concentrated, and as the state assumes increasing responsibility for the provision of crucial consumption facilities. (e) Urban space and the reproduction of labour-power are thus increasingly dependent upon and influenced by the level and form of state provision of necessary means of consumption. It follows from this that, to the extent that consumption becomes collectivized, the urban question becomes a political question.

Urban politics and the crisis of collective consumption

We have seen that Althusser's concept of a 'structure in dominance' indicates the potential development of a multitude of contradictions within any given capitalist society – contradictions internal to each of the three levels of the capitalist mode of production, contradictions between each of these levels, and contradictions between overlapping modes of production within the same society. Given Castells's argument that the urban system is a part of this social structure, it follows that the contradictions that develop in the whole will also develop in the part. To the extent that this is the case, they become manifest as 'urban problems' such as disjunctures between local labour availability and local labour requirements, planning failures, traffic congestion, shortages of building land and so on (see Castells 1976c, pp. 152–3).

For Castells, however, the urban system is not simply one part of the total social structure but is also a specific functional unit within it; it is the subsystem within which labour-power is reproduced. This means that, in addition to reflecting the contradictions within the system as a whole, it is the locus of a specific contradiction or set of contradictions that develops between the process of consumption and other key processes within the total system. Of particular significance here, according to Castells, is the contradiction between consumption and production; that is, between the need to reproduce labour-power and the need to produce commodities at the maximum possible profit.

The argument, quite simply, is that, although the capitalist system must secure the adequate reproduction of labour-power as a prerequisite of continued production and accumulation, individual capitalist producers find it less and less profitable to invest in the production of those commodities that are necessary for such reproduction to take place. The reason for this concerns not the inherent nature of the products concerned (housing, hospitals, educational facilities, etc.) but rather the peculiar character of the firms and industries involved. As one example, Castells cites the French house-building industry (1977a, pp. 149–69).

According to Castells, French capital has found it increasingly unprofitable to invest in the production of low-cost working-class housing, even though there is a desperate need for such housing from the point of view of both workers and industrial capital as a whole (the former because they need somewhere to live, the latter because labour-power must be reproduced cheaply and efficiently). Part of the reason for this is that this widespread need cannot be translated into 'solvent demand' (in other words, housing is an extremely expensive commodity which most workers cannot afford to buy), and to build housing to rent involves a long-term commitment of capital (and firms cannot afford to wait for many years before getting a return on capital). In addition to these problems of realizing profits, there are also problems of generating surplus value through house production. This is because the building industry is fragmented among many small producers, each employing only a few workers, and because of the lack of technological innovation in the industry as a whole.

Castells recognizes that the French case cannot be generalized across all capitalist societies at all points in time. He notes, for example, that the inadequate provision of working-class housing by the private sector is less marked in the United States than it is in France because of a more advanced level of building technology (for instance, factory-based prefabrication), easier availability of building land, a higher level of solvent demand (owing to the higher standard of living), and so on. Nevertheless, he does suggest that the French case is by no means unique: 'The housing question in France is not an exception, but a typical case, within the developed capitalist economy, at a certain phase of its evolution' (1977a, p. 158).

As Duncan (1978) has suggested, there is clearly a danger of drawing unwarranted generalizations from particular cases. Historical and comparative evidence suggests that different types of consumption facilities may fall short of social requirements in different societies at different points in time, and the question of whether and how such situations occur is necessarily contingent upon a range of specific factors which cannot be encompassed within a general theory. However, what is implicit in Castells's argument is that the *potential* for a crisis in the provision of commodities necessary for the reproduction of labour-power is inherent in the nature of capitalist commodity production. The reason for this is simply that production is concerned with exchange values while consumption is concerned with use values. There is, in other words, no necessary reason why what it is most profitable to produce should coincide with what is most socially necessary to consume, since the investment of capital is dictated by rates of return rather than need.

It is Castells's argument that this potential disjuncture between profit and need, exchange value and use value, production and consumption, has become increasingly manifest in different ways throughout the western capitalist world, and that this has resulted in 'lacunae in vast areas of consumption which are essential to individuals and to economic activity' (1978, p. 18). Left to itself, in other words, private capital has shown a marked inability to produce socially necessary facilities.

If this growing contradiction, which becomes manifest in housing shortages, inadequate medical care, lack of social facilities and so on, is not regulated in some way, then it must necessarily create new sources of political tension and strife. Resorting to Althusserian terminology, Castells suggests that 'Any fundamental contradiction unregulated by the system leads finally to an overdetermined contradiction within the political system' (1977a, p. 270). The regulation of system contradictions is, as we saw earlier, the function specific to the political level. It therefore falls to the state as the agency of social cohesion and the regulator of the total system to intervene in the process of reproduction of labour-power in an attempt to plug the gaps. This is why consumption becomes more and more collectivized and why the urban system as a whole is increasingly structured by state intervention.

Such an explanation for state intervention and the growth of collective consumption does, of course, appear strongly functionalist (system needs provoke system responses), although it is a central feature of this analysis that, while state intervention may overcome one set of contradictions, it necessarily generates another (i.e. the system is not a dynamic equilibrium, as in Parsonian sociology, but is inherently contradictory – see below, p. 199). Nevertheless, the functionalist assumptions on which this analysis necessarily rests clearly disturbed Castells as his work developed over the years, and increasingly he came to place greater emphasis on the analysis of the direct causes of state intervention (which he traces to the development of class struggle and urban social movements) than on the functional requirements which it is said to fulfil. This shift (which represents a move away from Althusser's theoretical structuralism in that it emphasizes the effectivity of people's actions) is not, however, as profound as may first appear, for the theory of the state which Castells employs has always contained both aspects. In other words, the theory entails two different kinds of explanations, one having to do with practices (the state does what it does as a response to class struggle), and the other having to do with structures (the state does what it does because of its structurally-determined role in the mode of production). Thus, as Castells increasingly emphasized the role of class struggle and urban social movements in shaping the pattern of state intervention, he was not so much breaking with his initial theory as shifting the emphasis between its two constituent dimensions. The problem, however, was always how to relate these two causal elements of the theory to each other, for it was by no means clear why or how the state's actions in response to class struggle should necessarily be consistent with its structurally-defined role in safeguarding the interests of the capitalist class and reproducing the relations of capitalist domination. Is it not possible that political pressures may dictate one course of action while system needs dictate another? How is it possible to hold both that the state responds to the (unequal) power exerted by different classes, and that its interventions are the expression of the structural needs of the system at any given time? Is it political power or structural requirements which shape the interventions of the state?

The theory of the state which lies behind all of Castells's work was derived originally from the work of Poulantzas (1973) who attempted to theorize the 'political instance' in its relation to the other levels of the capitalist mode of production. Poulantzas it was who attempted to introduce the analysis of class practices into structuralist theory:

> The originality of Poulantzas's work lies in his attempt to transcend the integrationist perspective of functionalist sociology. He does this by trying to graft the Marxist proposition that the class struggle is the motor of history onto Althusser's structural-functionalist conception of society. The theory of class is inserted between the structure and the state, so that the state is subject to a double determination. In the first place, it is determined directly by the structure as a specific functional level of that structure. Secondly, its functioning in practice, within limits determined by its place in the structure, is subject to the conditions of the class struggle, which are in turn determined, at least partially, by the structure (Clarke 1977, p. 11).

In terms of its *structural determination*, Poulantzas analyses the function of the state as its role in regulating the articulation of the different levels of the system as a whole: 'Inside the structure of several levels dislocated by uneven development, the state has the particular function of constituting the factor of cohesion between the levels of a social formation' (1973, p. 44). In other words, its location in the system is such that it must perform this function of system regulation. On the other hand, as a part of the system, it must also necessarily reflect the contradictions that develop within and between the other levels; indeed, it is precisely within the state (namely at the political level) that these contradictions come together and are manifested and 'condensed'. As Castells (1977a, p. 243) suggests, it is therefore at the political level that 'one may map the indices of change'.

In terms of its *determination by class struggle*, Poulantzas argues that the state is a condensation of the class struggle. In other words, while it is certainly not a neutral instrument of political administration as pluralist theory suggests, it is not a tool of any one class as is often claimed by economistic Marxist theories. Poulantzas's argument is basically that contradictions within the system give rise to class struggles, and that the state's response to these contradictions through its interventions is determined by such struggles. Thus, while its function is necessarily to maintain the system in the interests of dominant class interests, the way it achieves this is by responding to the political balance of class forces at any one time. Quite simply, the state cannot possibly perform its (structurally determined) function of maintaining system cohesion without responding to the political pressures exerted upon it from dominated as well as dominant classes, for to remain aloof from working-class claims would be to fail to intervene on the contradictions that have provoked such claims.

It follows from this argument that the state does not itself have power, but rather reflects through its interventions the political relations between different classes. Power, in other words, is a function of class relations and is revealed through class practices: 'The concept of power is constituted in the field of class practices. . . . Class relations are relations of power' (Poulantzas 1973, p. 99). The various institutions of the state are merely the organizations that express the relative power of different classes in any given 'conjucture'. It also follows from the argument that class practices are constituted at all three levels of the social formation; Poulantzas is heavily critical of the familiar dichotomy in Marxist analysis between classes in and for themselves, arguing instead that classes are constituted through their practices and that such practices develop (albeit unevenly) through economic, political and ideological struggles simultaneously. Political struggles are thus an inherent aspect of class practices (that is, classes do not first constitute themselves as economic categories and then engage in political struggles), although the political groupings (for example, parties) through which they are expressed cannot be directly reduced to economic categories owing to the relative autonomy between the levels. In other words, we do not find wage-labour and capital necessarily confronting each other directly at the political level, but this does not mean that the groups that do confront each other there are not engaged in class struggle.

It is evident from all of this that class practices bring about system change (since they are reflected in state intervention), but that such practices are in turn determined to some extent by the development of system contradictions. Class struggle is in this sense the link in the causal chain between contradictions in the system and state intervention which attempts to resolve them. The greater the contradictions, the greater will be the intensity of political struggle, and the more the state will intervene as a result. However, both Poulantzas and Castells then go on to argue that class practices are determined by the structure only *to some extent*. Thus, not only is there a relative autonomy between the different levels of the structure (the political is relatively autonomous from the economic), but there is also a relative autonomy between the levels of the structure and the practices to which they correspond (political struggles are not merely the expression of contradictions condensed at the political level). This is because practices do not simply express contradictions but bring them together and articulate them. Contradictions in the structure exist only through practices, and (as we saw in the last chapter with reference to the notion of theoretical practice) the very concept of practice entails the production of qualitatively new effects. This is why Poulantzas insists on 'conceiving of practice as a production, i.e. a work of transformation. It is important to see that in this sense a structural instance does not as such directly constitute a practice' (1973, p. 87). Similarly, Castells argues that political practice 'is not simply a vehicle of structured effects: it produces new effects. However, these new effects proceed not from the consciousness of men, but from the specificity of the combinations of their practices, and this specificity is determined by the state of the structure' (1977a, p. 125; see also p. 244). Practices are therefore determined by the structure in the sense that structural contradictions give rise to them, but they generate new effects within the system according to how they articulate these contradictions. The state thus performs its functional task in regulating the system by responding to the particular way in which different classes mobilize around system contradictions.

But if class struggle arising out of system contradictions is the immediate cause of state intervention, how does this enable the state to fulfil its regulative function in the system? Poulantzas's answer is twofold. First, the state organizes and unifies the divergent interests of different fractions of the capitalist class under the hegemony of the dominant fraction (monopoly capital): 'It takes charge, as it were, of the bourgeoisie's political interests and realizes the function of political hegemony which the bourgeoisie is unable to achieve. But in order to do this, the capitalist state assumes a relative autonomy with regard to the bourgeoisie' (1973, pp. 284–5). In other words, by reflecting in its policies the different interests of different fractions of capital (even if, on occasion, this necessitates the pursuit of a policy that is against the interests of the dominant fraction in the short term), the state maintains the unity of the capitalist 'power block' and thus acts in the long-term interests of monopoly capital which dominates the power bloc.

Second, while unifying an inherently fragmented capitalist class, the state also fragments the dominated classes. This it does in two ways. First, the legal system, the electoral system and so on produce and sustain an ideology of the individual through which members of these classes come to conceive of themselves and to live their lives as atomized individual subjects rather than as class agents (an argument that closely reflects Althusser's concept of the interpellation of individual subjects discussed in Chapter 5). Having created isolated individuals out of objective social relations, the state can then function 'to represent the unity of isolated relations founded in the body politic' (Poulantzas 1973, p. 134) – e.g. by representing the 'public interest'. Second, and more significantly from our present perspective, the state fragments the lower classes in the very process of responding to their political class practices. Precisely because the state is relatively autonomous of any one class, it is quite possible for it to cede concessions to dominated classes at the economic level provided this does not threaten the domination of capital at the political level: 'Within these limits it can effectively satisfy some of the economic interests of certain dominated classes. . . . While these economic sacrifices are real and so provide the ground for an equilibrium, they do not as such challenge the political power which sets precise limits to this equilibrium (p. 192). This, according to Poulantzas, is the explanation for the growth of the capitalist welfare state.

This argument is fundamental to Castells's analysis, for it explains how it is that the state may come to respond to working-class pressure, increase its spending on social items that benefit this class (even though this may not be in the immediate interests of the dominant class – for instance since it raises taxation), and yet still function in the long-term interests of monopoly capital by maintaining social cohesion. As he puts it,

> The state apparatus not only exercises class domination, but also strives, as far as possible, to regulate the crises of the system in order to preserve it. It is in this sense that it may, sometimes, become reformist. Although reforms are always imposed by the class struggle and, therefore, from outside the state apparatus, they are no less real for that: their aim is to preserve and extend the existing context, thus consolidating the long-term interests of the dominant classes, even if it involves infringing their privileges to some extent in a particular conjuncture (Castells 1977a, p. 208).

In the particular case of collective consumption provisions, state intervention performs this function of system maintenance in at least four different ways. First, it is essential to the reproduction of labour-power required by the various fractions of capital. Second, it regulates the class struggle by appeasing lower-class groups with economic concessions while leaving the relations of political domination intact. Third, it stimulates demand in the economy both directly (for example through state purchases from the private sector) and indirectly (through the multiplier effect), thereby combating crises of under-consumption/over-production. And fourth, by investing in unprofitable areas, the state counters the falling rate of profit in the private sector:

> Public investment, as we know, is an essential form of 'devaluation of social capital', a major recourse for counteracting the tendency toward a lowering of the profit margin. By investing 'at a loss', the general rate of profit in the private sector holds steady or increases in spite of the lowering of profit relative to social capital as a whole. In this sense, 'social' expenditures of the state not only thus favour big capital, but they are also indispensable to the survival of the system (Castells 1978, pp. 18–19).

So it is that the growth of collective consumption, brought about by the development of working-class struggle (which itself reflects the development of the contradiction within the system between profit and need, production and consumption), functions in the long-term interests of monopoly capital and allied fractions by aiding the reproduction of labour-power, regulating class conflict, orchestrating new solvent demand and countering the tendency for the rate of profit to fall in the private sector.

Two further points should be made about this argument. First, as we noted earlier, Castells has tended to shift the emphasis of his analysis between his earlier and later writings. This is revealed most clearly in the way in which he has applied his theory of state intervention to the specific question of urban planning (the political level within the urban system). In his earlier essays, urban planning is explained almost entirely in terms of its necessary function within the structure of regulating system contradictions: 'If one accepts the idea of the political system as regulating the system (concrete social formation) as a whole, according to the structural laws on which it is based, then urban planning is its intervention on a given reality in order to counteract the dislocations expressed' (1976c, p. 166). In his later work, however, and in the light of his empirical research in Dunkerque, much greater emphasis comes to be placed on planning as the expression and mediation of class relations: 'The political role of urban planning is due essentially to its capacity to act as an instrument of mediation and negotiation between the different fractions of the dominant class and between the various requirements necessary to the realization of their overall interests, as well as *vis-à-vis* the pressures and demands of the dominated classes' (1977b, p. 77).

As we have already seen, this shift represents more a modification of his earlier theoretical position than a fundamental break with it. It is true, of course, that the earlier emphasis on the functional determination of the state by its location in the structure assumes a general theory of the capitalist state whereas the later emphasis on the determinate role of class struggle recognizes that the character of state intervention will vary across different societies in different historical periods (hence Castells's call in his later writings for a 'theorized history of states' (1978, p. 181)). However, it is equally clearly the case that, just as the earlier formulation recognizes that class struggle is the means whereby structurally determined functions are achieved, so the later formulation recognizes that the state performs a regulatory role within the system as a result of its mediation between the demands of different classes and class fractions. The emphasis has changed but the components of the analysis remain the same, for both formulations necessarily include the elements of structure and function on the one hand, and practice and class struggle on the other. As we shall see in the next section, the tension between these two necessary aspects of the theory is in no way resolved by switching the primary focus of attention from one to the other.

The second point to be noted is that, although Castells argues that the growth of state intervention in the sphere of collective consumption has produced a number of positively functional effects (reproduction of labour-power, appeasement of class struggle, etc.), he then goes on to suggest that it nevertheless also generates a new set of contradictions within the system. These basically derive from the 'dislocation between the private control of labour-power and of the means of production and the collective character of the (re)production of these two elements' (1977, p. 279). In other words, the state pays the increasing cost of reproducing labour-power while private capital retains the profits created by this labour-power. The more the state is driven to increase its social provisions, the wider the gap becomes between its expenditure and its revenues. The result is a fiscal crisis of the state which, in the United States at least, has dramatically been reflected in a fiscal crisis of the cities (the most celebrated example being the near bankruptcy of New York City), and which has become manifest in other countries to a greater or lesser degree (for example through massive rate increases in British cities). As Castells puts it, 'The fiscal crisis of the inner cities was a particularly acute expression of the overall fiscal crisis of the state, that is, of the increasing budgetary gap created in public finance in advanced capitalist countries because of the historical process of socialization of costs and privatization of profits' (1977a, p. 415).

Although taxation may be increased in response to fiscal crisis, such a policy cannot resolve the problem, for taxation on profits would undermine the profitability of the private sector which the state must act to sustain, while taxation on wages (which Castells suggests has increased) (1978, p. 21) is limited and, in the long run, counter-productive (since it will tend to result in demands on capital for higher wages together with a heightened level of working-class mobilization):

> State intervention in the maintenance of essential but unprofitable public services has effectively been carried out at the cost of an inflationary and growing public debt, for the financing of these growing and indispensable public expenses could not be achieved through an imposition on capital (which refused to yield part of its profits) or, completely, through increased taxation – the eventual social struggles and political oppositions spelled out the limits of such a strengthening of state power at the expense of wage earners (Castells 1978, pp. 175–6).

Faced with an inflationary spiral and encroaching recession, the state reacts by cutting its level of expenditure and redirecting resources from the support of labour-power to the direct support of capital. The result is a crisis in the provision of collective consumption.

The basic problems – lack of housing, poor health care, inadequate schooling, poor transportation facilities, shortage of cultural amenities and so on – that led the state to intervene in the process of consumption in the first place thus reappear. What is different, however, is that the whole area of consumption has now become politicized; the more the state assumes responsibility for the provision of social resources, the more centrally involved it becomes in the organization of everyday life and the more everyday life is politicized as a result. If one function of this increased level of collective provision has been the appeasement of the lower classes, then it follows that a reduction in the level of such provision carries with it the possibility of a strong and politically organized lower-class reaction against the state itself (and hence against the political dominance of monopoly capital).

Castells is careful to argue that the politicization of the urban question does not necessarily result in an intensification of class struggle. This is because, as we saw earlier, system contradictions do not determine class practices but are rather articulated through such practices. Thus Castells writes:

> The permanent and ever extending intervention of the state apparatus in the area of the processes and units of consumption makes it the real source of order in everyday life. This intervention of the state apparatus, which we call urban planning in the broad sense, involves an almost immediate politicization of the whole urban problematic. ... However, the politicization thus established is not necessarily a source of conflict or change, for it may also be a mechanism of integration and participation: *everything depends on the articulation of the contradictions and practices* (Castells 1977a, p. 463; emphasis added).

The factor that determines how these contradictions will be articulated in terms of class practices and how effective these practices will be in terms of fundamental social change is political organization. Without socialist organization, contradictions will be reflected in an uncoordinated, fragmented and ultimately ineffective way:

> The role of the organization (as a system of means specific to an objective) is fundamental for ... it is the organization that is the locus of fusion or articulation with the other social practices. When there is no organization,

urban contradictions are expressed either in a refracted way, through other practices, or in a 'wild' way, a pure contradiction devoid of any structural horizon (Castells 1977a, pp. 271–2).

The role of political organization is to link contradictions in practice. This means not only bringing together different urban struggles (e.g. housing struggles, education campaigns and so on), but also locating urban struggles as a whole within the wider context of class struggle. A failure to achieve the first will result in the perpetuation of divisions between different groups such that concessions gained by one group will be won at the expense of another, and this can only result in the reproduction of the system rather than an effective challenge to it. A failure to achieve the second will limit any popular movement to reformism. This is because urban contradictions are secondary: 'Whatever the level and the content of the various "urban issues", they can all be characterized as secondary structural issues, that is to say, ones not directly challenging the production methods of a society nor the political domination of the ruling classes' (Castells 1977a, p. 376). It follows that urban struggles cannot themselves provoke fundamental social change, but can only effect limited changes within the confines of the urban system: 'a municipal revolution and nothing more' (p. 360).

Castells's thinking on the role and significance of urban movements has, like so many other areas of his work, changed considerably over the years. Basically, his ideas have developed through three distinct phases.

In his earliest writings, he was clear that to be effective, urban movements must be assimilated into the wider working-class movement (which he took to be synonymous with the Communist Party). On its own, urban protest will always be limited in its political effectiveness, but if it can be harnessed to the Communist Party, with its strong base in industrial class struggles, then it can come to play a crucial role in bringing about social change. This is because 'the working class cannot on its own . . . pose a socialist alternative in western Europe' (1978, p. 172). It has to forge popular alliances with other classes such as the 'new petty bourgeoisie', and urban issues facilitate the formation of such alliances in that the movements which develop around the crisis of collective consumption draw upon a wide range of social interests. Polluted air does not stop at the boundaries of middle-class suburbs; cuts in school budgets do not discriminate between working-class and middle-class students; the shortage of hospital beds affects professional workers as much as manual workers; and so on. Urban contradictions, in other words, are 'pluri-class' in their impact, and the protests which they generate thus provide the basis on which to build new, anti-capitalist and anti-state alliances.

In this first phase of his work, Castells saw the significance of such alliances (somewhat implausibly) as being realized in popular insurrection. As the urban crisis deepened, so the fusion of industrial muscle and popular protest represented by the development of 'urban social movements' would shake the system of class domination to its foundations. 'Urban power', claimed Castells, 'lies in the streets', and these new alliances would 'reopen the roads to revolution' (1977a. p. 378). The events in Paris in 1968 seem to have provided the model which Castells had in mind.

In the second phase of his work, he continued to argue that urban protest had to be channelled through the wider political struggle for socialism, but he came to see the role of urban social movements less in terms of popular insurrection and more as a means of widening the electoral base of the socialist and communist parties:

> The articulation of new social struggles with alternative democratic politics can lead to a Left-wing electoral victory based on a programme opening the way to socialism. For such a victory to be possible and not to get bogged down in the administrative underground of the bougeois state, it must not support itself on a coalition of dissatisfactions, but on the political and ideological hegemony of the socialist forces at the mass level. We know that this hegemony must necessarily depend on a transformation of mass consciousness, and that this transformation will not be brought about by televised electoral speeches but by and in struggle. In our historical conditions, the revolutionary's essential task consists above all in winning the masses. The battle for the masses replaces the battle of the Winter Palace (1978, p. 60).

This endorsement of an electoral strategy obviously reflected the influence of 'Eurocommunism' within the French Communist Party in the 1970s, but it was also consistent with the deeper shifts within Castells's overall theory. The Castells of the early essays could only theorize change in terms of insurrection given his emphasis on the structural determinations of the state's role and functions, for no matter who ran the system, the outputs would always necessarily be the same. As his work came to emphasize the causal significance of practices relative to structures, however, so the possibility was opened up for endorsing a parliamentary strategy in which people could have some effect on outcomes. The democratic road to socialism, in other words, came to be seen as viable only when the theory made room for human actors.

In the third and most recent phase of his work, however, much of this theory of urban social movements has been jettisoned. Following a study of tenants protest movements in two municipal housing estates in Paris, Castells came to the conclusion that urban movements should maintain some distance between themselves and left political parties if they were to stand any chance of maintaining their vitality and pursuing their particular concerns. Moreover, he went on to argue that the labour movement is itself effectively powerless to bring about social transformation in a world where the levers of economic control are globally organized, and that its narrow economistic concerns with workplace issues prevent it from addressing the wider concerns regarding the quality of life which lie at the heart of the urban question.

Following a wide ranging analysis of urban movements in the USA, South America and Spain as well as France, he concluded that to be successful, such movements needed to focus not simply on collective consumption issues (what he termed 'consumer trade unionism'), but also on the political question of state power and the cultural question of urban meaning. In Paris, for example, the tenants' movement was limited by its failure to address wider community and political issues; in San Francisco, the gay movement succeeded in transforming neighbourhoods around its own cultural identity and in challenging for power in City Hall, but failed to address the problem of collective consumption provision; and in the South American shanty towns, the squatters' movement exerted demands for urban services and established new cultural communities, but at the expense of political subordination to state power and patronage. Only in Madrid during the Franco regime did Castells find an example (in the Citizens' Movement) of an urban social movement which successfully combined all three dimensions of the urban question; for here, demands for urban services were coupled up with a challenge to authoritarian state power and the development of new urban cultural forms which emphasized the city as a use value for people rather than as a speculative playground for big capital.

Given the inherent weakness and limitations of the labour movement in the contemporary period, Castells concludes by arguing that urban social movements are the only channel through which popular pressures for change can be expressed. However, they too are ultimately powerless to transform the conditions of oppression which give rise to them, for they lack the means to change the economic system, to control the production and dissemination of dominant culture, and to challenge the might of the modern nation state. They are, in the last analysis, 'local utopias' which keep alive the challenge to domination and exploitation but which cannot themselves overcome it: 'Urban movements do address the real issues of our time, although neither on the scale nor terms that are adequate to the task. And yet they do not have any choice since they are the last reaction to the domination and renewed exploitation that submerges our world' (1983a, p. 331). They are, to paraphrase Marx, the sigh of the oppressed creature and the soul of souless conditions. We have come a long way from the events of May 1968.

Production, consumption and the city

Thus far in this chapter, I have concentrated almost exclusively on outlining the core theoretical propositions developed by just one writer in the neo-Marxist tradition, Manuel Castells. This emphasis is justified given the enormous impact of Castells's early writing on the reshaping of urban sociology in the 1970s, especially in Britain. As Harloe has observed, 'It would be an exaggeration to say that Castells's approach monopolised the development of the "new" urban sociology in Britain in the mid-1970s. . . . Nevertheless, the citations to his work, as well as the attention paid to a critical examination of it, indicate that Castells's writings were of central importance' (1981, p. 4). The centrality of Castells's work during this period was partly a reflection of the fact that his key papers, and his key book, were translated into English quite early on while foreign-language works by other writers remained relatively inaccessible. For much of this period, many of us in Britain remained largely ignorant of the political and intellectual context which had spawned Castells's theories and had little knowledge of the alternatives being proposed by other European Marxists, nor of the debates to which Castells's work was addressed (see Lebas 1982). But having said that, it remains the case that Castells's early writings succeeded in pinpointing many of the core issues and problems in urban studies at that time, and that (rather like Rex and Moore's work in the mid 1960s) they generated intense interest and argument mainly because they challenged existing orthodoxies and assumptions while pointing the way forward to a new research agenda.

By the mid 1980s, however, Castells's work was no longer so dominant. Gradually, the English-speaking audience became familiar with other European theorists as well as itself generating critiques of, and alternatives to, Castells's proposed paradigm. Furthermore, as we have seen, Castells himself criticized many basic aspects of his own earlier work, while (as we shall go on to see in the next two chapters) other writers began to develop new agendas for urban studies which reflected the changed conditions brought about by deepening economic recession, new patterns of political conflict and, most crucially, a sustained attack by radical right governments in Britain, the USA and other advanced capitalist countries on the very system of collective consumption which lay at the heart of Castells's theoretical concerns.

For the remainder of this chapter, therefore, I wish to broaden the discussion to go beyond mere exegisis and critique of Castells's writings and to focus in more general terms on some of the issues and problems which are raised in his work but which are not necessarily resolved there. I shall therefore take various key themes and ideas from Castells's writings as springboards for discussion of certain methodological and theoretical issues which have attracted argument and debate among other writers in recent years, and in this way the chapter will lay the foundations for an analysis of the questions surrounding space (Chapter 7) and consumption (Chapter 8) which remain central to much work within urban studies in the contemporary period.

Let us begin with problems of methodology, following which we may go on to consider issues concerning his substantive concern with analysing collective consumption.

Methodological questions

According to many of his critics, Castells's approach as exemplified in *The Urban Question* was (a) ahistorical, (b) ethnocentric, and (c) functionalist (see, for example, Duncan 1981, Harloe 1981, Mingione 1981).

The charge of ahistoricism was undoubtedly valid, for it was a feature of the Althusserian structuralist paradigm that it not only ignored history but resolutely set its face against historical explanations in which social causality is traced to specific events (the shooting of an Archduke, a sealed train through Germany, a famine, a battle or whatever) rather than being established in terms of the necessary outcome of structural conjunctures. Historical explanation was for

Althusser fatally tied to the problematic of the human subject (for it explains change as the product of human actions) and to the methods of empiricism (for its claims to knowledge are grounded in historical evidence), both of which his approach had already ruled out; history, in other words, directly contradicted the 'scientific' method of theoretical practice.

We need not dwell on this issue, for Althusser's dismissal of history has been widely criticized elsewhere (see especially Thompson 1978), while Castells has himself come to reject this recipe for theoretical formalism and to emphasize the need for what he terms 'theorised histories' (1978, p. 181). As we have seen, he recognized quite early on the barrenness of an approach which led to the application of pre-existing (and empirically-untestable) theoretical generalities while ignoring historical variations, and he criticized the tendency in his own earlier work towards 'coding' observations into conceptual categories without ever understanding the specific conditions which give rise to them. Along with most other urban researchers, therefore, Castells now argues for a theoretically-sensitive historical method.

The issue raised by this in terms of current debates, however, is how an historical method focusing on the specific conditions arising in specific times and places can be combined with the generalizing claims of theoretical explanation. As we saw in Chapter 1, this was precisely the problem addressed by Max Weber in his methodology of ideal types when he argued that sociological explanation entailed generalization through the identification and understanding of typical probabilities of action. Notwithstanding the infinite number of factors which could and did give rise to any given phenomenon, it was possible in his view to develop adequate though partial explanations by focusing on those features which were relevant to the concerns of the researcher, and by showing how people typically responded in subjectively meaningful ways to them. Ideal types were thus the tools by which general concepts could be applied to the analysis of historically specific conditions.

In contemporary urban studies, however, Weber's methodology has not been widely endorsed. Rather, with the collapse of the Althusserian paradigm, Marxist theorists have attempted to reconcile the search for general theories with a recognition of the significance of specific conditions by developing what has come to be known as a 'realist' method. I have discussed this methodology elsewhere (Saunders 1983) and I consider it again in the appendix to this book.

Briefly, it differs from Weber's approach to explanation by rejecting a notion of causality as a sequence of events (as in, for example, the claim that Calvinism helped to create the conditions in which capitalism could develop), and focusing instead on causality as an inherent property of things themselves. Causal explanation is in this way achieved when analysis reveals how the capacity of something to behave in a certain way has been realized (or has been prevented from being realized) by the conditions in which it is operating. Thus, to revert to a physical analogy developed by Sayer (1984a), a length of copper wire has the inherent capacity to conduct an electric current, but this capacity will only be realized under certain contingent conditions (dampness, for example, may hinder conductivity). The task of scientific explanation lies not in analysing the peculiar events leading up to this result (e.g. the fact that it had rained), but rather in identifying the inherent mechanism (in this case, the ionic structure of copper) which necessarily generates a given tendency (i.e. the capacity to conduct electricity), irrespective of whether this tendency is actually realized in any given case. Whereas Weberian ideal type analysis identifies one factor as important while ignoring others on the basis of the researcher's own concerns and interests, a realist methodology thus distinguishes what it sees as the 'necessary' properties of things from the 'contingent' factors which may affect their operation. Its concern is not so much whether things happen but how they happen.

Despite the claims of its adherents to the contrary, this methodology is not that different in its practical applications to research from the Althusserian approach. Where the Althusserians came to a problem already armed with their theory of an underlying structure and simply 'coded' their empirical observations in terms of this theory, social realists come to their research similarly equipped with a theory which purports to explain the necessary tendencies of things, and they then proceed to explain what they find by pinpointing effects as the realization of these tendencies, modified where appropriate by the intrusion of contingent factors. What is deemed 'necessary' is thus determined by the theory while the actual observations are accounted for by reference to the peculiar effects of contingencies which no theory could or should generalize about. Theory, in other words, tells you about the generalities of how things necessarily work, while empirical and historical research tells you why these things may not work as theorized in actually-observed reality. In this way (just as for Althusserianism) the theory is safeguarded from empirical disconfirmation (since theorized tendencies may or may not reveal themselves according to contingent historical conditions), but unlike Althusserianism, this approach has the attraction of enabling empirical study so as to identify the operation of contingent conditions, and therefore of taking account of the fact that, for example, not all capitalist societies look the same even though they are said to operate according to the same inherent logic.

Here then is the response of urban studies to Castells's call for 'theorized histories'. Yet it is a response which still asserts the primacy of theoretical over empirical knowledge, which still facilitates the development of theories which are in principle unfalsifiable (since the controlled experiment in which all contingent events are held constant is not usually feasible in social science), and which still enables claims to epistemological privilege to be put forward against other perspectives which can safely be dismissed as 'empiricist' because they fail to theorize the necessities which are held to underpin the operation of real world events. The collapse of Althusserian epistemology has encouraged the growth of empirical research, but the findings of such research (while worthwhile in themselves) are never allowed to intrude upon the initial theory which is meant to explain them. Thus it becomes possible, for example, to analyse the important differences between housing provision in two different capitalist countries – differences which reflect the organization of the building industry, the role of the state, the pattern of class relations and so on – while still concluding that these differences are the products of contingent historical events which do nothing to undermine a theoretical explanation which is held to apply equally to both (see, for example, Dickens *et al.* 1985). If you study the contingencies, the theoretical necessities can safely be left undisturbed to look after themselves.

It is important to emphasize that Castells himself has avoided such an approach in his later work. His analysis of urban social movements in *The City and the Grassroots*, for example, is developed on the basis of observation of different cases in order to derive tentative theoretical generalizations (e.g. regarding the significance of different types of demands and strategies exemplified by different types of movements). These theoretical insights are then applied and amended through further empirical investigation – a methodology of grounded theory which explicitly sets out to avoid the prior imposition of general theories and which enables an inter-penetration of theory and empirical research which is effectively precluded by the adoption of a realist methodology. This is a very different notion of 'theorized history' from that employed in realist social science, and it is one which owes more to the methodology of ideal type generalization than it does to this alternative approach. Unfortunately, however, a new 'realist' orthodoxy does seem to be taking root in urban studies at this time, and although this will not preclude empirical investigation in the way that Althusserianism did, it does carry familiar dangers of theoretical non-falsifiability and epistemological claims to privileged knowledge.

I shall return to this issue in the appendix, but for now we may go on to consider the second, and related, criticism which has been levelled against Castells's earlier methodology: namely, that it was ethnocentric.

An approach grounded in a Weberian methodology of ideal types is, in a sense, inherently ethnocentric, not simply because the concepts employed will reflect the value-conditioned interests of a given researcher at a particular time in a particular place, but also because the 'individual types' employed are always partial and one-sided and will thus always reflect one aspect of the phenomenon in question while ignoring others. This is not, however, a serious problem within Weberian sociology since ideal types can always be amended or developed in the light of new observations, and it is always open to other researchers to develop other pure types reflecting conditions in other social contexts.

Althusserian methodology is, however, very different. Its concepts are developed as generalities without content. Rather like Weber's generic as opposed to individual types, they are timeless and spaceless for they are held to apply to all societies in all periods. Thus, they are total rather than partial in their scope and, furthermore, because of the exclusive claim to scientificity, they are the only generalities which can be employed. There is no room in such an approach for the development of alternative conceptualizations of the world, for these are dismissed as 'ideological'. There is only one road to scientific truth.

In practice, of course, the generalities which Althusserian researchers employed were not derived mysteriously from some privileged theoretical insight into the inner workings of human society, but inevitably reflected specific conditions pertaining in particular places and times. Castells was no exception. Abstract and formalistic concepts developed on the basis of Althusser's three 'levels' within a mode of production were invested with content and meaning by Castells by drawing upon concrete and specific historical instances and elevating them to the status of timeless generalities. As Duncan pointed out, 'The concepts employed, such as the urban question, the housing crisis, the state, are at once ahistorical generalizations and highly specific historically' (1981, p. 239). Thus Duncan showed how the conception of the state (the 'political instance' within a 'capitalist mode of production') developed by Castells in fact owed much to the particular form of state power which was characteristic of French society at the time when he was writing. Similarly, the emphasis on the contradiction between capital accumulation and the reproduction of labour power culminating in a tendency to fiscal crisis, which was seen by Castells as inherent to capitalism, was very much a peculiar feature of particular western European capitalist countries during the 1970s. Yet these essentially individual concepts were put forward as generic, despite the fact that in other countries (Duncan gives the example of Sweden) they simply did not apply.

Duncan, incidentally, claims that this is a problem shared in common by Althusserian and Weberian methodologies, and he sees this tendency in Castells's earlier work as 'surprisingly reminiscent of the Weberian method of formulating ideal types' (p. 248). This, of course, is not the case, for although ideal types may similarly be partial in their scope, there is no attempt in this methodology to apply them as if they were general across all times and places. As we saw in Chapter 1, for example, Weber's ideal type of the city was grounded in an analysis of western European cities during a specific period of their history, and neither he nor anyone else ever tried to suggest that the emphasis he placed on fortification, autonomous legal systems and the rest was generalizable across all cities at all times. The reason why ethnocentrism was such a crucial problem in Castells's work, therefore, was not so much that he was arguing on the basis of a distinctive experience (France in the late 1960s) but that he was elevating this experience to the status of an all-encompassing generality.

What, then, of his later work? As we have seen, his theory of urban social movements has now been developed, not on the basis of prior generalizations, but through empirical studies in the USA, Latin America and Europe, plus secondary analysis of historical materials ranging from studies of the Comunidades of sixteenth-century Castilla to the black ghetto riots of 1960s America. Only as a result of such wide-ranging empirical analysis does he then propose a general theory which is said to apply 'across different cultures of the capitalist-informational mode of production and in our epoch' (1983a, p. 322) – a claim which is certainly broad, but which in specifying a time period is still rather more modest than that characteristic of his earlier theory.

There are, however, still problems in so far as Castells continues to underplay the specific context within which his observations are set. Pickvance (1985) has pinpointed the problem clearly, for he shows the way in which Castells takes urban movements in a very peculiar situation (Franco's Spain) to exemplify successful grass-roots mobilization and thereby generalizes from what the Madrid Citizen's movement did to develop a general theory while failing to appreciate the peculiar conditions in which they did it (notably the ban on political parties which meant that urban movements became an important substitute as vehicles for expressing popular demands and opposition). For Pickvance, it is not so much the nature of the movement (e.g. whether or not it encompasses the three concerns with collective consumption, state power and urban meaning) that is important in explaining its success or failure as the character of the times and places in which it appears, and he goes on to suggest that, for all the apparent changes in Castells's methodology over the years, his latest work is still marred by the tendency to abstract from specific contexts while ignoring the importance of variations between contexts: 'Referring back to Castells's earlier model . . . one can in fact see a striking *formal* parallel with the new model despite the change of content. In each case a single model is advanced, and an exemplar of an urban social movement pointed to in order to illustrate it. . . . In both cases contextual features were played down or ignored' (p. 36).

Duncan's criticism of the early Castells and Pickvance's criticism of the later work are both pointing to the same problem – namely, the tendency to establish generalizations through reference (in the first case tacit, in the second explicit) to specific cases with their own specific contextual conditions which render such generalizations highly problematic. Castells has not been alone in this, for as Szelenyi (1981a) recognized in an influential paper reviewing the problems in the 'new urban sociology', there was a strong tendency in much of the work conducted through the 1970s to take western capitalist cities as *the* paradigm of contemporary urbanism, and to ignore variations both between capitalist and non-capitalist (Third World or eastern European) societies, and within different western capitalist countries. It is precisely the growing recognition of this problem which has led researchers, whether wedded to a realist or ideal type methodology, to emphasize the need for comparative research in which historical and empirical differences are identified and explained rather than subsumed under general and all-embracing theories. In particular, it is clear that any conceptualization of 'the urban question' will need to be sensitive to the temporal and spatial context, for as Castells has himself argued, 'A city (and each type of city) is what a historical society decides the city (and each city) will be. Urban is the social meaning assigned to a particular spatial form by a historically defined society' (1983a, p. 302). This indicates that the meaning of urbanism will differ over different times and places as different interests struggle to realize the expression of their own values and aspirations. There can thus be no generic concept of urbanism.

The third area of criticism levelled against Castells's original methodology concerned its inherent functionalism. Again, Castells has himself agreed with this criticism (1985, p. 7), although the issues involved here are complex, and it is important to unravel them if we are to derive any lessons for the future.

Functionalist forms of explanation in the social sciences seek to account for the existence and persistence of social phenomena by analysing their effects. Phenomena are explained by pointing to the beneficial consequences which they have for social groups or social systems, such that once a social 'need' has been identified and it has been shown how this need is met by the existence of the phenomenon in question, the phenomenon itself is said to have been explained. The problem in such a logic of explanation is not that it analyses phenomena to discover their hidden or intended consequences, but that it takes these consequences as adequate grounds for the existence of the phenomena in the first place. There are two faults in this logic. The first is that social systems do not have 'needs' as such which have to be fulfilled. It is quite possible to argue that if something is not done (e.g. if capital does not make profit) then something will change in the system (e.g. firms will go bankrupt, people will lose their jobs and all sorts of pressures will mount for political and economic change), but this is quite a different proposition from that which says that capital *must* make profit. Unlike biological organisms which do have system needs and which die if those needs are not fulfilled, societies do not die, they change. The second fault in the logic is that, in deducing a cause from a consequence, functionalist explanations invert the temporal sequence of causality. Put another way, the tacit assumption is built into functionalism that someone or something is capable of recognizing system needs and of organizing social affairs so that these needs are met; for as Mennell, among others, has pointed out, 'Collectivities have no group mind, and therefore cannot merely be assumed to be goal-directed and purposive' (1974, p. 157). A teleological explanation thus normally depends upon the recognition of human agency in social affairs (e.g. the argument that the people running the government see a problem looming and act to forestall it), yet even explanations of this sort tend to be dubious given the limited capacity of any one group of actors either to anticipate problems or to act effectively to resolve them. Even the most powerful groups in our society, whether they be governments, big companies, banks, unions or professions tend to respond to short-term problems with little idea of the long-term consequences, and their actions generally have unanticipated results which may turn out to be quite different from those intended.

Both flaws in the functionalist logic can be found in the structuralist Marxism of the 1970s, but the problem of teleology is especially marked in this perspective given that it rules out any explanation involving conscious and purposive human agency. Castells's original analysis of collective consumption, and the theory of the state which this analysis entailed, was a case in point, for the growth of collective consumption in advanced capitalist societies was explained in terms of the functions which it performed in reproducing labour-power, and this argument itself rested on a theory of the state which saw it as necessarily performing certain functions on behalf of the dominant class, yet all of this was held to occur in the absence of any deliberate human intent.

As we saw earlier, the theory of the state which Castells employed was basically that developed by Poulantzas (1973). According to this theory, the capitalist state 'must' perform a regulative role within the mode of production of which it forms an integral part – this is the function of the political level. State intervention serves the purpose of fragmenting the working class while unifying the different fractions of the capitalist class within a 'power bloc' under the hegemony of monopoly capital. The long-term hegemony of monopoly capital is ensured by making short-term concessions to other classes as and when this is necessary, but the state 'cannot' pursue policies which fundamentally threaten the monopoly fraction's interests. This is what Castells meant when he argued in an early essay that, 'Not every conceivable intervention . . . is possible, because it must take place within the *limits* of the capitalist mode of production, otherwise the system would be *shaken* rather than regulated' (1976c, p. 166).

Although the state functions on behalf of monopoly capital, however, it is not subject to its dictates. There is a 'relative autonomy' between the economic and political levels of the system which means that, although big capitalist interests are hegemonic, they do not dictate what the state does. This, of course, follows from the structuralist foundations of the theory, for to argue that certain capitalists control or influence the state according to their own purposes (a so-called 'instrumentalist' conception of the state) would be to admit human agency into the heart of the explanation. Thus the state functions in certain necessary ways, but no one – not the capitalist class, nor the agents within the state system, nor any other interest in society – acts to ensure that it does so.

How, then, are these functions discharged and maintained? The answer given by Poulantzas and adopted by Castells is that the causal agency in the system is class struggle. Quite simply, the balance of class forces at any one time is reflected in state intervention (for example, the extension of collective consumption provisions to the working class at times when it is relatively strong) which then has the effect of damping down unrest and hence reproducing the hegemony of the dominant class fraction. Thus system contradictions generate an intensification of class struggle which in turn generates a state response which regulates the original contradictions. There is (to borrow a concept from Parsons's systems theory) a cybernetic process at work whereby the system regulates itself through perpetual feedback and adjustment. As Mennell observes, such cybernetic loops can provide a logical solution within functionalist theories to the teleology problem, for they explain how systems adjust to meet new needs without conscious human direction. However, as Mennell also observes, 'Empirical evidence for the existence of feedback has to be produced and explained in the usual way and the logical requirements for doing so extremely stringent' (1974, p. 160). In the case of Castells and Poulantzas, these requirements are not met on at least two counts.

First, it is by no means clear in their work why the cause of state intervention (class struggle) should *necessarily* result in functional effects (system regulation). Why is it not possible, as Szelenyi (1981b) suggested, for the state to be driven by an escalation of popular demands and mobilization to pursue policies that have a directly deleterious effect on the long-term profitability of monopoly capital? In their discussion of Poulantzas's state theory, Gold and his colleagues suggested that 'Although there is a fairly rich discussion of *how* the relative autonomy of the state protects the class interests of the dominant class, and of the functional *necessity* for such a state structure, there is no explanation of the social mechanisms which guarantee that the state will in fact function in this way' (1975, p. 38). The same criticism can be made against Castells, for his functional theory of the state rested wholly on the assumption that reform is always ameliorative as regards the working class and non-threatening as regards the long-term interests of monopoly capital. This argument always was dubious theoretically (for it can be argued that system change raises rather than regulates aspirations for further change (see Runciman 1966)) and unsubstantiated historically (for radicalism is often more intense during periods of reform than during periods of stability or retrenchment). Castells's assumption that political zeal varies inversely with political concessions rested on an astounding ignorance (sustained by his methodology) of how people typically understand and interpret their situations.

Second, it is impossible in this theory to disentangle empirically the cause and the effect. The only way we have of knowing that the working class is strong (and hence that the state should be responding with reforms) is when we see the state introducing reforms which benefit that class! The theory, in other words, rests on a classic tautology. Furthermore, as Pahl (1977b) suggests, it is immune to empirical evaluation since, no matter how far the state goes in supporting the interests of the working class, the theory always ensures in advance (a) that such interventions must be because the working class is strong at that time, and (b) that they must be in the interests of monopoly capital in that they will ensure system stability in the long run. The lack of any counterfactual condition in the theory means that, no matter what the state does, the theory will be able to cover it. As Lefebvre suggests, 'This structural (non-dialectical) analysis is not false. It is not true either. It is trivial. It bears no date. It can be true or false anywhere and everywhere' (1976, p. 66).

It is not clear how far in his later work Castells breaks with this functionalist mode of theorizing. He has claimed that the theory of the state which underpins the analysis in *The City and the Grassroots* is 'a total revision' of what was basically a Leninist theory employed in his earlier work. The basis for this claim is first, that the theory recognizes axes of domination other than class (Castells cites in addition autonomous state power, gender domination and cultural domination around ethnicity or nationality), and second that it sees the state less as the automatic pilot of monopoly capital and more as 'the crystallisation of class and other social struggles, that is both of processes of dominance of certain classes and groups and genders but also as the expression of the process of resistance to dominance by classes and social groups and genders'. Planning, he now says, is 'a battlefield which is, to some extent biased by the political domination imbedded in the state apparatus but at the same time wide open to whatever struggles develop in society' (1985, p. 8).

This formulation has not so much resolved the problems of the earlier theory as sidestepped them. To define the state as a battlefield in which the capitalist class and other dominant social interests command the high ground is to beg all the familiar questions of the relationship between state power and economic power on the one hand, and between structural necessities and political practices on the other. Castells seems to recognize the analytical weaknesses of his earlier theory, yet still seeks to apply its essential insights as if mere recognition of the problems is enough to overcome them. In *The City and the Grassroots*, for example, he asserts that 'The state is present in the capitalist mode of production, having a major repressive function and tending to represent the interests of the capitalist class' (p. 306), but how this function is maintained and how capitalist interests come to be represented is never examined. We are told that, 'The management of urban services by state institutions, while demanded by the labour movement as part of the social contract reached through class struggle, has been one of the most powerful and subtle mechanisms of social control and institutional power over everyday life in our societies' (p. 317), but this familiar argument still fails to explain the cybernetic feedback whereby services demanded by one class come to serve the interests of another. Similarly, in *The Economic Crisis and American Society*, published three years earlier, we again find the claim that, 'The intervention of the state is required by capital (in its process of accumulation and legitimization) and forced by labor (which demands a larger share of the product through forced socialized consumption)' (1980, p. 125), yet the necessary connection between functional effect and immediate cause is never explicated. We are told that, 'The intervention of the state takes place within the structural rules of capitalism for the purpose of overcoming the historical contradictions that arise during the latter stages of its development' (p. 130), yet the relation between structural constraints and political practices is never theorized, while the problem of attributing a 'purpose' to state intervention when the state itself is not an agent but a battleground is never considered. And we are warned that, 'The state cannot be seen as a pure instrument of the ruling class', nor is it 'an even mirror of the class struggle', but that, 'It is the product of a historical process characterized, in a capitalist society, by the continuous domination of capital' such that 'The state is the crystallization of this class domination, and its institutions will reflect fundamentally the interests of the bourgeoisie' (p. 153), yet nowhere in this essentially descriptive outline can we find an explanation of how class struggle comes to be refracted in such a way that economic domination is automatically translated into political domination in the absence of direct capitalist control of the state apparatus.

What I am suggesting, then, is that while much else has changed in Castells's work, the theory of the state has remained in its essentials very much the same. It is still basically a functionalist theory, and as such it still falls down on the fundamental problem of relating the structurally-necessary functions which the state is said to perform to the causes which are said to bring them about. It is not that such a theory is empirically false, for at a descriptive level it seems plausible to suggest that capitalist states do often respond to diverse interests while at the same time attempting to safeguard capital accumulation. The point, however, is that the theory employed by Castells, Poulantzas and others simply does not and cannot explain how this happens.

There is a crucially important lesson to be drawn from this. If it is true, as seems to be the case, that capitalist states do respond to the ebb and flow of political struggles, then simple instrumentalist theories which explain state outputs as the product of exclusive control by dominant class interests need to be rejected (as Poulantzas and Castells argue). Equally, if it is also true that such a response is uneven, and that some interests enjoy an 'inside track' within the state system, then simple pluralist theories which explain state outputs as the product of popular political pressures need also to be rejected (as Poulantzas and Castells also argue). This suggests that we need a perspective which explains both types of outcome – both the prevalence of key economic interests and the partial effects achieved by less powerful groups – yet this cannot be achieved by a single theory such as that proposed by Poulantzas and Castells since such an approach constantly collapses back into functionalism. Rather, we need to develop a mode of analysis which recognizes the crucial role of human agency in shaping state policy (as both instrumentalism and pluralism – and, for that matter, managerialism – do), but which also recognizes the potential and limitations of the different kinds of demands, interests and preferences which come to be expressed by different kinds of groups through different parts of the state system. Rather than choosing between theories such as instrumentalism, pluralism and managerialism as if they were mutually exclusive, we need in other words to understand their complementarity in the sense of tracing the contexts in which each of them is most likely to apply. This, in my view, is the only way out of the recurring problems which beset Castells's attempt to escape from functionalist teleology, and it is the logic behind the development of a 'dual theory of politics' in which the forces shaping the collective provision of consumption are seen as different from those shaping other aspects of state intervention and regulation. What such a dualistic theory might look like, and its relevance for understanding the activities of the state in a country like Britain in the contemporary period, are matters which are examined in Chapter 8.

This extended discussion of some of the methodological issues arising out of Castells's work over the years can usefully be drawn together by summarizing the three lessons which can be learned as regards future work in urban sociology. First, we saw that the development of general theories must be sensitive to the peculiarities of time in the sense that causal explanations must relate historical specificities to theoretical generalities. Both realist and ideal type methodologies provide means for doing this, the former through the distinction between contingency and necessity, the latter through the construction of partial 'individual types' which generalize from specific historical patterns of social organization. However, we also saw the dangers in a realist methodology of asserting untestable theories which remain immune to, and divorced from, historical analysis, and we concluded by reasserting the value of an ideal type methodology as the basis for hypothesis construction.

Second, we saw the importance of sensitivity to the peculiarities of space. Social relations vary, not only historically, but also geographically, and it is important to guard against a form of ethnocentrism in which generalizations built up on the basis of just one or two places are then extended to encompass all others. There is, in this sense, no general theory of 'the' capitalist state, but rather theories of capitalist states (see Duncan 1981, Jessop 1982, Paris 1983). Similarly, there can be no generic specification of 'the' urban question, but rather conceptualizations of the urban question as it appears in different places at different times.

Third, we saw the importance of guarding against functionalist forms of explanation by insisting on the pivotal role of human agency in any theory. As regards a theory of state power, this implies that we need to start, not by identifying the functions performed and then working backwards to discover their causes, but rather with an analysis of the pressures and demands being exerted by different groups, which will then enable us to work forwards in order to trace how these interests are realized or constrained within any particular system of state power. This implies an endorsement of theoretical pluralism (in that different theories may be seen, not as incommensurable, but as complementary) which in turn takes us back to a methodology of ideal types in which different aspects of reality may be identified and explained in terms of different complexes of causality.

These three themes – the use of ideal types in historical explanation, the dangers of confusing historically individual types with ahistorical and aspatial generic ones, and the need to combine types in any overall theory of state power – form the methodological guidelines for the argument developed in Chapter 8. The substance of that argument, however, is developed not from a critical analysis of Castells's methodology, but from reflections on and developments of his theoretical ideas concerning collective consumption, and it is to these that I now turn.

Substantive questions

In his earlier work, Castells specified 'the urban question' in terms of the organization of, and struggles over, collective consumption. In his later work, the urban is still conceptualized in this way, although two further dimensions are added – namely, state power (i.e. urban struggles are struggles against centralized, bureaucratic domination), and cultural meaning (i.e. urban struggles are struggles to impose new cultural forms in the face of domination by the mass media and the various centres of information control). In his later view, therefore, the focus on collective consumption is valid but partial and its essentially economic focus has to be complemented by an equal concern with political and cultural issues (1985, p. 7).

How useful or legitimate is it to conceptualize the urban in this way? In particular, how far can we follow Castells in seeing the issue of collective consumption as a necessary (if no longer sufficient) factor in the analysis of urbanism? The critical literature has focused on four related issues: the relation if any between cities as spatial units and the organization of collective consumption; the analytical separation of 'consumption' from 'production'; the distinction between 'individual' and 'collective' forms of consumption; and the significance of consumption as regards an understanding of class structure.

The first of these problems refers to the key theme of this book – namely the question of whether it is possible to identify some social process or object which corresponds to the spatial entity of the contemporary city. As we saw in Chapter 5, Castells believes that this is indeed possible, for cities in advanced capitalist countries represent the containers within which labour-power is produced and reproduced. They are spatial units for the reproduction of labour-power, and in so far as capitalist states have found it 'necessary' to socialize the costs of such reproduction through the development of welfare provisions, cities can thus be seen as units of collective consumption:

> 'What is an 'urban area'? A production unit? Not at all, insofar as the production units are placed on another scale (on a regional one at least). An institutional unit? Certainly not, since we are aware of the almost total lack of overlap between the 'real' urban units and the administrative segmentation of space. An ideological unit, in terms of a way of life proper to a city or to a spatial form? This is meaningless as soon as one rejects the culturalist hypothesis of the production of ideology by the spatial context. . . . What is, then, what is called an urban unit? . . . It is, in short, the everyday space of a delimited fraction of the labour force . . . it is a question of the process of reproduction of labour-power' (1977a, pp. 44–5).

This formulation has provoked two types of criticisms. One is that such a definition ignores other crucial processes which occur in cities and which 'must' be taken into account in any definition of urbanism (e.g. Lojkine 1977). The other is that it does not encompass the range of collective consumption in advanced capitalism, much of which is either aspatial or spatially organized on a scale beyond that of the city. In my view, the first of these criticisms is irrelevant while the second is profound.

The first criticism contains an obvious truth – cities are more than mere units of consumption. As we shall see in Chapter 7, for example, there is a very different tradition of Marxist urban research which sees the primary importance of the city, not in terms of consumption, but in terms of the production and circulation of capital. When we look at any major city and see the office blocks housing the headquarters of major companies, the factories producing all sorts of commodities, the road and rail links transporting these goods to their markets, the banks and retail outlets which speed up the circuit of capital between its money and commodity form, then it would indeed be fatuous to argue that all that is important about cities is the housing, schools, hospitals and other provisions which aid the reproduction of labour-power.

This, of course, is not what Castells is saying. As he makes clear in the afterword to *The Urban Question*, 'A concrete city (or an urban area, or a given spatial unit) is not only a unit of consumption. It is, of course, made up of a very great diversity of practices and functions. It expresses, in fact, society as a whole, though through the specific historical forms it represents. Therefore, whoever wishes to study a city (or series of cities) must also study capital, production, distribution, politics, ideology, etc.' (1977a, p. 440). His argument is not that collective consumption is the only important urban process, but is that it is the only specifically urban process. The acid test of this claim is not whether things other than consumption happen in cities, but is whether collective consumption is spatially limited to cities in the way Castells suggests.

Here the critics are on stronger ground. Mingione, for example, writes that, 'It is impossible to isolate "urban" needs from "non-urban" ones. The consumption process itself is not definable in a purely territorial context, it does not correspond to any "urban question" but is rather an important part of the general social question' (1981, p. 67). It is not just that consumption occurs in many different types and scales of spaces – in inner cities, in suburbia, in agricultural villages – but that its organization through the state takes two crucially different forms – namely, provision in kind (council housing, schools, old people's homes, children's homes) and provision in cash (housing allowances, student grants, pensions, family allowances). Provisions in kind are necessarily spatial in the sense that all objects entail spatial location and extension, but provisions in cash are not. Both, however, involve the state in providing the resources whereby people can reproduce themselves (albeit with different implications; as I shall argue in Chapter 8, provision in kind carries within it a potential for state control and direction which is not inherent in a system of money transfers). If the object is to focus on collective consumption and the reproduction of labour power then there seems little coherent rationale for analysing those forms of consumption which happen to be provided in kind within a given spatial setting, and those which take alternative forms.

Castells's definition of an object of analysis is, in fact, remarkably similar to Pahl's. Thus for Pahl, 'I tend to use the word "city" as shorthand for "a given context of configuration of reward-distributing systems which have space as a significant component". Thus housing and transportation are elements in my view of a city, family allowances and pension schemes are not. An *urban* resource or facility must have a spatial component' (1975, p. 10). The problem with both formulations is that what is a 'spatial resource' actually varies over time and between different countries. For example, in Britain the sale of council houses has resulted in a shift from state provision of spatial resources in kind (the construction and letting of housing) to state provision of non-spatial resources in cash (the growth of tax concessions on mortgage interest payments). The amount of public money going into housing is as great, if not greater, as before, yet on the Castells/Pahl definition, state support for urban consumption has declined dramatically. Similarly, recent moves by health authorities away from institutional and towards community-based care for the elderly, the handicapped and other such groups would qualify on this criterion as a reduction in collective consumption provision, yet the people themselves may be receiving more adequate support than before! At the heart of this sort of specification of the urban question, therefore, lies a taken for granted acceptance of current (ethnocentric) forms of state provision and budgeting as in some way the 'real' basis for urban studies; as governments shift between benefits in cash and benefits in kind, so urban sociology adjusts its research agenda accordingly!

It is clear from this that collective consumption is not an urban 'real object'. Rather, Castells's focus on spatial units of collective consumption as the object of urban research reflects his particular (and quite legitimate) interests. The reason why he is only interested in state provisions in kind is that the spatial dimension to such provisions carries with it the possibility of collective mobilization. When people are spatially concentrated on municipal housing estates, or when their children are brought together in the same place to be educated, or when they all rely on the same bus route to get them to work, or on the same local hospital when they are ill, a capacity exists for common organization which is not present among those who receive tax concessions through their pay packets or Giro cheques through the post. This is essentially the same point as was made in Chapter 1 regarding Marx's analysis of the city as an aid to the development of class organization and consciousness. Such a focus on spatial forms of consumption is fair enough, as long as it is recognized that this is only one aspect of the consumption question. What Castells has done, implicitly, is to set up an ideal type conceptualization of urban processes which excludes both non-consumption processes and consumption processes with no spatial component, for in this way he is able to focus on that slice of social reality which interests him most – namely, city-based movements oriented to welfare issues. As he himself recognizes at one point, 'The urban system is only a concept and, as such, has no other use than that of elucidating social practices and concrete historical situations in order both to understand them and to discover their laws' (1977a, p. 241).

It should come as no surprise to find that Castells's identification of the urban question is, notwithstanding his own claims to have discovered a 'real object', grounded in an ideal type construct. As Weber observed, 'All specifically Marxian "laws" and developmental constructs – insofar as they are theoretically sound – are ideal types' (1949, p. 103). Seen in this light, however, it is clear that there are no compelling grounds why we should accept this conceptualization of the urban question, for how we respond to Castells's research agenda will depend upon how we view its usefulness. For myself, I would argue that the restricted focus on spatial units of consumption precludes analysis of what are precisely some of the most interesting and pertinent issues regarding the sociology of consumption in the current period. In particular, it fails to address the question of why consumption provisions take the form they do (cash or kind) at particular periods (e.g. the growth of direct provision in kind through the 1960s as compared with the privatization of services in the 1980s), and what the implications are of any shift in this balance of provision. In other words, the problem with Castells's definition of the urban question lies in my view not in his focus on consumption, but in his concern to link this to spatial forms. As he himself recognizes, 'A "sociology of space" can only be an analysis of social practices given in a certain space. . . . Of course there is the "site", the "geographical" conditions, but they concern analysis only as the support of a certain web of social relations' (1977a, p. 442). As I read this, it is saying that the specification of sociological objects of inquiry entails a concern with objects and processes rather than with the spatial relations between these objects or the spatial location of these processes. If that is the case (and as we shall see in Chapter 7, such a view has been disputed), then the concern with consumption should not be hedged in and constrained by a lingering concern to locate it in the specific spatial context of the city.

Some writers have argued that the impossibility of correlating consumption (or any other process) with the city as a spatial unit makes it futile to search for a definition of urbanism (cf. Mingione 1981, p. 70, Paris 1983, p. 94). Others have been more positive in the sense that they have adopted Castells's focus on collective consumption as the basis for urban analysis while stripping it of any necessary spatial connotations. Dunleavy, for example, defines urban politics as 'the study of decision processes involved in areas of collective consumption' while stressing that, 'My usage of "urban" applies to collective consumption processes in any area of the country, without any specific spatial reference' (1980, pp. 2 and 3). In previous work, I too have suggested that the urban may be equated with collective consumption as the basis for a 'non-spatial urban sociology' (Saunders 1985b). The question of the social significance of space, and whether urban studies or any other social science can proceed in this way, will be considered in more detail in the next chapter. For the moment, however, we may simply note that whether or not we choose to designate collective consumption as 'urban' is merely now a matter of convention. What matters is not the label which we apply to the analysis of consumption issues, but how we proceed to study them, and this brings us on to the second area of criticism of Castells's substantive focus – the analytical split between consumption and production.

Where some critics have denied that collective consumption can form an object of analysis for urban sociology because it is not specific to cities, others have rejected it on the grounds that it reflects and perpetuates an artificial or even ideological division between two processes – production and consumption – which cannot be understood in isolation from one another. Castells, in other words, is said to have broken the fundamental methodological rule of dialectical materialism which, as we saw in Chapter 1, emphasizes the contradictory unity of the parts within the wider whole and hence denies the possibility of partial scientific analyses.

There is no shortage of such criticisms. For Mingione, 'The consumption process is only a partial aspect of the general production process. Production (in a strictly technical sense), distribution and consumption relations are highly interdependent and together form the social relations of production, i.e. the social structure. One cannot consider consumption processes separately from the other two aspects of the capitalist reproduction process' (1981, p. 66). Harloe's point is similar: 'It seems quite unhelpful to place a special emphasis on consumption considered in isolation from production, for they are inseparabie in the Marxist analysis of capitalism' (1979, p. 136), and Lojkine too is critical of any attempt to 'reduce policy simply to the "management of the reproduction of labour-power" (housing and social infrastructure) and exclude its economic dimension' (1977b, p. 142). Indeed, Lojkine it is who attacks the production/consumption division as 'ideological', arguing that it reproduces 'the ideological split – imposed by the ruling class – between factory life and life in the city' (1984, p. 219). Harvey too echoes this argument that the division between a sphere of work (production) and a sphere of community (consumption) is an artificial separation imposed by capitalism, and that analysis must go beyond such ideological appearances to uncover the essential unity of oppression which gives rise to struggles in both spheres: 'The separation between working and living is at best a surficial estrangement, an apparent tearing asunder of what can never be kept apart. And it is at this deeper level too that we can more clearly see the underlying unity between work-based and community-based conflicts' (1978b, p. 35). Some Marxist urban researchers – most notably Katznelson (1981) in the USA – have attempted to document the way this division between work and home, production and consumption, was brought about in the early development of capitalism, while a number of feminist researchers (e.g. McDowell 1983, MacKenzie and Rose 1983) have pointed to the significance of patriarchy and gender relations of domination in generating and sustaining it, and have tried to trace the 'underlying links' between the two spheres of domestic and industrial life (both of which, they point out, involve women in productive activity).

What, in the face of all this, can be said in defence of the sort of analytical distinction drawn by Castells between production and consumption? Is it useful or even possible to sustain an analysis of one without at the same time focusing on the other?

The first point to make about this is that Castells recognizes that production and consumption are interrelated. As Dunleavy points out, 'Castells has never suggested that the inter-relationships between production and consumption activity should be ignored' (1980, p. 47). As we have seen, his original concept of the urban system identified the three economic elements of production, consumption and exchange, together with the political and ideological levels, as all interrelating within the system. His focus on the consumption element as that aspect which was specific to the urban system was, furthermore, premised upon the recognition of its importance for capitalist production, not only through its role in reproducing labour-power, but also as a source of demand for the products of capitalist firms (e.g. the drug companies which supply the health service, or the builders who erect public housing) and as a means of counteracting falling profit rates by socializing costs which would otherwise be incurred by the private sector. Both in his work with Godard or Dunkerque (Castells and Godard 1974), where collective consumption was analysed precisely in terms of the contradiction between economic and social priorities which followed the development of two large industrial complexes, and in his subsequent work on the role of the state in the American economy (Castells 1980), he demonstrated a clear awareness of the wider economic and political significance of collective consumption provision.

Criticisms to the effect that Castells ignores the link between production and consumption are thus clearly unfounded. What really seems to be at issue in such criticisms, however, is how this link is theorized. It is my contention that what many of Castells's Marxist critics really find objectionable in his work is the recognition that consumption may generate its own effects, notably as regards the formation of social cleavages and political movements which cannot be theorized as mere phenomena of class power arising out of the organization of production. In other words, Castells's specific focus on consumption, while all the time relating it to production, class power and the role of the state in a capitalist economy, also opens up the possibility of identifying non-class bases of power and popular mobilization (as in his analysis of urban social movements) and non-class forms of popular aspiration and identity. In asserting the interrelation of production and consumption, what the critics are really asserting is the primacy of production and hence the centrality of a conventional class analysis. Castells recognizes the links between production and consumption, but what the critics seek to do is to reduce the analysis of consumption to the analysis of production. The way they do this is by equating consumption with reproduction.

Castells himself, of course, theorizes collective consumption in terms of its role in reproducing labour-power. The analysis is grounded in Marx's theory of value according to which 'The value of labour-power is the value of the means of subsistence necessary for the maintenance of its owner' (Marx 1976, p. 274). Marx argues that the 'necessary' level of such subsistence is determined socially, by what is considered 'normal' in any given society at any given time, rather than biologically, and that unlike other commodities, the value of labour-power therefore 'contains a historical and moral element' (p. 275). Thus, for example, the value of an unskilled worker's labour-power in England is higher than that of a similar worker in India precisely because working-class living standards are different in the two countries.

The obvious problem with this formulation is that it rules out even the possibility that a gap may develop between the level of subsistence necessary to reproduce labour-power and the level of provision for workers' consumption needs. Whatever the working class achieves in raising its living standards is automatically deemed necessary if its labour-power is to be reproduced satisfactorily from the point of view of capitalist employers. If it is in the long-term interests of the capitalist class that labour-power be reproduced adequately, and if the criterion for this is that workers must be in a position to consume up to the normal standards prevailing in their society at that time, then it follows that whatever workers receive in the way of wages or state services 'must' be necessary if the capitalist system of production is to continue to function properly. This proposition lays the basis for the logically impeccable yet historically absurd thesis that, say, centrally-heated council houses with garages and gardens, or the teaching of foreign languages and social studies in schools, or the provision of free meals in hospitals, or an increase in the level of old age pensions, must all in fact be necessary if capitalist firms are to continue to exploit labour-power and accumulate profits. Every working-class gain short of a fundamental transformation of the whole capitalist system thus turns out on closer inspection to be in the interests of the capitalist class (although each gain may also hasten the development of contradictions which threaten the system).

There has been growing dissatisfaction with this kind of reasoning in recent years. In his review of reproduction theories, Connell (1983, ch. 8) takes issue with the static conception which seems to be built into them – the assumption that time is simply a succession of repeated patterns and that human agency can do little to bring about system change. As he observes:

> If dynamics are not recognised, we have functionalism. . . . It is, I suggest, a problem embedded in the very language of 'social reproduction'. Reproduction analysis, to put it in the most general way, is based methodologically on a bracketing of history which, unless the most strenuous efforts are made to prevent it, must suppress the agency of people in creating history, in creating the very structures whose reproduction is being examined (1983, p. 148).

The insistence on theorizing 'consumption' as 'reproduction' reflects the basic premise of any Marxist urban theory that the organization of production plays a determinate role in shaping social processes. Consumption, therefore, has to be analysed in terms of its contribution to the production system – whether in terms of providing labour-power (as in Castells's original formulation) or more generally in underpinning the class relations around which production is structured. It is this initial starting point which leads to the functionalist arguments criticized by Connell, for although subsequent writers have attempted to avoid a simple reduction of consumption to production, and hence to recognize the specific effects which are associated with particular 'modes of consumption', such analyses continue to be flawed by their claims that production is both primary and determinate.

The clearest example of this can be found in a study by Preteceille and Terrail which explicitly sets out to avoid any simple reduction of consumption to production while at the same time retaining a notion of production as the determining factor. As they explain the problem with earlier formulations, 'A proper insistence on the determining character of the social relations of production has overshadowed not only the necessary analysis of the specific structure of modes of consumption, but also an analysis of the relations between the two spheres, which has been reduced to a single, mechanistic determination' (1985, p. 4). Yet as their analysis proceeds, so they too inevitably develop a strongly functionalist model which ultimately collapses back into precisely the sort of 'mechanistic reduction' which they set out to avoid.

Preteceille and Terrail begin by criticizing 'bourgeois theories' which, they say, take consumer preferences and demands as given without explaining their origins. In their view, needs expressed in the sphere of consumption can only be explained by analysing the way capitalist production is organized. To explain why people have certain needs as consumers, it is necessary first to understand the 'needs' of the production system – the need to renew labour power, to create new skills, to slot people into their work roles and to perpetuate the existing form of social organization. Although these needs are not necessarily met (which enables the authors to claim that their's is not a functionalist theory), they do tend to generate forms of consumption which are appropriate to their resolution. This is achieved when individuals 'internalize' system needs as their own – e.g. when they demand forms of education which will enable them to secure employment, or when they ask their doctors for medicines which will overcome depression or fatigue and thus enable them to continue to function as productive workers. Preteceille and Terrail never really explain how this process of internalization is accomplished, for as they themselves recognize, they lack a theory of social psychology, but it is evident from their argument that state provision is important in this process (i.e. the state provides for needs in a form which is consistent with those required by the production system – by laying down educational standards and curriculum contents, for example, or by emphasizing curative rather than preventative forms of health care), as is the 'ideological message' encoded in commodity exchange in the private sector (e.g. the image of the consumer as sovereign which is perpetuated despite the obvious real limits on consumers imposed by the limited purchasing power which reflects the wage system in the sphere of production).

In advanced capitalism, both individual and collective consumption has expanded, but it is crucial to the Preteceille/Terrail thesis that this has done little to meet people's real needs. Rather, as the intensity of production has been stepped up, so the need to consume has increased as a result: 'The need for an increase in consumption, and of new forms of consumption, is only a response to the demands of this increasing wearing out of the labour force, and its consequences. Thus in order to achieve the same result, the reproduction of the same labour power, it is necessary to have a higher level of consumption, and thus a higher real income' (1985, p. 107). If households can now buy vacuum cleaners, dishwashers and other such commodities, this is simply to facilitate the increased exploitation of female labour which is released to work more hours outside the home while still performing the necessary level of domestic duties within it. If car ownership has expanded, this is simply a reflection of the need for workers to travel greater distances in shorter times to their place of employment. If millions of working-class people can now afford foreign holidays, this is simply because their need for recuperation has intensified as a result of changes in the organization of their working lives.

This increased pressure has also led to increased demands for state provision – for nursery schools to allow mothers to return to employment, for public transport to whisk workers to and from their office and factories, and so on. Such provisions invariably fall short of people's real (but perhaps not consciously realized) needs. As they expand, so their costs begin to erode private sector profitability while their inadequacies foster resentment and stimulate yet further demands. Preteceille and Terrail recognize that different consumers will press for different kinds of demands and hence that the consumption sphere generates cleavages rather than alliances (as had been supposed in Castells's original theory), but again these divisions are explained by relating them back to production relations. Thus different groups of workers experience different material conditions in employment which then generate different needs as expressed through consumption:

> The low attendance by workers in theatres . . . is not only because of tiredness and lack of time, but is also the outcome of a lack of interest, of cultural distance, of a profound feeling that this is something for 'them', not 'us'. The same statement can be made about education and training, reading, health care or exercise. Capital weighs down on the dominated class and shapes its needs by constricting them. But this is not a 'purely' ideological process: it is a process with a material basis in the conditions of daily life (p. 175).

The political challenge facing the left is therefore seen as breaking down these restricted notions of need and generating new needs (hence new demands) among working people through changing their material practices (e.g. by radical innovations in local politics, by encouraging and supporting self-management schemes in industry, and so on).

The importance of this approach is that it recognizes that consumption generates some independent effects. As Preteceille (1985) makes clear in a later paper, one's position in the organization of production does not totally determine one's consumption pattern (inheritance of material and cultural capital, for example, varies widely between different people in the same class location), and consumption can act back upon the social relations of production (e.g. divisions between different groups of consumers expressing different needs may fragment a social class). Nevertheless, he continues to assert that production is determining in the sense that divisions expressed through consumption can only be explained in terms of the divisions generated through production. This argument directly reflects a functionalist theory of system needs.

Preteceille and Terrail deny that their's is a functionalist theory on the grounds that they recognize that system needs may not be met. Yet no sophisticated functionalist theory would claim that all system needs are inevitably met (see, for example, Merton 1968, on functions and dysfunctions). In fact, their analysis, which is centrally concerned to show how the needs expressed by individuals through consumption are the product of system needs created in the organization of production, not only begs all the familiar questions about how system needs are to be identified, but also directly mirrors more conservative functionalist theories in its emphasis on the internalization by individuals of system imperatives. As they put it, 'Social needs are, *essentially*, no more than the objective demands of the mode of production with regard to its agents' (p. 58). What is entailed here is a strong version of functionalist socialization theory in which individuals somehow learn to express in their everyday practices desires and preferences which are consistent with those required by a capitalist economy. How this is done remains a mystery, however, for (unlike Parsonian systems theory) we are offered no theory of the personality and cultural 'systems', nor of how they interrelate with the social, economic and political systems.

The result, predictably, is tautology: as in Castells's earlier formulations, so too in Preteceille and Terrail's analysis, any apparent improvement in the conditions of working-class life is explained simply as a reflection of changed system needs. The possibility that capitalism may be able increasingly to meet people's needs is ruled out from the start: the growth of car ownership, home ownership, foreign travel, educational opportunities and the rest is explained simply as the response of the system (mediated through the demands of its socialized members) to increased exploitation in production.

Now it has, of course, to be accepted that the social organization of consumption relates to, and to some extent reflects, the way production in society is organized. But then, every aspect of social life obviously relates in some way to every other aspect. It is certainly the case, for example, that people's location in the organization of production sets limits upon their range of action as consumers (we cannot buy a house, for example, if we lack a regular household income of the appropriate size), but this does not mean that consumption has to be analysed as functional to production (as in Castells's focus on the reproduction of labour-power), or as a response to production (as in Preteceille and Terrail's focus on the creation and intensification of needs). Every position we occupy and role we play sets limits upon our capacity for action in some other role, but this does not mean that we cannot analyse particular aspects of social life without all the time relating them back to some prior, holistic conception of the total 'system' of which they form a part.

There are, in short, no necessary grounds for asserting that consumption is determined by production, and that a sociological analysis of consumption must always proceed by way of an analysis of production. The fact that the two spheres are related does not mean that both are subject to the same logic, nor that one is necessarily a function of the other. It is therefore quite legitimate to identify consumption as a specific area for study (as Castells does), and thus to investigate the specific patterns of inequalilty, political struggle and cultural identity which develop there. Indeed, it is my contention that the repeated attempts by Marxist urban theorists to relate such inequalities, struggles and identities back to a more 'fundamental' class analysis grounded in a concern with production have not only led inevitably into functionalist culs-de-sac, but have also obscured our understanding of some crucial changes which are located in, and derive from, the organization of consumption itself, and which are having the most profound effects on our society as a whole, and on class relations in particular.

At the heart of these changes is the growing economic, political and cultural significance of the division between collective and individual forms of consumption. As I shall argue below and in Chapter 8, the basic class division between those who own and control the means of production and those who do not is today increasingly being overlaid by an equally important division between those who own and control crucial means of consumption and those who do not – i.e. a division, which cuts right across the class structure, between those with access to individual forms of consumption and those who are reliant on collective provision. This distinction between individual and collective consumption is basic to any sociological analysis of consumption in the contemporary period. Like the division between production and consumption, it derives out of Castells's work, and it too has been the subject of some critical argument and refinement.

The main problem is simply to determine what is designated by the term 'collective'. As Mingione suggests, 'If we add the adjective "collective" to the word "consumption" we raise a number of questions which French neo-Marxist urban sociology scholars have not answered. What can be called collective consumption and what individual consumption?' (1981, pp. 66–7). At first sight, this may look like academic semantic quibbling, but the implications of different definitions of collective and individual consumption can be significant.

In his earliest formulations, Castells took collective consumption to refer to 'consumption processes whose organization and management cannot be other than collective given the nature and size of the problems' (1976b, p. 75). In later works, however, he specified the term more clearly as referring to 'processes which are largely determined by state activity' (1978, p. 179). It is not always clear, therefore, whether consumption is 'collective' because it is communal (a view also found in Lojkine 1976) or because it is socialized. Many communally-consumed resources are supplied by the private sector (theatres, coaches, etc.) while many resources provided by the state are not communally-consumed (housing being the clearest example). Furthermore, there appears to be some confusion over whether 'collective consumption' is inherently collective given factors like size, accessibility and 'neighbourhood effects' (e.g. roads or city parks – see Friedman 1962, ch. 2), or is historically variable (as in the 'privatization' of certain aspects of consumption by the Thatcher governments in the 1980s in Britain).

These sorts of issues have been widely discussed in the literature (see Pahl 1977a and 1978, Saunders 1979, ch. 3), and as Harloe (1979) suggests, Castells himself seems to have settled on a definition which limits collective consumption to social provisions provided and managed by the state, irrespective of whether they are consumed individually or collectively. Even so, problems remain with such a formulation, for some goods or services may be provided by the private sector and dispensed or managed by the state (e.g. public housing or drugs), others will be provided and dispensed by the private sector yet subsidised or regulated by the state (e.g. owner-occupied housing or private medicine), and yet others will be provided and managed wholly within the public sector (e.g. state schooling or social work services). Such variations may have significant economic, political and ideological implications such that their subsumption under a single and all-embracing category is likely to prove unhelpful.

The clearest and most useful attempt to clarify the concept of collective consumption, and to distinguish it from individual consumption, has been made by Dunleavy. In his initial formulation (1980, ch. 2), he established five criteria for determining collective consumption. The concept, he argued, precluded money transfers, referred to services rather than commodities, and covered only those services which were collectively organized and managed, allocated on non-market criteria, and paid for at least partially out of taxation. In a later paper (1983), he then developed these ideas more rigorously in the form of a typology of consumption.

Following Castells, Dunleavy defines 'consumption' as 'the final appropriation of products by people'. This enables him to rule out of his analysis both the consumption by firms of raw materials which are transformed into some other commodity, and the provision by the state of transfer payments in cash (since money is not itself consumed but is used to buy objects which people then 'appropriate').

The next step in the analysis is to distinguish 'autonomous consumption' (where people consume what they have themselves produced) from 'commodified consumption' (where they consume things provided either by private firms through the market, or by professional interests through bureaucratic systems of allocation), and the latter category is then itself subdivided into 'individualized' and 'socialized' forms. For Dunleavy, individualized consumption refers to those goods and services marketed without state subsidy, while socialized consumption covers those provided either with subsidies or through non-market channels. Socialized consumption is then itself broken down into 'quasi-individualized consumption' (private goods marketed with a subsidy – e.g. owner-occupied housing), 'quasi-collective consumption' (private services provided with a subsidy, such as the theatre, or provided outside the market, such as voluntary welfare services), and 'collective consumption' proper (which is thus limited to public services which are either non-marketed – e.g. schools and health care – or marketed with a subsidy – e.g. public transport).

Dunleavy argues that 'socialized consumption' as conceptualized in this paper 'provides a clear analytical solution to the problems of delimiting a field of urban studies' (1983, p. 9). Urban sociology, therefore, is concerned with more than just collective consumption (for it encompasses quasi-individual and quasi-collective forms of provision) but with less than consumption as a whole, since it precludes analysis of individualized consumption (i.e. the consumption of unsubsidized private goods and services through the market), or of autonomous consumption (i.e. self-provisioning), or of cash payments made by the state in order to facilitate consumption. As I shall argue in Chapter 8, such a limited specification of urban studies seems arbitrary and unnecessarily restrictive, but the typology itself is enormously useful in clarifying the different forms of consumption, each of which may have very different implications in terms of patterns of inequality and political domination in contemporary capitalist societies.

The key implication, which Dunleavy himself traces in this and in other work, concerns the development of new forms of political cleavage arising out of the organization of consumption and cutting across the vertical lines of class cleavage generated in the production sphere. Even more than Castells, Dunleavy recognizes that consumption may be crucial in influencing political alignments.

As we have already noted, Castells recognized from his earliest writings that political mobilization around issues of collective consumption rarely occurred on straight class lines. His initial theory of urban social movements, for example, held that waged workers, professionals, white-collar workers and even petty-bourgeois small traders and capitalists could mobilize in common over consumption issues, and that this could enable socialist or communist parties to build broad, popular alliances in support of an overall challenge to the capitalist system despite the separation and antagonism of these different classes in respect of workplace politics.

This theory has been criticized and largely discredited. Pickvance (1977b), for example, took issue with what he called the 'urban fallacy' of assuming that groups which may share common interests in particular consumption issues will as a result be willing to join in a radical anti-monopoly capital alliance whose main aim is to transform the social organization of production. The idea that individuals whose economic situations (wages, conditions of work, standard of living, etc.) were in all other respects totally divergent may nevertheless somehow be forged into a unified political bloc fighting together for socialism simply because a local hospital was threatened with closure or a neighbourhood bus route was withdrawn was clearly little more than wishful thinking. Such an argument could only be entertained by totally ignoring the subjective dimension of the actors' own views of their situations, for while it is true that consumption issues can result in a willingness on the part of the middle classes to join with less privileged groups in limited protests over specific consumption issues, it is also obvious that this is unlikely to eclipse actors' awareness of the other factors which divide them.

Rather than assuming that consumption issues can unite classes which are normally opposed, it is empirically and theoretically more plausible to suggest that such issues may be expected to fragment classes which are normally unified. For every example of an urban movement which draws on a pluri-class social base, there are probably many more of consumption cleavages cutting through a single class and setting its members against each other. Like gender, ethnicity and nationality, consumption location tends to be class-divisive, and this is especially the case in a context (such as that in Britain since the late 1970s) where collective consumption provisions are being selectively cut back. As Harloe and Paris (1984) recognize, a government strategy of reducing public expenditure on consumption provision and of privatizing consumption wherever feasible is unlikely to generate any unified opposition because of the cross-cutting pressures which such a strategy generates. A 'crisis of collective consumption', far from provoking broad and radical opposition (as Castells originally assumed), is thus more likely to create political confusion, fragmentation and ineffectiveness.

In a later paper, Pickvance (1985) has made the further and crucially important point that consumption issues do not necessarily stimulate 'progressive' or socialistic popular responses. A policy of privatization, for example, may represent a threat to some working-class people while providing an opportunity for others. The sale of council houses may be experienced as an attack by those on the waiting list for council accommodation, but for those existing tenants who aspire to buy their homes, it represents an unprecedented chance to realize their personal objectives. Similarly, privatization of certain municipal services may hit those workers who provide the service (e.g. by reducing wage levels) while benefiting working-class ratepayers (e.g. by reducing charges). Again, therefore, we see the tendency to fragmentation rather than fusion, polarization rather than unification, associated with the politics of consumption.

This political fragmentation has been documented in the case of Britain by Patrick Dunleavy (1979, 1980) who explains the growing 'class dealignment' in voting patterns as in large part a product of the increasing significance of the division between the public and private sectors in areas such as housing and transport. Controlling for social class, he shows that home ownership and car ownership appear to be highly significant variables associated with conservative voting (home owners, for example, are almost twice as likely to vote for the Conservative Party as council tenants), and he argues from this that 'consumption location' is a major factor, equivalent to occupational class location, in shaping political alignments.

Dunleavy's analysis has received considerable empirical support from other sources. Work in Greater Manchester by Duke and Edgell, for example, shows a high degree of working-class political fragmentation consequent upon variations in consumption patterns, and concludes that 'Political party alignment is influenced more by overall consumption location than by social class' (1984, p. 195). Analysis of the 1983 general election result indicates the political significance of housing tenure as a major consumption cleavage, for among manual workers, the Labour Party attracted only 5 per cent more support than the Conservatives, and the major factor associated with working-class Conservative voting was home ownership. Indeed, among those who had purchased their council houses, no fewer than 56 per cent voted Conservative compared with just 18 per cent who voted Labour (Crewe 1983). Case study evidence, such as my own work in the London Borough of Croydon (Saunders 1979), also tends to support the view that public/private divisions, at least as regards housing, are a major basis of political alignment and mobilization in local politics, while cross-cultural research (e.g. Kemeny 1980) has suggested that high rates of privatized consumption of housing can generate a strongly conservatizing influence as regards people's orientation to the welfare state and collective provision generally. Furthermore, more recent work by Dunleavy himself suggests that consumption sector cleavages, which come into being as a result of increased state involvement in the provision of consumption, may react back upon state programmes as the public/private sector division assumes increasing ideological significance (Dunleavy 1985).

Such evidence must, of course, be treated with some caution. Dunleavy's analysis has, for example, been questioned by Franklin and Page (1984) who cite evidence to suggest that consumption issues such as housing policy do not figure centrally in voters' minds at election times, and who argue that political socialization is still far more significant in affecting voting behaviour than consumption location. Clearly more research is needed into the relation between consumption sector cleavages and political alignments before any clear evaluation of Dunleavy's thesis is possible, and such work will need to go beyond mere studies of voting to consider other (arguably more significant) indicators of political alignment and political ideology.

More important than this, however, is the need to extend Dunleavy's analysis of consumption sectors beyond the political context. Again taking housing as the example, it is now irrefutable that home owners in Britain have often been able to generate large and real material gains from their housing – gains which have not been available to public sector tenants (see, for example, Farmer and Barrell 1981). It is also highly plausible to suggest that home owners may experience much more control and autonomy in their everyday lives outside of the formal workplace than is possible for those who rent their accommodation from the state (see, for example, Ward 1985). Such economic and cultural aspects of consumption location are just as crucial for a sociological analysis of consumption sector cleavages as the political effects in terms of party alignment, but they receive scant attention in Dunleavy's work. As we shall see in Chapter 8, the significance of social relations of consumption for an understanding of class and inequality in a society like Britain goes beyond mere political realignment, for as Mingione (1981) suggests, we are witnessing a process of 'social disgregation' and 'social restratification' within society as a whole in which the changing organization of consumption is playing a pivotal role.

Such considerations have taken us a long way from Castells's original analysis of collective consumption. We have seen in this chapter that Castells's initial focus has to be reconceptualized. In particular, it is clear that the analysis of collective consumption has to be made more sensitive to the different patterns of state management, subsidy and provision, that a focus on consumption should be alert to the fragmentation and restratification of class relations in the contemporary period, and that consumption effects can and must be analysed on their own terms without constantly seeking to explain them in terms of the 'functions' they are held to perform for a system of capitalist production. We have also seen that Castells's attempt to conceptualize the city as a unit of consumption is unhelpful, and that a sociology of consumption can only be developed once we break with the specific spatial orientation which has characterized urban studies up to the present day.

Unlike most of the other approaches to the 'urban question' discussed in previous chapters, Castells's focus on issues of consumption does at least open up the possibility of a coherent research agenda. To adopt such an agenda, however, means dropping the hitherto distinctive focus on the city as an object of analysis, for the organization of consumption is no more spatially delimited than any of the other processes identified in earlier urban theories. Paradoxically, however, we reach this conclusion at a time when some urban theorists have begun to reassert the specific significance of spatial organization in social and economic life. Before developing a framework for the sociological analysis of consumption in Chapter 8, it is thus necessary to address head-on the issue which has rippled through the whole of this book so far of whether spatial forms in general, and the city in particular, can constitute a significant object of analysis for urban studies in the context of advanced capitalist societies. This is the concern of Chapter 7.

7 A non-spatial urban sociology?

One of the most important legacies of Castells's assault on urban sociology in his early work has been the recognition that theorists and practitioners alike have tended to identify phenomena as 'urban' when their causes lie not in the existence of cities, but in the organization of society as a whole. Although Castells's critique of such approaches was grounded in an epistemology which he and many others have subsequently come to reject, it is notable that, among all the changes in his work over the years since then, he has remained consistent in his view that such formulations are fundamentally flawed. In his reflections on *The Urban Question*, for example, he states that he still stands by the critique of urban sociology developed there: 'It contains some mistakes but basically I would not change much' (1985, p. 6).

One of the puzzles surrounding his work, however, is that having demolished urban sociology, he then set about rebuilding it around the concept of collective consumption. As we saw in the last chapter, this concept can, when suitably clarified and revised, provide the basis for a sociological research programme which is both coherent and pertinent to the analysis of key aspects of contemporary capitalist societies, but Castells's attempt to tie it to the analysis of cities was unsuccessful. State provision of means of consumption is not specific to cities, nor to any other spatial units save for the space bounded by nation-states themselves. Indeed, this is implicitly recognized by Castells himself in so far as his analyses of collective consumption, while located in cities, have not generally explored the significance of this spatial context. Even in *The City and the Grassroots*, it is apparent that his focus is on the social processes which he finds going on in urban areas rather than on the areas themselves. Andrew Sayer makes the point clearly when he suggests:

> Castells . . . repeatedly refers to space and 'urban space', but these turn out to be references to objects whose spatial structure and setting is then ignored. Certainly, when we talk about housing and factories we are referring to things which could not possibly be aspatial, but this hardly justifies the claim that

space is being discussed properly, for we are told nothing about the internal spatial organisation of these objects or their spatial relations with other objects. . . . What Castells offers is more in the nature of classification of objects, activities and social relations in 'urban space' rather than an analysis of their spatial form (1979, pp. 65–6).

Now it is important to clarify at the outset just what is at stake in the issues raised by this sort of criticism. Sayer is not claiming that Castells's analysis is *aspatial*, but that it is to all intents and purposes *non-spatial*. The distinction is crucial, for as we saw in Chapter 1, it is quite possible to argue that in the modern period spatial units below the level of the nation state have lost their social significance without also arguing that space is therefore totally irrelevant to social scientific analysis. Weber, Durkheim and Marx and Engels all believed that the city had been eclipsed as a significant economic, political or cultural unit, but they also all recognized that the spatial context of social action could and did still play an important role in sustaining or inhibiting the development of particular kinds of action. Their analyses, in other words, were not aspatial, for they understood how spatial proximity could, for example, help foster a sense of class consciousness among city-based factory workers, or could aid the erosion of a powerful collective morality, but they were non-spatial, in the sense that the explanations for such phenomena were located in changes current in the society as a whole which were not specific to cities or any other form of human settlement. Much the same point can be made in respect of Castells's work, for as we saw in Chapter 6, his focus on urban-based collective consumption provisions took space into account as a factor tending to promote or inhibit collective political mobilization, but his primary focus was on the contradiction between consumption and production within the economy as a whole. In short, a non-spatial social science does not preclude the possibility of analysing spatial organization as a secondary factor, but it does deny the relevance of spatial form as an object of study in itself.

In this chapter, we shall consider some of the contemporary theoretical work in geography and sociology which claims that space cannot be analysed simply as a secondary factor, and which thus develops a critique of non-spatial social science. Throughout this discussion, however, it is important to bear in mind that what is at issue is not whether, as one recent influential book repeatedly asserts, 'space matters' (Massey 1984), but how much it matters. No one is arguing for an aspatial sociology any more than an ahistorical sociology: the issue is simply whether space is so crucial to sociological explanation that it must be a central and primary constitutive element of any sociological analysis.

In this chapter we shall consider two streams of thought which assert the centrality of space to social analysis. The first, associated mainly with the Marxist geography of writers such as David Harvey and Doreen Massey, attempts to theorize space in terms of its role in the process of capital accumulation, circuits of capital and capitalist restructuring. The second, associated principally with the sociological theory of Anthony Giddens and with the realist sociology of writers such as John Urry, has connections with the first approach, but its focus is wider than simply the operation of the capitalist economy, and it attempts to theorize space as a constitutive element of social interaction. Both approaches are rich with theoretical insight, and both amply demonstrate the inadequacy of an aspatial social science, but neither in my view establishes the much more problematic case for placing 'space' (still less 'urban space' or the 'city') at the centre of social scientific inquiry.

As a prelude to this discussion, and by way of a summary of the core theme which has developed in earlier chapters, this chapter begins with a brief résumé of the problem of relating spatial categories to social processes – a problem which has been explicitly addressed by various different traditions within urban sociology during the twentieth century but which has thus far eluded a solution.

Beyond a sociology of the city

We saw in Chapter 1 that, despite their very different methodological approaches and substantive concerns, Marx, Weber and Durkheim all came to very similar conclusions as regards the analysis of urban questions. All agreed that the city played an historically specific role in the development of western capitalism (although as we also saw, even this has been disputed by later historians), but they all also argued that once capitalism had become established, the city ceased to be a theoretically significant entity. This was because it was no longer the expression and form of a new mode of production (Marx), or because it ceased to be the basis of human association, social identity and political domination (Weber), or because it no longer corresponded to the geographical boundaries within which the division of labour was integrated (Durkheim). To the extent that these writers discussed the city in the context of their analyses of capitalist–

industrial societies, they treated it either as an illustration of the most developed tendencies within such societies (class polarization, bureaucratic rationality, anomic social disorganization), or as a secondary condition of the development of certain tendencies (notably, class struggle or the erosion of the collective conscience). The city, in other words, was not treated as a significant object of analysis in its own right, nor were spatial units other than the nation state itself invested with any great sociological importance. Urban questions were addressed only in so far as they could contribute to a wider understanding of certain processes associated with modernity.

The development of urban sociology as a distinct sub-discipline with its own journals, departments, associations and professional chairs changed all this, for urban sociology was premised on the assumption that cities were theoretically important in their own right, that certain social phenomena were characteristic of and peculiar to urban areas, and that it was therefore possible and necessary to generate specific theories of urbanism in order to explain distinctively urban phenomena. These assumptions were reinforced academically by a judicious, selective and generally uncritical reading of certain key works by writers such as Tönnies and Simmel, and were sustained practically by the willingness of governments and certain private foundations to fund work which would generate explanations if not solutions for problems which were generally manifested in large cities, be they poverty, crime, mental stress, racial tension or whatever. In confronting such problems through empirical work and through participation in the fledgling town planning movement, sociologists were inevitably led to the basic problem of how the city was to be conceptualized, for only by resolving this question was it possible to identify the specific problems that urban sociology could analyse and the range of factors which it might identify in its search for explanations.

So it was that the search began for an 'urban' object of analysis. Other sociological sub-disciplines each had their own specific object – the family, crime, organizations, religion or whatever – and although all of these could be observed in cities, none of them could be colonized by this new sub-discipline as objects distinctively of cities. What was needed, and what was to prove so elusive, was the specification of some social process or phenomenon which could be related to a physically-bounded area within the confines of the nation state. The subsequent theoretical history of urban sociology has been the history of a search for a sociological entity corresponding to the physical entity of the city. It has been the history of an institutionalized sub-discipline in search of a rationale for its own existence.

We have seen that four principal 'solutions' have been put forward in response to this problem. None of them has been successful, although each of them has contributed much by way of empirical work (as in the Chicago school ethnographies – see Hannerz 1980, ch. 2) or through analysing processes which, while not distinctively 'urban', are nevertheless crucial to other areas of sociological research. The problems encountered within each approach, together with the empirical or theoretical legacy which they left behind, are summarized in Figure 1.

The first attempt to develop a distinctive conceptual framework for urban sociology was Robert Park's theory of human ecology. However, as we saw in Chapter 2, this approach was from its very inception torn between a concern to explain processes of city growth and differentiation on the one hand, and processes of human adaptation to environmental changes within society as a whole on the other. In terms of the former, Chicago human ecology was a theory of the city, but in terms of the latter it was a theory of unconscious processes of competition and adaptation which occur in any human aggregate.

This division was the product of a methodological confusion, for like Durkheim, Park sought both to ground knowledge in observation of the world and to discover underlying causal processes which could not be observed directly. This logical contradiction lay at the heart of the contradiction in the theory itself. As a theory of the (observable) city, there was no reason to limit analysis to the biotic level of human organization, for as Firey, Alihan and other critics pointed out, the city was as much a product of cultural processes as of biotic ones. As a theory of adaptation, by contrast, there was no reason to limit its empirical reference to cities, for as Hawley, Duncan and others went on to show, such processes could equally be analysed in relation to any social groups, organizations or institutions. Increasingly, therefore, a split developed within the ecological tradition. One set of researchers held on to the city as the empirical object of analysis but jettisoned the theoretical focus on biotic struggles, and in this way they continued the Chicago school ethnographic tradition but lost any coherent theoretical framework through which to order and situate their observations. The result was a long series of demographic mapping exercises produced by quantitative researchers, and a tradition of community studies produced by qualitative ones, but both

Definition of 'urban'	*Analytical tension*	*Legacy*
Ecological system	(a) theory of the city (observable processes) versus (b) theory of adaptation (non-observable biotic forces)	(a) community studies/ ethnographies (b) functionalist sociology
Cultural form	(Simmel) (a) sociology of number versus (b) sociology of modernity (Wirth) (a) demographic analysis versus (b) class/life cycle analysis	(a) theories of moral density (b) cultural theories of capitalism
Socio-spatial system	(Pahl) (a) sociology of spatial inequality versus sociology of the state (Rex) (b) sociology of the city versus analysis of social stratification	(a) corporatist state theory/studies of bureaucratic and professional domination (b) focus on consumption cleavages
Spatial unit of collective consumption	(a) theory of capitalist urbanism versus (b) analysis of state functions in reproducing labour-power	(a) political economy of space (b) sociology of consumption (non-spatial 'urban' sociology)

Figure 1 Sociological conceptualizations of urbanism

proved essentially non-cumulative and atheoretical. Meanwhile, a different set of researchers, following Hawley, held on to processes of adaptation as the theoretically specific problem for analysis, but severed this from the concern with the city or other spatial forms. This second approach increasingly drew upon and became integrated with functionalist systems theories which likewise focused upon adaptation as one of the basic functional prerequisites of human societies, and as it did so, so the initial concern with the city was eclipsed and finally abandoned. Today, therefore, we are confronted with a schism between atheoretical descriptions of city life and theoretical analyses of processes which have no necessary relation to cities.

A second attempt to develop a coherent basis for urban sociology is represented by the work of Tönnies, Simmel and, most significantly, Louis Wirth. Here, some causal relation is posited between demographic features of human settlements and the cultural patterns thought to be associated with them, yet as we saw in Chapter 3, the familiar tension between a concern with the city and a focus on specific sociological phenomena which were not specific to urban space soon resurfaced.

In the case of Simmel, this tension reflected the distinct concerns in his work with a sociology of number or size, and a sociology of modernity. The first led to an analysis of the social implications of the growth of large-scale forms of human association, while the second was more concerned with the significance of factors such as the development of monetary systems and the intensification of the division of labour. In his essay on the metropolis, Simmel ran these two areas of analysis together with the result that factors inherent to cities (i.e. population size) became confused with factors inherent to capitalist societies (e.g. the alienation born of the division of labour and monetary relationships). Metropolis was thus neither urbanism nor capitalism; it was both.

Wirth's essay was an attempt to clarify this distinction. He was careful to theorize urbanism in terms of just three variables (size, density and heterogeneity), none of which was inherently associated with any particular economic or social form of organization, and he then went on to hypothesize that an increase in these three variables would tend to generate an increase in distinctively urban patterns of social relations as identified in his ideal type of urbanism (i.e. anonymous, superficial, transitory and segmental relations). The problem with this approach is not (as is often suggested) that it is empirically false (i.e. that social relationships in cities are not as Wirth characterized them), for such a criticism fails to understand Wirth's project and rests on a misinterpretation of the ideal type method. Rather, the problem is that the three key variables appear not to be the principal ones in explaining variations in patterns of social life. As the work of Pahl, Gans and others revealed, factors such as people's class situation, their ethnic culture, and their stage in the family life cycle appear to be much stronger determinants of ways of life than are the demographic factors identified by Wirth. Once again, therefore, we are forced beyond the city, to a study of social relations in society as a whole, in order to explain what we find going on in the city.

Both ecological and cultural theories of urbanism thus appear inadequate as the basis for a distinctively urban social theory, although both have left some residues. Human ecology has spawned a community study tradition which has been rich descriptively despite its theoretical weaknesses. The main problems with such studies, however, are first, that the very lack of a theoretical framework has hindered comparison and hence generalization (they are, as Bell and Newby 1971, suggest, essentially non-cumulative), and second, that it is always unclear to what extent the findings from one community can be taken as common to all. As we shall see later in this chapter, the 'locality' as an object of analysis has recently reappeared in urban studies research, but such studies today are premissed on a rejection of the notion that localities are microcosms of the wider society, for their rationale is precisely to understand how and why social processes vary between different places. In any event, it is clear that community/locality cannot itself constitute a theoretical object for urban sociology, for what is of interest is not the place *per se* but the social processes which are generated or mediated through different places. We return to this issue below in the discussion of work by Massey, Urry and Giddens.

The residue from cultural theories of urbanism is a theoretical concern with the effects of size, spatial form and what Durkheim termed 'moral density' on social relationships. As we saw in Chapter 3, these effects cannot entirely be dismissed, although once we take account of more specifically sociological variables such as class, life cycle and sub-culture, they often turn out, in Dewey's phrase, to be 'relatively unimportant'. Nevertheless, some interesting and fruitful work has been done on the social implications of different spatial arrangements, and such research can prove of practical relevance to those concerned with city design and planning practices. Newman's analysis of *Defensible Space* (1972), for example, has been influential in documenting the possibilities of and constraints upon criminal activity which follow from different types of site planning and architectural design. More broadly, Hillier and Hansen's *The Social Logic of Space* (1984) shows how the physical layout of buildings, both internally and in relation to each other, functions to structure the social use of space and hence to order the social relationships between people. Nevertheless, it can still be argued that sociological variables should probably take precedence in any explanation of such phenomena. Human behaviour in formally similar spatial settings can vary widely according to the socio-economic and cultural characteristics of those involved (consider, for example, the dramatic changes documented by Ward (1985) when council-owned flats were sold into owner-occupation in Liverpool), and the tendency to physical reductionism and spatial determinism should always be resisted by analysing the diverse meanings which different social groups may invest in similar spaces. What this work does show, however, is that spatial arrangements (including factors such as size and density as well as layout) cannot be ignored in sociological analysis. As we shall see below, spatial arrangements can inhibit or facilitate certain types of social phenomena, in which case it is important to avoid an aspatial social science. Nevertheless, it is a giant step from here to an acceptance of the idea that spatial variables determine social phenomena in the way that Wirth tried to suggest.

In Chapter 4 we considered a third approach to urban theory. This was based on the three main propositions that space is inherently unequal, that different social groups use such power as they command in the market or through the state to achieve favourable locations and access to resources, and that the decisions made by strategically-placed gatekeepers are crucial in influencing the distribution of such resources among these different groups. Urban sociology was then defined in terms of its theoretical concern with the distributive consequences of urban managerial decisions and with conflicts between different 'housing classes' over the allocation of scarce and desirable resources. Subsequent analysis of these two questions, however, has indicated that neither urban managerialism nor the housing class concept can adequately specify peculiarly 'urban' processes, although the legacy of this approach is again of some interest.

The initial problem with Pahl's focus on urban managers was that it lacked clear criteria for determining which sorts of people were significant in shaping resource allocation and how far they were responsible for the pattern of distribution which resulted. This led to a reconceptualization of urban managers as local state bureaucrats mediating between the private sector, central government and the local population. Although this formulation resolved the problem of identification, it failed to clarify the question of managerial autonomy and discretion. Inevitably, Pahl himself was driven by the logic of his own analysis to investigate national political and economic processes and hence to undermine his original concern with the city as a system of resource allocation. So developed the all too familiar tension between the empirical focus on the city and the theoretical analysis of processes located outside and beyond it, for the ensuing investigation of national-level corporatism clearly had little to do with Pahl's initial interest in theorizing specifically urban processes.

The housing class concept fared even worse. The main reason for this was the confusion in Rex's work between empirical and conceptual criteria of identification and classification. Thus we saw in Chapter 4 that Rex sometimes identifies housing classes in terms of current housing tenure (owner-occupiers, council tenants, landlords, etc.) yet at other times identifies them in terms of the potential power of different social groups when they enter the housing market (blacks, one-parent families, etc.). There is, in other words, a tension in his work between an interest in housing tenure as a basis of inequality and political mobilization outside of the sphere of production, and a concern to demonstrate how access to a crucial consumption resource such as housing depends upon factors such as racial status. Clearly his theoretical interest is in the latter, but this means that the social divisions he draws correspond not to 'urban' classes but to strata and classes in society as a whole, and that his work leads not to a theory of the city but to a theory of social stratification in which race and ethnicity play a major role. This becomes clear in his later work with Sally Tomlinson where he argued that the major source of conflict in inner Birmingham was not housing, but education and jobs – i.e. resources which have nothing inherently to do with cities as such, but which form the basis for conflict between different groups which live, in the main, in the large conurbations. Just as the study of urban managers leads us beyond the city to an analysis of political power in society as a whole, so too the question of housing classes takes us away from an initial urban spatial focus into an analysis of class structure and its relation to divisions grounded in race, gender or whatever. Neither concept thus establishes the basis for a sociology of the city.

The legacy of this work is nonetheless important. The key point to emerge from Pahl's work in this period is that the state is today a crucial factor in determining people's life chances, and that it does not necessarily operate according to a strict capitalist logic. It follows from this that sociological analyses of class and market power grounded in the study of relations of production must be complemented by analyses of inequalities generated and sustained through bureaucratic systems of allocation. We do not have to endorse Pahl and Winkler's somewhat overblown theory of corporatism to recognize that the state is today a major 'actor' intervening in many aspects of people's lives, and that the interests shaped by its interventions may not correspond to the neat lines of cleavage between capital and labour which are still the basis of so many sociological analyses of power and inequality.

The legacy of Rex's housing class analysis is similar, for it too was premissed on the recognition that inequalities and political struggles over consumption resources were distinct from the class inequalities and class struggles arising out of relations of production in society. Although Rex's analysis was muddled, the focus on housing tenure as one major aspect of consumption-based inequalities was fruitful, for it stimulated a protracted (and currently unresolved) debate within urban studies over the significance of home ownership as a factor tending to fragment or even restructure the class relations arising out of a capitalist organization of production. As we shall see in Chapter 8, housing tenure is a key feature of consumption sector cleavages in the contemporary period, and Rex's initial formulation of the housing class concept, while flawed, did much to alert later researchers to the significance of such divisions. For our present purposes, however, the main point remains that analysis of such cleavages and divisions cannot be contained within an empirical focus on the city as an object of study.

The concern with the state and with the related issue of consumption, which ran through the neo-Weberian work of the 1960s and 1970s, became the explicit focus of the fourth attempt to theorize the city – that by Castells. Indeed, it was Castells who for the first time directly pointed to the problem in urban sociology of identifying an urban 'theoretical object', and in his early work he criticized previous approaches (including the Marxist analysis developed by Lefebvre) for fetishizing space by attributing causal properties to urbanism which were in fact aspects of the organization of capitalism. In his reformulation of the urban question, he argued that the city is theoretically significant as the spatial container within which labour-power is reproduced through state provision of necessary consumption resources, although in his later writings he expanded this conception by arguing that cities are sites of struggle where different groups seek to realize their goals, interests and values, not only in respect of state consumption provisions, but also in relation to questions of political power and cultural identity.

Clearly, although Castells included the spatial dimension within his definition of urbanism, space actually played a very minor role within his analysis. As Gottdiener (1984) suggests, once he had fastened on to collective consumption (and latterly, urban social movements) as his substantive focus, he was 'no longer interested in a theory of space per se, but rather in a theory of urban problems' (p. 203). This does not mean that he ignored space, for as he made clear in a paper in 1983, 'From the critique of the "spatialist theory" of social crises, it does not follow that space is unimportant and that the spatial dimension of the crisis should be ignored' (1983b, p. 3). Indeed, in this paper he went on (in terms somewhat reminiscent of his old adversary, Lefebvre) to argue that the spatial implications of the use of new technology were crucial in, for example, reinforcing hierarchical relations between different specialized locations and thus in separating centres of control and domination from the places of everyday life. Space, he argues, is inseparable from society, and the use of space is a product of struggles between dominant groups (capital, the state and men) and oppressed sections of society (workers, citizens, women) pursuing alternative projects and blueprints. As Kirby suggests, the image of space which Castells is proposing is analogous to that of a chessboard:

> Space thus becomes the chessboard upon which each and every person is located. The moves that the pieces make take place within the spatial constraints of the board and the directions that are permitted. Most importantly, if we remove the board, we can no longer understand the logic of the pieces that remain. In fact, this is at the heart of Castells's account: namely, that swift changes within the contemporary capitalist mode of production are dissolving the form of the chessboard (1985, pp. 9–10).

Nevertheless, what interests Castells is not the board but the pieces, not the city but the struggles which occur within it. Neither his original focus on collective consumption, nor his later interest in urban-based movements challenging for material resources, political power and cultural self-determination have any inherent connection to the city as an object of analysis. For him, the city is a space within which interesting things happen, but as we saw in Chapter 6, there seems little reason for restricting either the analysis of consumption, or the study of non-class political and cultural movements, to an exclusive focus on this space.

Like the other three approaches, therefore, Castells's analysis results in something of a dilemma. If it is to be understood as a theory of the city, then the focus on consumption is too narrow for it ignores the significance of other processes which also unfold in major urban centres, for consumption (or, indeed, state power and cultural domination) is no more specifically centred on the city than retailing, banking, manufacturing, transportation, recreation or any other core social processes. Indeed, Castells recognized as much when he argued at the end of *The City and the Grassroots* that urban social movements are ultimately utopian since they address problems, the solutions to which extend beyond the boundaries of their local areas. As he graphically puts it, 'When people find themselves unable to control the world, they simply shrink the world to the size of their community' (1983a, p. 331).

If, on the other hand, Castells's project is to be understood as a theory of consumption, then the focus on urban space is too restrictive, for it ignores any aspect of consumption and state provision which is either non-spatial (as is the case with the many subsidies and tax concessions associated with the 'hidden welfare state') or which is organized at a higher spatial scale (e.g. the various regional state bodies involved in areas like health care, training, transportation, and the like; clearly, the equation which Castells draws between consumption and the city, and production and the region, is both arbitrary and unconvincing, for both processes may be organized at both levels).

Just as human ecology split apart some fifty years ago into its constituent yet irreconcilable elements (the focus on the city and the focus on adaptation), so urban studies has today split along a very similar fault line. Notwithstanding the commitment to a dialectical method, Marxist as well as non-Marxist urban researchers are now to be found working in two distinct fields. One group has basically forgotten about the city as an object of analysis and has devoted itself to the analysis of issues concerning consumption. This group is to be found working, for example, on the welfare state and the inequalities associated with it, on studies of fiscal strain in state budgets, on analyses of local government services and the increasing conflicts between central and local government in the current period, on local political struggles around consumption issues, on the growth of the 'self-service economy' and domestic self-provisioning in the face of unemployment and welfare cut-backs, on privatization and its implications for class relations and social inequality, and so on.

Another group, by contrast, has held on to the city and other spatial forms as its distinctive object of inquiry but has foresaken any attempt to theorize the city in terms of a specific social phenomenon or process. This group is interested in cities and regions as spatial forms which in some way reflect, influence or help constitute wider economic and social changes and processes. Some researchers, for example, see spatial organization as important as an element in the system through which a capitalist mode of production operates (like Lefebvre, they therefore see the analysis of space as integral to the analysis of modern capitalism). Others focus on spatial organization as important in enabling and constraining the development of social processes generally (i.e. they see the analysis of space as integral to the development of any sociological explanation of why, how and when things happen in the way they do).

The first group is engaged in developing what we may term a 'sociology of consumption', or a 'non-spatial urban sociology', and we shall consider the main elements in such work in Chapter 8. The second group is engaged in developing a 'political economy of space' or, more generally, a mode of social analysis in which space plays a central role. It is with this second group that we shall be concerned for the remainder of this chapter.

The spatial aspect of economic organization

The attempt by some Marxist theorists from the 1970s onwards to develop a political economy of space was premissed on the unequivocal rejection of Castells's claim that urbanism constituted neither a 'real' nor a 'scientific' object. The point was made forcibly by Dear and Scott in setting out a framework for such work:

> A specifically *urban question* does indeed exist. It is structured around the particular and indissoluble geographical and land-contingent phenomena that come into existence as capitalist social and property relations are mediated through the dimension of urban space. . . . The city *is* a definite object of theoretical enquiry (1981, p. 6).

For them, the urban question therefore refers to the problem of how land comes to be used and managed through the interplay of classes and the state in modern capitalist societies. Put another way, the focus for research is to be the explanation of how the organization of socially-created space comes to reflect, express, mediate or influence the social organization of capitalism with all the contradictions which that mode of production is said to entail. Just as Marxist analysis has long recognized that time is socially produced as history, so too it must come to recognize how space is socially produced as geography.

An early example of this sort of approach was an influential paper in which Roweis and Scott (1978) set out to show how spatial organization may enter into the process of capital accumulation as a factor inhibiting the most economically rational pattern of investment. In particular, the private ownership of urban land may thwart the optimal use of space as individuals seek to maximize their locational advantages in ignorance of the overall effects which their decisions are having. Furthermore, having invested in plant and equipment in one place, capitalist firms are then to some extent committed to staying put, even though the original factors which drew them to that place are soon likely to be eroded as a result of the self-interested locational decisions of other capitalists. As Roweis and Scott summarize the problem: 'Capitalist social and property relations create two major contradictory tendencies around the issue of urban land. On the one hand, the logic of commodity production and the private appropriation of profit call for functionally efficient urban land-use patterns. On the other, the private ownership and control of urban land lead to a tendency away from such efficiency' (p. 63).

It is in this context that the state tries to organize its interventions in the urban land system. Lipietz (1980), for example, argues that state planning and regulation involves the attempt to organize space in the interests of capital, both by providing collective infrastructure and other resources which each individual firm needs but cannot or is not willing to provide itself, and by forcibly imposing a logic of capital against private landowners through, for example, the compulsory purchase of land for redevelopment or by means of zoning and other measures. As Lamarche (1976, p. 104) suggests, state planning clears and prepares the land in order for private capital to sow and harvest the best fruit. Yet as Roweis and Scott go on to point out, the state is always limited in what it can achieve by the fact of private property ownership. It cannot direct investment in any coherent and rational way and it cannot lay down an efficient spatial pattern which all capitalist firms are obliged to follow. Even the British land use planning system is essentially a system of negative planning, for when the local and strategic plans have been established, it is still the private sector which decides whether and where to develop (see, for example, Ambrose and Colenutt 1975).

There is, at the heart of the urban land question, a 'contradiction between the socialized production of urban land in its totality, on the one hand, and the privatization of concomitant benefits on the other' (Roweis and Scott, p. 72). This contradiction is expressed in class struggles, not only between capital and labour, but also between different branches of capital itself, with the state centrally embroiled in the ensuing conflicts while being unable to resolve them. Capital accumulation, therefore, does not simply take place across space, but is essentially tied up with, and affected by, the organization of space.

The key implication of such an approach is that space is much more than a mere 'container' within which certain social or economic processes work out. In the view of those committed to developing a political economy of space, the attempt by Castells and others to find a social process which is limited to a particular organization of space is wrong-headed, for the task is rather to see how particular spatial forms are produced by, and react back upon, processes embedded within a particular organization of production. Putting the point somewhat oversimply, while Castells sought to locate social processes in a spatial setting, these writers seek to locate spatial processes in their wider societal and economic context.

That this is putting things oversimply is due to the fact that most of those who have attempted to develop a political economy of space reject the idea that space and society are separate entities which have to be related theoretically, one to the other. As Smith suggests, an approach which sees space and society 'interacting', or which analyses one as a 'reflection' of the other, is too crude, for it assumes that we are dealing with two distinct objects when, in fact, social organization is inherently and necessarily spatial. As material beings in a material world, we do not simply inhabit spatial locations, but we actively create them and have to live with the consequences: 'We do not live, act and work "in" space so much as by living, acting and working we produce space' (Smith 1984, p. 85).

In one respect, the space which is produced in a capitalist society will itself be an expression of capitalist social relations. As Lamarche puts it, 'The city is necessarily made in the image of the society which builds it' (1976, p. 117). Thus, when capitalism is reproduced, so too is its spatial form, and when capital restructures in response to mounting crisis, so too space is restructured. However, existing spatial arrangements also constrain and shape the way in which capitalism is reproduced or restructured, for space is already to some extent 'fixed' or congealed in forms which may have expressed previous patterns of economic activity. As Lipietz observes, 'Society recreates its space on the basis of a concrete space, always already provided, established in the past' (1980, p. 61). If and when capital restructures, therefore, it is immediately confronted by an existing spatial form which constrains and mediates any changes. If space changes when capitalism changes, then it is also the case that capitalism changes in and through an existing geographical landscape which cannot simply be reshaped by an act of will. Any change in the organization of capitalism thus not only carries with it an inherent change in the way space is used, but it also reflects existing spatial arrangements. Capitalist crises are spatial phenomena, not only in the sense that they are expressed in geographical unheavals (the creation of industrial wastelands in one place, the exacerbation of problems of rapid growth and concentration in another), but also in that material space may shape or intensify them by the constraints that it imposes on possible 'solutions'.

Here, then, is the 'urban question' reformulated in terms of what Soja (1980, 1985) has termed a 'socio-spatial dialectic': 'The structure of organized space is not a separate structure with its own autonomous laws of construction and transformation, nor is it simply an expression of the class structure emerging from the social (i.e. aspatial) relations of production. It represents, instead, a dialectically defined component of the general relations of production, relations which are simultaneously social and spatial' (1980, p. 208). The argument here is that there is a homology between the social structure with its division between dominant and exploited classes, and the spatial structure, with its division between centres and peripheries, for both arise from the same common cause (the organization of capitalism), are expressions of the same thing, and simultaneously shape each other.

At the heart of this dialectic is the assertion that, 'The spatiality of social life is society materially constituted' (Soja 1985, p. 177). Problems which manifest themselves in space (e.g. uneven development between countries or regions) are the inherent expressions of the contradictions within a capitalist mode of production, contradictions which are mediated by existing spatial arrangements and which are exacerbated by the tension between the inertia of current patterns and the dictates of new economic imperatives. Similarly, the conflicts which arise over the use of space are the mediated expressions of the class conflict within capitalism itself between capitalists, workers and other strata and fractions. There can be no theory of space as such, but nor can there be an aspatial theory of capitalist society, for, to adapt a well-worn aphorism, capital does not accumulate, nor classes struggle, nor the state intervene on the head of a pin.

As Soja himself acknowledges, this sort of approach to space and urbanism owes much to the theories of Henri Lefebvre. As we saw in Chapter 5, Lefebvre argues that the use of space has become integral to the survival of capitalism. The contradictions identified by Marx and Engels in the nineteenth century have been managed by ensuring the reproduction of capitalism through the domination of space – both by opening up new areas of accumulation outside and within the capitalist core countries (e.g. through exploitation of the Third World and through new investment in the core countries in property development and the provision for mass consumption – the so-called 'second circuit' dominated by finance capital), and by organizing space as a hierarchical structure which can ensure continued capitalist hegemony in every nook and cranny of everyday life as well as within the system of production. For Lefebvre, it is no longer enough to transform the social relations of production, for what is needed in addition is a reappropriation of urban space itself (an argument which, as we saw in Chapter 6, has now been taken up to some extent in Castells's revised theory of urban social movements as attempts to impose alternative meanings and uses on to the city).

According to Soja, Marxist theory has for too long ignored these sorts of insights into the spatiality of capitalism. For him, Lefebvre's work provides the basis for a retheorization of space which places 'the production of space and its control over the reproduction of social relations at the center of the survival of modern capitalism' (Soja and Hadjimichalis 1979, p. 9). The theorist who, more than any other, has critically taken up the sorts of issues raised in Lefebvre's work and who has attempted to develop Marxist theory in order to analyse the ways in which space is produced and reproduced under capitalism is David Harvey. In a series of articles and in two key books (*Social Justice and the City*, published in 1973, and *The Limits to Capital*, published in 1982), Harvey has developed what one commentator calls, 'The most systematic attempt to relate the theory of accumulation to the specific geography of capitalism' (Smith 1984, p. 125). He has since the 1970s become to Marxist urban geography what Castells became to Marxist urban sociology. How then does Harvey seek to put theoretical flesh on the conceptual bones of the socio-spatial dialectic?

Although Harvey's work has undoubtedly been influenced by

Lefebvre's writings (e.g. in the emphasis on the central role played by finance capital in producing space and in the concern with tracing the circuit of capital through the production of the built environment), it by no means accepts the whole of Lefebvre's research programme. Indeed, Soja (1980) bemoans the fact that Harvey fails to follow Lefebvre in placing space at the centre of the analysis of contemporary capitalism. Thus, although both writers see space as crucial in capitalism's ever-more pressing search for a means to ensure its own reproduction, Harvey from the outset rejected Lefebvre's view (expressed in his concept of an 'urban revolution') that the organization of space has become the fulcrum around which the whole system balances or collapses:

> To say that urbanism now dominates industrial society is to say that contradictions between urbanism as a structure in the process of transformation and the internal dynamic of the older industrial society are usually resolved in favour of the former. I do not believe this claim is realistic. In certain important and crucial respects industrial society and the structures which comprise it continue to dominate urbanism (1973, p. 311).

For Harvey, the industrial sector is still the motor of capitalist development and the major source of change in capitalist societies. The urban system has therefore to be analysed in this context. Thus, the creation of space is largely a function of where big firms choose to site their head offices, their research and development centres, their assembly plants and so on; the money which flows into land and property development is governed by rates of profitability in the industrial sector; and the key role of the urban system lies in its significance as a means for realizing profits for industrial capital (e.g. through the increased demand for cars and other individual consumer goods consequent upon the spread of suburbanization). In short, the creation of the built environment is a product of the relentless drive for profitability on the part of capitalist industry.

Harvey argues that, just as individual firms try to establish a comparative advantage over their competitors by investing in new and more productive technology, so too they also attempt to secure a competitive edge by locating in relatively advantageous places (e.g. those nearest to sources of supply or to markets). Like many of the other writers discussed above, he recognizes that physical relocation is limited by the pattern of existing investment in 'fixed capital' (i.e. plant and machinery whose value is only gradually exhausted through each round of accumulation), and that current spatial arrangements thus represent a fetter on the possibility of adjusting to changing conditions. Firms, that is, have to weigh up the relative advantages of a new location against the devaluation of existing assets in the old one, and this may prevent them from moving, at least in the short run. Nevertheless, the drive to maximize returns results in a constant pressure on firms to close down in one place and open up in another, and dogged resistance to such pressures is likely to lead eventually to falling profits and ultimate bankruptcy as competitors reap ever-increasing advantages of location. It is in this sense that uneven geographical development is inherent to and necessary for capitalism. Every time the conditions of production and circulation change (e.g. with the introduction of new technologies, new transportation systems and the like), so a process of 'musical chairs' is sparked off in which certain places are abandoned to their fate:

> The social geography which evolves is not...a mere reflection of capital's needs, but the locus of powerful and potentially disruptive contradictions. The social geography shaped to capital's needs at one moment in history is not necessarily consistent with later requirements. Since that geography is hard to change and often the focus of heavy long-term investment, it then becomes the barrier to be overcome. New social geographies have to be produced, often at great cost to capital and usually accompanied by not a little human suffering (1982, p. 403).

Capitalist relocation – the restructuring of space – is thus an essential feature of capitalist restructuring in periods of crisis. However, Harvey goes on to argue that this continuing search for relative locational advantage is ultimately self-defeating, for given the private ownership of land (which he sees as an essential and necessary feature of any capitalist society), temporary advantages which enable firms to make excess profits will soon disappear in increased rent payments to private landowners. In other words, no sooner do industrial firms move to an area and begin to reap greater returns (e.g. through savings in transportation costs, labour costs or whatever) than these returns are whittled away through rising rents and land prices.

Harvey has devoted much of his work over the years to an analysis of the role of rent in capitalist economies. In his view, rent is the concept which links the analysis of capitalist production to that of space and the built environment: 'Rent is that theoretical concept through which political economy (of whatever stripe) traditionally confronts the problem of spatial organization' (1982, p. 337). Rent (which includes both regular rental payments and capitalized one-off purchase payments for the use of land) is an example of 'fictitious capital' in that it represents a claim over future revenue. Land, in other words, does not produce value, but as an essential condition of production, it enables those who hold title to it to demand a slice of the value created by those who produce on it. Rent, in other words, is a deduction from the surplus value created in industrial production.

Broadly following Marx, Harvey identifies four categories of rent. *Monopoly rent* is that which accrues to a landowner as a result of the ability of the user of the land to sell his or her commodities at a monopoly price. In agriculture, for example, a particular plot of land may be used to produce wine of a unique quality which can command a high price, and in this case, the landlord will be able to raise the rent accordingly. Similarly, according to Harvey, the owner of a central location in a city will be able to command a high monopoly rent given the unique advantages of that location for, say, offices or retail outlets.

Absolute rent, by contrast, is the return which a landlord can demand before even the worst quality land is released. In Marx's analysis of agricultural rents, absolute rent is significant since it represents a barrier to investment in farming and thus prevents the equalization of profit rates between agriculture and other sections of industry. Thus higher rates of profit in agriculture, consequent upon a lower than average organic composition of capital, will result not in the attraction of new investment (and hence a raising of the organic composition and a reduction of profits to the average level), but rather in a creaming off by private landlords. Applied by Harvey to the urban context, the concept of absolute rent refers to the ability of landowners and property developers to extract money through the maintenance of artificial scarcity. Aided by state agencies (which restrict land availability for various uses through zoning) and by financial institutions (which determine lending policies in relation to house purchase and industrial investment), landlords as a class are able to maintain scarcity and thus to extract artificially high rents from people who have no alternative but to pay them.

The other two types of rent are forms of *differential rent*. The first of these refers to the difference between the returns which a producer can achieve on a given site and the returns which can be achieved on the worst land. In agriculture, for example, the owner of a high fertility field can extract the surplus profit which can be made on this land relative to that which is possible on land at the economic margin of cultivation, and this has the effect of reducing surplus profits to an average level pertaining throughout the farming industry. The second type of differential rent accrues as a result of previous investment in the land which raises its productivity, for here too, the owner will attempt to claw back the increased profits which can thereby be achieved. Differential rent therefore functions to equalize profit rates among producers on different quality sites at differentially-advantageous locations. The better the site, in terms of the advantages it provides in reducing costs and increasing returns, the higher the rent will be (although as Ball (1977), points out, the exact level or rent charged and paid will reflect specific struggles between landowners and users and cannot be generalized theoretically).

Now this analysis of rent leads Harvey to what he terms an 'extraordinary' conclusion. As we saw above, the competitive struggle to achieve surplus profits involves both the search for improved technology and the search for advantageous location. However, the search for excess profits through new technology is ultimately self-defeating since short-run advantages are soon wiped out as all other competitors also invest in the new machinery, thus raising the organic composition of capital and lowering the average rate of profit in the system as a whole. All that happens is that the same number of producers now manufacture a larger number of commodities of a lower value, hence depressing rates of profit and hastening the onset of a crisis of over-accumulation which can only be overcome by driving some firms to the wall. What Harvey now adds to this classic Marxist analysis of crisis is that spatial relocation follows much the same sort of pattern, for the pursuit of excess profits in new locations simply results in increased rents and hence in a reduction of rates of return back to the average level. Individual firms have no option but to relocate in order to seize competitive advantage, yet having done so, they find that this advantage promptly disappears! Industry is thus perpetually chasing its own tail while wreaking havoc across different regions and countries as it abandons existing investments in a futile attempt to improve profit rates:

> Individual capitalists, acting in their own self-interest and striving to maximise their profits under the coercive pressures of competition, tend to expand production and shift locations up to the point where the capacity to produce further surplus value disappears. There is, it seems, a spatial version of Marx's falling rate of profit thesis (1982, pp. 389–90).

It is this insight which lies behind Harvey's attempt to develop Marx's analysis of crisis by integrating the question of space into the investigation of capital accumulation. Like Lefebvre, he argues that Marxist theory has to be developed to take account of the way in which crises of capitalist production have been overcome by opening up new possibilities of accumulation, but unlike Lefebvre, he goes on to demonstrate how each successive 'solution' has set in motion a new set of contradictions – contradictions which represent the unavoidable 'limits to capital' and which ultimately threaten the very future of humankind.

The analysis begins by identifying as a basic contradiction of capitalism the fact that competition between individual capitalists results in aggregate effects which run counter to their own individual and collective interests. For Harvey, this is demonstrated by Marx's analysis of the tendency for unbridled competition to result in a falling rate of profit and an over-accumulation of capital in the system as a whole. Harvey here closely follows Marx's own analysis in arguing that the drive to invest in new technology necessarily results in a crisis of over-accumulation which becomes manifest in gluts on the market, falling prices, idle productive capacity and rising unemployment:

> Here we can clearly see the contradictions which arise out of the tendency for individual capitalists to act in a way which, when aggregated, runs counter to their own class interest. This contradiction produces a tendency towards over-accumulation – too much capital is produced in aggregate relative to the opportunities to employ that capital (1978a, pp. 104–6).

Harvey describes this analysis as a 'first cut' at crisis theory. This does not mean that the analysis is in some way wrong or even approximate, for in his view it succeeds in pinpointing the basic reason for the chronic instability of capitalist economies. What he does mean is rather that the analysis is incomplete in the sense that it fails to appreciate how the capitalist system has come to terms with this inherent tendency to a crisis of over-accumulation. What is involved here is a 'switching' of investment at times of impending crisis out of the 'primary circuit' of industrial production and into a 'secondary circuit' involving investment by financial institutions in 'fixed capital' and what he terms 'the consumption fund'.

As we saw above, fixed capital refers to that portion of investment which does not offer an immediate return but which gives up its value gradually through successive periods of productive activity. The most obvious examples are assets such as factories and offices. The consumption fund is in some ways analogous in that it consists of those items which are not directly consumed but are rather used over a long period of time to facilitate consumption. Examples here include housing and various consumer durables.

It is Harvey's argument that, faced with falling rates of return in industry, capital responds by increasing investment in this secondary circuit, much of which entails investing in the built environment. Sometimes this takes the form of investment in fixed capital such as office blocks. It is for this reason that bouts of property speculation (such as the office boom of the early 1970s) so often occur at times of industrial decline, for the development of urban physical infrastructure represents an alternative channel of investment when rates of return in the primary circuit begin to fall. Alternatively, it may involve investment in the consumption fund. The explosion of suburbanization in the United States after 1945, for example, is explained by Harvey (1977) as a massive switch into the secondary circuit, facilitated by the state (through tax concessions to home-buyers and construction firms) and by financial institutions (through special credit arrangements), which not only opened up new investment possibilities, but also helped stimulate demand for the products of industry such as cars and petroleum. Furthermore, such investment in the consumption fund had the additional advantage of maintaining political stability by creating 'a large wedge of debt-encumbered home owners' (1977, p. 125) intent on working all hours to pay off their mortgages while all the time believing that they had a 'stake in the system' which was worth defending.

Such switches of investment are themselves problematic, however. For a start, new investment in fixed capital commits enormous sums to physical infrastructure which may prove inappropriate to capital's future needs. Furthermore, the ability to switch investment into the secondary circuit is dependent upon a massive increase in the power of financial institutions which, together with the state, become the effective co-ordinators and managers of the whole system through their control of credit. Yet this only adds to the chronic instability of the system as large sums of fictitious capital are directed into various secondary forms of investment which may or may not show a return and which may or may not prove necessary for future capitalist growth. The collapse of various banks following the end of the office boom in the early 1970s was just one example of how speculative investment in the secondary circuit may relieve the pressure of over-accumulation only to exacerbate the crisis at a later date when falling rates of return can trigger off financial panic and mad lurches in commodity and currency markets.

The problem, therefore, is that switching into the secondary circuit displaces rather than resolves the basic contradiction. Just as the scope for employing capital profitably in the primary circuit dries up, so too the secondary circuit soon becomes saturated:

> As the pressure builds, either the accumulation process grinds to a halt or new investment opportunities are found as capital flows down various channels into the secondary and tertiary [i.e. investment in research and development] circuits. This movement may start as a trickle and become a flood as the potential for expanding the production of surplus value by such means becomes apparent. But the tendency towards over-accumulation is not eliminated. It is transformed rather into a pervasive tendency towards over-investment in the secondary and tertiary circuits (1978a, pp. 111–12).

Just as the onset of crisis demands the mass devaluation of industrial capital, so too it results in the devaluation of fixed capital and the consumption fund. Empty office blocks and bankrupt cities are just as much a mocking reminder of the basic contradictions of capitalism as are industrial wastelands and failed companies.

Here, then, is Harvey's 'second cut' theory of crisis. Yet as with the first cut theory, a potential solution is apparently at hand. This is what Harvey refers to as the 'spatial fix', by which he means the search for new areas of the globe in which capital can invest. And it is here that the earlier argument about the functional necessity of uneven spatial development comes back into the analysis. The spatial fix involves movement across territory in an attempt to bolster rates of return on new investment, but this proves problematic in practice. For a start, it is hindered by territorial coalitions of workers, politicians and small businesses which exert pressure on big firms seeking to abandon one area in favour of another. 'People who live in the communities being "obsolesced" resist and resent the process for the most part. Community activism arises as a response to the pressures for change' (1977, p. 137). Yet the more successful such coalitions are, the more dramatic is the collapse when the firms eventually do leave or close down.

More significant than popular resistance, however, is the problem that redirection of investment into underdeveloped regions or countries, far from resolving the basic crisis of over-accumulation, simply exacerbates it by reproducing it on a wider scale. Capital in the new areas grows up and intensifies the competition which was at the heart of the problem in the first place, for it too begins to encounter the limits of over-accumulation and it too starts to search for its own spatial fix. Geographical space has thus become central to the survival of capitalism, for the opening up of new areas of investment is necessary to keep the machine going yet the more this is done, the more pressing the problems become. It is in this way that Harvey explains the outbreak of the Second World War as the product of imperialistic rivalries as Britain sought to close off the Commonwealth, Japan expanded into Manchuria, Italy looked for space in Africa and Germany pushed eastwards into Czechoslovakia and Poland. It is also in this way that he comes to the apocolyptic conclusion that the continuing search for a spatial fix today has set the world on a course of nuclear destruction. The 'third cut' theory of crisis, in other words, ends up in obliteration, for the use of the credit system and territorial expansion to put off the effects of the growing crisis of capital accumulation has now brought us to the point where only wholesale destruction on a massive scale could achieve the devaluation necessary for capital to re-establish the conditions of profitable investment.

Harvey's 'second cut' and 'third cut' theories of crisis represent a major attempt to demonstrate the significance of space for an analysis of how capitalism has responded to the over-accumulation problem. For him, space is far from incidental to the concerns of political economy, for the creation and recreation of the built environment (through investment switches into the secondary circuit) and the attempt to exploit uneven geographical development for profitable investment (through the 'spatial fix') represent the strategies by which impending crisis has at one and the same time been staved off and intensified. Yet Harvey's concern to relate the analysis of space to the theory of political economy is ultimately unconvincing. Three problems in particular arise out of his work.

The first is simply that his work is pitched at such a high level of abstraction that it is often difficult both to pin down the precise propositions which are being made and to see how his ideas can be related to concrete analysis. He himself admits, in the introduction to *Limits to Capital*, that the book represents 'the theory as an abstract conception, without reference to the history' (p. xiv), and it is noticeable that many of the reviews of this book commend it for its sophisticated treatment of Marxist theory while noting the failure to relate this theory to the specific issues of the built environment and the space economy. As Ball suggests, the discussion of space is the 'least satisfactory' part of the whole book: 'sweeping generalisations are presented on a take-it-or-leave-it basis, including the announcement of the next world war. Here the author seems to forget that there are limits to abstract theorising as well as to capital' (1983, p. 494).

Harvey tells us in the introduction to *Limits to Capital* that he set out to write a theory of urbanization under capitalism but ended up writing a general treatise on the capitalist mode of production itself. The explanation he gives for this slippage is that the use of a Marxist dialectical method necessitates a theoretical understanding of the whole prior to analysis of what he calls the 'bits and pieces'. Yet as we saw in our earlier discussion of the structuralist methodology of Castells, it is precisely this emphasis on theorizing the totality of social relations which in the end tends to inhibit understanding of specifics. The emphasis on holism and dialectics inevitably pitches analysis at such a level of abstraction that it becomes virtually impossible to translate the theoretical focus into empirically or historically relevant categories: 'This impasse is tied in part to the abstract realms of Hegelian philosophy and its holistic argument where such terms as totality and essence square uncomfortably with empirical analysis. It is precisely this philosophy of structure and holism that Harvey . . . and others adhere to . . . which frustrates the empirical examination of advanced societies by Marxist geographers' (Duncan and Ley 1982, p. 31).

The first problem with Harvey's work, therefore, is essentially a methodological one. Rather like the early Castells, his analysis is abstract, formalistic and ultimately untestable. The theory is not evaluated against historical evidence (indeed, Harvey argues that validity is to be sought in political practice rather than empirically) but is selectively illustrated with reference to historical examples (Duncan and Ley 1982, p. 50). Indeed, the generality of the approach 'makes the transition to historical analysis virtually impossible' (Ball 1983, p. 495), for having identified 'contradictions' theoretically, these are simply mapped on to the empirical world with little or no concern for the specific features of particular historical conditions. In short, the theory has its own existence apart from the world it is intended to explain, and the two rarely articulate with each other.

The second problem, which is also reminiscent in many ways of Castells's earlier work, is that Harvey almost entirely neglects the historical role of human agency in producing and reproducing social relations. Indicative of this is the way in which human agents always appear in Harvey's work in the guise of reified categories (he talks, for example, not of 'capitalists' but of 'capital': capital 'does' things, 'encounters' problems, 'responds' to crises) such that, 'substance, power, activity, and sometimes intentionality' come to be attributed not to people, but to abstract concepts (Duncan and Ley 1982, p. 37). As is so often the case in such teleological reasoning, it is but a short step from here to unwarranted functionalist explanation in which things happen because 'capital' requires them to (one example being the explanation of suburban expansion as a response to capital's need to find new outlets for its surplus capacity).

Even more striking, however, is the fact that many social categories do not appear in the analysis at all. Harvey's explanations revolve entirely around what 'capital' does: the labour movement, the women's movement, community action, not to mention politicians, administrators and the professions, have no historical role to play. The whole thrust of the analysis is taken up with the logic of capital accumulation and the problems which arise from it. Amazingly for a Marxist, class struggle is a mere postscript to the theory (crises may provoke some working-class response – e.g. in territorial movements which try to prevent 'capital' from relocating elsewhere) but is in no way central to it, for the major contradiction which drives the whole system forward towards its impending demise is not brought about by class action (or any other form of action) but is simply the result of competition between 'capitals' producing an unintended and dysfunctional aggregate effect. From Harvey's perspective, the inevitable crisis of capitalism is self-engendered; the working class stands by on the sidelines of history and at most plays a reactive role while 'capital' inflicts its own wounds as a result of the incessant drive to accumulate.

Furthermore, when Harvey does discuss class relations, his analysis is crude in the extreme. Although he does recognize that classes are often divided against themselves (1978b, p. 12), his analysis proceeds as if late twentieth-century America (for most of his empirical examples come from observations of Baltimore) were no different from mid nineteenth-century England. There is no cognizance of the problem posed by the growth of the middle class, or of the significance of the expansion of state employment, or of the importance of sources of collective identity outside of the workplace. The wage labour–capital relation is taken as fundamental to all social relations, reverberating 'to every corner of the social totality' (1978a, p. 125). Urban conflicts, such as those discussed in Castells's later work on grass-roots movements, are all simply 'displaced' class struggles, just as urban problems are simply displaced problems of over-accumulation. The state is simply an appendage or tool of 'finance capital', the junior partner in 'an almost conspiratorial tie-up between government and finance capital' (Bassett and Short 1980, p. 200). The whole analysis of class relations and political power is, as Mingione (1981, p. 69) suggests, 'oversimplified' and 'mechanical'.

The third, and from our present perspective most significant, problem in Harvey's analysis is that the theory ultimately fails to demonstrate what it sets out to prove – namely, that space is now central to the reproduction of capitalism. As we have seen, Harvey tries to demonstrate this in two ways: first, by relating the function of the built environment to the process of switching investment into the secondary circuit, and second, by emphasizing the 'spatial fix' as a major strategy for avoiding crises of over-accumulation. Neither argument is convincing.

The problem with the first is that the empirical object of the built environment does not correspond to the theoretical categories of 'fixed capital' and the 'consumption fund'. As Harvey himself recognizes, fixed capital need not be spatially 'fixed' (he gives the examples of ships and locomotives), and productive investment in the built environment thus represents just one example of investment in the secondary circuit of capital. Furthermore (as Harvey does not seem to recognize), much of the 'consumption fund' is not spatially fixed either (e.g. 'cutlery and kitchen utensils, refrigerators, television sets and washing machines', to take his own illustrations (1982, p. 229)). The equation of the creation of the built environment with the switching of investment into the secondary circuit is thus something of a sleight of hand, for what is being demonstrated is not the centrality of the built environment as an outlet for over-accumulation, but rather the need to find some new investment outlets which may or may not involve new geographical arrangements.

The only grounds which Harvey offers for focusing specifically on the significance of investment in new built forms is that, unlike investments in other types of fixed capital or consumption fund items, the construction of offices, factories, motorways, houses and the like physically constrains future patterns of investment change. As we have seen, this is a point which is repeated throughout the spatial political economy literature, but how significant is it as a major contradiction of advanced capitalism? Certainly there is no *inherent* reason to believe that what is built today will prove obsolescent, a barrier to further accumulation, tomorrow. Most of the physical infrastructure laid down in a country like Britain – the roads, railways, sewers, houses, schools, hospitals and even factories and office blocks – is intensively used over several generations and much of it, built in the Victorian period, is still in use today and has repaid the initial investment several times over. Nor does Harvey demonstrate why investment in this secondary circuit necessarily reaches saturation (see Gottdiener, 1985, p. 97). Clearly there is no necessary contradiction entailed in investing in the built environment. Some investments will prove short-lived and some will be abandoned as 'capital' searches for more favourable locations, but to elevate these cases to a generalized theoretical 'contradiction' around which an entire political economy of space can be woven seems somewhat ingenuous. Harvey's work demonstrates how Marxist theory can be applied to an analysis of the creation of the built environment, but it does not in any way demonstrate that analysis of the built environment is a central or even necessary feature of a political economy of contemporary capitalism.

Much the same can be said of his discussion of the so-called 'spatial fix'. Indeed, here even the application of the theory is tenuous, for as Forbes, Thrift and Williams observe, the analysis 'tails off as Harvey addresses the spatial dimension' owing precisely to the problems of applying a general and abstract theory of crisis tendencies to the specific issue of spatial forms (1983, p. 356). The discussion of the space economy at the end of *Limits to Capital* is fragmentary, consisting of one or two scattered insights and half-developed hunches, and it certainly does not add up to a coherent political economy of space. Harvey does succeed in demonstrating the inherent geographical unevenness of capitalist development, and he does point to some of the problems which this creates (e.g. the problems faced by the core regions of selling to the periphery when the latter cannot afford to buy, and the tendency for investment in peripheral regions to create problems later when these areas begin to compete with the core areas for markets for their goods), but the analysis hardly represents a coherent basis for Harvey's claim that geography has to be integrated into overall theories of crisis (1982, p. 425). Indeed, there is a tendency in all of this to fetishize space by treating such concepts as 'core' and 'periphery' as entities in themselves. As Browett points out in an interesting review of the spatial political economy literature, it is one thing to recognize that economic processes unavoidably develop unevenly across space, but it is quite another to argue from this that uneven development is 'functional', still less that space therefore represents an object of analysis. It is precisely the absence of *people* from this sort of analysis, of course, which creates the void which is filled in these theories by *places*:

> The consideration of spatial relationships and spatial conflicts whereby regions develop, have social relations with, and do things to, each other is at best mystifying. . . . If one is to personify space in terms of exploiting and exploited regions, then why not greedy, or lazy, or clever regions? (Browett 1984, p. 164).

Analysis of spatial categories can conceal more than it reveals. There are some very affluent areas, and some very prosperous people, in the 'depressed regions' of Britain, just as some of the poorest areas and most desperate people can be found in the 'soft underbelly' of the south-east. Indeed, when we move away from geographical categories to sociological ones, we often find that it is not areas which are affluent or depressed, but certain social groups who may be more concentrated in one type of area than another. Cameron's review of the evidence on deprivation in Britain's major conurbations, for example, found that particular groups – the elderly, blacks, unskilled workers and so on – were often in a similar situation irrespective of their location (Cameron 1980). While it is obviously true that recession and economic restructuring has different implications for different places, it is all too easy to forget that most people in Merseyside or Tyneside are not chronically unemployed, just as most people in Berkshire or Cambridge do not work as highly skilled computer programmers. It is people, not places, who become redundant, and it is people, not places, who enter into new technology industries. The danger in seeking to develop a political economy of space is that we resurrect the ecological fallacy (see Chapter 2) by focusing on aggregate spatial configurations while overlooking the social variability that exists within them.

This conclusion leads us to something of a paradox. On the one hand, we have seen that space is more than simply a passive backdrop or 'container' within which social processes occur, for spatial arrangements evidently influence and affect how these processes develop. Yet on the other hand, we have also seen that space is not a 'thing' with its own materiality and causal properties, for ultimately it has no independent existence other than as the relation between objects. The problem with concepts such as Soja's 'socio-spatial dialectic' is that they posit society and space as two distinct entities which interact, and such an approach thus ends up by fetishizing space as an active component in social relations.

Evidently what is required is an approach which rejects both the 'relationist' position, in which space is said to consist of nothing more than the relations between objects, and the 'absolutist' position, in which space is said to possess its own distinctive causal properties (for a discussion of these two positions, see Smith 1984, ch. 3, and Urry 1985). Such an approach will need to go beyond the mere repetition of the sorts of platitudes which abound in the spatial political economy literature (e.g. the constant insistence that space is created and that it acts back upon social organization) in order to identify *how* new forms of economic organization shape new spatial patterns, and *how* spatial reorganization may structure social relations.

A significant start in this direction has been made by the British Marxist geographer, Doreen Massey. In various books and articles, but most notably in her *Spatial Divisions of Labour*, Massey sets out to show, not simply that 'space matters', but how it matters.

Her starting point is a familiar one:

> Geography matters. The fact that processes take place over space, the facts of distance or closeness, of geographical variation between areas, of the individual character and meaning of specific places and regions – all these are essential to the operation of social processes themselves. Just as there are no purely spatial processes, neither are there any non-spatial social processes. . . . Geography . . . is not a constraint on a pre-existing non-geographical social and economic world. It is constitutive of that world (1984, pp. 52–3).

Similarly, she goes on to argue, in terms reminiscent of much of the spatial political economy literature, that space is socially constructed and that social processes are constructed over space: 'The reproduction of social and economic relations and of the social structure takes place over space, and that conditions its nature' (p. 58). But what is distinctive about Massey's analysis is that she then proceeds to demonstrate how social relations are affected by spatial location – how it is that location shapes whether and how things happen – and she achieves this through concrete historical and comparative analysis.

Her analysis focuses primarily on class relations. Her thesis is that class relations develop differently in different places according to the peculiarities of past and present forms of economic organization. It is therefore misleading to talk of, say, 'the' working class in a country like Britain as if all workers in comparable forms of employment were homogeneous, for class relations are geographically structured and class capacities vary across different places. The point is obvious enough – one has only to compare, say, miners in the Nottinghamshire and Yorkshire coal fields to realize that apparently common work situations may generate very different kinds of social and political practices in different locations, and that a blanket term such as 'traditional–proletarian workers' (Lockwood 1966) is somewhat inadequate when it comes to understanding such variations. Similarly, Massey herself shows how an apparently similar national-level change (decentralization of assembly plants employing a high proportion of female labour) can in fact work out very differently in different parts of the country according to the existing social character of the areas concerned.

Why, then, do things happen differently in different areas? Massey argues that specific local histories mediate the effects of contemporary changes. Successive rounds of investment in an area (reflecting the part played by the local economy in the wider national and international division of labour) lay down 'layers of activity' and establish distinctive social, political and cultural legacies which then affect how later changes work out. The closure of a coal mine does not wipe out the pattern of social relations built up over generations, just as a shift from an agricultural to a manufacturing base does not eclipse the cultural traditions of the old farming communities. Such historical variations in local 'civil societies' are enormously significant in affecting the locational decisions of capitalist firms (e.g. the decision to establish a new assembly plant in an area of 'green' labour where there is no history of trade union organization) and in shaping the response of an area to local economic restructuring or 'deindustrialization' (see also Murgatroyd and Urry 1983). They also help to explain how it is that one working-class area sustains a radical local political culture while another does not (see Duncan and Goodwin 1982).

Having established that different areas with different histories generate different patterns of class organization with different capacities for action, Massey then goes on to consider the significance of contemporary patterns of capitalist investment across space. Unlike Harvey, she stresses that capital does not roam free across the landscape, investing in one place and pulling out of another, for such decisions reflect struggles and conflicts involving management, workers and the state: 'The establishment of a spatial structure . . . is not just a matter of a simple calculation on the part of capital. Its success or failure can be a function of workers' own attitudes and strategies. . . . "The requirements of capital" do not always have it their own way' (p. 90). However, she also recognizes that new patterns of spatial organization of firms are emerging, and that these are having a significant effect on local class and gender relations.

She distinguishes three main spatial patterns in contemporary capitalist production which she terms 'part-process', 'cloning' and 'single location'. The part-process spatial structure entails the establishment of different functions of the firm in different locations (e.g. the headquarters in one place, research and development in another, and assembly in a third). In this case, both the hierarchy of control and that of the technical division of labour are spatially organized. In the cloning structure, by contrast, the whole production process is located in each different plant, but the headquarters is concentrated is just one of them. In this case, the hierarchy of control is spatially organized but the technical division of labour is not. Finally, many firms of course carry out all their functions in a single location, and in these cases there is no spatial hierarchy of control or division of labour.

This very simple schema enables Massey to detect an important tendency in current patterns of investment – namely the move towards part-process systems in which large firms are likely to locate their head offices in London (which now contains between 80 and 90 per cent of the total office value in the UK (Urry 1985)), their prestigious and well-paid research and development functions in areas (normally in the south-east) where they can attract scarce, highly-skilled professional workers, and their routine assembly plants in other (often 'depressed') regions of the country (or sometimes overseas) where it is possible to find pools of relatively cheap, often 'green', and predominantly female labour.

This emerging geographical pattern demonstrates three crucial points. First, it exposes the fallacy in broad-brush spatial theories which assume that 'capital' (conceptualized as a homogeneous thing) simply deserts one area in favour of another, for what is happening is rather that different functions are gravitating to different areas. Second, it also shows how new investment is occurring in all sorts of areas, including to some extent the 'declining regions', but that the different kinds of investment going into different types of areas is producing a spatial hierarchy of control in which London and the south-east is coming to dominate the rest of the country. And third, it shows how the spatial reorganization of capitalist production involves at one and the same time a recomposition of local social relations. The old heartlands of male-dominated trade unionism are being broken up and new reserves of labour (whether in old industrial areas, where women are taking up unskilled jobs as men lose their traditional skilled occupations, or in newer and smaller towns) are being tapped with enormous implications for traditional class and gender relations in these areas. It is not just capital, but the working class as well, which is undergoing geographical reorganization, and this spatial factor is therefore crucial to any understanding of contemporary class and gender relations.

Massey's work overcomes many of the problems in Harvey's analysis – notably in its recognition of how people help structure the future of places, and in its attempt to relate a general Marxist theory of capital accumulation and class struggle to the historically specific conditions of different locations. Yet we are still some way away from establishing a theoretical understanding of the social significance of space. Massey shows that places vary in significant ways and that 'general' processes in society 'as a whole' are actively constituted and mediated through locally-specific conditions. It is clear from her work, for example, that an aspatial analysis of, say, class or gender relations cannot be sustained in that such social relations vary in important ways according to local historical factors. But although her work shows the need to take account of spatial variations in any social analysis, it is still not clear how – or even why – a distinctive concern with space should be integrated into the heart of social theory. Space has been shown to matter empirically, but the question for social theory remains, so what?

The spatial aspect of social organization

Mainstream social science has never denied the significance of space to social analysis (see Harris 1983). Although the community study tradition did in the past sometimes fall into the fallacy of assuming that one place was just like any other, and that a study of one locality could therefore be generalized to the society as a whole, sociology and related disciplines have more usually been acutely aware of the distinctiveness of place and, in empirical research, have normally taken great care to select areas for study with reference to the peculiar features they exhibit. Rex and Moore, for example, did not just happen to select Birmingham for their study of housing and race relations (any more than I myself simply chanced upon Croydon for my work on community power). It comes as no real surprise, then, to learn that things happen differently in different places with different histories, for location is one of a number of variables routinely addressed in any adequate social scientific inquiry.

When reading through the literature discussed in the previous section, the suspicion arises that Marxist geographers have in recent years been busy constructing theoretical mountains out of conceptual molehills. Of course, space matters, just as time matters, and it makes no more sense to attempt to practice an aspatial social science than it does an ahistorical one. The question, however, is why identify space as peculiarly significant for social analysis? What makes location something more than simply one variable among many which need to be taken into account when developing explanations of why and how social phenomena develop as they do?

The most sophisticated response to this question has come from sociologists and geographers working within a realist epistemology. As we shall see in the appendix, realism seeks explanations for how things happen by positing the existence of necessary and inherent causal properties in things which may or may not be realized (or which may be realized in one form rather than another) according to the contingent conditions in which they occur. An adequate explanation for some social phenomenon will thus entail both a theoretical identification of its inherent causal powers (e.g. the inherent capacity of the working class to organize itself as a political force) and an empirical identification of the relevant contingent conditions which in a particular case have enabled or constrained the expression of such powers (e.g. the existence of radical parties, the growth of full employment, the fragmentation of the work process, or whatever).

It is this crucial distinction between (theoretically identified) necessities and (empirically variable) contingencies which has been employed by writers such as Sayer (1984a and b) and Urry (1981, 1985) to specify the social significance of space. These writers reject both the relational and absolutist conceptions of space and argue instead that space is a contingent feature of social organization.

Put simply, the argument is that things have causal properties which, to be realized, depend upon an interrelation with other things with other causal properties. The inherent tendencies of things to act in certain ways will thus only become manifest when they come into particular spatially-conjunctural relations with other things. Gunpowder has the inherent capacity to explode, but it will not do so unless it coincides in its spatial and temporal location with, say, a dry atmosphere and a lighted match. So too, it is with social relations. Class relations, for example, will develop in different ways and take on different forms according to the presence or absence in a given place of, say, large companies, public sector employers, service employment, and so on (see Urry 1981). Seen in this way, space is neither a container of social relations, nor an object which interacts with social processes, but is the expression of contingent relations between social objects.

This sort of approach rules out the possibility of a theory or political economy of space, for if space is the contingent conjuncture of objects which enables causal powers to be realized but which does not itself have such powers, then it is impossible to develop a general theory of how space operates:

> Because spatial terms are contentless abstractions, until we specify what kinds of object with what kinds of causal powers actually constitute spatial relations, there can be no abstract general theory of space that is applicable to all objects (Sayer 1984b, p. 282).

> It is impossible and incorrect to develop a general science of the spatial. The latter cannot be separated from the social in such a manner that a general set of distinct laws can be devised. This is because space *per se* has no *general* effects. The significance of spatial relations depends upon the particular character of the social objects in question (Urry 1981, p. 458).

This, of course, is precisely what is wrong with the notion of a 'socio-spatial dialectic', and it also explains why Harvey ultimately failed to develop his abstract and general crisis theory in the context of a specific concern with space. From this perspective, abstract and general theory is appropriate to an understanding of the causal properties of objects, but the analysis of how and whether these properties are realized through specific spatial conjunctures can only ever be empirical.

One crucially important point arises out of all this, and that is that if space is to be analysed in terms of the contingent interrelation of things, then general theories about the things themselves need not be spatial. As Sayer (1984a, p. 134) recognizes, it is quite possible and legitimate to have a non-spatial social theory – indeed, given that abstract theory cannot generalize about spatially-contingent conditions, this is not only possible and legitimate but inevitable. While empirical analysis of concrete social phenomena must take the spatial context (i.e. the coexistence of other phenomena) into account if it is to explain what is happening in a particular case (hence Massey's dictum that 'geography matters'), the development of general social theory need not and cannot do this.

Here, then, is the epistemological justification for what most sociologists have been doing all the time! When you engage in empirical research, it is crucial to take account of the peculiar combinations of phenomena which arise in any given place, for these affect how and whether particular processes develop. But when you seek to generalize theoretically about such processes, you do so without worrying too much about the spatially variable contexts in which they may occur. We have, it seems, rediscovered the *ceteris paribus* clause – theory suggests that certain things will tend to happen, other things being equal, while empirical research shows how such things do not happen in this way owing to other things being far from equal in particular spatial contexts.

I am not suggesting that social theory is necessarily aspatial, in the sense that theory should totally disregard the fact that social phenomena have a spatial existence and location, but in following the logic of Sayer's argument, I am suggesting that it is necessarily non-spatial in the sense that space is not and cannot be an object of theoretical inquiry. The search for a political economy theory of space, or a sociological theory of space, is a non-starter. As we saw in Chapter 1 in the discussion of Marx, Weber and Durkheim, general theories of social organization are not inherently spatial, but spatial forms become relevant to them as secondary factors affecting the ways in which particular processes (e.g. the growth of working-class consciousness or the erosion of collective morality) develop in particular situations.

It has taken a long and roundabout route to arrive at a very simple conclusion! Here, however, we could let matters rest and turn to more substantial and theoretically interesting questions were it not for the fact that the theoretical waters, already murky with concepts such as 'the socio-spatial dialectic', have in recent years been muddied still further by the intervention of a leading social theorist, Anthony Giddens. In a widely read, and even more widely cited, series of books, Giddens has sought to place a concern with space in general, and the city in particular, at the heart of modern social theory, and in doing so he has breathed new life into the corpse of spatial sociology. It is, therefore, necessary to conclude this chapter with a critical discussion of Giddens's theoretical position, for those who seek to emphasize the social significance of space and to deny the possibility of a non-spatial sociology have tended to use his work to justify their arguments (see, for example, Paris 1983, p. 221, and Kirby 1985, p. 8).

Giddens's theoretical interest in space arises out of his concern to develop what he calls a 'theory of structuration' which can transcend the long-standing dualism in social theory between action and structure. In essence, the theory of structuration holds that structures consist of rules and material resources which represent the conditions of action in the sense that they both enable and constrain action. Individuals are conscious, acting subjects who understand these conditions without necessarily consciously acknowledging them, and who draw upon these rules and resources in living their everyday lives. In doing so, their actions reproduce them, although normally unintentionally, and often not with the results which they anticipated. In this way, the structural properties of social systems are routinely reproduced and changed over time through the unintended consequences of the (consciously or unconsciously motivated) actions of human agents. As Giddens puts it, 'The structural properties of social systems are both medium and outcome of the practices they recursively organize' (1984, p. 25).

How, then, does space (still less the city) enter into this analysis? The answer, in terms of the earliest versions of the theory, is hardly at all! In *New Rules of Sociological Method* (1976), for example, Giddens first explicitly outlined the key concepts of his theory of structuration, concepts which still constitute the foundations of his theoretical work today, but nowhere in this book is space taken to be in any sense central to an understanding of social reproduction. In the third chapter there is a passing reference to what Giddens sees as the 'obvious' point that interaction is situated in a spatial, as well as a temporal, context, yet this is evidently considered to be so insignificant an observation that it is never picked up in the concluding chapter where he summarizes the key elements of the theory of structuration.

This neglect of the spatial dimension in the early formulation of the theory is significant, for it is clear that whereas Giddens was from the outset sensitized by the logic of his analysis to the importance of time (since the reproduction of social systems is essentially an historical process), the concern with space only emerged later. It is my contention that this later interest in space is simply a corollary to the interest in time and is not a necessary feature of the theory of structuration. Even in the later works, the treatment of space seems almost gratuitous, an appendage to the theory rather than an essential component of it.

This appendage was grafted on to the theory in his 1979 work, *Central Problems in Social Theory*. Here, like so many other advocates of the crucial importance of space, he begins by taking sociology to task for its neglect of the spatial dimension in social life:

> Most forms of social theory have failed to take seriously enough *not only the temporality of social conduct but also its spatial attributes*. At first sight, nothing seems more banal and uninstructive than to assert that social activity occurs in time and in space. But neither time nor space have been incorporated into the centre of social theory; rather they are ordinarily treated more as 'environments' in which social conduct is enacted (1979, p. 202)

Against this view of space as a passive environment, Giddens argues that space forms part of the 'setting' of interaction. A setting, he tells us, 'is not just a spatial parameter, and physical environment, in which interaction "occurs": it is these elements mobilised as part of the interaction' (1979, p. 207).

He illustrates the point with reference to the structuration of classes. In an argument not dissimilar from that of Massey and Urry, he holds that spatial separation is a 'major feature' of class differentiation, and that the geographical separation of classes helps foster and reproduce regionalized class cultures which constitute different constraints and possibilities as regards individual and collective action. It is thus impossible to explain how and why any particular class acts as it does in particular situations without understanding the specifics of time and place in which it acts. Put another way, we cannot theorize, say, 'the working class' without first appreciating that the people designated by this term act in a physical and social context which affects and reflects what they do by structuring the rules and resources available to them. It is therefore a mistake to theorize class aspatially since class relations are constituted and reproduced in varying spatial settings. Where something happens is thus central to the explanation of how and why it happens.

This argument leads Giddens in his later books (notably *A Contemporary Critique of Historical Materialism, volume I* and *The Constitution of Society*, published in 1981 and 1984 respectively) to suggest that urban sociology is 'not merely one branch of sociology among others' (1984, p. 366), but is pivotal to the entire discipline. This is because urban sociology is that part of the discipline which has articulated most closely with geography and which has recognized most explicitly the interrelation of social and spatial organization. This elevation of urban sociology from its status as a somewhat neglected backwater of the discipline to a position of eminence within the social sciences and social theory reflects Giddens's belief that a concern with space in general, and with urban space (i.e. cities) in particular, is crucial to the 'problem of order' which lies at the heart of all social analysis.

As he sees it, the problem of order can be conceptualized as the problem of how social systems are bound or integrated over time and across space. Following familiar terminology, he distinguishes between 'social integration' (which arises out of face-to-face interaction in situations of 'co-presence' or 'high presence availability'), and 'system integration' (which refers to the integration of social systems across temporal and spatial distance where social relations are maintained between people who are not physically 'co-present' – i.e. in conditions of high 'time-space distanciation').

Giddens argues that space is crucial to both social and system integration. As regards the former, he suggests that integration is routinely reproduced by actors moving through familiar 'time–space paths' which intersect with other actors moving along their time–space paths, with the result that particular 'regions' of our lives assume a pattern in terms of recurring sets of social relationships. This accomplishment of routine interaction within spatial–temporal settings is, according to Giddens, enormously significant as a factor making for a sense of 'ontological security', for it means that in most aspects of our lives, we do not have to think too much about what to do or how to behave, but simply get on with the business of doing whatever it is we do in particular places at particular times in interaction with others whom we routinely expect to encounter there.

This regionalization of everyday life within particular 'locales' then helps build up system integration. Because time–space paths are repetitive, action is channelled through, and itself reproduces, regions of life which become institutionalized:

> Social integration has to do with interaction in contexts of co-presence. The connections between social and system integration can be traced by examining the modes of regionalisation which channel, and are channelled by, the time–space paths that members of a community or society follow in

their day-to-day activities. Such paths are strongly influenced by, and also reproduce, basic institutional parameters of the social systems in which they are implicated (1984, pp. 142–3).

In traditional or 'tribal' societies, most of this routine activity takes place within a single physical setting in a situation of high co-presence. In such a situation, the accomplishment of social integration is simultaneously the accomplishment of system integration since there are few, if any, social relationships to be maintained and reproduced beyond the everyday face-to-face level.

As human beings extend their control over nature (what Giddens calls 'allocative resources') and hence expand their capacity for organizing themselves socially (through the use of 'authoritative resources'), so the social system is progressively 'stretched' over time and space as reliance on face-to-face interaction diminishes. It is then that the problem of system integration emerges, and it is then that the city develops as the means for ensuring it.

Giddens argues that a society's control over allocative and authoritative resources can only grow to any significant extent when the means for storing them has developed. The concept of 'storage' is self-explanatory when applied to allocative resources, for it refers to the means for keeping, say, grain and cattle for extended time periods. Applied to authoritative resources, it means primarily the ability to collate and keep information (e.g. through the development of writing). Such storage capacity is a source of power in social life, for Giddens defines power as control over rules and resources (both allocative and authoritative). The place where resources are stored thus becomes the dominant place in such 'class-divided' societies, and this place is the city. Thus the city in class-divided societies represents a 'power container', a centre of economic, military and political strength and intelligence, which both depends upon and dominates its rural hinterland. So it is that the city–country relation emerges as the key structuring principle of class-divided societies where the social system has been 'stretched' and where system integration rests upon the relations of domination and interdependence forged between cities and their hinterlands.

With the development of capitalism in western Europe from the eighteenth century onwards, this stretching develops further and the social system bursts out of the city–countryside relation as trade is extended to a world level. Time–space distanciation is thereby massively increased with innovations in transport, communications, systems of monetary exchange and so on. In such a situation, system integration now depends upon ties of economic interdependency between people who rarely, if ever, even know of each other's existence, let alone meet face-to-face. In these 'class societies', therefore, the link between social relationships and spatial location becomes ever more tenuous, and natural space itself, which once represented a major constraint on social life (e.g. through people's inability to cross water, to settle in infertile regions and so on), is now subordinated to a social logic. Space is commodified (land is bought and sold like any other commodity) and is socially created with little reference to its natural form (e.g. as in the city block pattern of north American urbanization).

The extension of allocative and authoritative resources in modern class societies enhances the power of the nation state which displaces the city as the crucible of power in society as it expands its sophisticated methods of surveillance and information storage. In a world system of nation states, the old city–country relation all but disappears and the city itself ceases to constitute a significant 'locale' or setting of action:

> With the advent of capitalism, the city is no longer the dominant time–space container or crucible of power: this role is assumed by the territorially-bounded nation state. . . . The development of capitalism has not led to the consolidation of the institutions of the city, but rather to its eradication as a distinct social form (1981, pp. 147–8).

This last point is particularly important for our present purposes, for it certainly qualifies (and arguably undermines) much of what Giddens says about the centrality of urban space to social theory. Like Marx, Weber and Durkheim, Giddens here recognizes that, while cities were crucial units of organization in pre-capitalist, pre-industrial 'class-divided' societies where the city–country relations was fundamental, they have ceased to be so in contemporary capitalist 'class societies'. Today, that is, the city has ceased to be a significant unit of social, economic or political life.

In class societies, according to Giddens, the principal 'locale' or setting of social relations is the 'created environment'. 'The old city–countryside relation', he says, 'is replaced by a sprawling expansion of a manufactured or "created environment" ' (1984, p. 184). Yet the created environment is everywhere! The countryside, with its fields, hedgerows, woodlands and national parks, has been created just as the cities have. While it is true that action tends to be situated in particular locales, it is also the case that the substantive content of that action is little influenced by the environment in which it is placed. Just as social life has to a large extent transcended the temporal dimension (e.g. we may work at night as well as in the day, and the rhythm of social life does not vary much between winter and summer), so too it has transcended the spatial dimension. What happens in a particular place is largely determined, not by the character of the place itself, but by the operation of the land market and the intervention of the state. Where there is no natural harbour we build one; where the land is of poor quality we raise its fertility with artificial chemicals; where a hill blocks our path we force a cutting or drive a tunnel; and where there is no sun to tan our bodies we construct a solarium.

Now Giddens is obviously right to insist that none of this renders space insignificant in the modern period. Particular 'locales' (which may 'range from a room in a house, a street corner, the shop floor of a factory, towns and cities, to the territorially demarcated areas occupied by nation-states' (1984, p. 118)) are still associated with particular routinized patterns of everyday interaction, and the way space is 'packaged' may be important in facilitating information storage and surveillance and hence in reproducing relations of power and domination. Nevertheless, our relative transcendence of space in modern social life does seem to suggest that where something happens may not be as crucial as Giddens believes to an explanation of why and how it happens.

His discussion of the created environment seems to revolve around two key points. First, he recognizes that geographical divisions are not as marked as they once were – every town centre looks much the same, every housing estate has a similar design, every workplace is organized in much the same pattern, and so on. Second, he also accepts that we are much less tied to specific areas than was the case in the past – physical transportation is more readily available, geographical mobility is common, and electronic communications have freed us from the constraints of space. Taken together, these two points indicate that for most of us most of the time, where we happen to do something is relatively unimportant in affecting how we do it. Yet this conclusion flies in the face of Giddens's theoretical insistence on the centrality of space to social theory.

The source of the problem lies in Giddens's use of the concept of 'locale'. I would agree with Kirby (1985, p. 9) that this concept is 'poorly articulated' in Giddens's theory, and that the use he makes of it is 'idiosyncratic'. In 'class-divided' (i.e. pre-industrial, pre-capitalist) societies, locale refers primarily to the city–country cleavage in that these were the principal settings of social life which affected how you lived and whose relation structured the pattern of system integration in the society as a whole. But, as Giddens recognizes, this structural principle of organization has now been eroded. The city is no longer the power container of the society, for this role has passed to the nation state, and the division between the city and its rural hinterland has dissolved. This means that Giddens's statement that, 'The city cannot be regarded as merely incidental to social theory but belongs at its very core' (1981, p. 140) is actually rather misleading, for like Marx, Weber and Durkheim before him, Giddens knows full well that the city has long since ceased to be a sociologically significant locale in class societies. Today, the fundamental 'locale' is, according to Giddens, the created environment, yet as we have seen, the created environment is everywhere. Giddens's argument is thus tantamount to saying that place has lost its significance, for if the locale which sets the meaningful context of action is anywhere and everywhere, then specific locations would seem to have become virtually irrelevant.

It is as a result of his attempt to avoid this conclusion that Giddens's analysis becomes confused and confusing. To save his new-found commitment to space, he introduces yet another concept – that of the 'region'. Regions are, in a sense, mini-locales – places like the home, the street or (still more confusing given his earlier argument) the city – where social relations are routinely constituted and reproduced. As Thrift (1983) suggests, the region is thus the place where social structure and human agency meet – regions are the nodes through which social systems are structured.

But what does all this actually mean? In what sense are these regions crucial in structuring social relations? How exactly does the home, the street or the city work as a setting of reflexive action? What is at issue here is the specification of the process whereby physical places enter into the constitution of social life.

Giddens's analysis at this point is very weak. If we consider what he says about the home, for example, his argument consists simply of demonstrating how even this mini-locale is itself regionalized such that different rooms are associated with different life activities at different points in the day. Space within the home, he says, is structured into core and periphery regions (e.g. the kitchen and the spare bedroom) and this is analogous to the regionalization of other, larger-scale, locales such as the division of the city into the core business district and the peripheral suburbs, or that of the world into metropolitan core countries and the less developed nations. But this is a highly formalistic analysis, identifying formal similarities of spatial organization in different locales while abstracting from their contents. It is also very unclear what we as sociologists are meant to make of it. That we move through the home in definable time–space paths, washing in the bathroom in the morning, eating in the dining room in the evening, and sleeping in the bedroom at night, is indisputable. But so what?

Notwithstanding Giddens's conclusions to the contrary, I believe that it follows from the logic of his own analysis that social theory, in so far as it has addressed contemporary industrial societies, has been quite right to treat space as a 'backdrop' against which social processes develop. Unlike time, which is inherently caught up in, and thus constitutive of, the reproduction of social life, space only enters into the 'constitution of society' in a contingent way. It is notable that many commentators on Giddens's recent work have pointed out that his theoretical discussion of time is far more developed than his treatment of space (see, for example, Urry 1985). This is not, in my view, a weakness or lacuna which can be filled through further theoretical work, for the concern with space does not derive necessarily from the theory of structuration, but is tacked on to it from outside. This is inevitably the case given that (as Sayer recognizes) spatial arrangements, and the presence or absence of phenomena in space, are contingent and their effects can only be analysed empirically. Of course social science should not ignore space, for it is one factor (among others) which will need to be addressed when seeking explanations for specific empirical processes. We cannot afford an aspatial social science, for social processes do work out differently in different places according to the specific conjuncture of relations which occur there, but nor can we countenance a social theory of space which seeks to make location and positioning a key factor in the analysis. Location is a contingent variable and to fetishize it is as dangerous as ignoring it.

The fact that space is not central to the theory of structuration as developed by Giddens becomes clear when we consider the theory's applications. Giddens himself cites Paul Willis's study, *Learning to Labour* (1977), as an illustration of how his theoretical ideas can be translated into empirical research (although as Giddens himself admits, the study was actually accomplished without benefit of the theory (1984, p. 326)). This study exemplifies Giddens's own concerns with how system integration is routinely and unconsciously accomplished through meaningful action which is enabled and constrained by the rules and resources available to people in their everyday lives, and which gives rise to consequences (in this case, continued working class subordination) which are often unanticipated, unintended and unwelcome to the actors themselves. Yet it is notable that neither Willis nor Giddens, when discussing this research, feel it necessary to focus explicitly on the issue of space. Nowhere does Giddens demonstrate, or even ask, how space enters into this process whereby working-class 'lads' reproduce the conditions of their own subordination. Indeed, he does not even question whether 'lads' from other parts of 'Hammertown', or from other towns elsewhere in the country, engage in different sorts of practices as a result of their different geographical locales and time–space trajectories. The fact that Willis clearly believes that his in-depth study of just twelve adolescent boys in one town can to some extent be generalized to thousands of other working-class boys in dozens of other towns, and that he explicitly argues that Hammertown represents 'an archetypal industrial town' with 'all the classic industrial hallmarks' (1977, p. 6), is all accepted without comment in Giddens's discussion of the study. Not only, therefore, did Willis carry out this research without drawing upon the abstract theory of structuration, but he also did it without elevating space to a central position within the analysis, and Giddens himself seems to accept and endorse this as entirely adequate!

The point is, of course, that Willis was quite justified in stressing the similarities and generalities between Hammertown and other industrial towns and cities in Britain. Spatial considerations obviously did enter into his study at a very early stage, for as in any other empirical research, he needed to select a site where he would be able to study the particular people and processes in which he was interested. Hammertown is not Cheltenham, and he presumably chose the former rather than the latter precisely because he needed an area characterized by particular kinds and combinations of phenomena – e.g. working-class concentration, reliance on heavy manual forms of employment, etc. – not found in certain other places. But having selected his 'locale', what he found when he went on to study the lads' subculture was not a product of their living in Hammertown; rather, it was a product of their *social* location as working-class youth living in a capitalist society. What was going on does not happen in the same way in every other place, but the theoretical explanation for it has little, if anything, to do with space.

Giddens is, I believe, right to emphasize the centrality of recent urban sociology to the core concerns of social theory, but he asserts this centrality for the wrong reasons. The promise of urban sociology lies not in its traditional concerns with space and cities, which Giddens seeks to resurrect, but in its substantive focus on particular processes which Giddens in his discussion totally overlooks. Theoretical attempts to generalize about space, whether in terms of a 'socio-spatial dialectic' or a theory of 'locale', always end up either in the repeated assertions of banal observations (e.g. that space is socially created, that things happen differently in different places, or that we routinely do different things and interact with different people in different locations), or in a theoretical impasse where the general theory fails to articulate with the analysis of space (as in Harvey's failure to relate the theory of capital accumulation and crisis to the question of spatial form, or Giddens's failure to demonstrate the centrality of space to the process of social reproduction).

Here, then, is the case for what I term a 'non-spatial' urban sociology. What I mean by this is that urban sociology, like all other branches of the discipline, is essentially concerned with particular social relations and processes. Like every other branch of sociology, it must, when analysing these relations and processes, take into account their spatial setting, for particular combinations of presence and absence in particular places will have an affect on how and whether these processes occur. Urban sociology cannot therefore be aspatial, any more than industrial sociology, the sociology of education or the sociology of deviance can. But like every other branch of sociology, it will not focus on these spatial arrangements as its object of study. What is distinctive to urban sociology is not a particular concern with space, still less with the city as a particular spatial entity, but a specific focus on one aspect of social organization inscribed in space. Work by writers such as Pahl and Castells over the last few years has been enormously suggestive in terms of its substantive focus, but has ultimately collapsed in the face of the attempt to tie social processes to spatial forms. Ever since the work of Robert Park early this century, urban sociologists have been developing theoretical insights which have been undermined by the insistent attempt to mould them to a concern with space. It is time to rid ourselves of this theoretical straitjacket. It is time to put space in its place as a contingent factor to be addressed in empirical investigations rather than as an essential factor to be theorized in terms of its generalities. It is time for urban social theory to develop a distinctive focus on some aspect of social organization in space rather than attempting to sustain a futile emphasis on spatial organization in society. It is time, in short, to develop a non-spatial urban sociology which, while recognizing the empirical significance of spatial arrangements, does not seek to elevate these arrangements to the status of a distinct theoretical object.

8 From urban social theory to a sociology of consumption

We have seen that urban social theory cannot be constituted around the object of the city or the problem of space. This then leaves us with the question of what, if anything, urban sociology is about, and what it has to contribute to an understanding of contemporary social problems and processes.

In Chapter 6, we saw that much of urban sociology in recent years has come to focus on a range of issues concerning processes of consumption in advanced capitalist (and to some extent, state socialist) societies. This focus on consumption is, I suggested, crucial to the analysis of social inequality and political alignments in the current period, and it provides a distinctive object of analysis for urban studies. Whether or not the analysis of consumption, divorced from the traditional concern with cities and urban space, can still be termed 'urban' is simply a matter of convention, though like Dunleavy, I believe it is useful to retain this designation so as to maintain the intellectual continuity of the field. For the remainder of this chapter, therefore, I shall refer to 'urban sociology' and 'the sociology of consumption' as interchangeable labels for the same set of theoretical and substantive concerns.

It is necessary to make one point of clarification at the outset. We saw in Chapter 6 that Dunleavy seeks to restrict 'urban analysis' to the study of specific types of consumption. In particular, he rules out any concern with what he calls 'autonomous consumption' (where people service their own consumption needs and preferences) and 'individual consumption' (where people consume goods and services marketed without state subsidy). He also wishes to exclude analysis of those state provisions made in cash rather than kind on the grounds that money transfers enhance consumer spending power but do not themselves function as means of consumption. In this chapter, I shall suggest that this specification of the problem is too narrow and restrictive, and I shall attempt to demonstrate how a sociological analysis of the different patterns of consumption – state provision in kind, state provision in cash, self-provisioning and marketed or privatized provisioning – is in fact central to an understanding of certain key features of contemporary social organization and the way it is changing.

The chapter is arranged as three sections. In the first I seek to identify what is distinctive to the forms of politics which arise around state consumption provision. I do this by developing a typology which contrasts the politics of consumption with the politics of production. Although these two spheres are obviously related, I suggest that they tend to vary in terms of the types of interests which mobilize around them, the forms of state institutions through which they are organized, the level of the state at which they are located, and the dominant ideologies and values which surround them. It also follows from this that different kinds of political theory may be appropriate to the explanation of different aspects of state intervention in the modern period.

The second section then develops this analysis by considering the sociological significance of the division between private and socialized forms of consumption. Drawing on the literature on 'housing classes' (discussed in Chapter 4) and 'consumption sectors' (discussed in Chapter 6), it is suggested that a major fault line is opening up in countries like Britain between a majority of people who can service their key consumption requirements through the market and a minority who remain reliant on an increasingly inadequate and alienative form of direct state provision. This division, arising out of the social relations of consumption, is, it is argued, becoming as if not more significant than the more familiar class divisions arising out of the social relations of production, for it is fundamentally influencing not only political alignments, but also material life chances and cultural identities.

This conclusion then leads into the final section of the chapter where I consider some of the recent literature on the 'informal economy', domestic self-provisioning, and alternatives to state control of consumption. Drawing on work from within (e.g. Gans and Castells) and outside (e.g. Gorz and Ward) the urban social theory tradition, I suggest that the experience of domination and alienation which inevitably characterizes the organization of production in the modern period may to some extent be countered in the realm of consumption where there is a real potential for people to exert some degree of control over their everyday lives. This potential can, however, only be realized if the state's role in consumption is fundamentally restructured so as to enable rather than constrain individual and collective self-determination.

The politics of socialized consumption

We begin by trying to establish what, if anything, is distinctive to the forms of politics which tend to develop around the provision by the state of means of consumption. Two points, arising out of the discussion in Chapter 6, need to be made by way of introduction.

The first is that an analytical focus on consumption does not imply that consumption and production are unrelated. As we saw in Chapter 6, production influences and sets limits upon consumption, both in the sense that we cannot consume what has not been produced, and in that the social organization of productive life generates different capacities for consumption among different groups of people. To take an obvious example, a low-paid or unemployed worker will be unlikely to be able to afford to buy a house, run a car, pay for private medical insurance, and so on.

Having said this, however, it is also obviously the case that consumption influences and sets limits upon production, both in the sense that we cannot go on producing goods or services which are not consumed (hence Harvey's concern with problems of 'over-accumulation' in late capitalism), and that consumption generates different capacities for production among different groups of people (hence Castells's concern with the role of consumption in reproducing labour-power). There is, therefore, an interrelation between the two spheres, not a one-way determination.

More important than this, however, is the fact that in most contemporary capitalist societies, the capacity to consume is not entirely governed by one's location in the process of production. As we noted in the discussion of Pahl's work in Chapter 4, the enhanced role of the state in providing for basic consumption needs such as housing, education, health care and transportation has created a distinct pattern of consumption in the modern period which need not, and often does not, directly reflect the organization of production. Today, that is, most households depend for part of their consumption capacity on earnings from employment of one or more members, but their overall consumption also reflects their use of state provisions as well as their own home-based activities. Household consumption capacity is thus shaped by three key factors – the ability to earn, the right to state services, and the capacity to self-provision. Leaving discussion of the last of these to later in the chapter, it is clear that determination of household consumption capacity cannot be read off from members' participation in the formal system of production, for state provision is subject, in part at least, to a political logic which does not necessarily reflect the economic logic of the market.

In the modern period, therefore, people's life chances reflect the articulation of two systems of power – the operation of labour and commodity markets on the one hand, and the operation of the state on the other. As most contemporary political theorists, including Marxists, recognize, these are not reducible to each other. It therefore follows, if people's consumption is determined partly by participation in the market and partly by dependence on the state, that analysis of their place in the organization of production (i.e. their class location) cannot by itself be adequate for an understanding of their place in the organization of consumption. Put another way, although production and consumption are interrelated, they are also distinct processes shaped to some extent by different factors. This is why it is both possible and fruitful to distinguish them analytically.

Some critics of the approach to be outlined here have nevertheless continued to assert that the distinction between production and consumption cannot be sustained, and that a dualistic analysis based on this distinction must therefore be rejected. Duncan and Goodwin, for example, suggest that, 'There seems little historical argument for so rigid a separation between production and consumption. Much state activity . . . [is] clearly connected with both' (1982, p. 87). Similarly, Harrington argues of such an approach that, '. . . by splitting up the empirical objects of the explanation, it draws attention away from any connection between them. For example, the relation between "production" and "consumption" emphasised in Marxist analysis becomes deemphasised when using a dualist model' (1983, p. 215). Such arguments are, of course, reminiscent of those developed by Mingione, Preteceille and others against Castells's work (see Chapter 6). But as we saw when we discussed this work, a specific focus on consumption does not negate the relation to production, but simply denies that the former is reducible to the latter or that both are subject to the same logic.

What is really at issue here is a question of methodology. What critics like Duncan and Goodwin and Harrington seem to be suggesting is that a focus on consumption must be rejected because it is not holistic (which in contemporary social science is tantamount to saying it is not Marxist). It is, of course, nonsense to suggest, as

Harrington does, that a conceptual distinction between production and consumption necessarily obliterates the relation between them. The crucial point is that, in order to analyse this relation empirically, it is necessary first to draw the distinction conceptually. Those who deny this do so because, armed with their holistic framework, they already 'know' what the relation is, for their Marxist theory tells them that consumption is a function of production, that the two 'apparently' separate spheres are actually 'moments of one process in which production is the real point of departure and hence also the predominant moment' (Marx 1973, p. 94). These theorists thus proceed from the whole to the parts knowing in advance what the interrelation of the parts will be.

The approach outlined here, by contrast, proceeds by developing partial understandings of aspects of the social world, and thus gradually builds up a picture of how the different 'parts' affect each other. If we take this route, then it is essential that we have a clear idea of how the aspects of reality in which we are interested are to be identified and distinguished from other aspects. It also follows that knowledge of the interrelation of the parts will be derived, not from *a priori* theory, but from empirical research in different places at different times. This is the logic of a Weberian ideal type methodology, and it is this logic which informs the analytical distinction between production and consumption.

This brings me on to the second basic introductory point arising out of the discussion in Chapter 6, and this concerns the generalizability of the approach to be developed here.

We saw in Chapter 6 that a major problem with much recent urban social theory is that it has sought to establish as theoretical generalities insights gleaned from specific countries at specific periods. At first sight, an approach grounded in a methodology of ideal types would seem destined to reproduce this ethnocentrism and ahistoricism, for ideal types are constructed on the basis of observation of concrete social phenomena in particular times and places. The framework developed below, for example, clearly reflects the political arrangements pertaining in Britain in the contemporary period, and various critics have argued that it does not apply to this country at other points in its history (Duncan and Goodwin 1982, p. 85), or to other countries (e.g. Australia (Paris 1983, Badcock 1984) or Scandinavian (Kalltorp 1984)) in the current period.

More careful consideration of an ideal type methodology, however, leads to the recognition that ideal types may be either 'generic' or 'individual' (see Chapter 1). Individual types, such as Weber's concepts of the city or bureaucracy, are not intended to be generalizable beyond the times and places to which they refer, but they are constructed on the basis of generic types (e.g. Weber's four types of social action) which are taken to be timeless and spaceless. So it is with the framework developed here. This consists of an individual type, referring to the contemporary British context, but is built up on the basis of certain core elements (of which production and consumption are two) which may be taken as generic. The elements of the framework are thus generalizable, but the specific relation posited between them is not. To say, therefore, that the framework does not apply to the nineteenth century, or to other countries today, is to miss the point, for a major objective of this approach is to develop a set of concepts which, in different combinations, may enable the development of historical and comparative hypotheses by identifying which aspects of this or that state system are similar and which are different. Given that I have myself used this framework in an analysis of municipal politics in Melbourne (Saunders 1984a) and in a study of different forms of state intervention in the Australian Capital Territory (Saunders 1984b), the charge of ethnocentrism brought by Australian-based critics such as Badcock and Paris is particularly galling!

Let us, then, proceed to develop the framework itself. This entails identifying some of the main dimensions on which political interventions in the two spheres of production and consumption may typically differ. There are, I suggest, four such dimensions which relate to (a) the kinds of interests or 'social base' mobilized, (b) the mode through which these interests mobilize, (c) the level of the state system at which they mobilize, and (d) the sorts of values and ideologies which inform the state's activity in each sphere. Let me stress again that what is being proposed is not an empirical model designed to replicate any given reality in all its messy complexity, but an ideal type framework which logically purifies and exaggerates certain tendencies found in reality but which is itself a one-sided abstraction which does not actually exist in this pure form at any time or in any place. The purpose of this framework is to clarify concepts as an aid to hypothesis construction rather than to replicate or represent some concrete situation, and having outlined the framework, I will go on to develop a key hypothesis about the nature of consumption politics in the contemporary period.

The social base

The distinction between a 'politics of production' and a 'politics of consumption' derives partly from the work of Castells, but more especially from developments within German 'critical' theory. The key writers here are Jürgen Habermas and Claus Offe.

From the 1960s onwards, Habermas has been arguing that Marx's political economy is inadequate for an understanding of late capitalism. This is partly because the increased significance of science in revolutionizing the forces of production has in his view undermined the labour theory of value, and partly due to the crucial role that the state now plays in managing the economy. In *Legitimation Crisis* (1976), Habermas brought together many of the themes explored in his earlier works by suggesting that the 'steering problems' in late capitalist societies have been displaced from the economic sphere of the market to the political sphere of the state. In taking upon itself the responsibility for directing and managing the future development of the society, the state has undermined traditional laissez-faire ideologies while at the same time creating enormous 'rationality problems' as regards how to secure and direct economic growth. Failure to resolve these problems threatens both the legitimacy of the system (which now rests mainly on the ability of the state to deliver on its promises) and the motivation of individuals to participate fully within it.

These ideas were taken up and explored by Claus Offe in his influential 1975 paper and in various other essays (many of which are reprinted in Offe 1984). He distinguished between two aspects of the state's role – its traditional 'allocative' functions (in which the conditions of capital accumulation are maintained in a purely authoritative way through, for example, control of the money supply or regulation of working conditions), and its newer 'productive' functions (in which the state directly provides the resources required for further capital accumulation by, for example, nationalizing key but unprofitable sectors of the economy or by providing welfare to support the reproduction of the labour force). Offe argued that while allocative functions could be discharged according to the relative pressure brought upon the state by outside interests, this was not possible in the case of productive functions which had in some way to be insulated from competitive political pressures if they were to achieve their necessary effect. Offe discusses various possible strategies through which such insulation could be achieved, but concludes that none can ensure that productive interventions do in fact accord with the requirements of the system. For him, therefore, the 'rationality problem' confronting the modern capitalist state is irresolvable.

Offe's distinction between two sets of state functions (allocation and production), each of which is determined in a different way, was reflected in various works published outside of Germany through the 1970s. Of particular significance was James O'Connor's *The Fiscal Crisis of the State*, published in 1973. Like Offe, O'Connor believed that the primary task of the capitalist state lay in supporting capital accumulation, and that this was achieved (to the extent that it was possible to achieve it) by different kinds of interventions. He distinguished two main types of state expenditure designed to realize this objective – 'social expenses' (i.e. spending on items such as law and order or social security which are necessary to maintain social order and legitimacy but which are unproductive and thus constitute a drain on profitability) and 'social capital' which contributes to capital accumulation either directly (in the form of 'social investment' designed to lower the costs of constant capital – e.g. spending on economic infrastructure) or indirectly (in the form of 'social consumption' which lowers the costs of variable capital by supplementing workers' living standards and thus reducing the necessary level of wages – e.g. spending on housing or health care). In O'Connor's view, escalating demands on all three areas of the state budget result in a fiscal crisis as the state attempts in vain to maintain profitability and suppress social unrest during a long-term economic decline.

O'Connor's distinctions, and in particular that between 'social investment' and 'social consumption' functions, are useful in pointing to the different kinds of interventions made by modern capitalist states, but are ultimately flawed by the functionalist assumptions which lie behind them. For O'Connor, all state spending serves the interests of capital in one way or another, yet as we saw in Chapter 6, spending on 'social consumption' in most western countries has arguably gone far beyond anything which can seriously be designated as 'necessary' from the point of view of capitalist firms. This is not to deny that welfare provisions may contribute in some way to private sector profitability, for as Castells and others have noted, they not only reduce necessary wage costs but also sustain demand for the commodities produced by drug companies, building firms and the like. Nevertheless, the primary beneficiaries of (and often, though not always, the driving force behind the growth of) such provisions are not generally capitalist enterprises, but are the people who consume the services (public sector tenants, patients, students or whatever) and/or the people employed by the state to provide them (social workers, doctors, teachers, etc.). These groups have gained in real material terms from the expansion of social consumption spending, and they have done so to some extent at the expense of private capital (see, for example, Bacon and Eltis 1978).

It is this insight which leads us, not only to distinguish between interventions of the state which directly support capital accumulation (e.g. provision of physical infrastructure such as road and rail links, provision of raw materials and energy such as steel, coal and gas and electricity, provision of financial grants and incentives, and so on) and those which directly support people's consumption requirements (e.g. provision of public housing, health services, schooling, public transport, and so on), but also to recognize that different kinds of interests are likely to be mobilized around these different types of intervention. Where the state intervenes in the organization or production, it is class-based organizations such as, in Britain, the Confederation of British Industry and the Trades Union Congress which respond, for such organizations are constituted in terms of the social relations of production. Where, on the other hand, the state is involved in direct provision for consumption, the typical pattern of mobilization is not generally class-based but arises out of the organization of sectoral interests which may (depending to some extent on the service in question) cut across classes according to the specific constituency of interests affected by the policy.

The distinction between different aspects of the state's role can thus be said to coincide, to some extent at least, with the distinction between political cleavages based on class and those based on consumption location. It is of course important to avoid any mechanistic reduction of political action to an objectively-defined social base. As Franklin and Page (1983) point out, sectoral interests do not automatically produce political cleavages but are mediated through people's political consciousness. Or as Pickvance (1977a) argued in relation to Castells's work, we should not simply assume that, having identified a 'social base', it will necessarily be mobilized into a social force. Nevertheless, we can suggest that, when and if people do mobilize or align themselves around consumption questions, their class interests (e.g. as workers organized through trade unions, professionals organized through credentialist associations, employers, managers and entrepreneurs organized through industrial federations, etc.) will tend to figure less centrally than their sectoral interests (e.g. as home buyers, as parents of schoolchildren, or as ratepayers). Typically, we would no more expect, say, owner-occupiers to mobilize around the issue of import controls than we would car firms to exert pressure over the issue of mortgage interest tax relief.

The mode of interest mediation

The next step in the analysis lies in the recognition that different kinds of interests not only mobilize around different aspects of the state's role, but they also organize their relationship to the state in different ways. Thus, while class-based producer interests typically participate in corporatist forms of state institutions, consumer interests generally have little option but to organize (to the extent that they organize at all) in the more public arena of competitive or pluralistic politics.

My argument here derives mainly from work in Britain from the late 1970s on the question of corporatism. As we saw in Chapter 4, the strong corporatist thesis developed by Pahl and Winkler was certainly over-ambitious, but later writers have attempted to refine and develop the concept by specifying more carefully the sorts of relations and processes involved, and by limiting its applications to certain particular areas of state activity.

Of particular relevance here is Cawson's work (1978, 1982), where he suggests that the division between monopolistic and competitive sectors of the economy has a parallel in the division within the polity between a relatively closed corporatist sector and a more open competitive sector. His notion of corporatism owes much to the approach of Philippe Schmitter (1974) who defines it, not as a new societal or state system (in the way Pahl and Winkler suggest), but as a distinctive way of organizing key interests within advanced capitalist countries. For Schmitter, as for Cawson, corporatism is thus a mode of interest mediation characterized by functional rather than territorial representation of interests, and by the participation of such functional interests in both the development and implementation of state policy. Although it often takes the form of tripartite arrangements involving capital, organized labour and the state, Cawson stresses that this is not a necessary feature, for corporatist mediation can and does develop in bipartite relations and may encompass various other producer interests (notably the professions such as the doctors) besides industry and the unions.

There is still considerable debate in the literature about the nature of existing corporatist relations. Mercer (1984), for example, argues that Cawson is mistaken when he cites the doctors as a major interest involved in corporatist arrangements in the British health care system. Similarly, where Jessop (1978, 1979) sees organized labour as very much a 'junior partner' in corporatist economic policy-making which is dominated by the relation between capital and the state, Middlemas (1979) detects the growth of a 'corporate bias' in British economic policy since the First World War in which organized labour has played the key role at the expense of capital. Such disputes are important, but they represent disagreements over the content of corporatist relations rather than over their existence. All of these writers agree that a new system of functional representation and mediation of interests has emerged side-by-side with the more traditional elective aspect of the state system and that effective power has increasingly shifted from the latter to the former. They also agree that it is producer (class) interests which have come to participate in these new arrangements (though which producer interests remains unclear) while other social interests have been excluded.

Summarizing all this, we may agree with Jessop that, in Britain at least, the political system has become 'bifurcated' between a sphere of electoral-democratic politics (the world of parliament, petitions and pressure groups) and a more closed sphere of corporatist mediation in which key producer interests come to be directly represented and involved in the making and implementation of state policy. This split tends to coincide with that between the politics of consumption and the politics of production. The modern state, in other words, is not a homogeneous entity, but consists of various institutions which tend to operate in different ways in different policy areas and which are differentially accessible to different kinds of interests. Furthermore, as we shall now see, these variations tend also to coincide with the different levels on which state intervention is organized.

The level of intervention

We saw in Chapter 4 that Pahl's concept of urban managerialism collapsed as he came to realize that local bureaucrats were not autonomous agents but were operating in a context of constraint in which the pressures from central government on the one hand, and from the local population on the other, were a major factor. The concept which eventually displaced that of urban managerialism in urban studies from the late 1970s was that of the 'local state', first coined by Cockburn (1977) in her study of the London Borough of Lambeth.

Cockburn both dismissed the idea of local autonomy and argued (in terms strongly reminiscent of Poulantzas) against analysing urban politics in terms of the goals and values of individual managers or politicians. For her, the 'local state' (by which she really meant little more than local government – see Duncan and Goodwin 1982) could only be understood as part of a unified capitalist state, and the provision of services at the local level simply reflected the requirements of capital as a whole. In this way, she equated 'local state' with 'capitalist state' (thereby denying any degree of local discretion or autonomy), and 'capitalist state' with 'the interests of capital as a whole' (thereby denying any effective degree of state autonomy from capital).

In the shift from urban managerialism to the local state, urban studies in Britain lurched from frying pan to fire. Where Pahl had over-emphasised local discretion and political autonomy, Cockburn now denied them! Clearly, as Boddy (1983) has argued, what is needed is some approach which can combine the strengths of Marxist state theory with the insights of mainstream political science which has long recognized that local government is more than simply a passive agent of central authority (e.g. see Rhodes 1980). To achieve this, it is necessary to return briefly to Jessop's discussion of the bifurcation of politics between corporatist and competitive sectors.

To the extent that Jessop's analysis is correct, it seems that the state today operates in two different ways. On the one hand, the traditional institutions of representative democracy (elections, lobbying, demonstrations, petitions and all the other paraphernalia of liberal-democratic systems) provide a forum for non-incorporated interests such as small business, welfare clients and consumers generally to press their demands; on the other, the corporatist sector, which is exclusive to representatives of functional producer interests such as industry, organized labour and the professions, operates mainly to develop policies which are consistent with the requirements of these key groups and which can therefore overcome to some extent the 'rationality' or 'steering' problem identified by writers such as Habermas and Offe.

The problem, however, is that according to Jessop there exists a 'contradictory unity' between these two modes of interest mediation, for popular pressures exerted through the democratic sector tend to undermine the commitments negotiated in the corporatist arena. There is, in other words, a recurring tension between rational planning and democratic accountability (a point which has also been noted by so-called 'new right' theories which seek to explain what they see as 'the ungovernability of Britain' – see Dearlove and Saunders 1984, for a review). This tension is overlaid by that between economic and social expenditure priorities identified in O'Connor's work, for the question of how to reconcile the demands of key producer interests with those of consumers is at one and the same time the question of how to reconcile corporatist economic strategies with electoral pressures on social spending.

One way in which these tensions may be mediated is through the location of different types of intervention, involving different modes of interest mediation, at different levels of the state system. As Friedland and his co-authors have noted, the more local the organization of state intervention, the more susceptible it is likely to be to popular mobilization and pressure:

> The electoral-representative arrangements which underpin municipal governments make them vulnerable to popular discontent . . . local governments are often important loci for popular political participation because they are structurally accessible, the point of daily contact between citizen and state. The relative visibility of local government policies and the relative accessibility of local government agencies make them a more susceptible target of political opposition than other levels of the state (1977, pp. 449, 451).

This crucial insight suggests that one way in which the tensions between different aspects of the state's role may be managed (whether intentionally or not) is through the removal of key services relating to production to higher levels of the state system. Certainly there is no doubt that producer interests generally find it easier to organize effectively on a regional or national level while consumer interests are most effective at a local level (I have demonstrated this both in respect of health and water services in England (Saunders 1985a) and through an analysis of the mobilization of bias in land use planning questions following the removal of municipal government in Melbourne (Saunders 1984a)). I am not here suggesting that local level politics are always open and pluralistic (what Cochrane has dismissively termed the 'pluralist and institutionalist myth that local government is more responsive than central government' (1984, p. 282)); only that consumers of state services are likely to find it less difficult to make their voices heard the closer to home the agency which is responsible for providing them. Put another way, if popular, non-class, interests cannot organize effectively at the local level, then it is unlikely that they will be able to organize effectively anywhere.

Two other points should also be emphasized about this argument. First, notwithstanding the criticisms advanced by Harrington (1983, p. 209) and Duncan and Goodwin (1982, p. 85), I am not here positing a new form of functionalist state theory in which the level at which a service is provided is explained in terms of the need to insulate it from, or tailor it to, this or that interest or pressure. The explanation for *why* particular aspects of policy are located at particular levels of the state system involves an historical analysis of various factors, and does not imply that there was some functional necessity impelling this pattern of distribution. One factor has undoubtedly been the deliberate and conscious intention on the part of governments to remove 'contentious', 'strategic' or 'expensive' aspects of public policy from the local level (this, for example, seems to have been the motive for nationalizing the social security system in Britain between the wars, for regionalizing water services in 1974, and for eroding local government autonomy since 1979; it was also the major motive behind the dismissal of the Melbourne City Council in 1981 when a residents/socialist coalition began to block new commercial developments in the central area). But other factors have also played their part. Furthermore, even where key powers have been relocated to higher levels of the state in a deliberate attempt to safeguard the interests of capitalist or other major producer groups, this has not guaranteed that the strategy has been successful. As Giddens notes in his theory of structuration, even purposive action has a nasty habit of producing unintended and undesired consequences. The 'steering problems' faced by the modern interventionist state are such that there can be no simple safeguard against failure, and when it comes to directing the use of state monopoly power, the clearest of intentions may turn out to have the most disastrous of consequences (see Hayek 1960). The argument outlined here is thus neither functionalist in the explanations it offers, nor functionalist in its expectations of outcomes.

The second point to note is that the tendency for consumption interventions to be focused on local, electoral levels of the state while production interventions gravitate towards higher level corporatist institutions, obviously takes different forms in different places at different times and is nowhere as clear-cut as the ideal type suggests. There is no country in the world where the national/local division corresponds neatly to that between production and consumption, or corporatism and pluralism, or class politics and sectoral politics. In America and in Norway, studies of business and union involvement in local affairs suggest that, 'Corporatism should not be restricted to the analysis of national politics' (Villadsen 1983, p. 22), and in Britain, studies of local planning (e.g. Flynn 1981 and 1983, Reade 1984, Simmie 1981) have claimed to find some evidence of local corporatist initiatives. Sharpe, too, argues that, 'There may now be emerging something that looks like a corporate dimension at the local level' (1984, p. 37), while other commentators have suggested that local political action 'may involve an important social class component as well as a consumption sectoral component' (Duke and Edgell 1984, p. 196). Cooke (1982) goes further in suggesting that the local arena has often been crucial in generating and sustaining class-based political cultures, and he argues that the relation between capital and labour is constantly surfacing at all levels of the state system.

Much of this work is valid and significant, and it would be foolish to deny that corporatist initiatives may emerge at local level or that people may organize around their class interests at this level. However, the crucial question is whether such patterns are *typical*, for in Britain at least, I believe they are not. Thus, when corporatist initiatives are launched at local level (e.g. in various contemporary local economic strategies) they not only prove very limited in scope, but they also tend to be largely ineffectual in anything other than propaganda terms. Similarly, the history of class mobilization at local level is generally one of short-term action and highly fragmented organization (hence the conspicuous absence in Britain of fully-fledged 'urban social movements'). The framework outlined here does not deny the possibility that elements of the politics of production may appear at local level, but it does rest on strong theoretical and empirical grounds for believing that such patterns are not typical and are rarely enduring.

The only significant exception to this pattern concerns the tendency for state consumption provisions in cash (i.e. the social security system) to be located centrally in most countries (see Dunleavy 1984, and Sharpe 1984). This is an important exception. As Sharpe suggests, it is partly a reflection of the fact that monetary payments are much more easily centralized than are services in kind. I would add to this the observation that the state has less inherent control over people when it gives them money than when it provides them with specific services or goods (a point I shall explore in the final section of this chapter), in which case the centralization of cash transfer payments (which in Britain followed the rebellion of the Poplar councillors over Poor Law payments in the 1920s) may represent an attempt to increase surveillance over that aspect of consumption which is least easily monitored and controlled.

The ideology

Thus far, we have been examining the external environment in which the state operates – the types of interests it encounters, the ways in which it articulates with them and the levels at which it deals with them. However, as Harrington notes, 'The influence of external forces will to some extent be modified by the attempt of professional groups within the state to assert their own interests' (1983, p. 214; see also Flynn 1986). We need, in other words, to return to the sorts of issues addressed in Pahl's work on urban managerialism, for although professionals and bureaucrats within the state do not generally operate in a political vacuum, nor are they normally totally insignificant in determining what the state does and how it does it.

The problem with Pahl's urban managerialism thesis was ultimately that he failed to theorize managerial discretion. To some extent, of course, this cannot be theorized, for the scope for action in any given case will depend on a range of empirically variable factors. However, we can take the theoretical analysis further than Pahl took it by first identifying in more detail the relations which managers are called upon to mediate, second, recognizing the sorts of professional/managerial ideologies and values which are likely to emerge in different situations, and third specifying under what conditions these values and ideologies are likely to prove paramount in shaping state outcomes.

The first point is self-evident from the foregoing analysis. Urban managers stand at the intersection of the politics of production and the politics of consumption. To the extent that these different spheres relate to different types of state intervention organized in different ways at different levels in respect of different kinds of interests, urban managers can be seen as mediating the tensions between economic and social priorities, corporatist and democratic strategies, central and local initiatives and class and sectoral interests.

The way they mediate these various cross-cutting pressures will depend upon their own values and interests, which are often technocratic and supposedly 'apolitical' (see, for example, Reade 1984), but whose content is likely to vary along a continuum from 'capitalistic' values at one extreme to 'public service' values at the other. In my work on health and water authorities in England

(Saunders 1985a), for example, it was apparent that the managers and professionals involved in the water authorities tended to reveal a commitment to a view of water as a commodity rather than a service (thus reflecting the significance of water as a means of production for private sector interests such as farmers, developers and industry), whereas health professionals and administrators stressed their role in providing for social need (albeit in a rather paternalistic way). Different types of ideology are thus appropriate to different types of state provision, and these ideologies and values are likely to permeate the policy-making processes within these different state institutions.

The significance of professional and managerial values will, however, depend upon the context in which the managers are operating. Managerial autonomy, I would argue, is a function of two key factors – the degree to which strategic producer interests are content to permit it, and the extent to which consumer interests can be held at arm's length. In national level corporate institutions, for example, it is likely to be highly circumscribed given the integration of producer interests into the policy process. In local level competitive institutions it may be more pronounced, though will be limited to the extent that the consumers of the service in question are able to force their views and demands on to the political agenda. Managerial autonomy is probably most developed in situations where, as in the English Regional Health Authorities, the service in question is of little interest to producers while the scale or level at which it operates (reinforced in this case by the absence of electoral mechanisms at the regional level in England) is beyond the scope of consumers to influence.

All of this reinforces the argument that the state in the modern period cannot be analysed as a single, cohesive entity. It is fragmented into different 'branches' (see, for example, Miliband 1969, ch. 3), each of which is internally differentiated into different levels and departments. Some parts of the system are elected, some are open to domination by bureaucratic or professional employees, and some effectively function as the mouthpiece of particular private interests. The different bits and pieces of the system operate according to different logics, are accountable to different publics and are responsible for managing different types of problems. The sheer organizational complexity of the state apparatus makes it virtually impossible for any one group to impose any single, transcendent strategy culminating in any one set of desired outcomes (hence the 'rationality problem' identified by Habermas and Offe). Theories of *the* state, which attempt to explain its overall operation in terms of a single general theory, should clearly be treated with some scepticism, for the possibility that any one group (be it the elected government or the capitalist class) or any one logic could dominate such a system seems highly implausible.

This, then, is the case for what may be termed a 'dualistic theory of politics'. By distinguishing the social base, mode of interest mediation, level of intervention and affinitive ideology typically associated respectively with the politics of production and the politics of consumption, it is possible to identify different aspects of politics which may best be explained by different political theories. In other words, we can move from the construction of an ideal type framework (summarized in Figure 2) to the development of specific hypotheses by recognizing that theories which have often been counterposed to each other as incompatible may in fact be complementary in the sense that they are appropriate to an understanding of different aspects of the political process.

	Politics of production	*Politics of consumption*
Social Base	Class interests	Consumption sector interests
Mode of interest mediation	Corporatist	Competitive
Level	Central state	Local state
Dominant ideology	Capitalistic (private property rights)	Public service (citizenship rights)
State theory	Instrumentalism (class theory)	Imperfect pluralism (interest group theory)

Figure 2 The dual politics thesis

What is being suggested here is not that all of these elements necessarily always line up with each other in all times and in all places, but that there is a tendency for the different elements to correspond in this way, and that (most crucially) to the extent that they do, the greater will be the relative applicability of one or other theory to understanding and explaining them. The dual politics thesis, in other words, is above all else an attempted solution to the relative autonomy problem discussed in Chapter 6, for it sets out to identify the different mechanisms which, in aggregate, result in the state both supporting the interests of dominant classes and responding to the demands of less powerful groups.

The basic hypothesis is very simple and may be stated in the form of two propositions. First, the state will operate in the interests of dominant classes the more its interventions are directed at the process of production, the more corporatist its organizational forms, the more centralized its operations and the more those in key positions are predisposed to support the principles of allocation grounded in rights of private property. Second, the state will be more responsive to the weight of popular opinion and various demands articulated by different sections of the population the more its interventions are directed towards provision for consumption, the more competitive or democratic its organizational forms, the more localized its operations and the more those in key positions are predisposed to support principles of allocation grounded in concepts of citizenship rights and notions of social need.

The first pattern is thus best explained in terms of instrumentalist theories which see the state as operating in the interests of dominant classes due to (a) the fact that key individuals and groups recognize that primacy must be accorded to capital accumulation in order to maintain all other state activity, (b) the fact that dominant class interests will often achieve direct access to key state institutions, and (c) the fact that most strategic state personnel at this level will be ideologically predisposed to support the rights of private property (see, for example, Miliband 1977). The second pattern, by contrast, is best explained by theories of imperfect pluralism which emphasize the relative openness and responsiveness of elected authorities to the pressures brought upon them by their constituencies, while also recognizing that the competition for the ear of government is unequal, and that political pressures will be mediated through the values of those responsible for managing the services in question (see, for example, Dahl 1963).

The framework outlined here can be used to develop other, more specific, hypotheses (e.g. it can be applied to the development of a theory of central–local state relations – see Saunders 1984c). It has been applied with some success in various empirical studies of urban politics, not only in my own work on Australian city government and on English regional authorities, but also in work such as that by Blowers (1984) on a planning conflict between industrial and environmentalist interests in Bedfordshire. And as we shall see in the next section, it can also provide the basis for a retheorization of social stratification in the modern period. In addition, however, this framework can help to clarify two fundamental issues which have been at the centre of recent debates in urban studies; namely, the problem of specifying an object of study, and the problem of explaining the relative autonomy of the state.

I have already suggested that urban studies may fruitfully be defined in terms of an interest in questions of consumption. We are now in a position to specify this object of study more rigorously, for we have seen that the analysis of consumption will generally entail a concern with the four dimensions identified in Figure 2. This specification of the object of study is, interestingly, broadly consistent with the proposition arrived at by Castells in *The City and the Grassroots*, for as we saw in Chapter 6, Castells now argues that the urban question relates to the issues of collective consumption, political power and cultural meaning. Castells's focus on collective consumption is reflected here in the division between producer and consumer interests, his focus on cultural meaning is reflected in the division between values of need and values of profit, and his focus on political power is broken down into its two constitutive elements of scale – local/non-local – and mode – democratic/non-democratic.

Seen in this way, the 'urban question' may be defined in terms of the tensions which arise in the contemporary period between consumption and production based interests, competitive and corporatist forms of politics, local and central levels of state power, and values of need or social rights as against values of profit or private property rights. Taken together, this cluster of related issues defines, not simply a coherent research agenda for urban studies, but also a set of problems which go to the heart of the issues facing modern industrial societies in the late twentieth century. The significance of the tension between producer interests and consumer interests is revealed in, for example, the battles of trade unions to save jobs even at the expense of higher prices or taxes, the concerns of the professions to preserve their legal monopolies even at the expense of consumer choice, the concerted attempts by capitalist firms and capitalist governments to bolster profits even at the expense of welfare provisions, environmental quality or (as in the case of the defence industry) growing threats to world peace. The significance of the tension between competitive and corporatist modes is revealed in the growing problems of secrecy and closure – the demands for freedom of information, the demands for greater political accountability, the mounting frustration with bureaucratic insensitivity and non-responsiveness. The significance of the tension between local and central state levels is revealed in the mounting chaos surrounding relations between central and local authorities in a country like Britain, in initiatives such as the 'new federalism' in the USA or the decentralization programme in France, and in the spread of local participatory, co-operative or self-help movements designed to claw back some degree of control and autonomy in an increasingly centralized system of power and domination. And the significance of the tension between values of need or social rights as against values of profit or property rights is revealed in the breakdown of the post-war ideological consensus, in the growing polarization of politics and society between collectivistic and individualistic solutions, in the divisions between the 'new left' with its attempts to rethink the socialist project and the 'new right' with its assertion of neo-liberal values, and in the widening gulf (discussed in the next section) between those who can service their needs through the market and those who must rely on the state.

These, then, are the sorts of issues addressed by urban studies when it takes consumption as its object of analysis, and they are issues which are central in determining the future shape of the society as a whole. It is for this reason that I suggested in Chapter 7 that Giddens is right when he claims that urban sociology has a place at the very core of social theory and social analysis, but this position reflects not its concern with the abstract problem of space, but rather its substantive concerns with a set of crucial contemporary themes.

The second major issue in urban studies which the framework developed here may help to resolve is the problem of how to explain the 'relative autonomy' of the state. As we saw in Chapter 6, structuralist Marxism was undoubtedly right in its observation that the modern capitalist state tends to operate in the long-term interests of dominant classes while responding in the short term to various popular interests, but the theory advanced to explain this was seen to be inadequate. The dual politics thesis can, however, explain how this happens, and it can do so in a way which is in principle testable. Thus, if a situation could be found in which productive interventions at central level organized through corporatist initiatives and managed by individuals supportive of private property were nevertheless determined by pluralistic competition between different interest groups (the acid test of general pluralist theories), or in which consumption interventions at local level organized through elective or participatory agencies and managed by progressive individuals were determined by the influence of dominant economic class interests (the acid test of general instrumentalist theories), then the thesis would be refuted. Unlike structuralist Marxist theories of relative autonomy, then, this approach specifies counterfactual conditions and hence recognizes the empirical criteria of its own invalidation. It also allows for further development and modification in the light of new empirical research findings.

This proposed solution to the relative autonomy problem reflects an explicit commitment in the dual politics thesis to theoretical pluralism – i.e. to the view that different theories can be applied in a complementary way to the analysis of different aspects of political processes. Such an approach has, however, been criticized by some commentators as 'eclecticism'. Paris, for example, describes the approach as 'unashamedly eclectic' and attacks it for taking 'analytical categories out of context from different and mutually contradictory theoretical frameworks' (1983, pp. 225 and 223). Similarly, Kalltorp is critical of the attempt to 'unite very different theoretical elements into one single framework', and he suggests that 'these theoretical perspectives to some extent contradict each other if their full ramifications are elaborated' (1984, p. 63).

Such criticisms must be refuted, for it is clear that this approach is not eclectic. It does not rip theories from their contexts and cobble together the various bits and pieces, but rather applies theories as integral wholes while also recognizing that their applicability is limited to particular aspects of the political process. Only if one denies the possibility that different kinds of processes may be subject to different kinds of social determinations will it make sense to attack the thesis as eclectic. This of course is precisely what many (though not all) Marxist theorists do deny through their assertion that one single theory must explain all aspects of the social totality. Yet as the failure of Marxist relative autonomy theories indicates, such an holistic approach collapses once it is recognized that an institution seen as a unity (i.e. the state in its entirety) may in fact be engaged in two or more different courses of action at the same time, for it then becomes necessary to break the apparent unity down in order to see how different factors are influencing different parts of the system in different ways. To accept the dual politics thesis, at least as a possible starting point, is to accept that Marx was not the fountainhead of all wisdom (and, similarly, that the liberal–democratic tradition is also partial in its applicability). The criticism of 'eclecticism', if taken seriously, would simply return us to the intellectually stagnant theoretical trenches of the 1970s when different schools of thought were able to seek shelter from their opponents rather than having to engage with alternative ideas which threatened to disturb their precarious ontological security. After all, some of the most exciting developments in twentieth-century social theory have come when writers have broken out of such trenches and have sought to combine insights from different traditions (e.g. as in German critical theory's attempt to relate Marx to Weber and Freud, or in Parsons's early development of a theory of action out of the ideas of Weber, Durkheim and Marshall).

Some critics (notably Pickvance 1982 and 1984) have accepted the need for theoretical pluralism but have argued that different approaches are best integrated by distinguishing levels of abstraction rather than types of processes, thereby enabling micro-level theories (he gives the example of urban managerialism) to 'nest' inside macro-level ones (such as structural Marxism). I would reject such a formulation, partly because the micro/macro distinction is in my view unsustainable (see, for example, Giddens 1984, ch. 3), and partly because I suspect that such an approach would simply result in a reduction of the 'micro' theory to the 'macro' one. However, Pickvance's argument does have the merit of emphasizing that some processes are more general or more powerful than others. Thus, referring back to Figure 2, it is clear that the various elements identified as constituting the 'politics of production' tend to set limits on the elements constituting the 'politics of consumption', for the concern to safeguard capital accumulation takes priority over the concern to cater for social need, the corporate bias tends to prevail over demands expressed through democratic institutions, the centre tends to extend its control over the locality, and the ideologies of private property tend to take precedence over ideologies of citizenship, both in law and in cultural forms of everyday life. That there is an unequal relationship between the left and right hand columns in Figure 2 is undeniable, for consumer interests are subordinated to producer interests on all dimensions, and current patterns of social and political change (e.g. the continuing erosion of local government powers) seem only to exacerbate this power imbalance. I shall address this particular issue again in the final section.

Consumption sector cleavages and social restratification

Just as the main social division arising out of the organization of production in capitalist societies is that between those who own and control the means of production and those who do not, so the main division arising out of the process of consumption in these societies is that between those who satisfy their main consumption requirements through personal ownership (e.g. through purchase of a house, a car, nursery schooling, dental treatment, medical insurance, pension schemes and so on) and those who are excluded from such forms of ownership and who thus remain reliant on collective provision through the state. And just as, in the sphere of production, the division between owners and non-owners is pertinent, not only in shaping the distribution of economic power and life chances, but also in influencing political alignments and cultural–ideological forms of life and consciousness, so too the division between owners and non-owners in the sphere of consumption is crucial politically and culturally as well as economically.

The growing significance of relations of consumption in countries like Britain reflects an historical process of political and economic change in which the prevailing 'mode of consumption' has shifted over the last 150 years or so from a 'market', through a 'socialized', to a 'privatized' mode, each of which is distinguished by the dominant form of property relations inscribed in the process of consumption.

In the first of these phases (dating in Britain to the period up to the mid nineteenth century), consumption was organized primarily through the market. In 1860, for example, there was no state system of income security other than that offered by the Poor Law, no state medical care (apart from lunatic asylums, vaccination and environmental health controls), no state education apart from grants to religious schools, no system of state housing, and no state-run public transport (see Mishra 1977, p. 92). This did not, of course, mean that there was no system of social support, but it did mean that people's consumption needs were met (to the extent that they were met) by a patchwork combination of private charity, self-help initiatives such as the friendly societies and building societies, and market purchase.

As Marxist theorists from Engels to Castells have argued, the basic problem in this market mode of consumption lay in the contradiction between low wages and high consumption costs. Housing provides the clearest example of this, for it is an inherently expensive commodity which could only be afforded by many people through gross overcrowding in shoddily-constructed and insanitary dwellings. In the nineteenth century, labour represented a major cost of production in most industries, and relatively low productivity meant that labour costs had to be kept to a minimum if profits were to be maintained, yet this in turn meant that many (though by no means all) workers could not afford to buy the provisions they and their families desperately needed.

Gradually – first by regulating the symptoms, and later by itself taking responsibility for rectifying the causes – the state intervened in the sphere of consumption. It is important to recognize that a number of factors contributed to this growth of intervention – ruling-class paternalism, fear of insurrection, and economic self-interest among them – but that pressure from the working class itself is probably not a major explanation. Popular hostility towards the state, fostered by the cynical operation of the Poor Law and sustained by a widespread view of the state as the instrument of the wealthy, led many working-class people and their leaders in the fledgling trade union and labour movement to suspect and distrust many attempts at social reform. The Housing Acts, for example, often resulted in the clearance of working-class areas with little or no provision for replacement, the early Education Acts forced working-class parents to send their children to school yet levied fees which were a burden on many, the Factory Acts inhibited the earning capacities of working-class households by limiting child and female labour, and even as late as 1911, the National Insurance Act obliged certain categories of workers to pay a compulsory weekly sum which many resented (not least because this undermined the voluntary and collective forms of security provision which they had built up through the friendly societies (see Green 1982)). It is not therefore surprising that, even with the extension of the franchise to working-class males in 1886, there was no popular thrust for reform, and none of the elections from then until the turn of the century were fought on social welfare issues (see Pelling 1968). To assert, as so many theories of the welfare state do, that collective provision emerged as a response to working class or popular agitation, pressure or mobilization is, in the case of Britain at any rate, a rewriting of history.

As state intervention was stepped up from the early, faltering steps taken by the Disraeli and Gladstone ministries, via the reforms of the pre-war Liberals under Lloyd George, through to the pragmatism of the inter-war governments in responding to the growing problems posed to the creaking Poor Law system by the onset of mass unemployment, so the market mode of consumption was slowly undermined and there emerged in its place the seeds of a new socialized mode which came to fruition with the Beveridge reforms following the end of the Second World War. The comprehensive system of national insurance introduced in 1946, coupled with far-reaching reforms in health care, housing, town planning and education, created a socialized system of support consisting on the one hand of cash payments (e.g. unemployment benefits, old age pensions, family allowances and supplementary benefits) and on the other of provision in kind. So it was that this new socialized mode of consumption to a large extent overcame the contradiction between low wages and high consumption costs by supplementing the former and lowering the latter.

Yet, as Marxist theorists have also argued, this system itself gave rise to a new contradiction – that between the socialized costs of welfare provision and the limited revenues available to pay for it. It was this contradiction which O'Connor pinpointed in his theory of fiscal crisis, and it is this which has sparked off a further change in the organization of consumption from a socialized to a privatized mode.

The origins of this transition in the British case go back to shortly after the war, while the transition itself is even now still in progress. Like the socialized mode which it is replacing, the privatized mode has a long gestation period and develops fitfully and unevenly across different aspects of consumption.

The first steps in this transition, which occurred very early on, involved the abandonment by governments and parties of the left of the universalistic welfare principle. In housing, health, education and pensions, the coexistence of private and public sectors came to be tolerated and, in some cases (such as the shift in Labour Party policy towards owner-occupation during the 1950s and 1960s) actively supported. This step was then followed swiftly by the abandonment of the free welfare principle as user charges were introduced into various welfare services (e.g. the battles in the post-war Labour governments over the introduction of prescription charges and charges for spectacles). The third step was to raise user charges to notional 'market' or commercial levels (e.g. as in the imposition of so-called 'fair rents' in the public housing sector in the early 1970s, or the erosion of subsidies to public transport in the early 1980s), and the final step lies in the transfer of ownership from the state to individual consumers (e.g. through the drive to sell off council houses or to privatize the State Earnings Related Pension Scheme) which is only possible when the service in question has been reorganized on commercial costing principles.

Two points should be emphasized about this transition. The first is that the move to privatized consumption may, and often does, still involve considerable state subsidy (e.g. tax relief on mortgage interest payments or school fees, discounted prices on council house sales, the use of public sector equipment in the private medical sector, and so on). Whether or not the aggregate level of state spending declines or increases as a result of such changes is therefore an open question, but what is clear is that there is no sign of a return to the nineteenth-century market mode in which the state played an insignificant role. It is not therefore the case, as Harloe has argued, that my analysis assumes that 'privatization involves withdrawal of state support with, eventually at least, a wholly free and private market' (1984, p. 229), for what is entailed in these changes is mainly a shift from one form of state support (provision in kind) to another (financial subsidy). It is quite likely that this will enable a reduction in the overall level of state spending, if only because it reduces the costs involved in managing and distributing resources in kind, but this is by no means certain.

The second point to emphasize is that there is nothing 'necessary' or 'inevitable' about these developments. I am not positing an historical evolutionary theory of consumption to match some of the cruder theories of social change in the sphere of production which have been associated with economistic Marxist theories over the years, for such tendencies can to some extent be checked, changed or perhaps even reversed as a result of changing economic and political conditions. Nevertheless, there are, I believe, strong grounds for arguing that a transition from a predominantly socialized to a predominantly privatized mode of consumption is now well under way in Britain (and possibly in other countries too), and that this transition is more likely to continue, albeit with various hiccups and diversions, than to be halted or reversed.

There are four factors that lead me to this conclusion, and these have to do with the crisis of socialized provision, the demand for privatized provision, the changed standard of living since the nineteenth century, and the momentum already gathered by the changes which have occurred. Taken together, these four factors suggest that, 'Collective consumption is proving to be not a permanent feature of advanced capitalism but an historically specific phenomenon' (Rose 1979, p. 23). The socialized mode of consumption will in the future, I suspect, come to be seen as having represented a period of transition between the decline of a market mode and the rise of a privatized mode – a period when the state performed a 'holding operation' in order to cover people's basic consumption needs until such time as they were able to reclaim responsibility for providing for these needs themselves.

The first factor which supports such an argument is that the welfare state is in crisis. Demands on state budgets are rising while the capacity to meet them is falling. The contradiction of the market mode has thus reappeared within the public sector in the form of a fiscal crisis, and the results are much the same as they were in the nineteenth century as the quality of welfare services dwindles and the services themselves begin to collapse. Even when the level of spending is increased, this tends not to enhance the quality of the service, for much of the money is syphoned off into administration and staff costs (see Bacon and Eltis 1978), while the primary beneficiaries of much welfare spending are in any case not the poor but the middle class, for it is they who make most use of the health services, of further and higher education, of commuter train services, and so on. As social expenditure has increased, so too has deprivation (Townsend 1979). The welfare state has reached saturation point.

Second, although popular support for certain aspects of the welfare system in Britain (notably the National Health Service) remains high, it is also ambivalent (Taylor-Gooby 1985). This reflects partly the worsening experiences suffered by many people when they come into contact with state consumer agencies (the long queues at the hospitals, the intrusions into one's privacy by the social security office, the bureaucratic insensitivity of the housing department and the irregularity of the local bus service) and partly the escalating costs incurred through local and national taxation required to keep these services going, but most of all it is a function of the increased popularity of, and aspirations for, private ownership solutions in the sphere of consumption. Where they can, most people today prefer to buy a car rather than rely on public transport, to buy a house rather than rent from the local authority, and so on. I shall explore the reasons for this later in this chapter, but here we may simply note that the shift to a privatized mode of consumption is in part a response to a shift in people's values.

Such a change in values would, of course, be of little consequence if people did not also have the financial means to realize such objectives. The third major factor behind the growth of a privatized mode of consumption is that, since the war, real incomes have been rising and, with the growth in the numbers of women employed, real household incomes have for many risen dramatically. The contradiction between low wages and high costs which characterized the nineteenth-century market mode of consumption is thus for many people no longer operative, for they can now afford many of the items which were out of the reach of their parents' or grandparents' generations. In Britain (and it happened somewhat earlier in the USA, somewhat later in some other European countries), car ownership became more common among working class and middle class alike through the first twenty years after the war while house ownership spread through these strata in the 1960s and 1970s to a point where today, 62 per cent of all households (and 40 per cent of working-class households) own or are buying their homes. Private pension schemes too have spread to many sections of the population (more than 11 million subscribers by 1975), and although schooling and health care are still predominantly state-provided, aspects of these services too have begun to shift from public to private sectors (e.g. the growth of private pre-school education, the increased fees for specialist tuition within the state system, parental purchases of educational capital equipment such as home computers, the growth in corporate subscriptions – by trade unions among others – to private medical insurance schemes, the spread of private 'fringe' medicine, the growth of private dental treatment, and so on). Nevertheless, with some 95 per cent of British children still attending state schools, and with less than 10 per cent of the population covered by private health insurance, these remain the two bulwarks of the socialized mode, and if the shift to a privatized mode is to proceed in the future, it is in these two areas that it will have to occur. As I shall suggest in the final section of this chapter, this is by no means inconceivable.

The final factor which suggests that the tendency to a privatized mode is more than simply an empirical trend which may be reversed at any time is that, once set in motion, it seems to take on a momentum of its own. The raising of public transport fares to cover reduced subsidies serves to encourage private car ownership; the raising of school meal charges to commercial levels serves to encourage private forms of catering; the raising of council house rents serves to enhance the attractiveness of house purchase; and the increased charges and lengthening waiting lists in the health service serve to encourage private health insurance. In all these cases, the more users who opt for a private solution, the poorer becomes the quality and the higher the price for those who remain in the dwindling socialized sector. This is what Hirschmann (1970) has referred to as the 'exit phenomenon', and as welfare services crumble, charges rise and more and more people seek alternative solutions, we may expect all those who can to exit from the system with increasing haste.

What all this suggests is that we are moving towards a dominant mode of consumption in which the majority will satisfy most of its consumption requirements through private purchase (subsidized where appropriate by the state through income transfers, discounts, tax relief or whatever), while the minority is cast adrift on the waterlogged raft of what remains of the welfare state. If this is the case, then the division between the privatized majority and the marginalized and stigmatized minority, which is already evident in respect of housing (Forrest and Williams 1980), is likely to grow wider and deeper as a fault line opens up in British society, not along the lines of class, nor even along the lines of gender or ethnicity (although race does coincide to a high degree with this division), but around the ownership and non-ownership of key resources for consumption.

Some urban analysts have begun to recognize the implications of this. Mingione (1981), for example, has discussed the 'disgregation' of the traditional class system and has identified a process of 'social restratification' in advanced capitalist societies in which class boundaries have become blurred and class allegiances fractured as new divisions have emerged around questions of consumption (or what he terms 'reproduction'). 'The main axis of the contradictions of modern societies', he writes, 'is progressively shifting from the economic sphere of production relationships to the social sphere of complex reproduction relationships' (1981, p. 11). Unfortunately, Mingione then attempts to reduce the consumption cleavages he has identified to a more traditional Marxist class analysis by arguing that exploitation by capital in the workplace spills over into consumption. As we saw in Chapter 6, such arguments are unhelpful and unnecessary, for what we are facing here is not a reflection of familiar relations of exploitation and domination, but the emergence of new ones. The key difference betwen the two, of course, is that whereas the class system is constituted in such a way that a minority excludes a majority from its power and privileges, the divisions arising out of consumption reveal an inverted pattern. The implications of this for an understanding of the distribution of life chances and the development of future lines of social conflict and cleavage are enormous, for the more important the consumption sphere becomes in people's lives, the more likely they are to see themselves as part of a majority with something to defend rather than (as in the class system) part of a majority with nothing to lose. The familiar metaphor of the 'triangle' of power and privilege is thus slowly turning upside down, for as regards consumption cleavages, the 'haves' are becoming a majority while the 'have-nots' – those who, by virtue of age, education, gender, race or religion cannot achieve private access to key consumption resources – are coming to form a small, fragmented, alienated and isolated minority whose response to their marginalization may vary from morose acceptance to violent and inarticulate reaction.

But how significant are these consumption cleavages? Is it realistic to suggest, as I have done, that they are becoming as important in shaping people's lives and in determining the pattern of social relations and conflicts as the more traditional class cleavages? My grounds for arguing thus, and for asserting that what Mingione calls a process of restratification is indeed taking place (and with crucial implications), are threefold. Consumption cleavages are, I suggest, important in shaping material life chances, in structuring political alignments, and in shaping cultural experiences and identities.

Back in the nineteenth century, when the market mode of consumption was dominant (and, incidentally, when most of our current theories of social stratification were first developed), people's class location was fundamental in determining their material well-being. If your wages were low, then your consumption capacity was stunted and many of your basic needs or requirements were therefore inadequately met. Certainly in Marx's day, but also to a large extent in Weber's, class power was therefore basic to an understanding of social inequality and domination.

Since then, as we have seen, the state has intervened directly and massively in both the production and consumption spheres. With around 7 million people in Britain employed in the public sector, and with millions more reliant on state provision of services such as education, health care, housing and general welfare, it is no longer axiomatic that class location is the fundamental basis of material life chances. As we saw in our discussion of Pahl's work (Chapter 4), resources today are allocated not only on the basis of market power, but also according to a political logic determined by the exercise of state power. Yet the significance of this change has not generally been recognized in theories of social stratification, for whether Marxist or Weberian, they continue to employ essentially nineteenth-century ideas to analyse late twentieth-century conditions. As we saw in Chapter 6, the cleavages which arise out of the use of allocative state power cannot be reduced to a Marxist class analysis, but neither are they examples of Weber's status groups (for they reflect differences in material life chances as much as attributions of prestige and 'social honour') or parties (for they do not necessarily organize in an attempt to control or influence the direction of state power). They are, rather, a distinct phenomenon of the distribution of power in the modern period, and as such they generate qualitatively different economic, political and cultural effects.

Some contemporary writers recognize this, but only up to a point. As we saw above, Mingione (1981), for example, accepts that a process of 'restratification' has occurred through changes in the organization of consumption, but he then tries to integrate these changes back into a conventional Marxist class theory by generalizing the concept of 'exploitation' from the sphere of production into the sphere of 'reproduction'. Similarly, Preteceille (1985) accepts that state provision of consumption goods and services can and does generate new inequalities and social divisions over and above those generated within the class system, but he too then suggests that such divisions are essentially derivative and secondary. This is because, first, people's class position fundamentally structures their access to state consumption resources just as it does when these resources are distributed through the market, and second, because consumption sectors are internally fragmented such that different consumers derive different benefits or incur different costs from state provisions according to their class position.

Preteceille's argument here is on the face of it a strong one, for there is now considerable evidence (including that which he himself presents on the basis of research in Paris) to support his contention that access to, and benefit from, state services often tends to reflect pre-existing class inequalities. Nevertheless, the conclusion which he draws from such evidence neglects two crucial points.

The first is that, as we have already seen, class is often a poor guide to a household's consumption location. Private cars, private superannuation schemes and insurance policies, home ownership and aspects or private health and education provision are commonly purchased in many capitalist societies (and sometimes in state socialist societies too (see Ward 1983, p. 187, on housing policy in Romania)) by large sections of the population including many working-class people. Indeed, as Pahl's recent work (discussed in the final section of this chapter) has shown, the key factor structuring access to consumption may often have less to do with class than with whether or not people have *any* form of paid employment, and whether or not households are able to draw on more than one income.

Seen in this way, class divisions *per se* are probably less salient in the explanation of differential patterns of consumption than divisions between the employed and the unemployed, or between single and multi-earner households (see Pahl 1984).

The second point to note in response to the sort of analysis offered by Preteceille is that, notwithstanding their internal fragmentation (and it is worth remembering here that classes too are internally fragmented), consumption sectors still share certain fundamental material interests in common. It may well be, to take his own example, that working-class children tend to get less out of the same state system of schooling than their middle-class counterparts, and even that working-class and middle-class parents seek different things from the school system (although this is less certain, and Preteceille's argument here rests less on empirical evidence than on the dubious theoretical determination of people's different 'needs' which we discussed and dismissed in Chapter 6), but the fact remains that, as public sector consumers, both sets of people share a common interest in, say, keeping state schools open, maintaining good quality and high levels of staffing, ensuring adequate provision of books and equipment, and so on. It is true that they may also differ among themselves in their views on syllabus content, disciplinary codes, patterns of assessment or whatever, but this does nothing to undermine their common and shared interest as state sector consumers, nor does it erode the significance of the major fissure between them and those other parents who send their children to private schools and whose interests lie in reducing levels of expenditure in the state sector, increasing state subsidies to the private sector, and so on. Furthermore, the relative distribution of resources between these two sectors will have a crucial bearing on the relative material life chances of each group. In other words, the initial pattern of educational advantage or disadvantage bequeathed on children by their position in the class system can be modified according to the allocation of resources within and between the two sectors. It may be, as Bernstein (1970) puts it, that 'education cannot compenste for society', but it is also clearly the case that it can influence and mediate patterns of inequality. One has only to think of the significance for the children of many skilled working-class families of the decision to expand higher education in Britain during the 1960s to see that the use of state power in the sphere of consumption can be significant in modifying the horizons of opportunity imposed by the class system in the sphere of production.

Much the same argument can be made in respect of other aspects of consumption such as housing. Here again it is undoubtedly true (as Rex and Moore's work indicated) that households on the same side of the public/private sector division nevertheless vary in their material well-being, and that these variations to some extent reflect their prior class situation. Council tenants in well-built houses with their own gardens are in a different situation from those living on the fourteenth floor of a crumbling, damp and vandalized tower block, just as owners occupying detached houses in their own grounds experience a different quality of life from those struggling to meet the mortgage repayments on a two-up, two-down inner city Victorian terraced property. Nevertheless, the different circumstances of people within each sector cannot undermine the interests that they share in common by virtue of their location in the organization of consumption. All owner-occupiers, for example, have a common interest in maintaining domestic property values, reducing interest rates, increasing state subsidies through tax relief, grants or other channels, and so on, and in this they come into conflict with the interests of all public sector tenants in reducing rents and improving maintenance and repair services through increased state spending on the public sector.

As in the case of education, furthermore, we can see how consumption location in respect of housing generates new patterns of material privilege and inequality over and above those deriving out of the organization of production. This reflects a number of factors. Owner-occupiers, for example, can raise additional money through loans secured on their property or through second mortgages which are often spent on other consumer items (it is estimated that up to half of the mortgage money advanced by British building societies in 1984 was actually spent on non-housing-related consumption such as cars, holidays and consumer durables). They also have the ability, within the limits of what they can afford, to choose their location, and this enables them to maximize benefits from spatially-fixed public goods such as schools or parks in a way that is not normally possible for public sector tenants. And in general, owner-occupiers do not have to worry too much about their financial viability as they approach old age, for not only is the mortgage then paid off (unlike the rental payments of the tenant), but the capital value of the house is an insurance which can substitute for the need to pay out large sums in insurance and pension payments through the working life (see, in relation to this, Kemeny's interesting work on the way privatized consumption of housing affects people's orientation to collective provision in other areas of consumption (Kemeny 1980)).

The major factor, however, which creates differential life chances between owners and non-owners of housing, and which can be of such significance that consumption location may actually come to outweigh class location in its economic effects, is the capacity of private house buyers to accumulate capital. This is one of the reasons in my view why, despite the obvious and crucial importance of other aspects of consumption provision such as education and health care, housing is the most basic element in the analysis of consumption relations (the other reason has to do with its cultural significance, discussed below).

I have discussed the issue of capital gains in housing at some length elsewhere (Saunders 1978), and I shall not repeat those arguments here. Suffice it to say that real gains can be and are made by owner-occupiers as a result of house price inflation (which tends to outstrip inflation of wages or of other commodity prices), favourable rates of interest on housing loans, government subsidies on house purchase (e.g. tax relief, improvement grants, discounts, first-time-buyer grants and all the other instruments developed by various governments to support private home ownership over the years) and the opportunity that owners have to use their own labour to increase the value of their dwellings. Farmer and Barrell (1981) estimate in the case of Britain that owner-occupiers achieved a staggering *real* annual rate of return on their capital of between 11.7 per cent (for those who stayed in the same house) and 15.7 per cent (for those who 'traded up') in the period from 1965 to 1979, and as they point out, no other form of investment could come anywhere near matching this rate of return over the same period.

Now it is true that this period was to some extent exceptional and that, in other periods, gains are likely to be less spectacular (see Edel 1982 and Williams 1982). It is also true, as Thorns (1982) has shown through comparative work in Britain and New Zealand, and as Edel and his colleagues (1984) have demonstrated historically in work on Boston, that those who gain most tend to be those who have most in the first place, and that some people during some periods may actually lose as a result of a relative decline in the value of their housing. Nevertheless, even Edel and his co-authors have to admit that the overall historical pattern for the last hundred years has been one of uneven but moderate gains, and when we consider that these have been secured in addition to the enjoyment by owner-occupiers of the use value of their houses (one cannot live in stocks and shares), and that owners can reap the full capital gain even though they probably only advanced a fraction of the initial purchase price (receiving the rest as a mortgage advance), it is clear that we are dealing here with a resource of immense economic significance.

The owner-occupied sector in Britain accounts for over 60 per cent of households (in countries like the USA and Australia, this figure is considerably higher). This suggests that a majority of the population today is in a position to accumulate some capital gains simply by virtue of its particular mode of consuming housing. It also indicates that, for the first time in our history, we are approaching a situation where millions of working people stand at some point in their lives to inherit a capital sum which (even if realized from a small terraced house and divided among several children) is likely to exceed anything they could hope to save through earnings from employment.

The sociological significance of this development cannot be overstated. Even seventy years ago, when Weber was writing, such large-scale inheritance of property would have been inconceivable. Today, however, it is starting to happen. As this process unfolds, so it will force social scientists to reconsider their nineteenth-century conceptions of class and inequality as simply phenomena of the organization of production. Taken together with the other material advantages enjoyed by owner-occupiers, and in the context of the significance of the public/private division in generating material inequalities in other areas of consumption such as education, pensions or health care, the inheritance factor is likely to demonstrate ever more clearly the significance of people's consumption location. Any analysis which continues to insist, in the face of these developments, on the primacy of class or the derivative nature of consumption is likely to prove less and less relevant to an understanding of patterns of power and privilege as the years go by.

What, then, of the political and cultural significance of these consumption-based cleavages? We have already considered their political significance in the discussion of Dunleavy's work in Chapter 6. There we saw that the public/private split (notably in respect of housing) has had a major bearing on political alignments, not only as regards voting behaviour, but also in relation to people's overall attitudes towards public spending and cuts in state services (see Duke and Edgell 1984). Dunleavy (1985) himself has suggested in a carefully argued paper that the sectoral divisions created by increased state welfare provision tend to react back on to the political process by changing the social basis of support for political parties, such that parties of the left increasingly draw their support not from the working class, but from a coalition of state sector workers and state sector consumers, while parties of the right come to represent a private sector constituency which similarly cuts across traditional class lines. This in turn fragments the working class and establishes a political agenda which is structured around the issue of state intervention such that the expansion of state spending in one period tends to provoke a backlash in another.

Other writers have come to similar conclusions. Drawing on a range of British empirical data, for example, Newby and his co-authors suggest:

> Those most dependent on state provision are most supportive of state spending in these areas, and vice-versa. The Labour Party thus appears to be representing a smaller and smaller minority rather than a clear majority of the working class. Post-war patterns of consumption (in particular housing) have thus served to integrate workers into capitalism as individuals: and in a directly economic (rather than simply ideological) way, providing them with a stake in the system of financial and property markets which in turn undermines their sense of class identity and hence their participation in class politics (1984, p. 23).

The crucial point here is that these political divisions are not simply the product of ideological determinations, but reflect in mediated form divisions based on real, economic interests. As I suggested at the start of this section, consumption sector cleavages are essentially expressions of specific sets of property relations, for just as social classes are distinguished first and foremost by the division between owners and non-owners of key means of production, so consumption sectors are distinguished above all else by the division between owners and non-owners of key means of consumption. It is the nature of property rights in means of consumption which gives rise to new patterns of economic inequality and new clusters of political alignment, and it is here too that we find the source of the cultural significance of consumption-based cleavages.

Two points need to be made about this. The first is, as Harloe (1984) rightly points out, that property rights in means of consumption may still be facilitated or underpinned by the intervention of the state. Home ownership, for example, is subsidized in most capitalist countries by one or another form of state support. As I emphasized earlier, the emergence of a privatized mode of consumption is not tantamount to a return to the nineteenth-century market mode. Nevertheless, with or without state subsidies, it does represent a fundamental break with the socialized mode in that property rights are transferred from the state to the consumer.

The second point is that the type of property represented in consumption is fundamentally different from that represented in production. Prouhdon recognized this when he argued in the latter case that 'property is theft', and in the former that 'property is freedom' (see Ward 1983, pp. 186–7). It has long been recognized in the more subtle traditions of socialist and libertarian thought that ownership of what Lafargue called 'property of personal appropriation' (defined as 'the food one eats . . . and the articles of clothing and objects of luxury . . . with which one covers and decks oneself' (no date, p. 4)) entails very different sorts of power and sets of social relations from those associated with capitalist private property in means of production. Thus Williams, for example, notes that, 'The legal institution of property covers a wide range of situations. . . . But clearly not all property has the same significance. . . . The spread of home ownership does not confer economic power in the sense of the rights to those properties giving a say in the direction of the British economy' (1982, pp. 19–20). Similarly, Ward writes that, 'Most of us . . . make a distinction between real property and personal property . . . the owner-occupied house, like the peasant's private plot, is personal property like clothing, not real property like the landlord's estate' (1983, p. 187).

Clearly, then, it is important to distinguish different types of private property ownership. Equally, however, it is also important to distinguish between individual and collective ownership within each of these types. For example, while agreeing with Williams that the rights and capacities of the home owner are qualitatively different from those of the factory owner, we should also recognize that they are also qualitatively different from those of the public sector tenant. The variations in types of property rights and relations thus include both the dimension of economic power (i.e. the capacity to accumulate and to dominate others by virtue of an exclusive control of resources) and that of individual autonomy, (i.e. the capacity to control, direct, benefit from the use of, and dispose of resources). Seen in this way, the person who owns a house lacks the economic power of the person who owns a factory but shares with the factory owner the individual control and autonomy which is denied to the tenant (for an extended discussion of these issues, see Newby *et al.* 1978).

These distinctions are of crucial importance, both for political argument over the consumption question, and for sociological analysis of the growth in the privatized mode. As regards the former, it is clear that current socialist thinking has largely forgotten the sorts of distinctions drawn by writers such as Proudhon and Lafargue, for the socialist attack on private property has too often been generalized across both production and consumption. One reason for this is that socialism evolved at a time when, under a market mode of consumption, few people enjoyed property rights in key means of production or consumption, and there seemed little likelihood, given the level of wages prevailing at that time, that mass ownership of either could be achieved other than by collective means. As Stretton has observed:

> It was a tragedy that socialism had to be born between the first industrial revolution and the second, when working families had scarcely any private resources and an appalling proportion of all private property was used by the few who owned it to exploit the labour of the many who didn't. . . . It is a terrible mistake to let the abuse of capitalist property discredit the idea of family property or to confuse commercial capital with the home capital which really has opposite possibilities (1974, p.76).

This 'terrible mistake' has, however, been further compounded in socialist thought by a traditional intellectual distaste for all forms of 'petty property' and the ways of thinking and acting associated with it. As Keat notes, 'For many socialists, capitalism is to be condemned not only as a system based on the exploitation of one class by another . . . but also for the individualistic character of its social relationships' (1981, p. 127). Owner-occupation, in particular, seems to provoke the same sorts of reactions among socialists today as the French peasantry did among Marxists a century or more ago, for personal property rights in a house are seen (as in Harvey's work, for example) as seducing the occupant into a hopelessly conservative support for the status quo. Every display of personal attachment to the home – the gnomes in the garden, the stone-cladding on the walls, the name on the garden gate – provides a further wincing reminder of the 'petty bourgeois' mentality thought to be associated with ownership of personal property. As Ward again acutely observes, the socialist antipathy to such forms of property is based on 'the fear that "the workers" will be at home papering the parlour when they ought to be out in the streets making a revolution' (1983, p. 186).

It is, however, not only important for socialist theory to rediscover the distinctions between different types of property rights, for this is also obviously crucial to the future sociological analysis of privatized consumption. We know surprisingly little about *why* people so often opt, when given the effective choice, for a private form of consumption, nor about how people experience privatized as against socialized provision. It is true, as Dunleavy (1983) suggests, that privatized consumption is sometimes effectively forced on to people (e.g. cut-backs in state provision of buses, day nurseries or dentists may leave those who can afford it with little option but to turn to private solutions). But it is surely also the case that people often actively seek out private solutions even where (as in the case of council house sales) the object of ownership remains unchanged. There is, it seems, something about private ownership and possession which itself is important to people, irrespective of the nature of the service or object in question.

This cultural dimension to the consumption question (which, precisely because it is a *cultural* phenomenon rather than something inherent to the objects themselves, is likely to vary in form and significance between different societies at different times) is as fascinating as it is under-researched. Here, we may simply float two points deserving of further consideration.

The first is that private ownership seems often to be associated with personal identity. Work by social psychologists, for example, suggests that adults as well as children depend upon their personal possessions as externalizations of self and as means of expressing their identity to themselves and to others (see, for example, Trasler 1982). Similarly, Goffman (1961), in his work on the way 'total institutions' attempt to mould their inmates through a process of 'mortifying the self', points to the significance of stripping people of their possessions as the first step in stripping them of their identities. As Bryant puts it, 'Human beings live in symbolic universes and they vest something of themselves in their personal belongings' (1978, p. 63).

It would seem plausible to suggest, therefore, that the opportunity to extend the scope of objects in one's environment in which one can claim some right of personal and exclusive possession may represent one means of asserting the self against the enveloping intrusions of 'mass society'. This, however, is only part of the story, for what ownership also offers, in principle at least, is an extension of the individual's capacity to *control* those objects.

Here, then, is the second aspect to the cultural dimension of privatized consumption; that private ownership entails exclusive rights of control, benefit and disposal, and thus represents a capacity for asserting personal autonomy in key areas of everyday life. As I shall argue in the next section, few of us can ever realistically aspire to asserting effective control over that part of our lives devoted to formal productive activity, but private consumption can offer an alternative outlet. Access to a car, for example, entails a certain degree of freedom of mobility for many people today and releases them from reliance on the pre-set routes and timetables of public transport. The purchase of private medical care or private schooling (which unlike private transport is not today generally available to most people in a country like Britain) would in principle similarly enhance the range of options available to people and would (if some means could be found for making it universally available) enable consumers to break out of the relationship of dependency and clientalism so often nurtured by state agencies such as hospitals and schools, and to assert a degree of control as purchasers enforcing property rights, rather than as clients relying on citizenship rights (just as in the nineteenth century, working-class members of friendly societies were able to exert control over the doctors, pharmacists and other professional producers whom they collectively employed and collectively dismissed (see Green 1982)).

Most significant, however, are the possibilities for control opened up by private ownership of dwellings. This is because home ownership represents rights of control over an everyday personal space of crucial significance. As Porteous observes, the home 'is the locus at which individual control of fixed physical space is paramount' (1976, p. 384).

We saw in Chapter 7 how Giddens argues that the 'stretching' of social systems across time and space has created a sense of 'ontological insecurity' in the modern world. Social relations, he suggests, have been displaced from their traditional spatial and temporal settings with the result that people have sought to re-establish some degree of autonomy, familiarity and inter-subjective meaning within the private realm. The popular desire for home ownership, I would suggest, is indicative of this response, for 'a home of one's own' is above all else a property right which ensures both a physical (spatially-rooted) and permanent (temporally-rooted, in perpetuity and across subsequent generations) location in the world where the owner can feel, both literally and metaphorically, 'at home'.

As autonomy has been eroded in the sphere of production, so it has been asserted through the desire for home ownership in the sphere of consumption. Ever since the nineteenth century, working-class people have responded to the intrusions into their lives of an uncontrollable world capitalist system of production by seeking to carve out 'a separate sphere in the sense of seeking out, in and through the fabric of everyday life, a distinct cultural space for gaining as much control as possible over the purpose and direction of our lives' (Rose 1981, p. 32). Whether or not this search for a separate sphere has been successful in re-asserting control and autonomy, and whether or not it is feasible in the modern world of multinational corporations and powerful nation states to continue to seek it through a private realm of consumption, are issues I shall take up in the next section.

Before that, however, it is necessary to draw this discussion to a conclusion by making four important points about what I have suggested as regards the capacity for control through private property rights in the sphere of consumption.

First, it is obviously the case that exclusive property rights may be vested in individuals or in groups of individuals. The privatization of consumption does not necessarily therefore entail the individualization of consumption. Assuming that my analysis is correct, and that the tendency to privatized consumption continues, this does not mean that individuals may not come together – e.g. in housing cooperatives, car pools, or even (as in the fledgling communal education initiatives currently developing in Britain among certain middle-class and Asian communities) in neighbourhood schooling arrangements – to form collective organizations for the provision of members' consumption needs. The point here is that individual property rights can be pooled in collective endeavours in a way that collective rights granted through national citizenship cannot easily be disaggregated. Collectivism may in this sense be an outgrowth of privatized consumption rather than (as is so often assumed) its antithesis. Certainly the future, as regards the emerging forms of consumption, is by no means predictable and need not result in a society of individualized and home-centred family units huddled around the video machine (although, of course, this is one possible pattern).

Second, the capacity of different social groups to exert control through private ownership is uneven. As consumption is currently organized, women, in particular, are often disadvantaged as compared with men. Freedom of mobility through car ownership, for example, is more often characteristic of the male than the female experience in most households. Similarly, the private home may represent a sphere of personal control for men, while it represents a place of work and subordination for their wives. Privatization of health care, too, can result (in the absence of any other changes) in an increase in the domestic burden for women who may be called upon to nurse aged relatives, tend to sick children, and so on. The point, then, is that the different modes of consumption offer different capacities for control, but that the ability to take advantage of these reflects other dimensions of power and inequality in our society, of which gender is one. And as Weber was well aware, a change in one dimension of power has no necessary implications as regards a change in any other.

Third, and related to this last point, the privatization of consumption only offers opportunities for control, self-expression and so on if consumers themselves have the financial capacity to service their requirements through purchasing the goods and services they need. At present, in a country like Britain, this clearly is not the case. Many households still cannot afford to buy a car, still less a house, a private pension, private medical insurance and the rest. It is for this reason that I have argued in this section that a major cleavage is opening up in the sphere of consumption between those who can afford to take advantage of the emerging privatized mode, and those who must remain reliant on the dwindling socialized mode. Most Marxist writers assume that such a division is inherent within a capitalist society – that the organization of production inevitably generates such inequalities and incapacities in the sphere of consumption. I have argued here and in Chapter 6 that this is not necessarily the case, and in the next section I shall try to suggest how a change in the form of state provisioning may overcome it. Nevertheless, for the moment it is important to remember that, like gender, class remains a factor in influencing access to key items of private consumption.

Fourth and finally, it is necessary to recognize that, if and as private means of consumption come to be generally available, so the rights of control and benefit associated with them may themselves be reduced. This is essentially the phenomenon referred to by Edel and his colleagues (1984) as 'partial mobility', or the process of going up the down escalator. Thus, as these writers point out, the more car ownership spreads, the more congested the roads become, and the less advantage there is to be had from running a car. Similarly, the more educational opportunities are opened up, the better qualified the population becomes, and the more any given credential becomes devalued. However, there is no 'iron law' which suggests that this will always be the case in every extension of consumption capacity. Furthermore, even if there were, it would only mean that enhanced consumption provision left people no better off in relative terms, for they would still have benefited in absolute terms. Sitting in one's car in a traffic jam may still be preferable to standing in the rain waiting for a bus, just as the opportunity to have twelve years schooling may still represent an improvement on six years, even if one is offered the same sort of job at the end. If, indeed, such enhanced consumption capacities entail, not only material improvements (i.e. more of this or that good or service), but also a change in the form in which consumption is achieved (i.e. more control over the goods or services in question), then these changes may be of much greater significance than the concept of 'partial mobility' allows. After all, tenants who buy their council houses experience no change in the material object which they consume (i.e. the house remains the same), but may experience an enormous change in the possibilities which open up in terms of how they can consume it. In sociological analyses of consumption, the quantitative question of how much people benefit must never be allowed to eclipse the equally important qualitative question of how they benefit. Put another way, as for production, so for consumption, analysis of social relations is as central as analysis of material means.

Privatized consumption, self-provisioning and the dual society

The various urban theories which we have explored in this book are to a large extent products of the time when they were developed. The human ecology of the Chicago school, for example, reflects the conditions of market capitalism in America in the period before the Great Depression and the growth of state intervention ushered in by the New Deal. The focus by Pahl and others on urban managerialism was in many ways the product of post-war welfare state capitalism in Britain at a time when the economy was still growing and when state social expenditures were rising rapidly. And the growth of Marxist urban theory during the 1970s reflected the onset of a new recession in the West which brought with it a crisis of state consumption provision and which seemed, in the context of the 1968 events in Paris, to offer the prospect of new forms of political struggle and new paths to a socialist transformation.

Writing in the context of the mid 1980s, none of these approaches any longer seems relevant. As we have seen, the market mode of consumption, on which human ecology theories were largely based, has long since disappeared, and the socialized mode, which generated theories of urban management, is now similarly in decline. Furthermore, the recession has deepened, the crisis of the welfare state has been exacerbated, but urban social movements have, in most western capitalist countries, all but disappeared (see Pickvance 1985). The neo-Marxist work of the 1970s thus seems to have been appropriate (within its own theoretical limitations) to an understanding of a particular transitional period in which the socialized mode was in crisis and the privatized mode was still in its infancy; but fifteen years on, it seems to have less and less analytical purchase on the new social forms which are emerging. Not for the first time, social change seems to be proceeding in advance of our theoretical capacity to understand it.

Most of the developed capitalist world has been in recession, now marked, now less so, since at least 1974. The reasons for this sustained recession and the high levels of unemployment associated with it are various – the end of the post-war 'long wave' of accumulation, the development of new capital-intensive technologies, the restructuring of the international division of labour, the saturation of the credit system, the fiscal crisis generated by 'unproductive' state expenditures, and so on – but irrespective of how they explain it, few commentators see any serious prospect of a return to the levels of economic growth and full employment which characterized the quarter-century after the war. In Britain, the recession has been more severe than in most other countries, and again this reflects a number of specific factors, which include the legacy of historically low levels of investment, the haemorrhaging of capital overseas, the peculiarities of the class sytem, and the impact of successive disastrous government policies culminating in the last-ditch return to neo-liberalism after 1979 (see Gamble 1981, and Dearlove and Saunders, 1984, ch. 8). Yet in Britain, as much if not more than in other western countries, the sustained slump cannot really be said to have resulted in a crisis of the society. Sporadic rioting in a few inner city areas in 1981, and again in 1985, an increasing bitterness in industrial relations (as exemplified by the miners' strike of 1984–5), and a growing polarization of party politics (with a new 'centre party alliance' coming through the middle) are all indicators of the severity of the country's economic decline, but what is striking about the current period is less the overt conflicts which have arisen than the sense of hopeless resignation which now pervades so much of social and economic life.

What this seems to suggest is that British society (and almost certainly other western capitalist societies too) is in some way 'adjusting', fitfully and with some difficulty, to changed economic conditions rather than 'collapsing' or 'transforming' in the face of them. Capitalist firms are adjusting through mergers and take-overs, through diversification and relocation, through shedding labour and reorganizing labour relations and the hierarchy of control. The state is adjusting through institutional reforms designed to block off popular aspirations (e.g. in the local government system), through stepping up social control and surveillance while backing out of a range of economic and social commitments, and through engineering a new political culture in which the 'legitimation crisis' prophesied by Habermas is to be averted through the denial of public responsibility for what are defined as individual problems. And the culture of everyday life is adjusting too as people seek to defend what they've got rather than assert what they want, and as they learn to trim their aspirations and to lower their hopes for the future. The prevailing mood of the time is fatalism, and no radical transformation of society was every born out of that.

There is, however, a paradox in all of this. Real earnings in Britain have continued to rise even as the recession has bitten deeper. At a time of record unemployment, when conditions in cities like Liverpool or Glasgow have degenerated to become among the worst in Europe, and when the per capita GNP of the country has fallen to a level around that of Portugal, Eire or Italy, the country has witnessed a spectacular and sustained consumer spending boom (much of it financed by mortgage credit). Ownership per head of consumer durables such as video machines is higher in Britain then anywhere else in the world. For many households, the 1980s must seem more like a boom than a slump.

It is not difficult to explain this apparent paradox. As Prime Minister Thatcher never ceased to remind her audiences, even with 15 per cent unemployment, over eight in ten people who could and wished to have paid employment did so. The 1980s, in other words, have been a period of massive social polarization in Britain in which perhaps three-quarters or more of all households have remained virtually untouched by mass unemployment (for as Urry notes, 'The majority of the labour force is rarely unemployed while a small but growing proportion bears much of the impact' (1983, p. 36), while a marginalized minority has either suffered chronic long-term unemployment (e.g. older workers made redundant and school-leavers who fail to find work), or has lurched from one insecure job to another. This polarization is expressed along a number of divisions – between different parts of the country, between different types of workers with different levels of skills or in different sectors of the economy, between the old, the young and the middle-aged, and between certain categories of male and female workers – but in every case it cuts through the traditional class system. It is not only the middle class who have been buying the video recorders and home computers, nor is it only the middle class who have been borrowing on the strength of home ownership to finance foreign holidays and car purchase.

Like the division between those who can increasingly afford privatized consumption and the marginalized minority which is being left reliant on a residualized state system of support, this major cleavage thus takes the form of a split between a majority of households which, at the very least, are 'getting by', and a minority which is struggling to cope in the face of negligible employment opportunities and declining state services. Those who are suffering the full impact of the recession are not the working class as such, but are fragments of the population, what Mingione (1985) calls the 'surplus population', groups such as the elderly, one-parent families and young blacks. The rest of us continue on our spending spree while (just occasionally) Toxteth burns.

The wave of consumer spending (which is generally directed at imported domestic goods and which therefore does little to stimulate demand for indigenous industry) is part of a process identified some years ago by Gershuny (1978) as the emergence of a 'self-service economy'. Gershuny's thesis is that the traditional, evolutionary model of socio-economic development, in which societies are said to 'progress' from primary production, through manufacturing, to a reliance on service industries, is over-simple. He recognizes that in Britain, employment in manufacturing has been falling while service employment has (until recently) been rising, but he also shows for a number of European countries including Britain that since the 1970s, people's expenditure on services has been falling while their purchases of goods have been rising! He explains this partly in terms of a proportion of service employment being consumed by industry rather than households (e.g. industrial cleaning or accounting services), and partly in terms of differential productivity in manufacturing and service industries (Gershuny 1985). Thus, he shows that productivity in the service sector (whether private or state) has lagged behind that in manufacturing with the result that households have found it increasingly expensive to buy, say, bus journeys, laundry services or cinema seats, but increasingly cheaper to purchase the cars, washing machines or videos which will enable them to provide equivalent services for themselves.

All of this led Garshuny to propose that work in what he termed the 'informal sector' of the economy was expanding at the same time as employment in the formal economy was contracting. People were no longer buying services for final consumption, but were buying the goods – televisions, power tools, freezers – which they could use as means of consumption (to entertain themselves, to refurbish their own houses, to store their own produce). Hence, what is developing is a self-service economy in which domestic work or self-provisioning is not only raising people's living standards (by enabling them to consume more services more cheaply), but is also expanding the scope for people to realize the potential of their own labour.

Now, all of this would seem to have considerable implications for an analysis of both the newly-emerging privatized mode of consumption, and the division associated with it between the majority of 'haves' and the residualized minority of 'have-nots'. In particular, it would seem but a short step from Gershuny's analysis of self-servicing to the argument that the decline of paid work is in some sense being compensated by the growth of self-provisioning in which workers, freed from the burdens of formal employment, are liberated into an alternative form of work characterized by greater autonomy, control and self-sufficiency. This is what Pahl, for example, seems to have had in mind in one of his early contributions to this literature when he suggested that reduced demands for paid labour, coupled with continuing state support for the surplus population, could actually prove beneficial for those who have more usually been defined as the marginal and the dispossessed:

> The formal economy appears to have shrinking manpower requirements both as its productivity increases and as the informal economy flourishes, growing, as it does, at a faster rate than the formal economy. Released from the realm of necessity by capitalism's inevitable desire to continue accumulation and to maintain rates of profit, and protected in the realm of freedom by the need of the state to maintain social control, it seems as though some workers are slipping out of their chains and walking out of the system's front door (1980, p. 17).

Gershuny, too, seemed attracted by the same sort of argument, for he tentatively suggested that the decline in paid work was being counterbalanced by the rise of the informal sector, and thereby held out the prospect of transforming people's whole experience of work.

Today, however, few (least of all Pahl himself) would hold to this view. The debate over the so-called 'informal economy' (a term which Pahl himself now rejects) has today developed into a dispute between, on the one hand, those who believe that it is a hopeless coping strategy which the non-employed are forced to adopt in order to ensure some degree of subsistence, and on the other, those who suggest that the non-employed are effectively excluded from informal work just as they are excluded from paid employment.

The first position is exemplified by the analysis developed by Mingione (1983, 1985). He sees the growth of informal activities (in which category he includes moonlighting, non-registered employment, informal self-employment, criminal activity, do-it-yourself, reciprocal exchanges and the like) as the way in which working-class people have attempted to ensure their own survival at a time when capitalism is in sustained recession and the state is under pressure to cut its spending. The responsibility for reproducing the surplus population has thus been shifted, for households must now carry more of the costs (in terms of time, money or both) which were once covered by wages or by welfare provisions. Drawing on his work in Italy, he suggests that this growth of informal activity not only fails to meet the needs of the surplus population (for they must now work longer hours for lower rates of subsistence), but also reproduces and perpetuates their subordination and poverty. Children, for example, are withdrawn early from school to help augment the family income, and this ensures that they remain unqualified, semi-literate and (in terms of the formal economy) virtually unemployable. Furthermore, self-provisioning on a subsistence level reduces demand for the products of local industry and thus gives an added twist to the crisis of formal waged employment, while at the same time it also reduces the state's tax revenue thereby whittling away the capacity of the welfare system to bolster household incomes.

For Mingione, then, the expansion of domestic self-provisioning is a phenomenon, not of choice, but of coercion, not of hope but of despair. It is 'a forced response of families to the situation of inflation and of crisis of the public or collective service industry sector' (1983, p. 323). The only grounds he can detect for possible optimism are that informalized consumption may foster a sense of communal solidarity and neighbourhood co-operation which could provide a basis for a political challenge and alternative to be mounted against the existing system of mass consumerism and social reproduction (an argument which would seem to echo Castells's hopes in the 1970s in regard to the crisis of collective consumption, and which in my view is just as utopian).

A rather different approach has been developed by Pahl (1984) as a result of his research in the Isle of Sheppey in Kent. This research leads Pahl both to reject his earlier speculative ideas concerning informal work as a substitute for paid employment, and to develop an alternative view of domestic self-provisioning to that advanced by Mingione. Basically, Pahl's conclusion is that informal work such as moonlighting is relatively rare, that home-based self-servicing on the Gershuny model is common among certain categories of households but not others, and that neither strategy is generally available to those members of households which are not locked into the formal economy of paid employment.

He argues that full-time paid work is indeed in decline, although he also notes that the full employment years of the 1950s and 1960s were probably somewhat unique. Thus, he shows historically that most households have relied upon a variety of work strategies by their various members, that they have not generally depended solely on the wages brought in by one 'breadwinner', and that periods of unemployment have been common. The post-war years, however, effectively incapacitated many households in the sense that they came to rely entirely on waged work while the resources which were necessary to sustain other work activities disappeared:

> In retrospect, the years when it was said they never had it so good, in the period of recovery after the Second World War, were the years of incapacitation. The messy back streets with their potential premises for small workshops were knocked down as part of slum clearance. The factories were rebuilt and rationalized. The unions got stronger and led their members to believe that collective solidaristic action would lead to a permanent position in the rising escalator of incomes. . . . The physical and social infrastructure of the post-war period was developed on an assumption of smooth and continuing growth. Households with a limited and narrow view of work as factory employment . . . had, perhaps for the first time in English history, lost the means of getting by with a household work strategy (1984, pp. 56–7).

Nevertheless, Pahl also shows that, with the onset of the recession, household self-provisioning has been increasing again. In terms reminiscent of Gershuny, he cites figures to show what have been quite spectacular increases in the sales of tools, home decorating products, and DIY equipment (up by 19 per cent between 1974 and 1980 compared with a rise in GDP over that period of 8 per cent), and he explains this in terms of the growth of home ownership, the increased costs of marketed services and the reduced hours spent in paid employment (1984, pp. 101–2). He also notes that those households which have been busy renovating their houses, repairing their cars or growing their own vegetables have often derived considerable personal satisfaction in the process – they are certainly not the cowed and coerced informal sector workers described by Mingione. Nor, however, are they the unemployed, for Pahl's key finding is that the households engaged in 'informal' or domestic work are also those with access to paid employment: 'Employment and self-provisioning go together, rather than one being a substitute for another' (1984, p. 236).

This point is crucial, for it underscores the argument developed here that the division between the employed and the unemployed tends to coincide with that between privatized and non-privatized consumers. Indeed, as Pahl goes on to point out, the same people who work in paid employment and who also work most in the home are also those who make most use of formal services purchased through the market. The line of exclusion is, it seems, drawn at around the same point no matter which aspect of resources we focus on. The households which earn money are the households which provide for themselves are the households which buy private sector services. They are also, as Pahl emphasizes, normally the households which own their own homes.

The reason, of course, is that money from paid employment (as well as the contacts and skills which may be built up there) is a condition of engaging in other forms of work (which require outlays of capital on materials) and of purchasing marketed consumption services. The unemployed 'are too poor to work informally' (p. 96). Furthermore, given that the house is the major focus of informal work, home ownership, too, would seem to be a condition of its development, for on the Isle of Sheppey at least, house purchase and renovation was a major strategy for acquiring capital (p. 183).

It is important to emphasize that none of this supports a class-reductionist thesis, for Pahl clearly establishes that it is household structure (i.e. the number of earners and the stage in the life cycle) rather than class which is (and in his view has always been) the key factor in shaping patterns of work. What his study establishes is the growth of a social polarization, not on class lines, but between households that can work (formally and informally) and those that cannot. There is, he says, a 'growing middle mass' (p. 324), and the fundamental cleavage in contemporary British society lies between it and the marginalized, residualized 'underclass':

> A process of polarization is developing, with households busily engaged in all forms of work at one pole and households unable to do a wide range of work at the other. ... The division between the more affluent home-owning households of ordinary working people and the less advantaged under-class households is coming to be more significant than conventional divisions based on the manual/non-manual distinction (1984, p. 314).

For the remainder of this chapter I shall take this polarization thesis as given, for the evidence and arguments which have been marshalled in support of it in this and the previous section are, I believe, overwhelming. I shall therefore turn to consider what might realistically be done about it. How, in other words, could changes be instituted which might break down this depressing and frightening cleavage in British society between the new privileged majority and the marginalized minority?

The solution, obviously, lies in somehow enhancing the consumption capacity of those at the bottom. At present, they are at the butt end of declining state services from which the majority are fast 'exiting', and they are excluded not only from what Dunleavy (1983) terms 'individual consumption' (i.e. the purchase of marketed goods and services), but also from what he calls 'autonomous consumption' (i.e. effective self-provisioning).

One way of doing this, of course, would be to bolster the state welfare sector – to build more council houses, increase staff in schools, pump more money into the National Health Service, raise subsidies to public transport, and so on. Yet not only is this probably the least realistic strategy given the availability of state revenues, it is also arguably the least attractive one. Most commentators with eyes to see recognize that, as Castells puts it, the demand for enhanced consumption provisions 'is too often understood in terms of more public housing and more social services. It is crucial to consider it in terms of different kinds of services and urban amenities' (1983b, p. 15). I would also add to this that it is crucial to consider it in terms of what people as consumers actually seem to want. 'When we build again', pleads Colin Ward, 'we need not a plan for housing, but an attitude that will enable millions of people to make their own plans' (1985, p. 120). And so of course it is with other consumption resources.

Could not socialized consumption provisions be democratized, then, to take account of consumer opinion? The dual politics thesis would suggest, for example, that welfare services can be made more accountable and controllable if they are locally organized and administered by elected bodies. The tendency in Britain is, of course, in the other direction, towards regional or national non-elected bodies such as the health authorities and the metropolitan public transport agencies; but even if local democratization could be brought about, its impact would be limited. As we saw when we discussed the dual politics thesis, consumer interests tend always to be subordinated to producer interests within the state system. Furthermore, the experience of local democratic initiatives suggests that most people pay them little heed, for no matter how much the housing department decentralizes its management offices, or the health authority delegates to its community councils, the consumers themselves still experience the services passively, as clients, and they act accordingly, grumbling here, grateful there, but never asserting control.

If the aim really is to make consumption provisions more accountable to people – i.e. to shift power from those (whether they be politicians, urban managers, state-employed professionals, public sector workers or private sector producers) who currently control these services to those who use them – then this implies a transfer of responsibility from the former to the latter. Effectively, this can only mean a transfer of property rights – rights to control and dispose of, as well as to use and benefit from, the resources in question. It implies, in other words, an extension (to all aspects of consumption, and to all sections of the population) of the privatized consumption mode. In practical terms, this could only be achieved through a move from state provision in kind to state provision in cash.

There tends to be a curious knee-jerk reaction on the left when this sort of proposal is floated. Ward (1985, p. 28) notes how concepts such as 'self-help' and 'mutual aid' have somehow become 'dirty words' for socialists, and Pahl (1984, p. 325) similarly despairs of the way collectivistic solutions have come to dominate socialist thinking as regards consumption as well as production. 'For a time', he says, 'ordinary people were prepared to go along with solidaristic collectivism as perhaps the only way to get major advances into citizenship. Now, it seems, the citizens of the middle mass are asserting themselves in their private lives' (p. 326).

As I suggested in the previous section, this 'middle mass' has been able to pursue a privatized solution to its consumption requirements owing to the increase in real household income which has taken place over the last hundred years. Bolstered in many cases by the 'hidden welfare state' of tax allowances and other financial benefits, its income from work is now enough to support purchase of the most expensive household consumption item – the house itself – and the time is probably fast approaching when, individually or corporately (e.g. through trade union or company subscription), it will be able to finance most elements of its health care needs too. The minority of households which do not enjoy regular wage income cannot, however, aspire to the private ownership solution under current arrangements. They cannot 'assert themselves in their private lives', either by purchasing services or by self-provisioning through purchasing means of consumption, but instead remain locked into dependency on whatever the state chooses to dispense.

State spending on consumption provisions in Britain accounts for around 25 per cent of the country's Gross National Product, or 60,000 million pounds in 1981–2 prices (see Le Grand and Robinson 1984). Of this, nearly half goes on transfer payments – mainly pensions, but also supplementary, child and unemployment benefits. The rest is distributed among provisions in kind, with education and health and personal services accounting for about 80 per cent of it, and housing and transport taking up the rest. Now suppose (leaving aside the question of any addition to the overall budget which may be deemed desirable) the money which currently goes to finance provisions in kind were reallocated, gradually over a period of years, to enhance people's ability to buy the goods and services they want. Such a redistribution of money would take account of variations in household needs and incomes and could take the form of 'negative' income tax payments, earmarked benefits such as increased child allowances, specific voucher schemes, or some combination of all three. This would generate, on average, an extra £2000 per household per year at 1981–2 prices, although some households would in practice receive very little extra (for as we have seen, many multi-earner households can already afford to finance most of their consumption needs without additional support), while others, including those who currently make up the marginalized minority of our society, would receive a large increase. In any event, such a system would have to establish a minimum income level so as to ensure that everyone could purchase at least that level of services to which they are currently entitled under the existing system of provision in kind. Judging by figures calculated by Patrick Minford and cited in Green (1986, ch. 6), this should not be too difficult to achieve.

The first effect of such a gradual transition in the mode of state spending would be to bring about a substantial redistribution of income in favour of the worst off. Under Minford's scheme, for example, people would pay for health insurance, schooling and pension arrangements, but the lower paid would receive in negative income tax and child benefits more than the total cost of such payments and would therefore be better off than they are under existing arrangements. Furthermore, a shift away from provision in kind would mean that lower income earners would no longer be compelled to pay through their taxes for services which they tend to under-use and from which more affluent people extract the most benefit.

A second effect of such a change would almost certainly be a reduction in the costs of most services. Privatization of consumption can, of course, increase costs since economies of scale may be lost, provisions may be duplicated by competing suppliers, and prices obviously include a profit component. Against this, however, administration costs could certainly be cut by overcoming the need to maintain the current levels of monitoring and surveillance entailed in a state system of allocation in kind. As Ward suggests, there is an 'appalling difficulty about the expensive business of looking after people. They would be better off if they simply had the cash to look after themselves' (1985, p. 94). Furthermore, competition between suppliers of services can be expected to reduce prices and costs as compared with a state system of monopoly provision which contains no mechanism for ensuring that service producers pursue the most cost-effective strategies. Not only this, but the individual and co-operative forms of control which would replace state provision are almost certainly less wasteful. As Ward notes in relation to public housing, for example, accommodation which is rented to tenants by the state tends to deteriorate much more rapidly than the equivalent sorts of buildings sold to equivalent sorts of people through the market sector: 'The transfer of council houses to their occupants is the best guarantee of their survival' (1985, p. 50). Much the same logic would seem to apply to other aspects of consumption provision as well.

A third and vitally important effect would be to break down the stark division which is now emerging between net recipients and net donors in the welfare system. My argument here is premissed on Dunleavy's recognition that consumption sector cleavages tend on., to arise around the provision of resources in kind. As he notes, in the case of 'generalized income transfers which are not tied to the consumption of specific commodities . . . we should find that the overall importance of consumption sector effects . . . is reduced' (1985, p. 10). The reason for this is simple. An integrated tax/benefit system of income transfers leaves no visible trace of who is reliant upon the state and who is not, for everyone appears in the market to purchase their consumption requirements as customers rather than as clients, and no one need feel stigmatized. As Simmel noted long ago, money carries no trace of its origins and is no respecter of status.

Fourth, such a change should enable all households to participate more fully than they can at present in informal modes of work. As Pahl suggests, 'Money is necessary to do all the other forms of work. . . . If there were a national minimum wage instead of the present system of benefits and allowances, the total amount of work done would almost certainly increase' (1984, p. 336). Not only, therefore, would the extension of transfer payments to cover health, education and so on enable people to assert themselves more effectively through the selection of the particular services they wished to purchase, but it would also enable them to develop, where feasible, their own modes of self-provisioning and mutual aid. People could, if they chose, form consumer co-operatives to organize for their children to be educated and they could come together in modern forms of the nineteenth-century friendly societies to employ doctors and dentists who would be made accountable to them. Or, if they preferred, they could instead purchase services on an individual basis, selecting the type of schooling they most preferred and the level of medical insurance which best suited their personal requirements. Either way, their capacity for controlling key aspects of their lives would be enormously enhanced.

The major effect of such a change, however, would be to bring about a fundamental redistribution of power in society – something which the existing welfare system has conspicuously failed to achieve. As the (socialist) theorist, Alec Nove, has recognized in his stimulating analysis of markets and state planning, 'With a given distribution of income (as egalitarian as the given society chooses it to be), *there is no better way* of enabling citizens to register their preferences than to allow them freely to spend their "money" (tokens) or their money. If this is denounced by the fundamentalist [Marxist] as a "market", so be it. . . . [N]o voting system can be a substitute because, first, the huge variety of preferences makes it an impossibly unwieldy task, and secondly . . . because this is not a matter of majority vote anyhow, since a minority is entitled to be supplied also (1983, p. 54, emphasis in original). Customers can exert power (albeit limited) within a market through their purses, pockets and pouches, but this is denied to the client within a system of state provision. Clients can complain, can vote, can demand, but in the end they have nowhere else to go, and no choice but to accept what is offered. They are, in short, *dependent* in a way that is never true of customers in a competitive market.

There is a tendency among conservatives and state socialists alike to doubt people's ability to take over such a degree of control and responsibility for their own lives. In one sense, such doubts are justified, for a century of escalating state control has undoubtedly eroded our capacities for making our own decisions about crucial aspects of our own lives. It is precisely because the system they defend has made us dependent that such conservative and socialist thinkers can argue that it would be folly now to bring about a shift in effective power from producers and state managers to consumers. But against this, a change of the kind envisaged here could be expected to revolutionize people's aspirations and expectations and to break through the grudging deference and hopeless fatalism which pervades so much of the state welfare system. After all, people already make decisions in their everyday lives which have a crucial bearing on their health and well-being – decisions about the food that they purchase, the shoes and clothing they dress their children in, and (in the case of the 'middle mass') the home that they will live in and the kind of pension and insurance arrangements that they require. A shift in other areas of consumption from state provision in kind to a policy designed to enable people to exert their own effective demand for what they want would extend the scope of such responsibilities, and there is no reason to assume that people who already make decisions and choices in one area would not also be able to make them in another.

Those who often deny this most vociferously tend to be those responsible for managing and providing the services in question, the 'professional hierarchies' of the welfare institutions who 'have convinced society that their ministrations are morally necessary' (Illich 1971, p. 12). These, of course, are the interests which stand to lose from any increase in effective consumer power, for they would lose their captive client constituency and would, for the first time since the socialized mode of consumption developed, have to address themselves to the demands of the consumers of their services.

Such a shift in power from producers to consumers is in my view the moral and political rationale which lies behind the future development of urban sociology as a sociology of consumption. In a recent and stimulating contribution, Herbert Gans has outlined what he terms a 'third paradigm' for urban sociology, which goes beyond the anti-collectivism of neo-ecology and the anti-individualism of neo-Marxism. What distinguishes this third paradigm is its emphasis on consumers rather than producers, an emphasis (exemplified in different ways in the writings of Pahl and Ward discussed above) on understanding what people want and on analysing how best they might achieve it. For Gans, 'Producers of goods and services probably have more power than consumers in all societies, because they play a central role in a communist economy, and because they have the incentives and resources to put pressure on government in a capitalist economy' (1984, p. 295). This producer power goes unchallenged by both neo-ecology (which speaks for private sector corporations) and neo-Marxism (which, despite its sympathy for 'an imagined coalition of the poor and the working class' actually resists the expressed aspirations of these groups and speaks mainly for academics who are themselves, of course, part of the public sector producer interest). The task, therefore is to develop an urban sociology:

> . . . beginning from the perspective of the users (be these customers or clients or constituents) and tracing the relationships and problems with the public bodies. This sociology would pay less attention than current ones on how public bodies are structured and function, or how they produce and reproduce – or reach users. Instead, the analysis begins with the interests of users, as perceived and felt by them, looking at producers and suppliers of services in terms of their ability and willingness to pay attention to, or ignore or manipulate, user demands and preferences (1984, p. 305).

Such a research agenda cannot, of course, ignore producers, for as we saw in Chapter 6, modes of consumption are related to modes of production, and a change in one will carry implications as regards change in the other. If, for example, a policy was adopted in which, wherever practicable, state provisions in kind were replaced by cash payments in one form or another, then this would certainly change the character and organization of agencies producing goods and services. Just as consumer co-operatives could develop, so too, for example, could producer co-operatives (e.g. teachers who share a particular ethos of education could come together to offer a particular kind of schooling). Furthermore, the redistribution of spending power away from state monopolies and towards those sections of the population who currently lack financial power in consumer markets would clearly create new patterns of demand and would (provided the minimum level of household income were established at a point sufficient to ensure that everyone could participate effectively in the market) bring forth new forms of supply to meet them.

Given this interrelation of production and consumption, it may well be asked why this 'third paradigm' in urban sociology should focus primarily on the latter. Why analyse people's experience as consumers rather than as producers? Why seek to liberate people through their use of goods and services rather than through their production of these goods and services? Why, in short, elevate consumption above production?

The answer is that, in the conditions pertaining in advanced industrial societies, liberation through the formal production sphere is almost certainly impractical. The sphere of consumption is as important and crucial as it is precisely because it is here that the potential exists for extending people's control over their own lives. In general, this potential does not exist in the sphere of production.

My argument here has much in common with that developed by André Gorz in his two books, *Farewell to the Working Class* (1982) and *Paths to Paradise* (1985). Both books start out from the assumption, shared by Pahl and many others, that the era of full employment in a single, paid job has finished. Technological developments have brought us to a point in the West where only 20,000 hours of labour are necessary in any one lifetime in order to produce all the items we need to consume. In such a situation, it is ludicrous to continue to assert that formal paid employment constitutes people's central life activity and identity: 'There can no longer be full-time waged work for all, and waged work cannot remain the centre of gravity or even the central activity in our lives. Any politics which denies this, whatever its ideological pretensions, is a fraud' (1985, p. 34). Gorz also argues that the Marxist project of liberating people in and through their labour is similarly fraudulent, since for most workers, labour is necessarily experienced as alienative. This, he says, is not simply because of the way capitalist production is organized, but is because of the inherent character of advanced production methods which are too large in scale and too diversified and fragmented in nature for anyone to experience creativity through their work or to seek to control the overall process. It follows from this that:

> For workers, it is no longer a question of freeing themselves *within* work, putting themselves in control of work, or seizing power within the framework of their work. The point now is to free oneself *from* work by rejecting its nature, content, necessity and modalities. But to reject work is also to reject the traditional strategy and organisational forms of the working class movement. It is no longer a question of winning power as a worker, but of winning the power no longer to function as a worker (1982, p. 67).

It is on the basis of such arguments that Gorz distinguishes two spheres within what he terms a future 'dual society'. One sphere is the realm of compulsion and necessity, what he terms the 'sphere of heteronomy'. It is here that the goods and services are produced which are conditions of the exercise of 'practical autonomy' in the other sphere of life. People, he suggests, could contribute 20,000 hours of labour to working in a planned and programmed system of production, in return for which they would earn sufficient to claim access to the various goods and services they required in order to pursue their other and more central life activities.

What is of interest in Gorz's work as regards our current concerns is less his futuristic blueprint than the arguments which lie behind it. Two points appear to be crucial. First, Gorz is clear that, even with the decline in paid employment, some necessary work remains to be done and this will always be experienced by most people as alienative and coercive:

> The division of labour is thus inevitably depersonalising. . . . There can never be effective self-management of a big factory, an industrial combine or a bureaucratic department. It will always be defeated by the rigidity of technical constraints. . . . It is thus impossible to abolish the depersonalisation, standardisation and trivialisation of socially determined labour without abolishing the division of labour through a return to craft production and the village economy. This is out of the question. . . . The point, then, is not to abolish heteronomous work, but only to use the goods it supplies and the way in which they are produced in order to enlarge the sphere of autonomy (1982, pp. 100–1).

It follows from this that, whether organized through a market or a planning system, the sphere of formal production cannot today offer the prospect of popular liberation or autonomous control.

The second argument is that personal liberation and control is nevertheless an essential feature of popular aspirations (one which has generally gone unrecognized in socialist movements), and that it can potentially be realized outside of people's formal working lives. Provided they have the necessary means (which they gain through work in the heteronomous sphere of production), people can therefore achieve control and self-determination away from formal work in what I have called the sphere of consumption.

It is important to emphasize that Gorz does not limit this sphere of autonomy simply to passive consumption of goods and services, but includes in it all the activities in which people may choose to engage other than through instrumental–economic necessity. 'The sphere of individual sovereignty', he notes, 'is not based upon a mere desire to consume, nor solely upon relaxation and leisure activities. It is based, more profoundly, upon activities unrelated to any economic goal which are an end in themselves' (1982, p. 80). It thus includes both passive and active consumption, or what Dunleavy terms 'individual' and 'autonomous' consumption. It includes, in other words, the use of means of consumption in 'informal work' and self-provisioning as well as consumption as an end in itself, DIY as well as TV.

Given his view that paid employment is no longer the central life activity (if, indeed, it ever was) and that self-management, identity and control can only be expressed outside of the formal production sphere, it is clearly crucial for Gorz that the realm of autonomy should determine the realm of heteronomy rather than vice versa. As he puts it:

> There can be neither morality nor relations informed by morality unless two conditions are fulfilled. First, there must exist a sphere of autonomous activity in which the individual is the sovereign author of actions carried out without recourse to necessity, alibis or excuses. Secondly, this sphere must be prevalent rather than subordinate (1982, p. 93).

Here, then, is the case for concentrating our attentions on the sphere of consumption prior to the sphere of production, and for attempting to expand the capacity for people to control their own lives in the consumption sphere by limiting the power of producers to control it. This also provides the justification for attempting as far as possible to limit state determination of human activities to the sphere of production while keeping state monopoly power away from the sphere of consumption. As Gorz says, 'There is no "good" government, "good" state or "good" form of power, and . . . society can never be "good" in its own form of organisation but only by virtue of the space for self-organisation, cooperation and voluntary exchange which that organisation offers to individuals' (1982, p. 118).

Here, too, is the case for Gans's attempt to forge a new sociology which goes beyond both the anti-collectivism of the right and the anti-individualism of the left, for it is clear that individualistic solutions in the sphere of consumption are not inconsistent with, and may to some extent require, collectivistic solutions in the sphere of production. Just as we saw earlier in this chapter that different social scientific theories which have generally been seen as incompatible may in fact be complementary in so far as they apply to the different spheres of production and consumption, so now we see that this is also the case with different political and moral philosophies. As Gorz recognizes, 'Economic liberalism gives rise to demands for state control and . . . state control provokes demands for liberalisation. The point, however, is not to choose one or the other; but to define the field in which both can be cogently put into effect' (1982, p. 114). The privatized mode of provision is thus appropriate to the sphere of consumption, but the state may still have a crucial role to perform in the sphere of production in order to ensure that the conditions of autonomy in the former are maintained and reproduced.

Just how state power could or should be used in the production sphere in order to safeguard the autonomy of the consumption sphere is, however, a problem requiring further consideration and analysis. Gorz himself fails to provide a satisfactory answer, for having argued at the beginning of his analysis that the modern system of production does not allow for any effective popular control, he is forced at the end (e.g. 1985, pp. 57–8) to posit the existence of a social consensus as the basis for determining collective decisions as to what needs to be produced and how. The possibility that such a consensus could ever exist is, to say the least, dubious, as is his belief that it is possible to retain a technical division of labour without perpetuating a hierarchy of authority and stratification (1985, p. 77).

Various of Gorz's critics (and there have been many, for his analysis strikes at the heart of traditional Marxist theory and practice) have suggested that the partial liberation which he offers does not go far enough. Production, they assert in familiar vein, remains primary and determinant over consumption, in which case Gorz's attempt to carve out a niche of personal autonomy in respect of the latter is doomed. Ignoring his tightly-argued demonstration that freedom in the sphere of formal work is a chimera, for example, Godard concludes his critical discussion of Gorz's work by asking with a rhetorical flourish, 'Is this not to prescribe the hopelessness of significantly changing the logic (of functioning) of the large-scale apparatuses of production and control of the state machine? Can we change ways of life without also changing the ways of producing and governing?' (1985, p. 335).

In contrast to these critics, I would suggest that Gorz probably goes too far. What is wrong with his analysis is not that it seeks to establish autonomy in only one sphere, for this is entirely realistic, but that he fails to show how the other sphere will accommodate and adjust to this. It is for this reason that I have outlined an altogether more modest proposal – namely, a reform of the state's role in consumption involving a shift from direct provision to cash transfers – for while this will not usher in a new age of freedom and self-determination, it will enormously enhance people's capacity for controlling and determining certain core aspects of their lives, and it does appear to be an attainable goal.

Such issues and arguments are, of course, open to further debate, elaboration and critical analysis. As Pahl notes, 'The sociology of consumption is not well developed' (1984, p. 106; see also Moorhouse 1983). But provided we can shake off the legacy of a long strain of intellectual thought which asserts that consumption is simply a derivative of production, then such a sociology does hold out considerable promise. As Gans suggests, 'If citizens want anything from sociology, it is informational help in escaping exploitation and domination, and in maximising their control over their own lives' (1984, p. 306). Urban sociology, understood as a sociology of consumption, can, I believe, help provide such information and point the way to such control. In focusing on that sphere of life which provides the greatest potential for the expression of individual autonomy, urban sociology is uniquely equipped to chart a path out of the 'iron cage' which Weber believed was encompassing the whole of modern society. In the problem of consumption, therefore, urban sociology has not only at long last discovered an object of analysis; it has helped identify one of the core questions of the modern age.

Appendix A note on the empirical testing of theories

It has been suggested at various points in this book that empirical testability is one important criterion of theoretical adequacy. We saw in Chapter 6, for example, that Marxist theories of the relative autonomy of the state ultimately fail to explain what they describe because they are essentially tautologies which are immune to empirical evaluation. The reason for this is that the concept of relative autonomy combines two opposing principles into a single general statement which cannot support counterfactual conditions, for to argue that the state both supports the long-term interests of monopoly capital and responds to the interests of non-capitalist classes without specifying the conditions under which these two contradictory tendencies become operative is simply to provide a self-confirming theory which is descriptively accurate but devoid of explanatory power. It was for this reason that it was suggested in Chapter 8 that a dualistic perspective may prove fruitful, for by distinguishing those situations in which capitalist interests are dominant from those in which the state responds to different interests engaged in competitive struggles with one another, it is possible to develop a range of hypotheses that may be assessed in the light of empirical research.

One possible objection to this whole argument, however, is that it betrays a naive view of the relation between theory and empirical evidence. Thus social scientists have increasingly come to recognize that the traditional assumption behind positivist research that 'facts' can be assembled through direct experience of the social world must be treated with some caution. It is now generally agreed that knowledge cannot be the product of unmediated experience through the senses, but that the way in which we come to 'see' the world is in some way dependent upon the theoretical assumptions and conceptual frameworks that we apply to it. As we saw in Chapter 1 when discussing the problems with Durkheim's sociological method, what we take to be 'facts', and thus 'evidence' and 'proof' for our assertions, will depend upon the way we conceptualize the world. There is no 'pure' observation, no neutral body of evidence, no 'facts' that are independent of prior conceptual assumptions.

If observation is theory-dependent, then resort to empirical evidence to arbitrate between competing theoretical explanations is clearly problematic. As Hindess suggests in relation to Popper's arguments regarding the need for empirical falsification in science, 'If all observation is to some extent theoretical, then how is it possible to maintain that all knowledge is reducible to observation and that theory is to be tested against the "facts" of observation?' (1977, p. 18). The point is not simply that theory determines where we look, but that it to some extent governs what we find.

The theory dependency of empirical research findings does not, however, undermine my earlier argument that empirical testability is an essential condition of theoretical adequacy. Three points need to be considered.

The first is that theory dependency does not imply theory determinacy. There is, in other words, no reason to suggest that different theoretical perspectives cannot agree on common areas of conceptualization and common criteria of empirical evidence. To argue otherwise would be to suggest that different theorists always talk past one another, never engage in meaningful debate and mutual criticism, and never concur over what is actually happening in the world; yet this is clearly not the case. For example, although they certainly disagree over the explanations they offer, and sometimes disagree over criteria of adequate or valid empirical evidence, conflict and consensus theorists nevertheless broadly agree on the sort of evidence that may indicate the perpetuation or break-down of social order. Similarly, while we may doubt, say, Castells's reasons for predicting the growth of urban social movements, and we may criticize the very concept of an urban social movement, none of this precludes the possibility of Castells and his critics agreeing on the existence or non-existence of such movements in a particular place at a particular time on the basis of the criteria which Castells himself puts forward.

The point is, therefore, that any theory employs both relatively high- and relatively low-level concepts, and that there is always likely to be a fairly broad conceptual 'lower common denominator' between different perspectives. As Andrew Sayer notes in his defence of Marxist methodology, ' "Looking at the evidence" need not imply an empiricist notion of observation as theory-neutral, but in relation to concepts like "socialization of consumption", those employed in observation are liable to be of a "*lower order*". That is, they are unlikely to be exclusive to Marxism' (A. Sayer 1979, p. 48). Thus Sayer distinguishes between the (correct) view that evidence is theory-laden and the (incorrect) view that it is therefore theory-determined. Different theories share a broad (though low-level) area of agreement regarding their conceptualization of the world and their criteria of empirical evidence, and, this being the case, the theory dependency of empirical research need not rule out some degree of empirical evaluation of different theories, nor need it result in a collapse into cognitive relativism (see also A. Sayer 1984a, Ch. 2).

Before leaving this point, and as a prelude to the second point, it is important to take issue with one aspect of Sayer's argument concerning his critique of Hirst's rejection of epistemology which we discussed briefly in Chapter 5. It will be recalled that, in criticizing Althusser's epistemological imperialism, Hirst came to the conclusion that there are no epistemological principles divorced from particular discourses that can determine the correct mode of scientific analysis. We cannot, that is, criticize any given perspective simply on epistemological grounds, although different perspectives can be attacked on criteria internal to their own discourse. While himself rejecting Althusser's position, Sayer also rejects Hirst's argument as 'fatuous' and 'silly' on the grounds that it assumes that 'all observation is completely theory-determined' (A. Sayer 1979, p. 73). For Sayer, in other words, a rejection of epistemology is tantamount to an endorsement of cognitive relativism (despite the fact that Hirst has stressed that his is not a relativist – or, indeed, any other epistemological – position).

Given our endorsement of Hirst's argument in Chapter 5, it is clearly necessary to answer this criticism, for we have seen that Sayer is quite justified in arguing against the theory determinacy view of observation. The point is, however, that Hirst's argument does not entail such a view. Hirst and his various co-authors do not necessarily deny that different discourses may agree on epistemological principles; only that any one epistemology can be taken as self-evident and thus as the basis for rejecting alternative approaches grounded in alternative methodologies. His critique of epistemology suggests simply that no approach can be dismissed on the grounds that it is epistemologically invalid because no general epistemology can be self-justifiable. This does not, however, imply that different discourses cannot engage in mutual criticism based on common agreement regarding what is to count as a valid mode of analysis or adequate empirical evidence.

Neither Sayer nor other like-minded critics of Hirst's position have been able to demonstrate the superiority of one epistemological position over others. In his critique, for example, Collier suggests that, for knowledge to be possible, it must be assumed that reality is structured in a certain way:

> If our faculties of knowledge depend for their possibility on the structure of the world outside them in this way, why should we not assume that the world really has that structure and hence makes them possible, rather than that they have the additional magic ability to force the world into a knowable form which it doesn't have in itself? (Collier 1978, p. 16).

The answer, of course, is that there is no reason why we should not *assume* that our concepts develop in such a way as progressively to map and hence reveal the real structure of the world, and that dialectical materialism is the method that is most appropriate to such a voyage of discovery since 'its result depends on the structure of external reality, not on us' (Collier 1978, p. 19), provided we always remember that this is a starting assumption which is not an *a priori* truth (as Althusser seems to believe), and which cannot in itself justify the rejection of other approaches based on other initial assumptions. It is not Hirst and his colleagues who must 'come clean', as Sayer and Collier both suggest at the end of their respective papers, but rather those Marxist theorists who claim to work with a privileged epistemology yet who have failed to demonstrate the source of its superiority. It does seem that the hostility shown by many academic Marxists towards Hirst's arguments is born of a fear of losing the 'scientific' basis of their political analyses, the paradox being (as Hirst himself has shown) that it is precisely this claim to scientific privilege that has so consistently weakened rather than strengthened the political impact of Marxism over the last hundred years.

What is specific to the Marxist method is, as we saw in Chapter 1, the distinction that it draws between essence and phenomenal appearance, and hence its claim to be able to explain the latter through the discovery of the former. This leads us to consider the second point relating to the question of empirical testability; namely, that Marxist laws cannot and should not be tested through any simple notion of empirical falsification. Sayer's paper is again relevant here.

Sayer argues, quite justifiably, that the Marxist method involves the attempt to discover necessary tendencies (such as the tendency within capitalism for the rate of profit to fall), and that the question of whether or not these tendencies are realized is contingent on a variety of empirical conditions (for example the mobilization of counteracting tendencies to prevent the rate of profit from falling). Drawing an analogy with the natural sciences, he argues that, just as the chemical laws of combustion are not falsified if a particular pile of gunpowder fails to explode when a flame is applied (since, for example, it may be damp), and just as the law of gravity is not falsified whenever aeroplanes fail to drop from the sky, so too Marxist laws cannot be rejected as false simply because they fail to become manifest in particular situations. He then argues on the basis of this that Marxist theories cannot be subject to the test of empirical falsification (since this ignores the question of counteracting tendencies), or even to the test of their success in guiding political practice (since political intervention changes the situation to which they refer). He concludes that 'In social science there are no "tests", only applications' (A. Sayer 1979, p. 33).

This argument reflects Sayer's commitment to what has become known as 'realist' philosophy. As we saw in Chapter 6, this is an approach to social scientific explanation which seeks to identify the inherent capacities of things to act in certain ways. Unlike empiricist approaches, which see causality in terms of correlation between events (whenever A occurs, then so too does B), realist philosophy argues for a conception of causality in terms of generative mechanisms. Theoretical progress thus entails identification of the 'necessary' mechanisms which tend to produce given tendencies. The fact that such tendencies may not become manifest in observation is due to the operation of contingent factors which obviously cannot be theorized, but whose effects can be examined in given empirical cases. Thus, for example, it may be held that there is a necessary and inherent tendency in capitalism for the rate of exploitation of labour to increase. This will itself tend to generate an intensification of class struggle between labour and capital, but the form that such struggles take (e.g. worker absenteeism, industrial sabotage, strikes, demonstrations, revolutions), and, indeed, whether or not they occur at all, will reflect the particular historical conditions pertaining at any given time in any given place (e.g. the character of the labour movement, the nature of dominant ideologies, the strength of state coercion, etc.). The important point about all this is that, even if events do not seem to bear out the theory, this does not invalidate it, for events reflect contingent conditions while theory is concerned with necessary mechanisms which exist irrespective of whether they become manifest.

One confusing aspect of this approach which is immediately apparent concerns the distinction between 'necessities' and 'contingencies', for what is a necessity (and thus capable of being theorized) from one point of view may be a 'contingency' (and thus incapable of being theorized) from another. Thus, taking the above example, the 'contingent' factor of the nature of the labour movement can itself be re-translated into a 'necessary' one by a simple shift in the types of research questions we set ourselves. We could presumably develop an argument to the effect that placid labour movements are necessarily generated by, say, the tendency for real wages to rise as capitalism develops, and the contingent condition in this case would be that factors sometimes arise (e.g. the quadrupling of oil prices in the early 1970s) which depress living standards and which therefore prevent this placidity from becoming manifest. There are, in other words, no obvious guidelines (other than the researcher's own value-conditioned interests) for determining what is necessary and what is contingent.

There is, however, an even more thorny problem with this whole approach which is basically that it becomes possible to posit virtually anything as a 'real' and 'necessary' tendency, given that contingent events or 'counteracting tendencies' can always be appealed to in order to save the theory. What is to stop us identifying through our theories all sorts of causal mechanisms which may or may not exist?

Realist philosophy attempts to guard against this by stipulating three steps in the construction of any explanation. The first is observation in which we detect empirical regularities in the world (e.g. all swans are white, apples fall downwards, capitalist economies lurch into crisis every few years). The second step is then to develop plausible explanations relating to the mechanism which may be generating these regularities (e.g. that the genetic make-up of swans inhibits pigmentation in the feathers, that a gravitational force exists which draws all objects to the centre of the earth, or that competition between capitalists tends to drive overall rates of profit downwards). As we saw when we discussed Derek Sayer's notion of 'retroduction' in Chapter 1, this second stage is necessarily conjectural, for we are not and cannot be sure that the mechanisms we have posited are the real ones. It is for this reason that the third step – experimental checking – is so crucial, for it is here that contingent conditions are as far as possible held constant so as to identify the causal mechanisms which are actually generating the observed effects.

The problem when we come to apply this method to the social world, however, is that this third experimental stage is not normally possible. There are many reasons why this is so – among them, the fact that there are too many variables to hold constant, that sociological experiments in controlled conditions destroy the situation which is being studied, and that enormous ethical problems are raised in any attempt to experiment with people's lives. Realists generally accept this. One of the leading realist philosophers, for example, admits that the crucial third stage of experimental verification cannot be carried through in social explanation:

> The central argument of this study ... has turned on the possibility of experimental activity.... [I]t is clear that experimental activity is impossible in the social sciences ... there is a general problem of confirmation (or corroboration) and falsification in the non-experimental sciences (Bhaskar 1978, pp. 244–5).

This would seem to throw considerable doubt over the application of a realist methodology in the explanation of social phenomena, for while we may be in a position to observe regularities and to conjure up various plausible explanations for them in terms of the operation of 'necessary tendencies', we cannot follow through to the crucial third stage of examining whether or not these tendencies actually exist when contingent conditions are held constant. We never know, for example, whether there is, as Marxist theory tells us, a real tendency in capitalist societies for the rate of profit to fall, for the contingent events which operate in the opposite direction (e.g. increased investment in 'Department I' industries, or increased rates of exploitation of labour in 'Department II' industries) occur simultaneously, and it is impossible to examine the effects of a rise in the ratio of constant to variable capital independently of these 'counteracting tendencies'.

What then is to stop us developing any theory of necessity when we know that it cannot be checked through controlled experimental conditions? Andrew Sayer (1984 a) provides two checks. First, he says that it is normally possible, though by no means easy, to find independent corroborative evidence for the existence of a necessary tendency. Second, he suggests that fanciful theories can be eliminated by exposing the weaknesses in the explanations which they offer of the generative mechanisms at work. Thus, for example, my pet theory that there are no elephants in Surrey because I go round the county once a month scattering mustard seed which keeps them away can be rejected first, by seeking independent evidence (e.g. were there elephants in Surrey before I began my monthly ritual?), and second, by demonstrating the inadequacy of the mechanism (e.g. by looking at the effect which mustard seed has on elephants) (see Sayer 1984a, pp. 198–200). This, however, does not really answer the problem. For a start, the refutation of the theory rests on a controlled experiment (testing the effects of mustard seed on elephants) which we have already seen is not possible in the case of social theories. And second, the independent corroboration (e.g. evidence that Surrey has never had elephants) can simply be dismissed as itself the result of other contingent conditions (e.g. the effects of climate) which do nothing to undermine the theorized necessary mechanism regarding the inherent tendencies of mustard seed as an elephant deterrent.

My theory concerning the inherent tendencies of mustard seed is, as Sayer says, trivial, but the lessons to be learned from it are not. In my view, the growth of realist approaches in urban studies during the 1980s is effectively leading to a repeat of the sorts of claims being advanced by Althusserian philosophy in the 1970s.

As we saw in Chapter 5, Althusserianism gained its adherents through its claim that there was but one scientific method and that alternative approaches were essentially ideological. This brash assertiveness eventually collapsed as researchers came to realize, not only that this method hindered empirical work (in that it denied the possibility of knowing the world other than through theory), but also that (as Hirst showed) there could be no meta-epistemology which could possibly justify Althusser's claims to a privileged insight into reality.

Liberated from the yoke of Althusserian epistemology, many people (among them, Castells) began to discuss the need for more empirical research, and a few actually began to do it. In particular, they began to assert the importance of historical analysis as the means for explaining how and why things came to be as they are. This tendency, however, carried the clear danger of heresy against some cherished Marxist principles (as is obvious in Castells's later work), for to argue that history could explain causality was to undermine a belief in scientific laws governing human affairs. Various neologisms were coined in an attempt to resolve these difficulties. What was required, we were told, was not a return to 'empiricism' (bad), but the development of 'theoretically-informed empirical research' (good);

not 'bourgeois history' (bad) with its preoccupations with unique events and key individuals, but 'theorized histories' (good) which would situate these events and individuals within the laws and universal tendencies of which they were but an expression. What all this amounted to was a call for selective empirical and historical research which would not produce new knowledge so much as illustrate and 'confirm' existing knowledge gleaned through a thorough grounding in Marxist theory. The theory, in other words, was to be preserved while allowing empirical research to develop within its boundaries. What was needed was an approach which would subordinate history to theory and which would guarantee the immunity of the latter from the results of the former. Realism was the epistemology which was seized upon to fulfil this requirement.

Part of the attraction of realism has been that it seems to offer many of the old epistemological certainties which disappeared with the collapse of Althusserianism. Just as Althusser distinguished his 'science' from everybody else's 'ideology', so now realists such as Bhaskar (and in urban studies, Sayer or Urry) distinguish their knowledge of 'real' causal mechanisms from everybody else's 'superficial' knowledge of the manifest pattern of events. As the very name implies, to be a 'realist' is to distinguish oneself from others who by definition have only a tenuous grasp of 'reality'.

Realism's atttraction also lies in its offer of an approach which justifies the desire to hold history at arm's length from theory. This is achieved through the basic distinction between necessary causes and contingent conditions. As we have seen, necessary causes are identified by means of theory while contingent conditions are identified empirically (even though in practice, the distinction between what is necessary and what is contingent seems to hinge entirely on what it is the researcher is interested in looking at). This means that realism accords to empirical and historical research the task of identifying the contingencies which are mediating the real motive forces which have already been identified through the theory.

What we have here is a revised and more subtle form of Althusserianism. Unlike Althusserianism, realism does make room for empirical work – indeed, it demands it. Like its predecessor, however, it accords explanatory primacy to causes which can only be identified theoretically and which, in the absence of controlled experiments, remain effectively immune to falsification even though there may be no evidence that they are operating or even that they exist. The 'necessities' are simply asserted while the catch-all category of 'contingency' takes care of all the problems. In this way, awkward empirical or historical 'events' play second fiddle to theoretical certainties (for as Urry (1985) suggests, echoing Harré, realism involves not an 'event ontology' but a 'thing ontology'), and these certainties are invariably derived from Marxism (for there are, as far as I know, no examples in contemporary social science of non-Marxist realist work).

The growing attraction of realism is that it not only makes existing theories immune from falsification while still enabling empirical research, but it also carries the added bonus that other people's theories (which may be objected to on political grounds) can be dismissed as methodologically unsound. Non-Marxist approaches can all be condemned as superficial – as looking only at manifest events while failing to appreciate the deeper real causes which have brought them about. Monetarist economics can be dismissed in this way because it lacks an understanding of the 'real' value movements which underpin price movements; pluralist political theory can be dismissed because it fails to understand how 'real' class relations underpin the superficial cleavages and alliances which arise over particular issues; and Weberian sociology can be dismissed because it fails to understand how the values, beliefs and motives which give direction to people's actions are simply the expression of 'real' material forces operating in a given mode of production. Realism, in short, provides a spurious intellectual justification for asserting a left orthodoxy and discounting alternative approaches by presenting political and moral values and beliefs as if they were scientifically derived. The irony, of course, is that this was precisely the complaint voiced by earlier generations of radicals against positivism!

The third main point I wish to make about the problem of empirical testability concerns the question of testing within as opposed to between theories, for it follows from our earlier discussion of Hirst's critique of epistemology that the specification of counterfactuals and of the criteria by which they can be identified empirically will be specific to particular discourses.

My insistence on the importance of counterfactuality refers only to the necessity of any theory to support the possibility of disconfirming instances and to stipulate the criteria by which such instances may be recognized in empirical research. Theories should not be merely self-confirming tautologies, but should be open to empirical test in accordance with conditions that they themselves lay down. To the extent that different approaches can agree on these conditions, they can be evaluated empirically against each other; to the extent that they cannot so agree, they can be evaluated empirically only on their own terms. But to the extent that they fail to provide such conditions, they cannot be evaluated empirically at all, in which case any claim they make to scientific knowledge can safely be ignored.

It is on this basis that I would justify the dualistic approach developed in Chapter 8, for as we saw there, such an approach can sustain counterfactual testing in terms of the argument that different types of political strategies tend to be associated with different aspects of the state's role performed at different levels of its organization. It was not, of course, suggested that this is universally the case, but only that this may be taken as an ideal-typical framework within which empirical research on a variety of different cases may fruitfully proceed. The significance of this approach, in other words, is that it enables the development of hypotheses that are not true by definition but that can be amended, developed, further specified or even abandoned in the light of empirical evidence from different studies of different aspects of state activity in different countries at different times. It therefore facilitates the development of Castells's call for a 'theorized history of states' in a way that Castells's own use of the concept of relative autonomy did not.

One final point should be made in conclusion, and this concerns the possible criticism that an insistence on counterfactuality and empirical testability is inconsistent with a rejection of general epistemological principles. Such a criticism would appear valid in the sense that my argument does point to a universal principle (internal testability) by means of which all perspectives are to be evaluated, and this reflects my assertion that sociological explanations that are inherently immune from empirical evaluation, even on their own terms, in effect explain nothing. Those who remain content to accept such 'explanations' will obviously reject my emphasis on counterfactuality. However, for those approaches that seek to go beyond tautology and resolute faith, an insistence on counterfactuality does not represent an unwarranted epistemological intrusion since it does not attempt to impose external and general principles regarding correct procedure or universal criteria of empirical adequacy (for such questions are determined within discourses), but merely holds that some such criteria must be specified. This is a minimal epistemological principle, yet it is one that much of the literature discussed in the later chapters of this book fails to address.

Further reading

General texts

Martin Slattery's *Urban Sociology* (Causeway Press 1985) provides in ch. 2 probably the most basic and introductory review of urban social theory which is currently available, while *Structures and Processes of Urban Life* (Longman 1983), written by Ray Pahl, Rob Flynn and Nick Buck, discusses various key theories in the context of historical and empirical evidence. More detailed, but also more dated, discussions of approaches prior to the development of the 'new urban sociology' in the 1970s can be found in Leonard Reissman's *The Urban Process* (1964) and Rosemary Mellor's *Urban Sociology in an Urbanised Society* (1977). More recently, Les Kilmartin, David Thorns and Terry Burke have published *Social Theory and the Australian City* (George Allen and Unwin 1985) which contains useful reviews of ecological, Weberian and Marxist perspectives, as does Keith Bassett and John Short, *Housing and Residential Structure* (Routledge & Kegan Paul 1980). The Open University's D202 course on *Urban Change and Conflict* is also a valuable source (see especially Dunleavy's contribution in units three and four). For those who wish to follow up specific approaches in more detail, I identify below a few key references in respect of each chapter.

Chapter 1: Social theory, capitalism and the urban question

Marx's discussions of the urban question are scattered and fragmented, although an important reference is undoubtedly part 1c of Marx and Engels (1970), in which the town–country division is considered in the context of the development of the division of labour in society. This may usefully be read alongside some of the later chapters of the first volume of *Capital* (1976– notably chs. 26, 27 and 30–32), which also contains a short discussion of the causes and effects of capitalist urbanization (pp. 811–18 in the 1976 edition), although this latter theme is more fully elaborated in Engels (1969a, b). The best secondary source on all this is Lefebvre (1972), although this is unfortunately not available in English translation. Giddens (1971, ch. 2) is, however, a useful and readily accessible source.

Weber's essay on the city can be found in Weber (1968, ch. 16) or in a separate publication edited and introduced by Martindale (Weber 1958). As was suggested in Chapter 1, this essay has suffered some neglect within sociology – even Martindale's introduction focuses more on work by other writers such as Park and Wirth than it does on Weber – but there are short, useful discussions of it in Mellor (1977, pp. 189–94) and Bendix (1966, pp. 70–9). In my view, however, by far the best discussion of Weber's essay can be found in ch. 2 of *The City: Patterns of domination and conflict* (Macmillan 1982) by Brian Elliott and David McCrone. Philip Abrams's essay (1978) is also important, not only for its discussion of Weber, but also for its review of Marxist historical debates over the city in the feudal period.

The principal reference with regard to Durkheim's discussion of urbanization is Durkheim (1933, see especially pp. 1–10, 18–28, 181–90 and 256–301). This work has rarely been discussed in the context of its contribution to urban sociology, although S. Lukes, *Emile Durkheim: His Life and Work* (Allen Lane 1973, ch. 7) provides a thorough and critical review of its main arguments while J. Eldridge, *Sociology and Industrial Life* (Nelson 1973, pp. 73–91) is useful on the concept of anomie and its relation to Durkheim's discussion of a new nationally organized guild system.

Chapter 2: The urban as an ecological community

Probably the most concise statement of Park's theory is his essay on human ecology which was first published in the *American Journal of Sociology*, vol. 42, 1936, and which is contained in Park (1952, ch. 12). This collection of Park's essays should also be consulted for ch. 15 (in which he discusses the concept of natural areas in the context of his sociological method) and ch. 19 (a paper originally written in 1939 in which he comes to his final conclusions on the biotic–cultural distinction). His original essay on the city is also included in this collection, and can also be found in Park and Burgess, *The City* (University of Chicago Press 1925; re-issued in 1967), which contains other important contributions by Burgess (his famous paper on concentric rings) and McKenzie.

Of the avalanche of critical discussions of the Chicago school, the most important is probably that by Alihan (1938, especially chs. 2, 3 and 4), part of which is reprinted in G. Theodorson, *Studies in Human Ecology* (New York: Harper Row 1961). The Theodorson collection also contains papers or excerpts by Wirth, Robinson, Firey, Hawley and others, in addition to short summaries of the various papers by the editor. Hawley's reformulation of human ecology is summarized in his 1968 paper, although this should be read in conjunction with his earlier book (Hawley 1950, especially ch. 4). Brief and useful résumés of the ecological tradition can be found in Robson (1969, pp. 8–15 and 35–8) and Berry and Kasarda (1977, ch. 1); and further critical commentaries are provided by Reissman (1964, ch. 5), Mellor (1977, ch. 6) and Castells (1977a, ch. 8). Chapter 2 of Hannerz (1980) is also well worth consulting, not only for a summary of Chicago school theory, but also for a very readable review of much of its ethnography.

Chapter 3: The urban as a cultural form

Simmel's essay on the metropolis and mental life first appeared in English translation in Wolff (1950), though it has subsequently been reprinted elsewhere (e.g. in K. Thompson and J. Tunstall, *Sociological Perspectives* (Penguin 1971)). Wirth's 1938 essay on urbanism as a way of life has also subsequently appeared in a number of edited collections including P. Hatt and A. Reiss, *Cities and Society*, 2nd edn. (New York: Free Press 1957) and A. Reiss, *Louis Wirth on Cities and Social Life* (University of Chicago Press 1964). The Reiss collection also contains Wirth's essays on the ghetto (1927) and human ecology (1945), as well as his unfinished but important article on rural–urban differences. Useful supplementary reading on Simmel includes his essay 'On the significance of numbers for social life' (in Wolff 1950, Pt II, ch. 1) and the piece on 'Group expansion and the development of individuality' included in Levine (1971). Levine's introduction to this latter collection is also useful on Simmel's formalism, his sociological emphasis on number, and his relation to Park's later work.

The history of urban–rural dichotomies in sociology is discussed and summarized in Pahl (1968), which is also an important article in its own right for the critique that it develops of any attempt to relate cultural patterns to spatial locations. The other major contribution to this debate is by Gans (1968) who shows that, at most, Wirth's theory of urbanism applies only to deprived groups in inner-city areas of high population turnover. See also Dewey (1960) for an evaluation of the effects of location on cultural patterns, and the final chapter in Lewis (1951) for a critique of Redfield's work on folk culture. Mellor (1977, ch. 5) provides a critical overview of this whole tradition, while Williams (1973) develops a fascinating argument regarding the ideological significance of rural and urban imagery in western capitalism (see especially chs. 1 and 25; also his article on 'Literature and the city' in the *Listener*, vol. 78, 1967, pp. 653–6). M. P. Smith's *The City and Social Theory* (1980) contains exhaustive chapters on Wirth and Simmel which can also be recommended.

Chapter 4: The urban as a socio-spatial system

The original concept of a socio-spatial system is set out in Pahl (1970, ch. 4) and in ch. 7 of the second edition of *Whose City?* (Pahl 1975). The latter is a collection of Pahl's essays which clearly documents the shift in his thinking on urban managerialism from the earlier conception of managers as independent variables (as in ch. 10) to the later recognition of their mediating role in a context of economic and political constraint (ch. 13). This shift is clarified and discussed in Williams (1978) and Norman (1975). Its relation to Pahl's later writings on corporatism is never made entirely clear in Pahl's own work, although his 1979 article perhaps comes closest to spelling out the common methodological and theoretical position that lies behind his approach to both urban managerialism and corporate state strategies (cf. his argument on p. 34 that 'The process of resource allocation has certain common elements no matter what the scale of organization. . . . '). His discussions of corporatism can be found in Pahl (1977b, c), and these should be read alongside the two articles by Winkler (1976, 1977).

On the concept of housing classes, see Rex and Moore (1967, chs. 1 and 12), Rex (1968), and, for the various amendments made in the light of later criticisms, Rex (1971), on the problem of multiple value systems, Rex (1977) where the emphasis shifts from current tenure to potential access, and Rex and Tomlinson (1979, pp. 20–4 and chs. 5 and 8). This last reference also contains a methodological appendix in which recent Marxist work is attacked for its metaphysical assumptions and a Weberian emphasis on meaningful action and the use of ideal types is asserted and defended. The most important critique of the housing class model remains Haddon (1970), but see also Davies (1972, chs. 3 and 4), Couper and Brindley (1975) and C. Bell, 'On Housing Classes', *Australian and New Zealand Journal of Sociology*, vol. 13, pp. 36–40. Lambert *et al.* (1978) provide a useful evaluation of both the managerialist and housing class concepts in chs. 1 and 7, while my work on urban politics (Saunders 1979) also provides a fairly comprehensive review in chs. 2 and 3.

Chapter 5: The urban as ideology

Most of the relevant work by Lefebvre is still unavailable in English, although the flavour of his arguments can be sampled in Lefebvre (1976), especially ch. 1, section 7 (which contains an attack on Althusserian Marxism). Lefebvre's ideas are discussed in the final chapter of Harvey (1973) and in Castells (1977a, ch. 6).

Perhaps the most useful secondary sources, however, are Soja and Hadjimichalis (1979), Soja (1980), Martins (1982) and Gottdiener (1984 and 1985, ch. 4). Soja is one of Lefebvre's strongest advocates, while Martins and Gottdiener provide very useful accounts contrasting Lefebvre's approach with that of Castells.

Castells's critique of urban sociology (including the work of Lefebvre) is contained in two early papers (1967a, b) and in *The Urban Question* (1977a, chs. 5–8). These should be read in the light of Althusser's papers on Marxist methodology, especially chs. 3, 6 and 7 in Althusser (1969), and his discussion of ideology in his 1971 paper. A useful guide to Althusser's arguments can be found in A. Callinicos, *Althusser's Marxism* (Pluto Press 1976), especially chs. 2 and 3, while his approach has been subjected to a merciless critique from a humanist position by E. Thompson in his essay on 'The poverty of theory', which is contained in a book of the same title published in 1978 by the Merlin Press.

The key chapter in *The Urban Question* as regards Castells's formal conceptualization of his object of analysis is ch. 10, and much of his later work represents a gradual retreat from the position set out there. Significant milestones in this retreat include the 1975 Afterword to the English edition (which is important both for the auto-critique of his earlier formalism and for its clarification of the conceptualization of urbanism in terms of collective consumption) and ch. 1 in Castells (1978).

Chapter 6: The urban as a spatial unit of collective consumption

A simple introduction to the earlier Marxist work in urban sociology can be found in M. Harloe, 'The New Urban Sociology' (*New Society*, 5 October 1978). Mellor's article 'Marxism and the Urban Question' (in M. Shaw, ed., *Marxist Sociology Revisited*, Macmillan 1985) and Lebas's trend report (*Current Sociology* 1982) provide more detailed and critical overviews.

Castells provided useful summaries of his earlier position in ch. 2 of his 1978 collection and in two other papers – 'The class struggle and urban contradictions' (in J. Cowley *et al.*, *Community or class struggle?*, Stage 1 1977), and 'The wild city' (*Kapitalistate*, no. 4/5, 1976, pp. 2–30). For the later work, the key reference is, of course, *The City and the Grassroots*, although his retrospective reflections in Castells (1985) are also interesting.

Marxist approaches to theorizing the capitalist state are discussed and reviewed in Gold *et al* (1975), in Saunders (1979, ch. 4), and Dearlove and Saunders (1984, ch. 7). The problem encountered by structuralist Marxism in relating structures to practices, and in explaining the relative autonomy of the state is ably diagnosed by Clarke (1977) and Hirst (1977), while the specific problems in Castells's initial treatment of urban social movements are discussed by Pickvance (1976b, 1977a). Pickvance's 1985 paper addresses Castells's more recent work on such movements, as does ch. 1 of S. Lowe's *Urban Social Movements* (Macmillan 1985). The conceptualization of collective consumption is discussed by Pahl (1977a) and Dunleavy (1980, 1983); the latter, of course, is also the key source on the political significance of consumption sector cleavages – a concept which is developed in his 1979 article and his 1980 book, and which is applied in, among others, his 1985 paper.

Chapter 7: A non-spatial urban sociology?

For general discussions of the production of space from a Marxist standpoint, see N. Smith, *Uneven Development* (Basil Blackwell 1984), and M. Dunford and D. Perrons, *The Arena of Capital* (Maxmillan 1983). Soja's 1980 and 1985 papers are important for the discussion of the 'socio-spatial dialectic', which he claims to derive from a reading of Lefebvre. Harvey's work is not always as coherent and consistent as it might be, although his 1978a paper is probably a good place to start. Useful secondary accounts of Harvey's work are contained in Gottdiener (1985) and Bassett and Short's *Housing and Residential Structure* (1980), although neither addresses the arguments in *Limits to Capital*. Duncan and Ley (1982) provide a good critique.

Urry's approach can best be gauged by his 1981 and 1985 papers – the latter appears in a collection, edited by Gregory and Urry, which also contains important contributions by, among others, Sayer, Thrift and Giddens. Gregory interviews Giddens in *Society and Space* (vol. 2, 1984, pp. 123–32), but the key references on Giddens on space can be found in his 1979 (ch. 6), 1981 (especially pp. 140–50) and 1984 (especially ch. 3 and pp. 355–68) books. The latter is given an extended review by Thrift in *Sociology* (vol. 19, 1985), while I elaborate my arguments against Giddens's treatment of space in 'Anthony Giddens: Urban space man' (in D. Held and J. Thompson, eds., *Critical Theory of the Industrial Societies*, Cambridge University Press 1986).

Chapter 8: From urban social theory to a sociology of consumption

The dual politics thesis is set out and elaborated in a number of places, but see especially my paper with Alan Cawson ('Corporatism, competitive politics and class struggle') in R. King's edited collection, *Capital and Politics* (Routledge & Kegan Paul 1983), and my 'Reflections on the dual politics thesis: the argument, its origins and its critics' (in M. Goldsmith, ed., *Urban Political Theory and the Management of Fiscal Stress*, Gower 1986). This latter reference discusses the eight major criticisms which have been made against this approach (for examples, see Duncan and Goodwin 1982; Harrington 1983; Sharpe 1984; and Dunleavy 1984).

The discussion of socialized and privatized consumption is based mainly on my 1984 paper, 'Beyond housing classes' (*International Journal of Urban and Regional Research*, vol. 8, pp. 202–7). The same issue of the journal contains an empirical evaluation of the consumption sector cleavage argument by Duke and Edgell, and a critique of my paper by Harloe. Obviously, Dunleavy's various papers are central to much of this discussion (for a critique see Franklin and Page 1984), as is Mingione's 1981 discussion of restratification.

The further reading relating to the final section of the chapter suggests itself. Pahl (1984) is probably the key reference on the 'informal economy', though Gershuny's work is also important, as is Mingione's rather different approach. All three have contributions in N. Redclift and E. Mingione, eds., *Beyond Employment* (Basil Blackwell 1985). Gorz's ideas on the 'dual society' and the liberation from work appear mainly in his 1982 book, and are developed in Gorz (1985). Ward's libertarian anarchist approach to housing is set out in a number of essays collected together in Ward (1983), though his *When we build again* (1985) is a more polished statement of his position. Also to be recommended in his study of the inter-war plotlands, *Arcadia for All*, jointly authored with D. Hardy, and published by Mansell (1984), for not only does this demonstrate the strong popular desire to exert autonomy through personal property, but it also shows the extraordinary lengths to which the state will go to thwart such aspirations.

References

Abrams, P. (1978), 'Towns and economic growth: some theories and problems', in P. Abrams and E. Wrigley (eds.), *Towns in Societies*, Cambridge University Press

Abu-Lughod, J. (1961), 'Migrant adjustment to city life: the Egyptian case', *American Journal of Sociology*, **67**, pp. 22–32

Alihan, M. (1938), *Social Ecology: A Critical Analysis*, New York: Columbia University Press

Althusser, L. (1969), *For Marx*, Allen Lane

Althusser, L. (1971), 'Ideology and ideological state apparatuses', in L. Althusser, *Lenin and Philosophy and Other Essays*, New Left Books

Ambrose, P. and Colenutt, B. (1975), *The Property Machine*, Penguin

Bacon, R. and Eltis, W. (1978), *Britain's Economic Problem: Too Few Producers*, Macmillan

Badcock, B. (1984), *Unfairly Structured Cities*, Basil Blackwell

Ball, M. (1977), 'Differential rent and the role of landed property', *International Journal of Urban and Regional Research*, I, pp. 380–403

Ball, M. (1983), Review of 'Limits to Capital', *Society and Space*, *1*, pp. 494–5

Bassett, K. and Short, J. (1980), *Housing and Residential Structure*, Routledge & Kegan Paul

Becker, H. (1959), 'On Simmel's "Philosophy of Money"', in K. Wolff (ed.), *Georg Simmel 1858–1918*, Columbus: Ohio State University Press

Bell, C., and Newby, H. (1971), *Community Studies*, Allen & Unwin

Bell, C., and Newby, H. (1976), 'Community, communion, class and community action', in D. Herbert and R. Johnson (eds.), *Social Areas in Cities*, John Wiley

Bendix, R. (1966), *Max Weber: An Intellectual Portrait*, Methuen

Benton, T. (1977), *Philosophical Foundations of the Three Sociologies*, Routledge & Kegan Paul

Bernstein, B. (1970), 'Education cannot compensate for society', *New Society*, 26 February, pp. 344–7

Berry, B., and Kasarda, J. (1977), *Contemporary Urban Ecology*, Collier Macmillan

Beshers, J. (1962), *Urban Social Structure*, New York: Free Press

Bhaskar, R. (1978), *A Realist Theory of Science*, Harvester Press

Blowers, A. (1984), *Something in the Air: Corporate Power and the Environment*, Harper and Row

Boddy, M. (1983), 'Central-local government relations: theory and practice',

Political Geography Quarterly, **2**, pp. 119–38
Browett, J. (1984), 'On the necessity and inevitability of uneven spatial development under capitalism', *International Journal of Urban & Regional Research*, **8**, pp. 155–76
Bruun, H. (1972), *Science, Values and Politics in Max Weber's Methodology*, Copenhagen: Munksgaard
Bryant, C. (1978), 'Privacy, privatisation and self-determination', in J. Young (ed.), *Privacy*, Chichester and New York: Wiley
Burger, T. (1976), *Max Weber's Theory of Concept Formation*, Chapel Hill, North Carolina: Duke University Press
Burgess, E. (1967), 'The growth of the city: an introduction to a research project', in R. Park and E. Burgess, *The City*, University of Chicago Press
Cameron, G. (1980), 'The future of the conurbations', in G. Cameron (ed.), *The Future of the British Conurbations*, Longman
Castells, M. (1976a), 'Is there an urban sociology?' in C. Pickvance (ed.), *Urban Sociology: Critical Essays*, Tavistock
Castells, M. (1976b), 'Theory and ideology in urban sociology', in Pickvance (ed.), *Urban Sociology*
Castells, M (1976c), 'Theoretical propositions for an experimental study of urban social movements', in Pickvance (ed.), *Urban Sociology*
Castells, M (1977a), *The Urban Question*, Edward Arnold
Castells, M (1977b), 'Towards a political urban sociology', in M. Harloe (ed.), *Captive Cities*, John Wiley
Castells, M (1978), *City, Class and Power*, Macmillan
Castells, M (1980), *The Economic Crisis and American Society*, Basil Blackwell
Castells, M (1983a), *The City and the Grassroots*, Edward Arnold
Castells, M (1983b), 'Crisis, planning and the quality of life: managing the new historical relationships between space and society', *Society and Space*, **1**, pp. 3–21
Castells, M (1985), 'From the urban question to the city and the grassroots', Urban and Regional Studies *Working Paper*, no. 47, University of Sussex
Castells, M., and Godard, F. (1974), *Monopolville: l'enterprise, l'état, l'urbain*, Paris: Mouton
Castells, M., and Ipola, E. (1976), 'Epistemological practice and the social sciences', *Economy and Society*, **5**, pp. 111–44
Cawson, A. (1978), 'Pluralism, corporatism and the role of the state', *Government and Opposition*, **13**, pp. 178–98
Cawson, A. (1982), *Corporatism and Welfare*, Heinemann
Clarke, S. (1977), 'Marxism, sociology and Poulantzas' theory of the state', *Capital and Class*, **2**, pp. 1–31
Cochrane, A. (1984), Review of 'Corporatism and welfare', *International Journal of Urban & Regional Research*, **8**, pp. 281–2

Cockburn, C. (1977), *The Local State*, Pluto Press

Collier, A. (1978), 'In defence of epistemology', *Radical Philosophy*, **20**, pp. 8–21

Cooke, P. (1982), 'Class interests, regional restructuring and state formation in Wales', *International Journal of Urban & Regional Research*, **6**, pp. 187–204

Connell, R. (1983), *Which Way Is Up?*, George Allen and Unwin

Coser, L., (1965), *Georg Simmel*, Englewood Cliffs, NJ: Prentice-Hall

Couper, M., and Brindley, T. (1975), 'Housing classes and housing values', *Sociological Review*, **23**, pp. 563–76

Crewe, I. (1983), 'The disturbing truth behind Labour's rout', *The Guardian*, 13 June, p. 5

Dahl, R. (1963), *Modern Political Analysis*, Englewood Cliffs, NJ: Prentice-Hall

Davie, M. (1937), 'The pattern of urban growth', in G. Murdock (ed.), *Studies in the Science of Society*, New Haven, Conn., Yale University Press

Davies, J. (1972), *The Evangelistic Bureaucrat*, Tavistock

Davies, J., and Taylor, J. (1970), 'Race, community and no conflict', *New Society*, **9**, pp. 67–9

Dawe, A. (1970), 'The two sociologies', *British Journal of Sociology*, **21**, pp. 207–18

Dawe, A. (1971), 'The relevance of values', in A. Sahay (ed.), *Max Weber and Modern Sociology*, Routledge & Kegan Paul

Dear, M. and Scott, A. (1981), 'Towards a framework for analysis', in M. Dear and A. Scott (eds.), *Urbanization and Urban Planning in Capitalist Society*, London and New York: Methuen

Dearlove, J. and Saunders, P. (1984), *Introduction to British Politics*, Polity Press

Dennis, N. (1968), 'The popularity of the neighbourhood community idea', in R. Pahl, *Readings in Urban Sociology*, Pergamon Press

Dewey, R. (1960), 'The rural–urban continuum: real but relatively unimportant', *American Journal of Sociology*, **66**, pp. 60–6

Dickens, P., Duncan, S., Goodwin, M. and Gray, F. (1985), *Housing, States and Localities*, Methuen

Duke, V. and Edgell, S. (1984), 'Public expenditure cuts in Britain and consumption sectoral cleavages', *International Journal of Urban & Regional Research*, **8**, pp. 177–201

Duncan, J. and Ley, D. (1982), 'Structural marxism and human geography: critical assessment', *Annals of the Association of American Geographers*, **72**, pp. 30–59

Duncan, O. (1957), 'Community size and the rural–urban continuum', in P. Hatt and A. Reiss, (eds.), *Cities and Society* (2nd edn), New York: Free Press

Duncan, O. (1959), 'Human ecology and population studies', in P. Hauser and O. Duncan (eds.), *The Study of Population*, Chicago: Chicago University Press

Duncan, O. (1964), 'Social organization and the ecosystem', in R. Faris (ed.), *Handbook of Modern Sociology*, Chicago: Rand McNally

Duncan, O., and Schnore, L. (1959), 'Cultural, behavioural and ecological perspectives in the study of social organization', *American Journal of Sociology*, **65**, pp. 132–46

Duncan, S. (1981), 'Housing policy, the methodology of levels and urban research: the case of Castells', *International Journal of Urban & Regional Research*, **5**, pp. 231–54

Duncan, S. and Goodwin, M. (1982), 'The local state: functionalism, autonomy and class relations in Cockburn and Saunders', *Political Geography Quarterly*, **1**, pp. 77–96

Duncan, S. and Goodwin, M. (1985), 'The local government crisis in Britain, 1979–84: Part 2, Centralising local policy', *Geography Discussion Papers*, new series, no. 14, London School of Economics

Dunleavy, P. (1980), *Urban Political Analysis*, Macmillan

Dunleavy, P. (1983), 'Socialised consumption and economic development', paper presented at the Anglo-Danish seminar on Local State Research, University of Copenhagen (September); revised version forthcoming in *International Journal of Urban & Regional Research*

Dunleavy, P. (1984), 'The limits to local government', in M. Boddy and C. Fudge (eds.), *Local Socialism?*, Macmillan

Dunleavy, P. (1985), 'The growth of sectoral cleavages and the stabilization of state expenditures', paper presented at the Fifth Urban Change and Conflict Conference, University of Sussex (April); revised version forthcoming in *Society and Space*

Durkheim, É. (1933), *The Division of Labour in Society*, Toronto: Macmillan

Durkheim, É. (1938), *The Rules of Sociological Method*, New York: Free Press

Durkheim, É. (1952), *Suicide: A Study in Sociology*, Routledge & Kegan Paul

Edel, M. (1982), 'Home ownership and working class unity', *International Journal of Urban & Regional Research*, **6**, pp. 205–22

Edel, M., Sclar, E. and Luria, D. (1984), *Shaky Palaces: Homeownership and Social Mobility in Boston's Suburbanization*, New York: Columbia University Press

Elliott, B., and McCrone, D. (1975), 'Landlords as urban managers: a dissenting opinion', in M. Harloe (ed.), *Proceedings of the Conference on Urban Change and Conflict*, Centre for Environmental Studies

Elliott, B. and McCrone, D. (1982), *The City: Patterns of Domination and Conflict*, Macmillan

Engels, F. (1969a), *The Condition of the Working Class in England*, Panther Books

Engels, F. (1969b), 'The housing question', in K. Marx and F. Engels, *Selected Works*, vol. 2, Moscow: Progress Publishers

Farmer, M. and Barrell, R. (1981), 'Entrepreneurship and government policy: the case of the housing market', *Journal of Public Policy*, **2**, pp. 307–32

Firey, W. (1945), 'Sentiment and symbolism as ecological variables', *American Sociological Review*, **10**, pp. 140–8

Flynn, R. (1981), 'Managing consensus: strategies and rationales in policy-making', in M. Harloe (ed.), *New Perspectives in Urban Change & Conflict*, Heinemann

Flynn, R. (1983), 'Co-optation and strategic planning in the local state', in R. King (ed.), *Capital and Politics*, Routledge & Kegan Paul

Flynn, R. (1986), 'Urban politics, the local state and consumption', in M. Goldsmith (ed.), *Urban Political Theory and the Management of Fiscal Stress*, Gower

Forbes, D., Thrift, N. and Williams, P. (1983), 'Social relations in space: books in 1982', *Society and Space*, **1**, pp. 355–64

Ford, J. (1975), 'The role of the building society manager in the urban stratification system', *Urban Studies*, **12**, pp. 295–302

Forrest, K. and Williams, P. (1980), 'The commodification of housing; *Working Paper*, no. 73, Centre for Urban and Regional Studies, University of Birmingham

Franklin, M. and Page, E. (1984), 'A critique of the consumption cleavage approach in British voting studies', *Political Studies*, **32**, pp. 521–36

Freund, J. (1968), *The Sociology of Max Weber*, Allen Lane

Freund, J. (1978), 'Émile Durkheim', in T. Bottomore and R. Nisbet (eds.), *A History of Sociological Analysis*, Heinemann

Friedland, R., Fox Piven, F., and Alford, R. (1977), 'Political conflict, urban structure and the fiscal crisis', *International Journal of Urban and Regional Research*, **1**, pp. 447–71

Friedman, M. (1962), *Capitalism and Freedom*, University of Chicago

Gamble, A. (1981), *Britain in Decline*, London, Macmillan

Gans, H. (1962), *The Urban Villagers*, New York: Free Press

Gans, H. (1968), 'Urbanism and suburbanism as ways of life', in R. Pahl, *Readings in Urban Sociology*, Pergamon

Gans, H. (1984), 'American urban theories and urban areas: some observations on contemporary ecological and marxist paradigms', in I. Szelenyi: (ed.), *Cities in Recession: Critical responses to the urban policies of the New Right*, Sage

Gershuny, J. (1978), *After Industrial Society: The emerging self-service economy*, Macmillan

Gershuny, J. (1985), 'Economic development and change in the mode of provision of services', in N. Redclift and E. Mingione (eds.), *Beyond Employment*, Basil Blackwell

Gettys, W. (1940), 'Human ecology and social theory', *Social Forces*, **17**,

pp. 469–76
Giddens, A. (1971), *Capitalism and Modern Social Theory*, Cambridge University Press
Giddens, A. (1974), 'Introduction' to A. Giddens (ed.), *Positivism and Sociology*, Heinemann
Giddens, A. (1976), *New Rules of Sociological Method*, Hutchinson
Giddens, A. (1979), *Central Problems in Social Theory*, Macmillan
Giddens, A. (1981), *A Contemporary Critique of Historical Materialism*, vol. I, Macmillan
Giddens, A. (1984), *The Constitution of Society*, Polity Press
Godard, F. (1985), 'How do ways of life change?', in N. Redclift and E. Mingione (eds.), *Beyond Employment*, Basil Blackwell
Goffman, E. (1961), *Asylums*, New York: Doubleday Anchor Books
Gold, D., Lo, C., and Wright, E. (1975), 'Recent developments in Marxist theories of the capitalist state', *Monthly Review*, **27**, pp. 37–51
Gorz, A. (1982), *Farewell to the Working Class: An Essay on Post-Industrial Socialism*, Pluto Press
Gorz, A. (1985), *Paths to Paradise: On the Liberation from Work*, Pluto Press
Gottdiener, M. (1984), 'Debate on the theory of space: toward an urban praxis', in M. Smith (ed.), *Cities in Transformation*, Sage
Gottdiener, M. (1985), *The Social Production of Urban Space*, Austin: University of Texas Press
Gray, F. (1976), 'The management of local authority housing', in Conference of Socialist Economists Political Economy of Housing Workshop, *Housing and Class in Britain*, Conference of Socialist Economists
Green, D. (1982), 'The welfare state: For rich and for poor?', *Institute of Economic Affairs Papers*, no. 63
Green, D. (1986), *The New Right*, Harvester Press
Habermas, J. (1976), *Legitimation Crisis*, Heinemann
Haddon, R. (1970), 'A minority in a welfare state society', *New Atlantis*, **2**, pp. 80–133
Hall, P., Gracey, H., Drewitt, R., and Thomas, R. (1973), *The Containment of Urban England*, vol. 1, George Allen and Unwin
Hannerz, U. (1980), *Exploring the City*, New York: Columbia University Press
Harloe, M. (1975), 'Introduction' to M. Harloe (ed.), *Proceedings of the Conference on Urban Change and Conflict*, Centre for Environmental Studies
Harloe, M. (1977), 'Introduction' to M. Harloe (ed.), *Captive Cities*, John Wiley
Harloe, M. (1979), 'Marxism, the state and the urban question: critical notes on two recent French theories', in C. Crouch (ed.), *State and Economy in Contemporary Capitalism*, Croom Helm
Harloe, M. (1981), 'New perspectives in urban and regional research:

Progress and problems', in M. Harloe (ed.), *New Perspectives in Urban Change and Conflict*, Heinemann

Harloe, M. (1984), 'Sector and class: A critical comment', *International Journal of Urban & Regional Research*, **8**, pp. 228–37

Harloe, M., Issacharoff, R., and Minns, R. (1974), *The Organization of Housing*, Heinemann

Harloe, M. and Paris, C. (1984), 'The decollectivisation of consumption', in I. Szelenyi (ed.), *Cities in Recession*, Sage

Harrington, T. (1983), 'Explaining state policy-making: a critique of some recent "dualist" models', *International Journal of Urban & Regional Research*, **7**, pp. 202–18

Harris, R. (1983), 'Space and class: a critique of Urry', *International Journal of Urban & Regional Research*, **7**, pp. 115–21

Harvey, D. (1973), *Social Justice and the City*, Edward Arnold

Harvey, D. (1974), 'Class monopoly rent, finance capital and the urban revolution, *Regional Studies*, **8**, pp. 239–55

Harvey, D. (1977), 'Government policies, financial institutions and neighbourhood change in United States cities', in M. Harloe (ed.), *Captive Cities*, John Wiley

Harvey, D. (1978a), 'The urban process under capitalism: a framework for analysis', *International Journal of Urban and Regional Research*, **2**, pp. 101–31

Harvey, D. (1978b), 'Labour, capital and class struggle around the built environment in advanced capitalist societies', in K. Cox (ed.), *Urbanization and Conflict in Market Societies*, Methuen

Harvey, D. (1982), *The Limits to Capital*, Basil Blackwell

Hawley, A. (1944), 'Ecology and human ecology', *Social Forces*, **22**, pp. 144–51

Hawley, A. (1950), *Human Ecology: A Theory of Community Structure*, New York: Ronald Press

Hawley, A. (1963), 'Community power and urban renewal success', *American Journal of Sociology*, **68**, pp. 422–31

Hawley, A. (1968), 'Human ecology', *International Encyclopedia of Social Science*, **4**, Macmillan and Free Press

Hayek, F. (1960), *The Constitution of Liberty*, Routledge & Kegan Paul

Heraud, B. (1975), 'The new towns: a philosophy of community', in O. Leonard (ed.), *The Sociology of Community Action*, Sociological Review Monograph, no. 21

Hill, R. (1977), 'Two divergent theories of the state', *International Journal of Urban and Regional Research*, **1**, pp. 37–44

Hillier, B. and Hanson, J. (1984), *The Social Logic of Space*, Cambridge University Press

Hindess, B. (1977), *Philosophy and Methodology in the Social Sciences*, Harvester Press

Hindess, B. (1978), 'Class and politics in Marxist theory', in G. Littlejohn,

B. Smart, J. Wakeford and N. Yuval-Davis (eds.), *Power and the State*, Croom Helm

Hirschmann, A. (1970), *Exit, Voice and Loyalty*, Cambridge, Mass.: Harvard University Press

Hirst, P. (1975), *Durkheim, Bernard and Epistemology*, Routledge & Kegan Paul

Hirst, P. (1976), *Social Evolution and Sociological Categories*, George Allen and Unwin

Hirst, P. (1977), 'Economic classes and politics', in A. Hunt (ed.), *Class and Class Structure*, Lawrence & Wishart

Hirst, P. (1979), *On Law and Ideology*, Macmillan

Holton, R. (1984), 'Cities and the transitions to capitalism and socialism', *International Journal of Urban & Regional Research*, **8**, pp. 13–37

Illich, I. (1971), *Deschooling Society*, New York: Harper & Row

Jessop, B. (1978), 'Capitalism and democracy: the best possible political shell?', in G. Littlejohn, B. Smart, J. Wakeford and N. Yuval-Davis (eds.), *Power and the State*, Croom Helm

Jessop, B. (1979), 'Corporatism, parliamentarism and social democracy', in P. Schmitter and G. Lehmbruch (eds.), *Trends Toward Corporatist Intermediation*, Sage

Jessop, B. (1982), *The Capitalist State*, Martin Robertson

Jones, G. (1973), *Rural Life*, Longman

Kalltorp, O. (1984), Review of 'Social Theory and the Urban Question', *Scandinavian Housing and Planning Research*, **1**, pp. 61–4

Katznelson, I. (1981), *City Trenches: Urban Politics and the Patterning of Class in the United States*, University of Chicago Press

Keat, R. (1981), 'Individualism and community in socialist thought', in J. Mepham and D. Ruben (eds.), *Issues in Marxist Philosophy*, vol. 4: *Social and Political Philosophy*, Harvester press

Keat, R., and Urry, J. (1975), *Social Theory as Science*, Routledge & Kegan Paul

Kemeny, J. (1980), 'Home ownership and privatisation', *International Journal of Urban & Regional Research*, **4**, pp. 372–88

Kirby, A. (1985), 'Pseudo-random thoughts on space, scale and ideology in political geography', *Political Geography Quarterly*, **4**, pp. 5–18

Lafargue, P. (no date), *Evolution of Property from Savagery to Civilization*, Calcutta: Sreekali Prakasalaya

Lamarche, F. (1976), 'Property development and the economic foundations of the urban question', in C. Pickvance (ed.), *Urban Sociology: Critical Essays*, Methuen

Lambert, J., Paris, C., and Blackaby, B. (1978), *Housing Policy and the State*, Macmillan

Lebas, E. (1982), 'Urban and regional sociology in advanced industrial societies', *Current Sociology*, **30**, pp. 7–130

Lebas, E. (1980), 'Some comments on a decade of marxist urban and regional research in France', in Political Economy of Housing Workshop, *Housing, Construction and the State*, London, Conference of Socialist Economists

Lefebvre, (1968a), *The Sociology of Marx*, Allen Lane

Lefebvre, (1968b), *Le droit à la ville*, Paris: Anthropos

Lefebvre, (1970), *La révolution urbaine*, Paris: Gallimard

Lefebvre, (1972), *La pensée marxiste et la ville*, Paris: Castermann

Lefebvre, (1976), *The Survival of Capitalism*, Allison & Busby

Lefebvre, (1977), 'Reflections on the politics of space', in R. Peet (ed.), *Radical Geography*, Chicago: Maaroufa Press

Le Grand, J. and Robinson, R. (1984), 'Privatisation and the welfare state: An introduction', in J. Le Grand and R. Robinson (eds.), *Privatisation and the Welfare State*, Allen and Unwin

Levine, D. (1971), *Georg Simmel on Individuality and Social Forms*, University of Chicago Press

Lewis, O. (1951), *Life in a Mexican Village: Tepozilán Restudied*, Urbana: University of Illinois Press

Lipietz, A. (1980), 'The structuration of space, the problem of land and spatial policy', in J. Carney, R. Hudson and J. Lewis (eds.), *Regions in Crisis*, Croom Helm

Lockwood, D. (1966), 'Sources of variation in working class images of society', *Sociological Review*, **14**, pp. 249–67

Lojkine, J. (1977), 'Big firms' strategies, urban policy and urban social movements', in M. Harloe (ed.), *Captive Cities*, John Wiley

Lojkine, J. (1984), 'The working class and the state: the French experience in socialist and communist municipalities', in I. Szelenyi (ed.), *Cities in Recession*, Sage

McBride, W. (1977), *The Philosophy of Marx*, Hutchinson

McDowell, L. (1983), 'Towards an understanding of the gender division of urban space', *Society and Space*, **1**, pp. 59–72

McKenzie, R. (1967), 'The ecological approach to the study of the human community', in R. Park and E. Burgess (eds.), *The City*, University of Chicago Press

MacKenzie, S. and Rose, D. (1983), 'Industrial change, the domestic economy and home life', in J. Anderson, S. Duncan and R. Hudson (eds.), *Redundant Spaces in Cities and Regions?*, Academic Press

Mann, P. (1965), *An Approach to Urban Sociology*, Routledge & Kegan Paul

Martins, M. (1982), 'The theory of social space in the work of Henri Lefebvre', in R. Forrest, J. Henderson and P. Williams (eds.), *Urban Political Economy and Social Theory*, Gower

Marx, K. (1964), *Pre-capitalist Economic Formations*, New York: International Publishers

Marx, K. (1969), 'Preface to "A contribution to the critique of political economy"', in K. Marx and F. Engels, *Selected Works*, vol. 1, Moscow:

Progress Publishers

Marx, K. (1973), *Grundrisse*, Penguin

Marx, K. (1976), *Capital*, vol. 1, Penguin

Marx, K., and Engels, F. (1969), 'Manifesto of the Communist Party', in K. Marx and F. Engels, *Selected Works*, vol. 1, Moscow: Progress Publishers

Marx, K., and Engels, F. (1970), *The German Ideology*, Lawrence & Wishart

Massey, D. (1984), *Spatial Divisions of Labour: Social Structures and the Geography of Production*, Macmillan

Mellor, J. (1977), *Urban Sociology in an Urbanized Society*, Routledge & Kegan Paul

Mennell, S. (1974), *Sociological Theory: Uses and Unities*, Nelson

Menzel, H. (1950), 'Comment on Robinson's "Ecological correlations and the behaviour of individuals"', *American Sociological Review*, **15**, p. 674

Mercer, G. (1984), 'Corporatist ways in the NHS?', in M. Harrison (ed.), *Corporatism and the Welfare State*, Gower

Merton, R. (1968), *Social Theory and Social Structure*, New York: Free Press

Middlemas, K. (1979), *Politics in Industrial Society*, Andre Deutsch

Miliband, R. (1969), *The State in Capitalist Society*, Weidenfeld & Nicolson

Miliband, R. (1977), *Marxism and Politics*, Oxford University Press

Mills, C. (1959), *The Sociological Imagination*, Oxford University Press

Milner, H. (1952), 'The folk–urban continuum', *American Sociological Review*, **17**, 529–37

Mingione, E. (1981), *Social Conflict and the City*, Basil Blackwell

Mingione, E. (1983), 'Informalization, restructuring and the survival strategies of the working class', *International Journal of Urban & Regional Research*, **7**, pp. 311–39

Mingione, E. (1985), 'Social reproduction of the surplus labour force: the case of southern Italy', in N. Redclift and E. Mingione (eds.), *Beyond Employment*, Basil Blackwell

Mishra, R. (1977), *Society and Social Policy*, Macmillan

Moore, R. (1977), 'Becoming a sociologist in Sparkbrook', in C. Bell and H. Newby (eds.), *Doing Sociological Research*, George Allen and Unwin

Moorhouse, H. 'American automobiles and workers dreams', *Sociological Review*, **31**, pp. 403–26

Morris, R. (1968), *Urban Sociology*, George Allen and Unwin

Murgatroyd, S. and Urry, J. (1983), 'The restructuring of a local economy: the case of Lancaster', in J. Anderson, S. Duncan and R. Hudson, (eds.), *Redundant Spaces in Cities and Regions?*, Academic Press

Newby, H. (1977), *The Deferential Worker*, Allen Lane

Newby, H., Bell. C, Rose, D. and Saunders, P. (1978), *Property, Paternalism and Power*, Hutchinson

Newby, H., Vogler, C., Rose, D. and Marshall, G. (1984), 'From class structure to class action: British working class politics in the 1980s', paper presented at seminar on Geographical Aspects of Social Stratification, University of London (September)

Newman, O. (1972), *Defensible Space: Crime Prevention Through Urban Design*, New York: Collier

Nisbet, R. (1966), *The Sociological Tradition*, New York: Basic Books

Norman, P. (1975), 'Managerialism: a review of recent work', in M. Harloe (ed.), *Proceedings of the Conference on Urban Change and Conflict*, Centre for Environmental Studies

Nove, A. (1983), *The Economics of Feasible Socialism*, George Allen & Unwin

O'Connor, J. (1973), *The Fiscal Crisis of the State*, New York: St Martin's Press

Offe, C. (1975), 'The theory of the capitalist state and the problem of policy-formation', in L. Lindberg, R. Alford, C. Crouch and C. Offe (eds.), *Stress and Contradiction in Modern Capitalism*, Lexington Books

Offe, C. (1984), *Contradictions of the Welfare State*, Hutchinson

Pahl, R. (1968), 'The rural–urban continuum', in R. Pahl (ed.), *Readings in Urban Sociology*, Pergamon

Pahl, R. (1970), *Patterns of Urban Life*, Longman

Pahl, R. (1975), *Whose City?* (2nd edn), Penguin

Pahl, R. (1977a), 'Collective consumption and the state in capitalist and state socialist societies', in R. Scase (ed.), *Industrial Society: Class, Cleavage and Control*, Tavistock

Pahl, R. (1977b), 'Stratification, the relation between states and urban and regional development', *International Journal of Urban and Regional Research*, 1, pp. 6–17

Pahl, R. (1977c), 'Managers, technical experts and the state', in M. Harloe (ed.), *Captive Cities*, John Wiley

Pahl, R. (1977d), 'A rejoinder to Mingione and Hill', *International Journal of Urban and Regional Research*, 1, pp. 340–3

Pahl, R. (1978), 'Castells and collective consumption', *Sociology*, 12, pp. 309–15

Pahl, R. (1979), 'Socio-political factors in resource allocation', in D. Herbert and D. Smith (eds.), *Social Problems and the City*, Oxford University Press

Pahl, R. (1980), 'Employment, work and the domestic division of labour', *International Journal of Urban & Regional Research*, 4, pp. 1–20

Pahl, R. (1984), *Divisions of Labour*, Basil Blackwell

Paris, C. (1983), 'Whatever happened to urban sociology?' *Society and Space*, 1, pp. 217–25

Park, R. (1952), *Human Communities*, New York: Free Press

Parsons, T. (1951), *The Social System*, New York: Free Press

Parsons, T., Bales, R., and Shils, E. (1953), *Working Papers in the Theory of Action*, New York: Free Press

Pelling, H. (1968), *Popular Politics and Society in Late Victorian Britain*, Macmillan

Pickvance, C. (1976a), 'Introduction: historical materialist approaches to urban sociology', in C. Pickvance (ed.), *Urban Sociology: Critical Essays*, Tavistock

Pickvance, C. (1976b), 'On the study of urban social movements', in Pickvance (ed.), *Urban Sociology*

Pickvance, C. (1977a), 'From social base to social force; some analytical issues in the study of urban protest', in M. Harloe (ed.) *Captive Cities*, John Wiley

Pickvance, C. (1977b), 'Marxist approaches to the study of urban politics', *International Journal of Urban and Regional Research*, **1**, pp. 218–55

Pickvance, C. (1982), Review of 'Social Theory and the Urban Question' and 'City, Class and Capital', *Critical Social Policy*, **2**, pp. 94–8

Pickvance, C. (1984), 'The structuralist critique in urban studies', in M. Smith (ed.), *Cities in Transformation: Class, capital and the state*, Sage

Pickvance, C. (1985), 'The rise and fall of urban movements and the role of comparative analysis', *Society and Space*, **3**, pp. 31–54

Porteous, J. (1976), 'Home: the territorial core', *Geographical Review*, **66**, pp. 383–90

Poulantzas, N. (1973), *Political Power and Social Classes*, New Left Books

Preteceille, E. (1985), 'Collective consumption, urban segregation, social classes', paper presented at the Fifth Urban Change and Conflict conference, University of Sussex (April); to be published in *Society and Space*

Preteceille, E. and Terrail, J. (1985), *Capitalism, Consumption and Needs*, Basil Blackwell

Reade, E. (1984), 'Town and country planning', in M. Harrison (ed.), *Corporatism and the Welfare State*, Gower

Redfield, E. (1941), *The Folk Culture of Yucatan*, University of Chicago Press

Redfield, R. (1947), 'The folk society', *American Journal of Sociology*, **52**, pp. 293–308

Reissman, L. (1964), *The Urban Process*, Collier Macmillan

Rex, J. (1968), 'The sociology of a zone of transition', in R. Pahl (ed.), *Readings in Urban Sociology*, Pergamon

Rex, J. (1971), 'The concept of housing class and the sociology of race relations', *Race*, **12**, pp. 293–301

Rex, J. (1977), 'Sociological theory and the city', *Australian and New Zealand Journal of Sociology*, **13**, pp. 218–23

Rex, J., and Moore, R. (1967), *Race, Community and Conflict*, Oxford University Press

Rex, J., and Tomlinson, S. (1979) *Colonial Immigrants in a British City*, Routledge & Kegan Paul

Rhodes, R. (1980), 'Analysing inter-governmental relations', *European Journal of Political Research*, **8**, pp. 289–322

Robinson, W. (1950), 'Ecological correlations and the behaviour of individuals', *American Sociological Review*, **15**, pp. 351–7

Robson, B. (1969), *Urban Analysis*, Cambridge University Press

Rose, D. (1979), 'Toward a re-evaluation of the political significance of home ownership in Britain', paper presented at CSE Housing Workshop, University of Manchester (February); subsequently published in revised form in Political Economy of Housing Workshop, *Housing, Construction and the State*, Conference of Socialist Economists

Rose, D. (1981), 'Home ownership and industrial change: the struggle for a separate sphere', *Urban and Regional Studies Working Paper*, no. 25, University of Sussex

Roweis, S., and Scott, A. (1978), 'The urban land question', in K. Cox (ed.), *Urbanization and Conflict in Market Societies*, Methuen

Runciman, W. (1966), *Relative Deprivation and Social Justice*, Routledge & Kegan Paul

Saunders, P. (1978), 'Domestic property and social class', *International Journal of Urban and Regional Research*, **2**, pp. 233–51

Saunders, P. (1979), *Urban Politics: A Sociological Interpretation*, Hutchinson

Saunders, P. (1983), 'On the shoulders of which giant? The case for Weberian political analysis', in P. Williams (ed.), *Social Process and the City*, Sydney: Allen and Unwin

Saunders, P. (1984a), 'The crisis of local government in Melbourne', in J. Halligan and C. Paris (eds.), *Australian Urban Politics*, Sydney: Longman

Saunders, P. (1984b), 'The Canberra tea party: bureaucracy, corporatism and pluralism in the administration of the Australian Capital Territory', in P. Williams (ed.), *Policy, Politics and the City*, Sydney: Allen and Unwin

Saunders, P. (1984c), 'Rethinking local politics', in M. Boddy and C. Fudge (eds.), *Local Socialism?*, Macmillan

Saunders, P. (1985a), 'The forgotten dimension of central-local relations: Theorising the regional state', *Government and Policy*, **3**, pp. 149–62

Saunders, P. (1985b), 'Space, the city and social theory', in D. Gregory and J. Urry (eds.), *Social Relations and Spatial Structures*, Macmillan

Sayer, A. (1979), 'Theory and empirical research in urban and regional political economy: a sympathetic critique', *Urban and Regional Studies Working Papers*, no. 14, University of Sussex

Sayer, A. (1984a), *Method in Social Science*, Hutchinson

Sayer, A. (1984b), 'Defining the urban', *Geojournal*, **9**, pp. 279–85

Sayer, D. (1979), *Marx's Method*, Harvester Press

Schmitter, P. (1974), 'Still the century of corporatism?' *Review of Politics*, **36**, pp. 85–131

Sharpe, J. (1984), 'Functional allocation in the welfare state', *Local Government Studies*, **10**, pp. 27–45

Simmie, J. (1981), *Power, Property and Corporatism*, Macmillan

Sjoberg, G. (1960), *The Pre-Industrial City*, New York: Free Press

Sjoberg, G. (1964), 'The rural–urban dimensions in pre-industrial transitional and industrial societies', in R. Faris (ed.), *Handbook of Modern Sociology*, Chicago: Rand McNally

Smith, M. (1980), *The City and Social Theory*, Basil Blackwell

Smith, N. (1984), *Uneven Development*, Basil Blackwell

Soja, E. (1980), 'The socio-spatial dialectic', *Annals of the Association of American Geographers*, **70**, pp. 207–25

Soja, E. (1985), 'Regions in context: spatiality, periodicity and the historical geography of the regional question', *Society and Space*, **3**, pp. 175–90

Soja, E. and Hadjimichalis, C. (1979), 'Between geographical materialism and spatial fetishism: Some observations on the development of marxist spatial analysis', *Antipode*, **11**, pp. 3–11

Stacey, M. (1969), 'The myth of community studies', *British Journal of Sociology*, **20**, pp. 134–45

Stretton, H. (1974), *Housing and Government*, Sydney: Australian Broadcasting Commission

Swingewood, A. (1975), *Marx and Modern Social Theory*, Macmillan

Szelenyi, I. (1981a), 'Structural changes of and alternatives to capitalist development in the contemporary urban and regional system', *International Journal of Urban & Regional Research*, **5**, pp. 1–14

Szelenyi, I. (1981b), 'The relative autonomy of the state or state mode of production?', in M. Dear and A. Scott (eds.), *Urbanization and Urban Planning in Capitalist Society*, Methuen

Taylor-Gooby, P. (1985), *Public Opinion, Ideology and Social Welfare*, Routledge & Kegan Paul

Thompson, E. (1978), *The Poverty of Theory*, Merlin Press

Thorns, D. (1982), 'Industrial restructuring and change in the labour and property markets in Britain', *Environment and Planning 'A'*, **14**, pp. 745–63

Thrift, N. (1983), 'On the determination of social action in space and time', *Society and Space*, **1**, pp. 23–58

Tönnies, F. (1955), *Community and Society*, New York, Harper & Row

Torrance, J. (1974), 'Max Weber: methods and the man', *European Journal of Sociology*, **15**, pp. 127–65

Townsend, P. (1979), *Poverty in the United Kingdom*, Penguin

Trasler, G. (1982), 'The psychology of ownership and possessiveness', in P. Hollowell (ed.), *Property and Social Relations*, Heinemann

Urry, J. (1981), 'Localities, regions and social class', *International Journal of Urban & Regional Research*, **5**, pp. 455–74

Urry, J. (1983), 'De-industrialisation, classes and politics', in R. King (ed.), *Capital and Politics*, Routledge & Kegan Paul

Urry, J. (1985), 'Social relations, space and time', in D. Gregory and J. Urry (eds.), *Social Relations and Spatial Structures*, Macmillan

Villadsen, S. (1983), 'Urban Politics: central control versus local demands', University of Copenhagen, Institute of Political Studies, *Central Control, Local Communities and Local Politics*, report no. 10

Walther, U. (1982), 'The making of a new urban sociology', in R. Forrest, J. Henderson and P. Williams (eds.), *Urban Political Economy and Social Theory*, Gower

Walton, P. and Gamble, A. (1972), *From Alienation to Surplus Value*, Sheed & Ward

Ward, C. (1983), *Housing: An Anarchist Approach*, Freedom Press

Ward, C. (1985), *When We Build Again*, Pluto Press

Weber, M. (1948a), 'Science as a vocation', in H. Gerth and C. Mills (eds.), *From Max Weber: Essays in Sociology*, Routledge & Kegan Paul

Weber, M. (1948b), 'Politics as a vocation', in Gerth and Mills, *From Max Weber*, Routledge & Kegan Paul

Weber, M. (1949), *The Methodology of the Social Sciences*, New York: Free Press

Weber, M. (1958), *The City*, Chicago: Free Press

Weber, M. (1968), *Economy and Society*, New York: Bedminster Press

Westergaard, J. (1977), 'Class inequality and corporatism', in A. Hunt, (ed.), *Class and Class Structure*, Lawrence & Wishart

Williams, P. (1978), 'Urban managerialism: a concept of relevance?', *Area*, **10**, pp. 236–40

Williams, P. (1982), Property, power and politics: home ownership and social relations', paper presented at the Association of American Geographers annual conference, San Antonio, Texas (April)

Williams, R. (1973), *The Country and the City*, Chatto & Windus

Willis, P. (1977), *Learning to Labour*, Saxon House

Winkler, J. (1975), 'Corporatism', *European Journal of Sociology*, **17**, pp. 100–36

Winkler, J. (1977), 'The corporate economy: theory and administration', in R. Scase (ed.), *Industrial Society: Class, Cleavage and Control*, George Allen and Unwin

Wirth, L. (1927), 'The ghetto', *American Journal of Sociology*, **33**, pp. 57–71

Wirth, L. (1938), 'Urbanism as a way of life', *American Journal of Sociology*, **44**, pp. 1–24

Wirth, L. (1945), 'Human ecology', *American Journal of Sociology*, **50**, pp. 483–8

Wirth, L. (1964), 'Rural–urban differences', in A. Reiss (ed.), *Louis Wirth on Cities and Social Life*, University of Chicago Press

Wirth, L. (1967), 'A bibliography of the urban community', in R. Park and E. Burgess, *The City*, University of Chicago Press

Wolff, K. (1950), *The Sociology of Georg Simmel*, Glencoe, Ill.: Free Press

Young, K., and Kramer, J. (1978), 'Local exclusionary policies in Britain: the case of suburban defence in a metropolitan system', in K. Cox (ed.), *Urbanization and Conflict in Market Societies*, Methuen

Young, M., and Willmott, P. (1957), *Family and Kinship in East London*, Routledge & Kegan Paul

Index

Abrams, P. 28, 50–1
Abu-Lughad, J. 104, 105
agency, human 155, 169–70, 181, 213, 214, 217, 227, 231, 266–7, 270, 284 *see also* structural determinacy
alienation 13, 92, 94, 111–12, 246, 290, 347–8
Alihan, M. 67–8, 69–70, 80, 244
Althusser, L. 163–8, 169, 174–8, 179, 180, 183–6, 190, 192, 196, 206, 207–8, 354, 355, 359, 360
Ambrose, P. 254
anomy 13, 44, 48, 50, 54, 101
architecture *see* design; space, symbolism of
autonomous consumption *see* self-provisioning
autonomy: of cities 34–5, 38, 50–1; of individuals 11, 238, 290, 309, 326–32, 345–51; of state 126, 127, 215, 307; of urban managers 124–6, 131, 132, 137–8, 248–9, 299, 304, *see also* relative autonomy; self-management

Bacon, R. 297, 316
Badcock, B. 293
Bales, R. 82
Ball, M. 261,266
Barrell, R. 237, 323
base/superstructure *see* economy, relation to society
Bassett, K. 262
Becker, H. 96–7
Bell, C. 87, 247
Bendix, R. 35, 37
Benton, T. 43
Bernstein, B. 321
Berry, B. 66, 71
Bhaskar, R. 358, 360
Blowers, A. 308
Boddy, M. 300
Brindley, T. 144
Browett, J. 269–70
Bruun, H. 33
Bryant, C. 328
building industry 158, 190–1, 208, 322
building societies 116, 123, 312
built environment *see* space, production of
bureaucracy 13, 86, 93, 128–9; ecological analysis of 81; power of 128–9, 132–3, 304, 309; *see also* producer interests; state employees; urban managerialism
Burger, T. 31
Burgess, E. 58–9, 66–7, 76, 104, 114, 115

Cameron, G. 270
capitalism and urbanization *see* urbanization
capitalist mode of production 24, 80, 184–7, 190, 193–6
Castells, M. 9, 10, 79, 154, 156,

Castells, M. – cont.
162–3, 168–228, 231–2, 234, 235, 236, 238, 240–1, 250–2, 253, 255, 257, 266, 267, 287, 290, 291, 292, 296, 308, 312, 338, 340, 353, 359, 362
Cawson, A. 134, 298–9
central–local government relations 125, 133, 161, 299–304, 307, 309; *see also* state, local
Chicago school *see* human ecology
city: as microcosm of society 25–6, 50, 81, 186–7, 221; as object of urban analysis 7, 11, 13–16, 25–8, 38, 49–51, 52, 61, 64, 81–3, 95–7, 98, 108–13, 114, 119–20, 122, 138–9, 143, 149–50, 152, 158, 170–1, 176, 212, 219–24, 234, 238, 240–1, 242–53, 277, 282, 287, 308–9, 351; as power container 281–3; definitions of 34–5, 99, 120, 186–8, 212, 220, 222, 253; in Antiquity 22, 36, 38, 49–50; in Middle Ages 15, 23–4, 34–8, 48–9, 50–1, 187, 281; preindustrial 50–1, 76; relation to country *see* urban–rural dichotomy; *see also* urbanism; urbanization
Clarke, S. 193
class; alliances 201–3, 235; as determining ways of life 109; constituted spatially 271–4, 279, 303; dealignment 236, 324–5; distribution in city 74–5, 115–19; not sole basis of power 226, 235, 267–8, 290, 295–8, 301, 312, 318, 320, 340; 'restratification' 318, 320; struggle as cause of state intervention 194–7, 214–15, 296–7, 313; struggle between landowners and industrialists 24, 26–7, 152, 162, 194, 255, 267, 356; working class as revolutionary force 15, 25, 26–7, 333–4; *see also* housing classes; urban politics
Cochrane, A. 301
Cockburn, C. 297–300
Colenutt, B. 254
Collier, A. 355
community 53–66, 84–5; studies 70–1, 244, 247, 274; *see also* locality
Comte, A. 53, 55
conflict 27, 145–6, 353; *see also* class; urban politics
Connell, R. 227, 228
consensus 55, 59–60, 64, 350, 353; *see also* legitimation
consumption: alienative 111; collective 172–4, 175–6, 186, 192, 195, 199–200, 201–3, 213, 219–24, 232–5, 240, 251, 308, 315, 338; cultural significance of 328–32; economic significance of 232, 238, 319–24, 332; fund 257, 262–3, 268; ideological significance of 148–9, 229, 325; market mode of 312–13, 319, 327, 333; privatized 10, 223, 229, 233, 236, 312, 314–19, 325–32, 341–6, 350; relation to production 121, 136, 139, 159, 173, 188, 190, 224–32, 235, 238, 258, 263, 290, 291–3, 311, 346, 350–1; reorganization of 11, 340–51; role in determining life chances 136, 147, 148–9, 226, 292, 319–24; sectoral cleavages 9, 148–9, 150, 226, 230, 235–8, 250, 290, 295–8, 312–32, 344; socialized mode of 312–14; sociology of 8, 9, 10–11, 150–1, 184, 222–3, 232, 238, 245, 289–351; source of control

290, 347–51, *see also* autonomy; typology of 233–4; *see also* reproduction; welfare state
Cooke, P. 303
co-operatives 87, 309, 330, 344, 346–7
corporatism *see* state
Coser, L. 90, 92
Couper, M. 144
Crewe, I. 237

Dahl, R. 307
Darwin, C. 16, 47, 53, 55–6, 58
Davie, M. 66
Davies, J. 123, 143–4
Dawe, A. 33, 79
Dear, M. 253–4
Dearlove, J. 301, 333
democracy 38, 93, 128–9, 196, 202–3, 299, 300, 308, 341
Dennis, N. 84
density, sociological significance of 46–7, 56, 75, 98, 99, 105, 107–8, 112–13, 246
design 247–8, 283
determinism *see* structural determinacy
Dewey, R. 112–13, 247
dialectic 16–17, 19, 34, 88, 89–90, 157, 164, 184, 224, 252, 266, 292, 310, 355; *see also* methodology, Marx's socio-spatial dialectic
Dickens, P. 208
differentiation/division of labour 15, 23, 46–8, 56, 57, 64, 73–5, 81, 86, 92, 93–4, 96, 99, 101–2, 103, 107–8, 115, 246, 348, 350
domestic self-provisioning *see* self-provisioning
dual politics thesis 10, 217–18, 291–311, 341, 352, 362
dual society thesis 348
Duke, V. 236, 303, 324
Duncan, J. 266, 267
Duncan, O. 77, 79, 81–2, 106, 244
Duncan, S. 134, 191, 205, 210, 211, 218, 272, 292, 293, 300, 302
Dunleavy, P. 9, 148, 224, 225, 233–4, 236–8, 289, 303, 324, 328, 340, 344, 349
Durkheim, E. 9, 13–16, 38–51, 53–5, 56, 60, 61, 62–3, 65, 67, 70, 75, 86, 94, 95, 101, 241, 242, 244, 247, 277, 282, 284, 352

ecology *see* human ecology
economy, relation to society 18, 75, 82, 127, 129–31, 133, 136, 184–7, 192–7, 214, 216, 292, 295, 298–301
Edel, M. 323, 331
Edgell, S. 236, 303, 324
education 135, 145, 321, 329, 330, 331–2, 344
Elliott, B. 35–6, 38, 119, 123
Eltis, W. 297, 316
employment 136, 145, 336, 347; *see also* unemployment
Engels, F. 9, 15, 16, 21–8, 152, 241, 312
epistemology *see* methodology
essence/appearance 17–18, 20–1, 24, 28, 38–9, 40–1, 43, 225, 293, 355

Farmer, M. 237, 323
feudalism 23–4, 28, 35–8, 51, 185; *see also* guilds
Firey, W. 68–9, 244
fiscal crisis 199, 210, 296, 314, 316; *see also* state expenditure; taxation
Flynn, R. 134, 303, 304
Forbes, D. 269

Ford, J. 123
formalism 88–9, 95, 180–1, 285
Forrest, R. 318
Franklin, M. 237, 297
freedom *see* autonomy; urbanism, association with freedom
Freund, J. 34, 89, 90
Friedland, R. 301
Friedman, M. 233
functionalism: and dual politics thesis 302; and human ecology 78–9, 81–3, 245; and marxism 192, 212–17, 219, 228, 230–1, 267, 296–7

Gamble, A. 185, 333
Gans, H. 104, 107–10, 111, 112, 246, 290, 346, 350, 351
gatekeepers *see* urban managers
gemeinschaft 86–8
gender 215, 225, 235, 251, 273, 330–1, 335; female work 229, 272, 273–4, 331
Gershuny, J. 335–7, 339
gesellschaft 86–8
Gettys, W. 70, 80
Giddens, A. 9, 10, 37, 44, 141, 182, 242, 247, 277–88, 302, 309, 311, 329
Glass, R. 84
Godard, F. 179–80, 226, 351
Goffman, E. 326
Gold, D. 214–15
Goodwin, M. 134, 272, 290, 293, 300, 302
Gorz, A. 290, 347–51
Gottdiener, M. 251, 269
Gray, F. 136
Green, D. 313, 329, 343
guilds 23, 35, 36–7, 48–9, 92

Habermas, J. 295, 300, 305, 334
Haddon, R. 119, 142–3, 147, 148
Hadjimichalis, C. 257
Hall, P. 14
Hannerz, U. 244
Hansen, J. 247
Harloe, M. 119, 123, 124, 176, 204, 205, 225, 233, 236, 315, 325
Harrington, T. 292, 302, 304
Harris, R. 274
Harvey, D. 9, 10, 11, 154, 155–6, 225, 242, 257–69, 272, 274, 276, 287, 291, 327
Hawley, A. 10, 52, 67, 71–7, 78–80, 82, 244, 245
Hayek, F. 302
health services 134–5, 222, 299, 301, 304–5, 314, 316, 317, 329, 331, 342, 344
Hegel, F. 17, 184
Herraud, B. 84
heterogeneity *see* differentiation
Hill, R. 134
Hillier, B. 247
Hindess, B. 32, 33–4, 177, 353
Hirschmann, A. 317
Hirst, P. 43, 177–8, 354–5, 359, 361
Holton, R. 28
home: as locale 284–5; split from work 225
housing: capital gains from 144, 147, 237, 322–4, 339; determines life chances 119, 139, 322–4; expression of contradictions 25–6, 190–1, 312–13; high rise 132; municipal 115–19, 135, 142, 144, 148, 222, 227, 236, 314, 322, 332; owner-occupied 115, 116–19, 142, 147, 149, 231, 234, 236–8, 248, 250, 263, 298, 314, 317, 322–4, 326, 329–32, 339, 342, 343; source of identity 328; *see also* landlords
housing classes 115–19, 139–50,

248–50, 290, 322
human ecology 10, 13, 15, 44, 48, 52–83, 98, 100, 114, 152, 170, 171, 176, 182, 244–6, 332; as ideology *see* ideology; biotic/cultural distinction 55, 59, 60–6, 67–9, 80; concentric rings model 58–9, 66–7, 76, 104, 114; criticisms of 66–71, 78–81; ecological fallacy 67, 270; methodology of 60–6, 69–70, 71–2; reformulations of 71–83

ideal types 30–3, 34–5, 40, 85, 104, 106–7, 206–7, 209, 218, 219, 293–4; biotic/cultural distinction as 69–70; Castells's approach and 176–7, 209, 210, 223; class as 141, 145; concentric rings as 66; urbanism as 99, 105–7, 246
idealism 17, 70, 156, 165
ideology: distinct from science 19–21, 154–6, 162–82, 359, 361; human ecology as 76, 79–81, 152, 172, 182; level of CMP 166, 185; of state provision 304–5, 324–5; production/consumption split as 224–5 *see also* consumption, relation to production; social science as 18, 152, 154–5, 171; urban analysis as 28, 112, 152–82
Illich, I. 345
individualism 36, 46, 59, 87–8, 90–5, 100–1, 102, 106, 159, 327; ideologically constituted 167, 196; opposed to collectivism 157, 309, 330, 350
informal economy *see* self-provisioning
inner city 8, 58–9
investment 254, 262–5, 272–5
Ipola, E. 177, 179

Jessop, B. 134, 218, 299, 300
Jones, G. 106

Kalltorp, O. 293, 310
Kasarda, J. 66, 71
Katznelson, I. 225
Keat, R. 39, 63, 327
Kemeny, J. 237, 322
Kirby, A. 251, 278, 283–4
Kramer, J. 123

labour theory of value *see* value
Lafargue, P. 326, 327
Lamarche, F. 254, 255
Lambert, J. 136, 150
land development 253–5, 257, 258, 263, 302; *see also* planning; space, production of
landlords 117–18, 123, 142, 144, 147, 260
landowners, conflict with industrial capitalists *see* class
Lebas, E. 168, 174, 204
Lefebvre, H. 10, 22, 24, 25, 28, 154–63, 168, 170, 171, 181, 182, 215, 250, 251, 253, 257–8, 262
legitimation 128, 155, 295, 334
Le Grand, J. 342
leisure 158, 349
Levine, D. 89, 91, 92, 97
Lewis, O. 105, 106
Ley, D. 266, 267
life cycle 107, 247
Lipietz, A. 254, 256
local government *see* central–local relations; state, local
locale 280, 282, 283–4, 286
locality, significance of 81, 109–10, 119, 247, 252, 271–5, 322; *see also* central–local

locality – cont.
relations; community; state local
Lockwood, D. 272
Lojkine, J. 220, 225, 233

McBride, W. 19
McCrone, D. 35–6, 38, 119, 123
McDowell, L. 225
McKenzie, R. 57–8, 59, 64, 139
Mackenzie, S. 225
managerialism *see* urban managerialism
Mann, P. 105
market: as principle of capitalist organisation 130; as source of power 127, 341–6
Marx, K. 9, 13–29, 34, 37, 38, 49–51, 73, 87, 93, 137, 140, 152, 153, 157, 178, 188, 204, 222, 226–7, 241, 250, 257, 260, 262, 277, 282, 284, 293, 310
Massey, D. 9, 10, 241, 242, 247, 271–4, 277, 279
materialism 17, 166; *see also* dialectic; methodology
Mellor, J. 92, 95
Mennell, S. 213, 214
Menzel, H. 67
Mercer, G. 298
Merton, R. 230
methodological individualism 29, 39, 63, 78, 131–2, 139–40
methodology: Althusser's 164–6, 175–6, 207–8, 354, 359–61; Castells's 162–82, 205–19; Durkheim's 38–44, 352; epistemological privilege 17–21, 34, 153, 155, 163, 166, 174, 177–9, 208, 209, 293, 354–5; Hawley's 71; Lefebvre's 154–6; Marx's 16–21, 178, 184, 353–4, 355, *see also* dialectic; Parks's 53, 61–2, 63–6; pluralistic 310–11, 353; Simmel's 88–90; Weber's 28–34, 206, 292–3, *see also* ideal types; *see also* essence/appearance; idealism; ideology; materialism; positivism/empiricism; realism; relativism; retroduction; testing of theories
metropolis 7, 88–97
Middlemas, K. 299
Miliband, R. 305, 307
Mills, C. 68
Miner, H. 106
Minford, P. 343
Mingione, E. 205, 221, 224–5, 232, 238, 268, 292, 318, 319, 320, 335, 337–8, 339
Mishra, R. 312
money: as leveller 93, 95; as source of autonomy 93, 221, 303–4, 344, *see also* market; not urban phenomenon 96, 234, 289; *see also* transfer payments; welfare state, provision in cash or kind
Moore, R. 114–19, 123, 139–51, 204, 274, 322
Moorhouse, H. 351
Morris, R. 107
Murgatroyd, S. 272

needs, identification of 227, 228–31, 321
'New Right' 8, 133, 205, 300, 309
Newby, H. 84, 87, 247, 325, 326
Newman, O. 247
Nisbet, R. 13, 85, 93
Norman, P. 124
Nove, A. 344–5

O'Connor, J. 296, 301, 314
Offe, C. 295–6, 300, 305

ontological security 280, 329–30
overaccumulation 197, 261, 262, 264, 268, 291; *see also* profit, falling rate of
owner-occupation *see* housing

Page, E. 237, 297
Pahl, R. 9, 10, 104, 107, 109–13, 117–41, 142, 147, 150, 172, 215, 222, 233, 245, 246, 248–50, 287, 291, 298, 300, 304, 319, 320–1, 332, 336–7, 338–40, 341, 344, 346, 347, 351
Paris, C. 218, 224, 236, 278, 293, 310
Park, R. 10, 52–66, 68, 69–70, 71, 74, 79, 97, 101, 115, 139, 170–1, 244, 287
Parson, T. 82, 214, 231, 311
Pelling, H. 313
pensions 317, 322
Pickvance, C. 137, 175, 211, 235, 236, 297, 311, 333
planning 118, 128, 130, 133, 134, 152, 156–7, 198, 200, 216, 254–5, 301, 303, 308, 346
pluralism 217, 298–9, 300–1, 307, 361
polarization 8, 10–11, 334–5, 340 *see also* consumption, sectoral cleavages
politics *see* state; urban politics
Popper, K. 353
Porteous, J. 329
positivism/empiricism 39, 43, 44, 63, 65, 66, 70, 124, 164, 165, 174, 176, 177, 206, 352, 356, 361
Poulantzas, N. 183, 193–6, 213–15, 217, 300
power: function of class 194; function of property 326, 344–5; receeding locus of 138; storage of 281; system property 168–9, 193; Weber's analysis of 127–9; *see also* bureaucracy; producer interests; professionals; state
Preteceille, E. 228–31, 292, 320–1
privatization *see* consumption, privatized; welfare state, privatization of
producer interests 73, 297–9, 300–1, 305, 308, 311, 341, 345–7, 349
production *see* consumption, relation to production; space, production of
professionals, power of 132, 134–5, 297, 298, 300, 304–5, 308, 345
profit, falling rate of 129, 197, 226, 261, 262, 296, 356, 357–8
property 317, 325–32, 341; development *see* land development; inheritance 230, 324
Proudhon, P. 326, 327

race 8–9, 114, 116–17, 133, 144, 145–6, 215
rationality: economic calculation 37, 93, 94; of capitalism 31, 35, 254; of state 128, 295–6, 300, 305
Reade, E. 134, 303, 304
realism 39, 44, 63, 64, 66, 70, 206–8, 218, 242, 275–6, 355–61
Redfield, R. 102–4, 105, 106–7, 112
Reissman, L. 52, 102, 107
relative autonomy 186, 194, 195–7, 214–15, 307, 309–11, 352; *see also* economy; ideology; state

relativism 32–3, 178, 354
rent 56–7, 259–61
reproduction: criticisms of concept of 227–32; equation with consumption 226, 228, 318; Giddens's theory of 278, 286; of labour power 173, 188–9, 190–2, 197, 220, 226–7, 291, 296; of social relations 158–9, 160
retroduction 19–21, 34, 357
Rex, J. 10, 114–19, 123, 139–51, 204, 245, 249–50, 274, 322
Rhodes, R. 300
riots 8–9, 118, 210, 333
Robinson, R. 342
Robinson, W. 67
Robson, B. 79
Rome, ancient 22, 50, 185
Rose, D. 225, 315, 330
Roweis, S. 254–5
Runciman, W. 215

Saunders, P. 107, 134, 147, 148, 206, 224, 233, 237, 294, 301, 304, 307, 323, 333
Sayer, A. 178, 207, 240–1, 275, 276, 285, 353–6, 358–9, 360
Sayer, D. 18, 19–21, 357
Schmitter, P. 298
Scott, A. 253–5
self-management 162, 348
self-provisioning 9, 12, 234, 289, 290, 291, 309, 312, 335–40, 344, 349
Sharpe, J. 303
Shils, E. 82
Short. J. 262
Simmel, G. 10, 34, 88–97, 98, 100, 101, 102, 112, 113, 139, 243, 245, 246, 344
Simmie, J. 134, 303
size, sociological significance of 7, 34, 56, 57–8, 77, 90–2, 93, 94, 95, 96, 98, 99, 100–1, 107–8, 112–13, 246–7
Sjoberg, G. 51, 105
Smith, M. 94
Smith, N. 255, 257, 271
social security *see* transfer payments
socialism; comparison with capitalism 120, 128, 130, 320; development of 25, 26–7, 88, 327; social base of 235, 325; strategy for 153, 202, 235
Soja, E. 10, 154, 256–7, 258, 271
space: commodification of 157–8, 282; contingent 275–7, 287–8; functional differentiation of 56–9, 64–6, 67, 70, 75–6; inherently unequal 120, 124, 132, 248; object of analysis 10, 11, 120, 153, 156–7, 172–3, 223, 240–88, 309; production of 153, 155–61, 181–2, 253, 255, 257–9, 271, 282–3; relational 270–1, 275; restructuring of 255–6; significance for capital accumulation 157–8, 242, 253–74; social significance of 49, 50, 119, 120, 122, 159–60, 172–3, 188–9, 224, 238–9, 241, 243, 247–8, 251, 255, 274–88; 'socio-spatial dialectic' 255–7, 271, 276, 287; symbolism of 54, 60, 68, 159, 162, 181, 187; variations across 218, 247, 261, 271–4
Spencer, H. 53, 55, 94
Stacey, M. 110, 120
state: agency of unity 49, 87, 160, 185, 192, 193–4, 195–6, 200, 213, 263; corporatism 8, 9, 126–31, 133–5, 138, 249–50, 298–303, 305;

determinant of life chances 119, 135, 136, 249, 291–2, 319–20; employees 123, 135, 297, 319; expenditure 197, 199, 226, 295–7, 315, 325, 342, *see also* fiscal crisis; taxation; limitation of 349–50; local 125, 187, 299–304, *see also* central–local relations; Marxist theories of 192–200, 210, 213–18, 307, 309; power container 282; relation to economy 49, 124–5, 126, 129–32, 133–4, 136, 192–200, 215–17, 226, 249–50, 254, 263, 268, 295–7, 350, *see also* economy; Weber's analysis of 126–9; *see also* democracy; dual politics thesis; pluralism; power; welfare state
status groups 143, 146–7, 148, 319
Stretton, H. 327
structural determinacy 183, 192, 193, 195, 202–3, 213; *see also* agency
structuration theory 278–87, 302
suburbs 107–8, 115–16, 144, 145, 159, 258, 263, 267
Swingewood, A. 17
Szelenyi, I. 211, 214

taxation 196, 199, 233, 308, 315, 316, 337, 342
Taylor, J. 143
technology, social effects of 129–30, 251, 347–8
teleology: in human ecology 78–9; in marxism 213, 214, 267
Terrail, J. 228–31
territory *see* space
testing of theories 19, 21, 30, 32–4, 180, 181, 206, 207–8, 209, 215, 266, 352–62; counterfactuality 215, 309–10, 352, 361–2
third world 161, 257, 264–5
Thompson, E. 206
Thorns, D. 323
Thrift, N. 269, 284
time 76, 87–8, 218, 275, 278–81, 285, 329
Tomlinson, S. 142, 143, 145–6, 149, 249
Tönnies, F. 10, 86–8, 95, 243, 246
Torrance, J. 31
totality *see* dialectic
town/country division *see* urban/rural dichotomy
Townsend, P. 316
trade unions 130–1, 134, 274, 298–9, 308, 317, 338
transfer payments 135, 314, 342, 344; not local 303–4; not urban 120, 221–2, 233, 234, 287; *see also* money; welfare state
Trasler, G. 328

unemployment 8, 262, 313, 321, 333, 334–5, 337–40
urban managerialism 10, 121, 122–41, 150–1, 169, 248–50, 299–300, 304, 311, 332
urban politics: black movements 145–6, 152, 161, *see also* race; conflict over urban resources 118–19, 121; defined 224; mass movements 102, 161; political alignments *see* consumption, sectoral cleavages; class, alliances; urban social movements 152, 181, 192, 200–4, 208, 210–11, 226, 235–6, 251, 252, 257, 303, 333, 353; women's movements 152, 251, *see also* gender; *see also* consumption;

urban politics – cont.
housing classes; state; welfare state
urban/rural dichotomy 7–8, 15, 21–4, 38, 84–8, 94, 98–100, 102–7, 110–13, 158, 281, 282, 284; rural–urban continuum 99, 103, 106–7, 110, 113, 114, 171
urban social movements *see* urban politics
urban sociology, definition of *see* city, object of analysis
urbanism; as culture 10, 52, 84–113, 159, 171, 187, 212; associated with freedom 48, 54, 91, 93, 95, 100–1, 107, 153, 162; associated with problems 14, 25, 48, 54, 59, 84, 102, 106–7, 190; associated with progress 47–8, 84, 111
urbanization and rise of capitalism 14–15, 23–8, 35–8, 46–9, 50–1, 88, 95

validity of theories *see* testing of theories
value, Marxist theory of 18, 136, 158, 226–7, 260, 295
values: in society 116, 129, 143–5, 316; in sociology 33, 39, 79, 106–7, 127, 181, 357; of urban managers 121, 123, 128, 304–5
Villadsen, S. 303

Walther, U. 163
Walton, P. 185
Ward, C. 238, 248, 290, 320, 326, 327, 340, 341, 343, 346
Weber, M. 9, 13–16, 28–39, 40, 49–51, 60, 86, 93, 95, 98, 106, 114, 126–9, 131, 136, 139–41, 146–7, 148, 176–7, 206, 210, 223, 241, 242, 277, 282, 284, 294, 331, 351
welfare state: alternatives to 340–6, 349–50, 351; crisis of 200, 295–7, 316, 333, *see also* fiscal crisis; cuts in spending 8, 133, 236, 308, 324–5, 328, 337, *see also* state, expenditure; functions of 189, 192, 213, 229, 296; privatization of 8, 9, 223, 236, *see also* consumption, privatized; provision in cash or kind 221–2, 223, 289–90, 303–4, 314, 315, 341–6; 351, *see also* transfer payments; *see also* consumption; education; health; housing; producer interests; professionals; state; urban managerialism
Westergaard, J. 134
Williams, P. 123, 132, 269, 318, 323, 326
Williams, R. 25, 27, 84, 111–12
Willis, P. 285–6
Wilmott, P. 104
Winkler, J. 129, 130–1, 133–4, 250, 298
Wirth, L. 10, 48, 53, 61, 97–104, 112, 113, 139, 168, 170–1, 172, 187, 245, 246–7, 248
Wolff, K. 90, 91, 93, 94, 96
women *see* gender
women's movement *see* urban politics
working class *see* class

Young, K. 123
Young, M. 104

zone of transitiion 58–9, 114, 117